I0868868

Collaborative Convergence and Virtual Teamwork for Organizational Transformation

Jingyuan Zhao
Department of Political Science and Department of Geography, University of Toronto, Toronto, Canada

IGI Global
PUBLISHER of TIMELY KNOWLEDGE

Published in the United States of America by
IGI Global
Business Science Reference (an imprint of IGI Global)
701 E. Chocolate Avenue
Hershey PA, USA 17033
Tel: 717-533-8845
Fax: 717-533-8661
E-mail: cust@igi-global.com
Web site: http://www.igi-global.com

Copyright © 2021 by IGI Global. All rights reserved. No part of this publication may be reproduced, stored or distributed in any form or by any means, electronic or mechanical, including photocopying, without written permission from the publisher. Product or company names used in this set are for identification purposes only. Inclusion of the names of the products or companies does not indicate a claim of ownership by IGI Global of the trademark or registered trademark.

Library of Congress Cataloging-in-Publication Data

Names: Zhao, Jingyuan, 1968- editor.
Title: Collaborative convergence and virtual teamwork for organizational transformation / Jingyuan Zhao, editor.
Description: Hershey : Business Science Reference, 2020. | Includes bibliographical references and index. | Summary: "This book addresses the design and implementation of e-collaboration technologies, and their use in business today establishing the important links between the use of e-collaboration technologies and behavioral patterns in the workplace"-- Provided by publisher.
Identifiers: LCCN 2020018656 (print) | LCCN 2020018657 (ebook) | ISBN 9781799848912 (hardcover) | ISBN 9781799858379 (paperback) | ISBN 9781799848929 (ebook)
Subjects: LCSH: Organizational change. | Virtual work teams. | Communication--Technological innovations. | Business enterprises--Computer networks.
Classification: LCC HD58.8 .C6355 2020 (print) | LCC HD58.8 (ebook) | DDC 658.4/022--dc23
LC record available at https://lccn.loc.gov/2020018656
LC ebook record available at https://lccn.loc.gov/2020018657

British Cataloguing in Publication Data
A Cataloguing in Publication record for this book is available from the British Library.

All work contributed to this book is new, previously-unpublished material. The views expressed in this book are those of the authors, but not necessarily of the publisher.

For electronic access to this publication, please contact: eresources@igi-global.com.

Editorial Advisory Board

Eric Andonoff, *University of Toulouse 1, France*
Narinder Kumar Bhasin, *Amity University, India*
Rafik Bouaziz, *University of Sfax, Tunisia*
Mohamed Amine Chaabane, *Higher Institute of Business Administration, Tunisia*
Youngkeun Choi, *Sangmyung University, South Korea*
Jean Constant, *Hermay.org, USA*
Sindy DeLaTorre Pacheco, *Universidad Autónoma de Coahuila, Mexico*
Christopher B. R. Diller, *University of Nebraska at Omaha, USA*
Fatma Ellouze, *Faculty of Economics and Management, Sfax Tunisia, Tunisia*
Dorina Gnaur, *Aalborg University, Denmark*
Joel Helquist, *Utah Valley University, USA*
Hans Hüttel, *Aalborg University, Denmark*
John Kruse, *MITRE Corporation, USA*
Salvatore Nizzolino, *Sapienza University of Rome, Italy*
Ramaraj Palanisamy, *St. Francis Xavier University, Canada*
Spyros Papadakis, *Hellenic Open University, Greece*
Sofia Th Papadimitriou, *Hellenic Open University, Greece*
Anupama Rajesh, *Amity University, India*
Dominik Siemon, *Technische Universität Braunschweig, Germany*
Timo Strohmann, *Technische Universität Braunschweig, Germany*
Nazim Taskin, *Massey University, New Zealand*
Jacques Verville, *EM – Normandie, France*
Yu Zhonggen, *Beijing Language and Culture University, China*

Table of Contents

Detailed Table of Contents

This chapter examines the post-convergence process of organizing ideas that are generated during collaborative idea generation activities. The method presented reduces the impact of organizing brainstorming ideas on individual participants by dividing the organization activity into smaller, discrete tasks that can be completed individually, and in parallel, by the participants. The entire pool of brainstorming ideas is subdivided into smaller pools and each participant is then tasked with organizing one of the subsets of ideas. The results show that by dividing up the overall activity into subtasks, the subjects experienced a more favorable environment. Furthermore, the subjects were able to work through their subset of ideas and produce results that were similar to those performing the full sort of the entire pool.

Process flexibility has been investigated for intra-organizational processes, but it is still an open issue for collaborative processes (CP), each of which is defined as a set of intra-organizational processes that interact together. In the literature, the version-based approach is largely used in the field of business process management (BPM) to cope with process flexibility. However, BPM practitioners can face difficulties in a multi-version environment. So, the following questions arise: How can we use the version-based approach to easily model flexible CP? Does an appropriate version exist for a given situation or is it necessary to create a new one? The chapter answers these questions recommending a solution for the modeling of CP versions and the retrieval of the adequate CP version for a given situation. This solution comprises (1) a meta-model to consider the modeling of the CP versions, (2) an ontology-based approach to model and query the context of use of CP versions, and (3) a framework to provide support for both the modeling of CP versions and the context querying.

Nowadays, information technologies are catching growing attention and their application to English language learning is also prospering. Using a Foreign Language Classroom Anxiety Scale and College English Test Band 4, this study explored the different impacts of e-collaborative learning via QQ group and traditional multi-media learning on learning outcomes and anxiety among tertiary students. Around 70 participants were involved in different styles of learning and instruction and received both surveys and tests. The results showed that QQ group-based e-collaborative learning could significantly decrease anxiety but no significant gain was found in learning outcomes compared with traditional multi-media learning. Correlation between learning outcomes and anxiety was also studied, which resulted in no significant findings. Both disadvantages and advantages of this study were discussed, and future research was recommended as well.

The increases in complexity of patient care, healthcare costs, and technological advancements shifted the healthcare delivery to interprofessional collaborative care. The study aims for identifying factors influencing the quality of team collaboration. The study examines the impact of trust and technology orientation on collaboration with the mediating effects of communication, coordination, and cooperation. The results of the study validate that (1) collaboration has positive and significant relationship with coordination, and cooperation; (2) trust has positive and significant relationship with communication, coordination, and cooperation; and (3) technology orientation has positive and significant relationship with cooperation but not with communication and coordination. The research and managerial implications of these factors are given in the discussion. The results can be used by healthcare professionals and managers to advance their understanding on the impact of trust and technology on collaboration mediating communication, coordination, and cooperation practices.

Continuous increase in computing power and more available data contribute to AI maturing, enabling an efficient and powerful human-AI collaboration. As a result, the nature of work will change, and more and more AI will be involved in joint work. In this study, the authors introduce the so-called Virtual Collaborator (VC), an equal partner in digital collaboration, and report the results of a conducted online study. Based on the results of our study and current research, the concept of a VC was constructed,

to count losses and cost. The big question which has emerged that whether e-collaboration between banks and technology continues to be the key to success for finding solutions to the problems in this new environment which COVID-19 has created. This chapter examines the way the digital banking collaboration between banks and Fintech can resolve the problems provided by the COVID-19 pandemic and control the impending economic fallout in India and across the world.

Problem-based learning (PBL) is central to the degree programmes at Aalborg University (AAU), but if one is a member of the teaching faculty with a degree from another institution, it is unlikely that one is familiar with PBL. In this chapter, the authors describe the development of an ongoing experiences with PBL Exchange, a web-based platform whose goal is to facilitate the transfer and development of knowledge and skills within PBL project supervision by means of a web-based crowdsourcing approach that makes it easy to exchange and discuss one's specific problems and experience with project supervision. The goal was to build a new community of practice from a network of practice, but this has turned out to be difficult. The authors discuss and analyze their experiences and suggest technical and social developments that may be able to facilitate the creation of community of practice.

This chapter deals with the continuous professional development required in the teaching profession with a focus on the European Union, embracing the education sector as a whole socio-anthropological structure with similar needs and expectations. In particular, the topic of professional networking and mobilities, analyzed under the effect of the Erasmus Plus program, emphasizes the need for a new perspective. Social network analysis improves the understanding of particular behavioral patterns promoted by the implementation of European education policies in public education networking. The chapter contributes to policymakers in the field of education and training in the education sector.

The COVID-19 pandemic is affecting communities worldwide today in many novel ways. The rapidity at which the disease is transmitted and the amount of information available in real-time creates a unique situation. This research, based on qualitative remediation at the community level, provides a fertile ground from which significant patterns are emerging. The authors reviewed the literature available as well as over 100 individual sites of local administrations, faith-based, NGOs, local charitable and community initiatives. It is premature to project an accurate picture of how to alleviate best the distress caused by a pandemic. However, some significant and credible patterns have emerged that lead to conclude that, next to transparency, initiatives based on proactive use of peer to peer e.communication, direct e.outreach, and e.collaboration between parties lead to constructive and successful initiatives.

The objective of massive adaptation of digital payments by the banks with the support of the central bank of any country along with their government agencies is to improve customer services and satisfaction in the online payment systems in place of cashless and paperless payment systems. There are very few researches that have focused to measure the higher customer satisfaction based on factors like trust, risk-free, secure, transparent, accountability of banks, fintech, regulator, and payment system operators. This chapter analyzes the impact of digital banking and fintech in the Indian banking system, initiatives taken by RBI, NPCI, and the government to build the strong trust of customers in online payment systems to ensure improvement in customer services with higher customer satisfaction.

The advancement in information technology has transformed the world. There has been a tremendous impact of information technology on contemporary vocational education. This chapter highlights the impact of information technology on vocational education paradigm in China. In general, education paradigm has gone through three stages: empirical imitation education, computer-aided education, and data-driven education. China's vocational education is experiencing a transformation of paradigm from teaching support to learning support. This work is focused on how to construct a learning support paradigm in China's vocational education system through information technology. The Open University of China creating an innovative approach to learning support paradigm is discussed and three key elements of strategy for constructing a learning support paradigm of vocational education through information technology are presented in the chapter.

Preface

Virtual teams are work arrangements where team members are geographically dispersed, and work interdependently through the use of electronic communication media to accomplish one or more organization tasks. Virtual teams enable organizations to pool the talents and expertise of employees and non-employees by eliminating time and space barriers, and connect knowledge workers together over time and distance to combine effort and achieve common goals (Bell & Kozlowski, 2002; Kozlowski & Bell, 2003; Dulebohn & Hoch, 2017). Over the past several decades, there has been an explosive growth in organizations' use of virtual teams to organize work. In the competitive market, virtual teams represent a growing response to the need for fasting time-to-market, low-cost and rapid solutions to complex organizational problems. Nowadays organizations are increasingly investing in virtual team to enhance their performance and competitiveness. The performance of virtual teams depends on organizational structures and team integration, e.g. composition of the team, business goals, and technological solutions (Ale Ebrahim et al., 2011; Großer & Baumöl, 2017). Organizations have rapidly deployed technology solutions, such as collaboration tools and cloud computing, which enable their employees to work remotely and continue organizational operations, especially during a time of crisis such as the COVID-19 pandemic.

Virtual team members mostly interact through information and communication technologies due to the geographical distance existing between teammates. Research has found that this lack of face-to-face interaction creates new challenges for organizations and their managers. Most of these challenges are related to processes involved in interpersonal relationships such as communication and collaboration. As geographic, temporal, and cost constraints move organizations toward virtual teamwork for increasingly complex tasks, research on the impact of groups attempting to solve business problems without face-to-face communication becomes more critical (DeLuca & Valacich, 2005; Kauffmann & Carmi, 2017). Media Synchronicity Theory suggests that communications media with low synchronicity (e.g. e-mail, bulletin board) may be appropriate for conveyance of information, whereas media with high synchronicity (e.g. video conference) may be more desirable for convergence on shared meaning. Today convergence happens all over the collaboration space. For example, VoIP, PSTN and computer networks are converging; synchronous and asynchronous collaboration technologies are converging and evolving into on-demand collaboration tools.

Collaborative convergence has been identified as a pattern that characterizes how teams execute activities that are part of a collaboration process (Briggs et al., 2003; Seeder et al, 2017). Under a variety of conditions, teams using collaboration technologies and techniques may produce more idea of higher quality than individuals who do not use such support (Fjermestad & Hiltz, 1998; Dennis & Wixom, 2002; Dennis, Minas & Bhagwatwar, 2013; Paulus et al., 2013; Seeder et al, 2017). The pressure to interact efficiently with team members with different language and cultural backgrounds leads to the foregrounding of certain strategies and organizational dynamics that facilitate viable communication. Collaboration technology focuses on cooperation and organization processes, such as communication, coordination and coproduction. Collaborative convergence focuses on content, such as creation, storage, sharing and use of information and knowledge. Collaboration technology and collaborative convergence ensures an organization to be more effective and efficient (Yahia et al., 2012; Cha et al., 2015; Nickerson & Goby, 2018).

There are unsolved issues of design and implementation of collaboration technologies for virtual teams and their collaborative convergence. In particular, virtual teams are becoming more common in today's businesses. Virtual teams as a form of organization are playing a key role in the process of organizational construction and transformation. This book is an innovative collection of the latest research findings on virtual teamwork and collaborative convergence for organizational transformation. This book covers significant topics such as collaboration technologies in virtual teamwork, design and evaluation of collaborative convergence in organizational settings, collaboration technologies impact on organizational transformation as well as Web-based tools, Web-based asynchronous conferencing tools, collaborative learning tools, group decision support systems, teleconferencing suites, workflow automation systems, and document management technologies. More importantly, the book analyzes and discusses successful organizational transformation requiring a holistic understanding of the issues linked to team and workplaces, communication and integration, technological barriers and sociocultural factors. The book is organized into 14 chapters which provide insight on collaborative convergence and virtual teamwork for organizational transformation as a whole.

Chapter 1 (Executing Collaborative Brainstorming Idea Organization Through Distributed and Parallel Sorting) examines the post-convergence process of organizing ideas that are generated during collaborative idea generation activities. The method presented reduces the impact of organizing brainstorming ideas on individual participants by dividing the organization activity into smaller, discrete tasks that can be completed individually, and in parallel, by the participants. The entire pool of brainstorming ideas is subdivided into smaller pools and each participant is then tasked with organizing one of the subsets of ideas. The results show that by dividing up the overall activity into subtasks, the subjects experienced a more favorable environment.

Chapter 2 (A Version and Context-Based Approach to Easily Model Flexible Collaborative Processes) discusses on how we can use the version-based approach to easily model flexible CP and whether an appropriate version exists for a given situation or whether it is necessary to create a new one. This chapter answers these questions recommending a solution for the modeling of CP versions and the retrieval of the adequate CP version for a given situation. This solution comprises (i) a meta-model to consider the modeling of the CP versions, (ii) an ontology-based approach to model and query the context of use of CP versions, and (iii) a framework to provide support for both the modeling of CP versions and the context querying.

Chapter 3 (The Impact of E-Collaboration and Traditional Learning Styles on Learning Outcomes and Anxiety) explores the different impacts of e-collaborative learning via QQ group and traditional multi-media learning on learning outcomes and anxiety among tertiary students. Around 70 participants are involved in different styles of learning and instruction and received both surveys and tests. The results show that QQ group-based e-collaborative learning could significantly decrease anxiety but no significant gain was found in learning outcomes compared with traditional multi-media learning. Correlation between learning outcomes and anxiety was also studied, which resulted in no significant findings. Both disadvantages and advantages of this study are discussed and future research is recommended as well.

Chapter 4 (Factors Influencing Interprofessional Collaboration in Healthcare Environment: An Empirical Analysis) aims to identify factors influencing the quality of team collaboration. The chapter examines the impact of trust and technology orientation on collaboration with the mediating effects of communication, coordination and cooperation. The research and managerial implications of these factors are given in the discussion. The results can be used by healthcare professionals and managers to advance their understanding on the impact of trust and technology on collaboration mediating communication, coordination and cooperation practices.

Chapter 5 (Human-AI Collaboration: Introducing the Virtual Collaborator) introduces the so-called virtual collaborator, an equal partner in digital collaboration and report the results of a conducted online study. Based on the results of our study and current research, the concept of a VC is constructed, which consists of potential roles, tasks, level of autonomy and behavior. This construct can be used as a guideline to design and implement a VC in collaboration scenarios.

Chapter 6 (E-Collaboration in Educational Organizations: Opportunities and Challenges in Virtual Learning Environments and Learning Spaces) explores the use of Virtual Learning Environments (VLE) to support Learning Spaces in Schools/Universities and illustrates their advantages to enhance e-collaboration and its key dimensions. In particular this chapter emphasizes in the development of e-collaborative experiences at Schools/Universities based on LMSs to support both students and educators in their complex work. The chapter highlights discussion themes raised by e-collaborating in VLEs and generally in Learning Spaces. Proposals for further development of e-collaboration and conclusions are drawn and commented.

Chapter 7 (An Investigation of Collaborative Consumption Engagement and the Interaction With Self-Identity) investigates the relationships between motivation factors and collaborative consumption engagement and explore the moderating effect of self-identity on that relationship. This study collects data from 228 college students in South Korean through a survey method. The research results include: the more sustainability or economic benefits participants perceive in collaborative consumption platforms, the more they are engaged in collaborative consumption; a positive relationship between perceived sustainability and collaborative consumption engagement is stronger for participants in collaborative consumption platforms high rather than low in interdependent self-view.

Chapter 8 (Impact of COVID-19 Lockdown on Digital Banking E-Collaboration Between Banks and Fintech in Indian Economy) raises the question of whether E Collaboration between banks and technology continues to be the key to success for finding solutions to the problems in this new environment which COVID 19 has created. This particular research examines the way the digital banking collaboration between banks and Fintech can resolve the problems provided by the COVID 19 pandemic and control the impending economic fallout in India and across the world.

Chapter 9 (The Challenge of Building Communities about PBL Supervision: From Networks of Practice to Communities of Practice) describes the development and ongoing experiences with PBL (Problem-based learning) Exchange, a web-based platform whose goal is to facilitate the transfer and development of knowledge and skills within PBL project supervision by means of a web-based crowd-sourcing approach that makes it easy to exchange and discuss one's specific problems and experience with project supervision. The goal is to build a new community of practice from a network of practice, but this has turned out to be difficult. This chapters claims technical and social developments may be able to facilitate the creation of community of practice.

Chapter 10 (Teachers' Networking, Professional Development and Motivation Within EU Platforms and Erasmus Plus Programme) deals with the continuous professional development required in the teaching profession with a focus on the European Union, embracing the education sector as a whole socio-anthropological structure with similar needs and expectations. In particular, the topic of professional networking and mobilities, analyzed under the effect of the Erasmus Plus program, emphasizes the need for a new perspective. Social network analysis improves the understanding of particular behavioral patterns promoted by the implementation of European education policies in public education networking. The chapter contributes to policy-makers in the field of education and training in the education sector.

Chapter 11 (Communication in the Age of a Global Pandemic: Qualitative Remediation at the Community Level) provides a fertile ground from which significant patterns are emerging, based on Qualitative Remediation at the community level. The authors reviewed the literature available as well as over 100 individual sites of local Administrations, Faith-Based, NGOs, local charitable and community initiatives. It is premature to project an accurate picture of how to alleviate best the distress caused by a pandemic. However, some significant and credible patterns have emerged that lead to conclude that, next to transparency, initiatives based on proactive use of peer to peer e.communication, direct e.outreach, and e.collaboration between parties lead to constructive and successful initiatives.

Chapter 12 (Study of Increasing Adoption Trends of Digital Banking and Fintech Products in Indian Payment System and Improvement in Customer Services) presents that the objective of massive adaptation of digital payments by the banks with the support of the Central Bank of any country along with their Government agencies is to improve customer services and satisfaction in the online payment systems in place of cashless and paperless payment systems. This chapter analyzes the impact of digital banking and Fintech in the Indian Banking System, initiatives taken by RBI, NPCI, and the Government to build the strong trust of customers in online payment systems to ensure improvement in customer services with higher customer satisfaction.

Chapter 13 (Vocational Education Paradigm Transformation Through Information Technology: An Innovation Case Study of China) highlights the impact of information technology on vocational education paradigm in China. China's vocational education is experiencing a transformation of paradigm from teaching support to learning support. This work is focused on how to construct a learning support paradigm in China's vocational education system through information technology. The Open University of China creating an innovative approach to learning support paradigm is discussed and three key elements of strategy for constructing a learning support paradigm of vocational education through information technology are presented in the chapter.

Jingyuan Zhao
Department of Political Science and Department of Geography, University of Toronto, Toronto, Canada
2020 September

REFERENCES

Ale Ebrahim, N., Abdul Rashid, S. H., Ahmed, S., & Taha, Z. (2011). The Effectiveness of Virtual R&D Teams in SMEs: Experiences of Malaysian SMEs. *Industrial Engineering and Management Systems, 10*(2), 109–114. doi:10.7232/iems.2011.10.2.109

Bell, B. S., & Kozlowski, S. W. J. (2002). A typology of virtual teams: Implications for effective leadership. *Group & Organization Management, 27*(1), 14–49. doi:10.1177/1059601102027001003

Briggs, R. O., de Vreede, G. J., & Nunamaker, J. F. (2003). Collaboration engineering with ThinkLets to pursue sustained success with group support systems. *Journal of Management Information Systems, 19*(4), 31–64. doi:10.1080/07421222.2003.11045743

Cha, K. J., Kim, Y. S., Park, B., & Lee, C. K. (2015). Knowledge Management Technologies for Collaborative Intelligence: A Study of Case Company in Korea. *International Journal of Distributed Sensor Networks, 11*(9), 368273. doi:10.1155/2015/368273

DeLuca, D., & Valacich, J. S. (2005). Outcomes from conduct of virtual teams at two sites: Support for media synchronicity theory. In *Proceedings of the 38th Annual Hawaii International Conference on System Sciences* (p. 50b). Los Alamites, CA: IEEE Computer Society. 10.1109/HICSS.2005.481

Dennis, A. R., & Wixom, B. H. (2002). Investigating the moderators of the group support systems use with meta-analysis. *Journal of Management Information Systems, 18*(3), 235–257. doi:10.1080/07421222.2002.11045696

Dennis, A. R., Minas, R. K., & Bhagwatwar, A. P. (2013). Sparking creativity: Improving electronic brainstorming with individual cognitive priming. *Journal of Management Information Systems, 29*(3), 195–216. doi:10.2753/MIS0742-1222290407

Dulebohn, J. H., & Hoch, J. E. (2017). Virtual teams in organizations. *Human Resource Management Review, 27*(4), 569–574. doi:10.1016/j.hrmr.2016.12.004

Fjermestad, J., & Hiltz, S. R. (1998). An assessment of group support systems experimental research: Methodology and results. *Journal of Management Information Systems, 15*(3), 7–149. doi:10.1080/07421222.1998.11518216

Großer, B., & Baumöl, U. (2017). Virtual teamwork in the context of technological and cultural transformation. *International Journal of Information Systems and Project Management, 5*(4), 21–35.

Kauffmann, D., & Carmi, G. (2017). The Mediating Effect of Interpersonal Trust on Virtual Team's Collaboration. *International Journal of Knowledge Management, 13*(3), 20–38.

Kozlowski, S. W. J., & Bell, B. S. (2003). Work groups and teams in organizations. In W. C. Borman, D. R. Ilgen, & R. J. Klimoski (Eds.), Handbook of psychology: Vol. 12. *Industrial and Organizational Psychology* (pp. 333–375). Wiley.

Nickerson, C., & Goby, V. P. (2018). Convergence and collaboration: Co-creating meaning within culturally diverse workforces. *The International Journal of Organizational Analysis, 26*(5), 941–952. doi:10.1108/IJOA-03-2018-1390

Paulus, P. B., Kohn, N. W., Arditti, L., & Korde, R. (2013). Understanding the group size effect in electronic brainstorming. *Small Group Research, 44*(3), 332–352. doi:10.1177/1046496413479674

Seeber, I., de Vreede, G. J., Maier, R., & Weber, B. (2017). Beyond Brainstorming: Exploring Convergence in Teams. *Journal of Management Information Systems, 34*(4), 939–969. doi:10.1080/07421222.2017.1393303 PMID:29399005

Yahia, N. B., Bellamine, N., & Ghézala, H. B. (2012). *On the Convergence of Collaboration and Knowledge Management.* https://arxiv.org/abs/1202.6104

Chapter 1
Executing Collaborative Brainstorming Idea Organization Through Distributed and Parallel Sorting

Joel Helquist
Utah Valley University, USA

Christopher B. R. Diller
University of Nebraska at Omaha, USA

John Kruse
MITRE Corporation, USA

ABSTRACT

This chapter examines the post-convergence process of organizing ideas that are generated during collaborative idea generation activities. The method presented reduces the impact of organizing brainstorming ideas on individual participants by dividing the organization activity into smaller, discrete tasks that can be completed individually, and in parallel, by the participants. The entire pool of brainstorming ideas is subdivided into smaller pools and each participant is then tasked with organizing one of the subsets of ideas. The results show that by dividing up the overall activity into subtasks, the subjects experienced a more favorable environment. Furthermore, the subjects were able to work through their subset of ideas and produce results that were similar to those performing the full sort of the entire pool.

Changes in technology and connectedness have yielded a proliferation of tools that enable collaboration between individuals. These collaborative tools vary in sophistication and in the types of collaboration that are enabled, from simple instant messaging to complex Group Decision Support systems. Despite the proliferation of tools and vast body of research, many challenges still exist in making collaboration a simple and reliable approach for broad use. These challenges impede the effectiveness and efficiency

DOI: 10.4018/978-1-7998-4891-2.ch001

Copyright © 2021, IGI Global. Copying or distributing in print or electronic forms without written permission of IGI Global is prohibited.

with which individuals and groups can solve problems. Even worse, these challenges keep people away from collaborating (Denning & Yaholkovsky, 2008).

One such collaborative challenge revolves around the ability of large groups to collaborate effectively (Helquist, Kruse, Meservy, & Deokar, 2011; Kruse, Helquist, & Adkins, 2008; Thorpe & Albrecht, 2004). An increasing amount of research is currently underway on crowdsourcing various tasks and harnessing the wisdom of the crowds. These large groups pose a problem as they often do not lend themselves to traditional collaboration tools and methodologies as their characteristics are different.

Two of the key characteristics of large group collaboration are the proximity of the participants and the synchronicity of the collaboration (Helquist, Kruse, & Nunamaker Jr., 2009). Traditional collaboration has focused extensively on synchronous, face-to-face interaction, often led by a facilitator. However, due to physical and logistical constraints, large groups often require the use of physically distributed and asynchronous collaboration (Helquist, Kruse, Deokar, & Meservy, 2013). The increased number of participants, geographic distribution of participants, and asynchronous interaction all increase the complexity of the collaborative engagement (de Vreede, Briggs, van Duin, & Enserink, 2000). These factors can lead to more content being created during ideation and can complicate coordination among participants as they cannot easily communicate, focus attention, or achieve group understanding as they might in a smaller face-to-face group.

Collaborative work activities can be organized by what is called the "patterns of collaboration" (de Vreede & Briggs, 2019; de Vreede & Briggs, 2018). These patterns include the following:

- Generate: Brainstorming to identify solutions to the issue at hand.
- Reduce: Moving from many brainstormed ideas to a few worthy of more attention.
- Clarify: Improving the understanding of the brainstorming ideas.
- Organize: Organizing the ideas into groups or buckets to understand relationships.
- Evaluate: Identifying the ideas that provide the most value or utility.
- Build commitment: Improving the level of buy-in among the stakeholders.

The first stage, generate, is a classic ideation phase where groups brainstorm ideas. The next two steps, reduce and clarify, are convergence activities enable the group to reduce the content by summarizing and combining the brainstorming content. The overall effort of these two activities is to focus and make the content more valuable or usable by identifying the ideas most worthy of further consideration.

The organize phase allows the group to structure and synthesize the content. The brainstorming ideas are grouped into categories or buckets. Typically, this process is handled through a facilitator that guides the group through the organization process. However, in a large group setting, this activity becomes increasingly difficult to execute. Because the tasks inherent in changing the organization or structure of brainstorming ideas is normally a group-level activity, there is a need for an increased level of communication and collaboration between the collaborators.

Without increased coordination or facilitation, the actions of the participants will tend to result in task collisions, confusion and wasted effort. Thus, existing collaborative activities are also largely serial as the participants are forced to work together as a group, even with a facilitator, to avoid these collisions and reach some form of consensus with regard to the final organization phase output.

This research investigates organization activities in an effort to further understand the potential for changing current collaborative processes and tools with respect to large groups. The goal is to improve tools and methodologies that will enable large groups to collaborate effectively and efficiently in a distributed, asynchronous context. This paper is organized as follows. First, literature is presented regarding collaboration and different approaches to conducting collaborative work, followed by research questions, the approach of this research project, results, application, and conclusion.

LITERATURE REVIEW

Post-Generate Phase Challenges

Idea generation, or divergence, activities have received considerable attention in the literature (Anson, Bostrom, & Wynne, 1995; Briggs, de Vreede, & Nunamaker Jr., 2003; Nunamaker Jr., Briggs, Mittleman, Vogel, & Balthazard, 1996; Romano Jr., Briggs, Nunamaker Jr., & Mittleman, 1999; Valacich, Dennis, & Nunamaker Jr., 1992). Brainstorming is the activity that dominates the category and it is used extensively across collaboration modalities. It is low complexity and can be performed easily in parallel, by distributed participants, or even asynchronously, as it requires minimal collaborative coordination or interaction between the participants. Although there may be qualitative benefits to working in concert (e.g., the ability to see others' ideas while brainstorming), this is not a requirement. Each individual is able to submit ideas in parallel, yielding a low overhead way to generate content.

In contrast, convergence, and the subsequent organization, evaluation, and consensus building activities, tend to have much higher requirements for use (Briggs et al., 2003). These activities are of a much higher complexity and require more collaboration and interaction from the participants. These activities take many forms, but generally, they aim to move the group from having unstructured or semi-structured, and often repetitive, content to having a more coherent, structured, and succinct output of value for a particular end. Unlike the parallel brainstorming tasks, these post-ideation phases typically requires the group to work serially - considering, synthesizing, aggregating, and prioritizing the content together. These activities require a higher level of collaboration and interaction between the participants, creating an increased level of difficulty and cognitive load.

One of these activities that is typically performed serially and through a facilitator is organization. In this task, the participants group the brainstorming ideas into similar buckets. The facilitator typically guides the group as they review the brainstorming ideas, clustering similar thoughts, removing non-solutions, and trying to better understand the overall pool of ideas.

Work from Chen et al (1996) illustrates that satisfaction levels dip when groups move from divergence (idea generation) activities to convergence and subsequent (idea organization) activities. Similarly, the amount of time required by the group is greater for convergence activities than divergence activities. The end result is that the groups typically enjoy generating content while coalescing and organizing that content is more time consuming, laborious, and less satisfying.

Unlike divergence, the post-brainstorming activities have received little attention in the literature (Briggs et al., 2003). More specifically, the organization pattern of collaboration has not received much, if any, attention in the literature (de Vreede & Briggs, 2019). Recently, new research has come out investigating the reduce and clarify phases that constitute convergence (Seeber, Merz, Maier, de Vreede, & Weber, 2017; Seeber, 2019; Seeber, de Vreede, Maier, & Weber, 2017). More work is still needed to understand these convergence activities. Furthermore, the lack of literature regarding organization leaves a void in knowledge regarding a critical component of collaborative work. As a consequence, there exists a need to conduct exploratory research to further understand the complexities of organization as well as methodologies and tools for mitigating those complexities.

Facilitated Collaboration

Considerable research has been conducted over the years to examine different methodologies to plan and execute collaborative activities. One approach to collaboration is to use a skilled facilitator to lead and guide the group through the various collaborative activities. Research shows the productivity gains that can be achieved by using a skilled facilitator to guide the participants through the collaborative stages (Adkins, Younger, & Schwarz, 2003; Anson et al., 1995; Griffith, Fuller, & Northcraft, 1998; Schwarz, 2002; Zhao, Nunamaker Jr., & Briggs, 2002). As the director of the collaborative group, the facilitator performs a critical role for the group, significantly impacting the productivity and success of the group.

Despite the productivity gains from using a facilitator in collaborative sessions, many organizations have stopped using facilitators. Research by Briggs, et al (2003), investigates the reasons why facilitated collaboration sessions have become less common. Their results indicate that successful facilitators possess unique skillsets and develop organizational knowledge through facilitating various groups. Over time, these facilitators' skills and abilities are recognized and they tend to be moved to other critical non-facilitation duties within the organization.

Even when the facilitator is present, various contextual factors can increase the difficulty of executing the facilitator role. As the size of the group increases, the facilitator must be able to accommodate and direct an increasing number of participants (Helquist, Kruse, & Adkins, 2006b). Additionally, an increasing number of participants tends to increase the volume of content generated by the group. Finally, during the more complicated, and often serial, convergence and organization activities, there are often an increased number of participants that are involved in the decision-making processes. All of these increase the complexity and the load on the facilitator (Helquist, Kruse, & Adkins, 2006a). These factors are further compounded when the participants are geographically distributed and/or working asynchronously. As a result, we believe that there is a potential to improve the effectiveness and efficiency of collaborative work in these challenging environments through the use of innovative communication tools and facilitation methods.

Collaboration Engineering

Briggs, et al (2003), proposed a new collaboration methodology called Collaboration Engineering to enable groups to design collaborative engagements that minimizes the need for a skilled facilitator during the actual conduct of the group work. Collaboration Engineering can be defined as follows (de Vreede & Briggs, 2019):

An approach to designing collaborative work practices for high value tasks, and deploying them to practitioners to execute for themselves without ongoing support collaboration experts (p. 108).

This approach divides the overall collaborative process into separate component activities, called thinkLets, which can be assembled by a facilitation expert into various workflows depending on the context. The idea is that this experienced individual can set the workflow a priori and the semi-skilled participants are then able to follow the collaborative workflow without a facilitator to guide the interaction. This approach to collaboration increases the number of contexts in which collaboration can be successful (de Vreede & Briggs, 2019; de Vreede & Briggs, 2018). However, despite the improvements associated with thinkLets, the challenges of large, distributed, asynchronous groups still remain (Helquist, Deokar, Meservy, & Kruse, 2011).

Participant-Driven Group Support Systems

Participant-driven Group Support Systems (PD-GSS) is a different approach to collaboration that also enables collaboration in contexts without a facilitator (Helquist, Kruse, & Adkins, 2008; Helquist, Kruse, & Nunamaker F., Jr., 2010). PD-GSS utilizes a crowdsourcing methodology to divide up large collaborative tasks into discrete, smaller, more manageable tasks. Each participant is then able to complete various tasks independently and autonomously. Participants are also regularly asked to evaluate aspects of the product and are then polled to determine where further effort should be applied. The product evolves as the participants evaluate the product, identify opportunities for work, and then the participants perform that work. By breaking up the product into small, discrete tasks and leveraging the participants' individual efforts, PD-GSS enables the entire group to make progress through the collaborative workflow by providing a lattice of structure that would normally be furnished by a facilitator.

This design provides some advantages as compared with traditional, facilitated collaboration as well as the thinkLets approach. First, since participants are working in parallel and anonymously, PD-GSS provides an effective mechanism for working in distributed environments (Helquist, Deokar, et al., 2011). Similarly, the design minimizes dependence on communication and coordination between the participants; the system guides the participants and leverages their judgment in a somewhat dynamic workflow. As a result, PD-GSS also enables asynchronous collaboration. Lastly, the crowdsourcing approach actually benefits from an increasing number of participants. Large groups provide more judgment for evaluating the product, and more resources with which to complete the discrete tasks, expediting the overall collaborative process (Dennis & Valacich, 1993).

Research Objective

The overarching objective of this research project is to explore one of the core activities that is common after convergence, *idea organization*. The goal of this research is to further understand the idea organization task within the PD-GSS paradigm so that collaboration can be improved with large, asynchronous, and distributed groups.

DISTRIBUTED, PARALLEL SORTING

This research examines the organization activity of grouping or clustering brainstorming ideas. Typically, this activity immediately follows the brainstorming and convergence stages; the participants identify similar ideas within the brainstorming content and group them. In traditional, facilitated collaboration, this idea organization is performed serially through facilitator-led discussion. It is a time-consuming process that requires the participants to serially consider contributions and come to a certain level of agreement in their organization.

As part of the PD-GSS paradigm, the overall clustering activity can be broken down into smaller tasks. Each participant is assigned a subset of ideas from the overall list of brainstorming ideas. The participant then works autonomously to create clusters from the ideas received. This process is then iterated with other participants receiving other subsets of brainstorming ideas and performing their own clusters. In this fashion, each individual works independently to cluster a subset of the full set of ideas; the individual subset sorts are then combined to form the final sort of all the brainstorming content.

By decomposing the overall sorting process into more manageable tasks, the PD-GSS approach enables each participant to continue their parallel work, avoiding the bottleneck of having to work together converging. These discrete tasks also accommodate participation in distributed and in asynchronous environments. Distributed, parallel sorting aims to address the challenges of organization and improve end user satisfaction by leveraging the larger number of participants and reducing the burden on each individual participant while removing the requirement of a skilled facilitator.

METHODOLOGY

Research Questions

This research project is exploratory in nature due to the lack of extant literature. As such, two research questions are examined:

1. Does working on a subset of ideas, rather than the full list of ideas, reduce the burden on the participants?

Sorting a subset of ideas, rather than the full list of ideas, may lead to a reduced burden on the participants. Alternatively, sorting a subset of ideas may still lead to a comparable burden.

2. Can sorting a subset of ideas yield a result that is comparable to a full sort?

One of the risks of providing only a subset of ideas to organize is that the participant may not have the entire context from which to organize. Individuals that sort the entire pool of ideas are able to see and process the entire body of information that needs to be categorized, improving the context and vision. It is possible that reducing the contextual awareness of each participant, by limiting the number of ideas to sort, will hinder the overall quality of the final sort.

Experimental Procedure

An experiment was conducted to examine these research questions. Subjects were randomly assigned to one of three treatments, each with varying quantities of ideas to organize. These ideas were generated by a previous collaborative group. The subjects all used the ThinkTank commercial collaborative software to create the clusters for their subset of ideas. Each subject completed a pretest survey, watched a brief training video on the ThinkTank software and how to use it to complete the sorting task. Additionally, all subjects were given printed instructions that reinforced the video instructions.

After completing the sort in ThinkTank, the subject completed a post-survey to gather various self-report measures before leaving the experiment.

Independent Variable

The independent variable is the number of ideas to be sorted by each subject. Three different treatments were used:

- Condition A required the subject to sort all 110 brainstorming items
- Condition B required the subject to sort 55 randomly-selected brainstorming ideas
- Condition C required the subject to sort either 36 or 37 randomly-selected brainstorming ideas

Dependent Variables

Several self-reported measures were gathered via the post-survey to examine the first research question regarding the burden of participation. These subjective measures included the following:

- Perceived difficulty of the sorting task
- Level of fatigue
- Satisfaction with the process
- Satisfaction with the results

The second research question, the effectiveness or quality of the final sort, was assessed via Normalized Clustering Error (NCE). NCE provides a quantitative metric to compare each subject's sort to a sort generated by an expert facilitator (Roussinov & Chen, 1999). The participant's sort is compared with the expert sort to identify the number of correct associations, as compared with the expert sort, as well as the number of incorrect associations. The NCE value ranges from zero to one. Zero means that the two sorts are identical (a perfect result). One means that there are no similarities between the two (a completely incorrect result).

In this research, the expert facilitator sorted the entire pool of brainstorming idea (110 items) while two of the three treatment groups only sorted a subset of these ideas. In order to run the NCE calculation, the facilitator's sort was pruned to leave only the same brainstorming ideas that the subject sorted. In this fashion, NCE metrics can be derived for all subjects' sorts regardless of the treatment or number of ideas sorted.

In condition A, each subject sorted all 110 items individually. This treatment served as the control group. Since each individual sorted all of the items, each individual completed a full sort and thus their full sort could be compared with the full expert sort to generate the NCE value.

Conditions B and C required the subjects to sort a subset of either 55 ideas or 36 or 37 ideas, respectively. These treatments required the pruning of the expert facilitator sort before the NCE calculation could be run.

Participants

All of the subjects were recruited from a Management Information Systems class. In total, 352 subjects participated in the experiment. Condition A consisted of 56 subjects. Condition B consisted of 122 subjects. Condition C consisted of 174 subjects.

RESULTS AND DISCUSSION

Self-Reported Measures

The first set of analyses investigated the impact of dividing up the task on the self-perception measures in the post-survey, including ratings of difficulty, fatigue, and satisfaction.

Difficulty was rated using a seven-point Likert scale from 1, "not at all difficult", to 7, "very difficult". Helmert contrasts were used to investigate the differences between the three treatment conditions. The means and standard deviations are presented in table 1.

Table 1. Mean Difficulty Rating by Condition

Treatment	N	Mean	St. Dev.
A	49	3.59	1.74
B	96	2.93	1.60
C	201	3.00	1.66

Treatment A, the full 110 item sort, yielded significantly higher difficulty ratings than treatment B, $t(343) = -2.287$, $p = .023$, and treatment C, $t(343) = -2.244$, $p = .025$. No significant difference was observed between treatments B and C. Subjects sorting a subset of the full ideas reported experiencing significantly less difficulty than those completing the full sort.

Fatigue was measured comparing pretest ratings of fatigue with post-test ratings using paired t-tests. Each question utilized a seven-point Likert scale to respond to the phrase, "I am mentally fatigued right now". The response range was from 1, "strongly disagree", to 7, "strongly agree". The means and standard deviations for fatigue from both the pre and post-tests are shown in table 2.

Table 2. Pre-test and Post-test Fatigue Levels by Condition

Treatment		N	Mean	St. Dev.
A	Pre	50	2.96	1.59
	Post	49	3.98	1.68
B	Pre	100	3.05	1.70
	Post	96	3.13	1.58
C	Pre	202	2.84	1.56
	Post	201	2.92	1.56

Treatment A produced a significant increase in the level of fatigue, $t(48) = -5.43, p < .001$. No significant differences were found in treatments B and C, as the change from pre to post was only a slight increase. The subjects sorting the entire set of ideas experienced an increased level of fatigue while the subjects sorting a subset of the full set did not.

The first satisfaction measure assessed the subject's satisfaction with the process. This measure utilized a seven-point Likert scale with 1 representing "very dissatisfied" to 7 representing "very satisfied". Helmert contrasts were used to compare the treatments. The means and standard deviations by condition are shown in table 3.

Table 3. Mean Satisfaction with the Process by Condition

Treatment	N	Mean	St. Dev.
A	49	4.59	1.72
B	96	5.02	1.26
C	201	5.15	1.27

Treatment A was significantly worse than treatment C, $t(61) = -2.132, p = .037$. No significant differences were found between treatments A and B or between treatments B and C. Reducing the number of ideas to be organized to 36 or 37 yielded higher satisfaction with the process ratings than sorting all 110 ideas.

The final self-reported measure examined was satisfaction with the results. This question also used a seven-point Likert scale from 1, "very dissatisfied", to 7, "very satisfied". The means and standard deviations by condition are presented in table 4.

Table 4. Mean Satisfaction with the Results by Condition

Treatment	N	Mean	St. Dev.
A	49	4.51	1.65
B	96	5.06	1.24
C	201	5.16	1.20

The Helmert contrasts revealed that treatment A subjects were significantly less satisfied with the results than treatment C subjects, $t(61) = -2.614, p = .011$. Treatment A subjects were also significantly less satisfied with the results than treatment B, $t(76) = -2.068, p = .042$. No significant difference was found between treatments B and C.

The subset sorting treatments produced significantly higher ratings of satisfaction with the results than the full-sort treatment.

Quantitative Results

The efficacy of each subject's sorting was assessed using the NCE metric. NCE ranges from zero, indicating a perfect match between the expert facilitator's sort and the subject's sort, to one, indicating no matches between the two sorts. Table 5 shows the NCE means and standard deviations by treatment.

Table 5. Mean NCE Values by Condition

Treatment	N	Mean	St. Dev.
A	55	.742	.08
B	121	.725	.10
C	172	.709	.12

A test of homogeneity of variances, Levene statistic, indicated that the variances are not homogenous. Accordingly, comparison of the means was examined using the Welch statistic. No significant differences in NCE values were identified between the three treatments, $F(2, 168.2) = 2.644$, $p = .074$. All three treatments produced the same quality sorts as compared with the expert facilitator.

Relationship Between Qualitative and Quantitative Results

One additional analysis was conducted to examine the relationship between the self-reported, perceptual measures measuring the burden of the task and objective performance on the sorting task itself. Partial least squares (PLS) was selected as the data analysis technique and WarpPLS was the software used to conduct the analysis (Kock, 2010, 2011, 2013).

The PLS model was defined to show the self-reported measures loading an exogenous latent variable representing the burden on the participants. This latent variable has a direct link with the endogenous performance latent variable, which is constructed of the quantitative sorting effectiveness metric (NCE).

The indicator loadings and cross-loadings for this analysis are presented in Table 6. These loadings examine the assumption that each indicator variable reflects only one latent construct (Kock, 2010). All of the indicator variables load properly on their respective latent constructs and are significant.

Table 6. Indicator Loading and Cross-loadings

Indicator	Loading: Burden	Loading: Performance	p-value
Difficulty	0.619	0.026	< 0.001
Fatigue	0.506	0.178	< 0.001
Satisfaction with Results	0.835	-0.070	< 0.001
Satisfaction with Process	0.833	-0.056	< 0.001
NCE	0.000	1.000	< 0.001

Table 7 shows the correlation among the latent constructs using the average variance extracted (AVE) to assess discriminant validity. For each latent construct, the square root of the average variance extracted should be higher than any of the other correlations for that latent construct. The data conforms to this standard and the correlation is significant at a $\alpha = 0.05$ significance level.

Table 7. Correlation Among Latent Constructs

	Burden	Performance
Burden	0.712	-0.123
Performance	-0.123	1.000

Figure 1 shows the structural model with the R^2 value for the endogenous latent variable performance as well as the path coefficient. The relationship between the two variables is significant, $p < .01$; an increase in the perceived burden affects a decrease in performance effectiveness. However, while significant, this relationship only accounts for 2% of the variation in performance. This low R^2 value is likely due, in part, to the simplistic model and the single exogenous latent variable. Further research in this area is warranted to further analyze a model that captures additional exogenous latent variables and paths.

Figure 1. PLS Structural Model Results

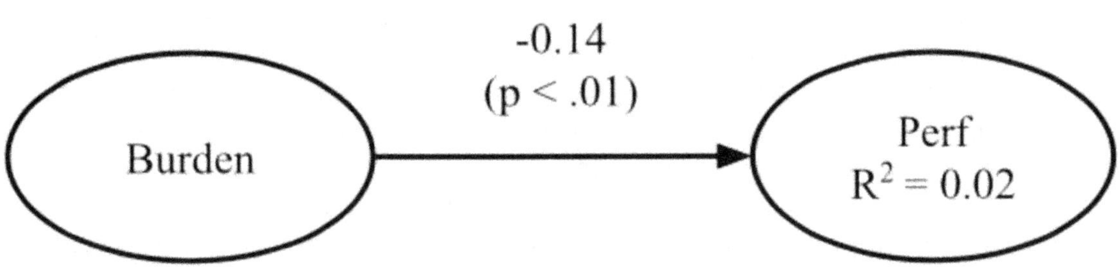

APPLICATION

The ability to break up and perform collaborative tasks in a distributed and asynchronous manner opens up many possibilities for practical application. While distributed and asynchronous divergence is straightforward and relatively common, convergence and subsequent collaborative activities are not. The core activities in these phases revolve around transforming information to make it more useful. Typically, this requires some form of shared understanding among the group members that is generated through a facilitator.

This research into idea organization, however, shows that it is possible to successfully divide up and delegate a task that was previously thought to not be easily divisible. Moreover, the participants in this task have been able to successfully create idea clusters and populate them without the benefit of seeing the full range of ideas available. This implies that the participants can, in some cases, successfully contribute in structuring and transforming information into a collaborative product with incomplete information.

The driving force behind this research was to identify realistic means for making large-scale PD-GSS a reality. Participants have a limited capacity for attending to the wealth of information developed by large groups. If each participant has limited attention, the collaboration process must present individuals with limited information on issues. Currently, this is not done and users are required to invest a great deal of effort, or those running the process simplify the task. The underlying idea behind PD-GSS is to break up the collaborative task into smaller tasks that can be successfully performed by individuals. In effect, it is trying to perform collaborative work as an aggregation of discrete individual actions. This approach allows practitioners to scale collaborative processes beyond the typical group sizes that are seen today. In fact, this approach allows collaboration owners to leverage the wisdom of the crowds and apply crowdsourcing resources to collaborative tasks.

Beyond improving the ability to scale and distribute collaboration, this approach may also yield a decrease in the complexity of the processes and associated support. For instance, once convergence and organization tasks can be performed in a more mechanistic and predictable fashion, the dependence on a skilled facilitator for process guidance is decreased. By lowering the costs of collaboration, both financially and in terms of complexity, practitioners and researchers may be able to open up a broader variety of tasks to group-derived solutions. This may also help to minimize the bias and influence of facilitators, which can be introduced through traditional facilitation (Briggs, De Vreede, Nunamaker Jr., & Tobey, 2001).

Additionally, breaking up and distributing organization tasks may enable collaborators to engage a broader population of participants. Currently, participation in convergence and organization tasks requires a high degree of attention and commitment as participants are asked to look at all of the data and work to develop shared understanding in order to contribute to the transformation of the information. When it is possible to break up these tasks, it is also possible to get the marginal value of contributions of many less committed people as they can be asked to participate on simpler tasks for shorter durations.

In looking for an illustrative example of where this approach might be beneficial, it is best to select a class of problem that is difficult both in terms of scale and task complexity, and also has limits on the general commitment level of the participants. Often, public policy and planning issues meet all three of these requirements. Regional transportation issues, for example, can be solved in any number of ways and are of interest to the majority of adults in the community. Nevertheless, solution sets are usually developed by small numbers of professionals augmented with highly motivated individuals and special interest groups that will participate in public meetings. Government officials may be able get some broader public input through surveys or interviews, but these typically are of more use in gauging support rather than formulating options. Through a series of divergence and organization activities, the government officials may be able to take a large group from the initial problem to a recommended solution. This example assumes an on-line web site that can host the collaborative activities.

The first step in this process would be a divergence task to brainstorm ideas for addressing a problem or situation. In this example, the government might post a question to the public such as, "how can the city of Springfield improve rush hour traffic?" The public participants would then openly brainstorm ideas. In the next round of the process, the government could utilize the clustering activity investigated in this effort to organize all of the previously developed ideas. Successive rounds of brainstorming and clustering could also be utilized to flesh out pros, cons, constraints, resources and timing associated with each cluster. Voting can also be integrated into the process at any point to decrease the number of issues or details being considered by the group. Ultimately, with only brainstorming, clustering and voting, a very large group can collaborate to produce a detailed and substantive product that better reflects public sentiment than can typically be achieved today.

The same approach could be utilized in more traditional, face-to-face, collaborative settings. A meeting facilitator would conduct the traditional divergence brainstorming activities as usual. However, instead of working as a full group to organize and transform all of the material from the divergence activities, subsets of smaller groups could work through subsets of the divergence material.

CONCLUSION

The objective of the parallel sort is to divide the collaborative phase of idea organization into smaller tasks to reduce the impact on individual collaborative participants. By completing partial sorts rather than full sorts, the subjects experience an easier environment. Additionally, it affords the possibility for asynchronous and distributed participation in sorting tasks, which would allow collaboration with large groups.

This work is in line with existing research that calls for more investigation of collaboration that is beyond or expanding the scope of what is typically defined as collaboration (de Vreede & Briggs, 2019; de Vreede & Briggs, 2018). de Vreede and Briggs (2019) point out that traditional collaboration uses and resources have changed dramatically over the years. Considerable research still needs to be conducted to examine what are the best practices for handling these crowdsourced, collaborative projects.

Analysis of the self-reported measures provides support for the idea that the partial sort treatments produce a less demanding experience. Subjects reported being less fatigued and found the experiment less difficult. Similarly, partial sorting produced higher levels of satisfaction with the collaborative process as well as the end result. Ideally, the decreased impact from participating in collaboration may lead to improved motivation to participate in collaboration and to stay engaged in the collaboration. Future research is needed to investigate this impact.

The quality of the final sorting was no different between the three treatments. These results lend support for the idea that even though the treatment conditions only sorted a subset of ideas, this limited view of the entire brainstorming pool did not hinder their ability to accurately organize the brainstorming ideas. The implication of this finding is important in the support of the PD-GSS paradigm, as each participant can contribute to the overall group effort while both lowering requirements on each individual and potentially speeding the organization process

The next research challenge is to investigate methods to aggregate these partial subsorts into one full sort that constitutes the summation of the group work. In this fashion, individuals can work independently, categorizing subsets of ideas, while the system aggregates these individual subsets into a meaningful whole. Research is currently underway in this area. One of the first studies constructed a weighted graph to aggregate all of the partial sorts (Helquist, Diller, & Kruse, 2019). A partitioning algorithm was used to partition the graph and assign brainstorming ideas to specific buckets. These buckets were also compared against sorts from an expert facilitator. The results show that this aggregation method is feasible and that it benefits from a crowdsourced approach of adding more labor (i.e., partial sorts from each individual participant).

The results from these crowdsourced organization tasks may not quite be a finished product but they may serve as the starting point for a group to further refine the organization and proceed on to voting and prioritizing activities.

While not yet complete, this work is producing promising results that are interesting to both researchers and practitioners. As mentioned previously, for researchers, this is an entirely new area that needs to be explored. The notion of dividing up tasks and recompiling the final sorts in a PD-GSS fashion aligns closely with many of the same themes and goals of crowdsourcing, which is becoming a large area of research. Many questions exist as to the specifics of executing a PD-GSS collaborative process that enables the proper decomposition of large tasks into smaller, discrete tasks.

From a practitioner perspective, these results provide interesting application into new methods for executing collaborative activities. One such approach is that a facilitator may choose to decompose one larger collaborative group into smaller collaborative group, each smaller group working on a subset of the problem concurrently. The implication from this approach is that not only does it reduce the burden on each participant but it also reduces the time to achieve a first draft of an organized set of ideas. This approach may yield participants that are more eager to stay engaged and participate in the collaborative activities due to the decreased burden. It may also open up participation to those with less time or commitment than is typical today. The most important implication may be that people can begin to perform higher value collaborative work with less process management. By lowering the barriers to collaborative work, practitioners can open up a broader variety of problem sets to collaborative solutions.

REFERENCES

Adkins, M., Younger, R., & Schwarz, R. (2003). Information technology augmentation of the skilled facilitator approach. In *Proceedings of the 36th Annual Hawaii International Conference on System Sciences*. Computer Society Press. 10.1109/HICSS.2003.1173776

Anson, R., Bostrom, R., & Wynne, B. (1995). An experiment assessing group support system and facilitator effects on meeting outcomes. *Management Science*, *41*(2), 189–208. doi:10.1287/mnsc.41.2.189

Briggs, R. O., de Vreede, G.-J., & Nunamaker, J. F. Jr. (2003). Collaboration engineering with ThinkLets to pursue sustained sucess with group support systems. *Journal of Management Information Systems*, *19*(4), 31–64. doi:10.1080/07421222.2003.11045743

Briggs, R. O., De Vreede, G. J., Nunamaker, J. F. Jr, & Tobey, D. (2001). ThinkLets: achieving predictable, repeatable patterns of group interaction with group support systems (GSS). In *Proceedings of the 34th Annual Hawaii International Conference on System Sciences*. Computer Society Press. 10.1109/HICSS.2001.926238

Chen, H., Houston, A., Nunamaker, J. F. Jr, & Yen, J. (1996). Toward intelligent meeting agents. *Computer*, *29*(8), 62–70. doi:10.1109/2.532047

de Vreede, G. J., & Briggs, R. (2018). *Collaboration Engineering: Reflections on 15 Years of Research & Practice*. Retrieved from https://aisel.aisnet.org/hicss-51/cl/processes_and_technologies_for_team/4/

de Vreede, G.-J., & Briggs, R. O. (2019). A Program of Collaboration Engineering Research and Practice: Contributions, Insights, and Future Directions. *Journal of Management Information Systems*, *36*(1), 74–119. doi:10.1080/07421222.2018.1550552

de Vreede, G.-J., Briggs, R. O., van Duin, R., & Enserink, B. (2000). Athletics in electronic brainstorming: asynchronous electronic brainstorming in very large groups. In *Proceedings of the 33rd Annual Hawaii International Conference on System Sciences*. Computer Society Press. 10.1109/HICSS.2000.926627

Denning, P. J., & Yaholkovsky, P. (2008). Getting to "we." *Communications of the ACM, 51*(4), 19–24. Retrieved from file:///Users/avd108/Documents/articles/Denning,Yaholkovsky-2008.pdf

Dennis, A. R., & Valacich, J. S. (1993). Computer brainstorms: More heads are better than one. *The Journal of Applied Psychology*, *78*(4), 531–537. doi:10.1037/0021-9010.78.4.531

Griffith, T. L., Fuller, M. A., & Northcraft, G. B. (1998). Facilitator Influence in Group Support Systems: Intended and Unintended Effects. *Information Systems Research*, *9*(1), 20–36. doi:10.1287/isre.9.1.20

Helquist, J., Diller, C. B. R., & Kruse, J. (2019). Crowdsourcing Convergence: Aggregating Partial Clusters to Facilitate Collaborative Convergence. *Proceedings of the 52nd Hawaii International Conference on System Sciences. (HICSS 2019).* Retrieved from https://scholarspace.manoa.hawaii.edu/handle/10125/59492

Helquist, J. H., Deokar, A. V., Meservy, T. O., & Kruse, J. (2011). Dynamic collaboration: Participant-driven agile processes for complex tasks. *ACM SIGMIS Database*, *42*(2), 95–115. doi:10.1145/1989098.1989104

Helquist, J. H., Kruse, J., & Adkins, M. (2006a). Developing large scale participant-driven group support systems: An approach to facilitating large groups. In R. H. Sprague Jr, R. O. Briggs, & J. F. Nunamaker Jr. (Eds.), *First HICSS Symposium on Field and Case Studies of Collaboration*. Los Alamitos, CA: IEEE Computer Society Press.

Helquist, J. H., Kruse, J., & Adkins, M. (2006b). Group support systems for very large groups: A peer review process to filter brainstorming input. *Proceedings of the Americas Conference on Information Systems*.

Helquist, J. H., Kruse, J., & Adkins, M. (2008). Participant-driven collaborative convergence. In *Proceedings of the 41st Annual Hawaii International Conference on System Sciences*. Computer Society Press.

Helquist, J. H., Kruse, J., Deokar, A., & Meservy, T. O. (2013). Enabling large group collaboration. In Collaboration Systems: Concept, Value, and Use (pp. 128–142). M.E. Sharpe, Inc.

Helquist, J. H., Kruse, J., Meservy, T. O., & Deokar, A. (2011). Facilitating large group collaboration. In Collaboration Science, Technologies, Processes and Applications: Vol. Advances i. Armonk, NY: M.E. Sharpe, Inc.

Helquist, J. H., Kruse, J., & Nunamaker, F., Jr. J. (2010). Participant-driven approach to autonomously cluster brainstorming ideas. In E-Collaboration Technologies and Organizational Performance: Current and Future Trends. IGI Global.

Helquist, J. H., Kruse, J., & Nunamaker, J. F. Jr. (2009). Synchronicity and group ability to autonomously cluster brainstorming ideas. *International Journal of e-Collaboration*, *5*(4), 67–81. doi:10.4018/jec.2009062605

Jr, N. (1996). Lessons from a dozen years of group support systems research: A discussion of lab and field findings. *Journal of Management Information Systems*, *13*(3), 163–207. doi:10.1080/07421222.1996.11518138

Kock, N. (2010). Using WarpPLS in e-collaboration studies: An overview of five main analysis steps. *International Journal of e-Collaboration*, *6*(4), 1–11. doi:10.4018/jec.2010100101

Kock, N. (2011). Using WarpPLS in e-collaboration studies: Descriptive statistics, settings, and key analysis results. *International Journal of e-Collaboration*, *7*(2), 1–18. doi:10.4018/jec.2011040101

Kock, N. (2013). Using WarpPLS in E-Collaboration Studies: What if I Have Only One Group and One Condition? *International Journal of e-Collaboration*, *9*(3), 1–12. doi:10.4018/jec.2013070101

Kruse, J., Helquist, J. H., & Adkins, M. (2008). Large-scale collaboration for ill-structured problems. *Thirteenth International Command and Control Research Symposium.*

Romano, N. C. Jr, Briggs, R. O., Nunamaker, J. F. Jr, & Mittleman, D. (1999). Distributed GSS facilitation and participation: Field action research. In *Proceedings of the Thirty-Second Annual Hawaii International Conference on System Sciences*. Computer Society Press. 10.1109/HICSS.1999.772737

Roussinov, D. G., & Chen, H. (1999). Document clustering for electronic meetings: An experimental comparison of two techniques. *Decision Support Systems*, *27*(1–2), 67–79. doi:10.1016/S0167-9236(99)00037-8

Schwarz, R. (2002). *The skilled facilitator: A comprehensive resource for consultants, facilitators, managers, trainers, and coaches*. John Wiley & Sons.

Seeber, I. (2019). How do facilitation interventions foster learning? The role of evaluation and coordination as causal mediators in idea convergence. *Computers in Human Behavior*, *94*, 176–189. doi:10.1016/j.chb.2018.11.033

Seeber, I., de Vreede, G.-J., Maier, R., & Weber, B. (2017). Beyond Brainstorming: Exploring Convergence in Teams. *Journal of Management Information Systems*, *34*(4), 939–969. doi:10.1080/07421222.2017.1393303 PMID:29399005

Seeber, I., Merz, A., Maier, R., de Vreede, G.-J., & Weber, B. (2017). Convergence on self-generated vs. crowdsourced ideas in crisis response: comparing social exchange processes and satisfaction with process. *50th Hawaii International Conference on System Sciences (HICSS 2017)*. Retrieved from https://orbit.dtu.dk/en/publications/convergence-on-self--generated-vs-crowdsourced-ideas-in-crisis-response-comparing-social-exchange-processes-and-satisfaction-with-process(53fc726c-c3e5-4cd2-8810-1f860c9dbd92).html

Thorpe, J., & Albrecht, C. C. (2004). Characteristics of large group support systems. In *Proceedings of the 37th Annual Hawaii International Conference on Systems Sciences*. Computer Society Press.

Valacich, J. S., Dennis, A. R., & Nunamaker, J. F. Jr. (1992). Group Size and Anonymity Effects on Computer-Mediated Idea Generation. *Small Group Research*, *23*(1), 49–73. doi:10.1177/1046496492231004

Zhao, J. L., Nunamaker, J. F. Jr, & Briggs, R. O. (2002). Intelligent workflow techniques for distributed group facilitation. In *Proceedings of the 35th Annual Hawaii International Conference on Systems Sciences*. Computer Society Press. 10.1109/HICSS.2002.993940

Chapter 2
A Version and Context-Based Approach to Easily Model Flexible Collaborative Processes

Fatma Ellouze
Faculty of Economics and Management of Sfax, Tunisia

Mohamed Amine Chaabane
Higher Institute of Business Administration, Tunisia

Eric Andonoff
University of Toulouse 1, France

Rafik Bouaziz
Faculty of Economics and Management, University of Sfax, Tunisia

ABSTRACT

Process flexibility has been investigated for intra-organizational processes, but it is still an open issue for collaborative processes (CP), each of which is defined as a set of intra-organizational processes that interact together. In the literature, the version-based approach is largely used in the field of business process management (BPM) to cope with process flexibility. However, BPM practitioners can face difficulties in a multi-version environment. So, the following questions arise: How can we use the version-based approach to easily model flexible CP? Does an appropriate version exist for a given situation or is it necessary to create a new one? The chapter answers these questions recommending a solution for the modeling of CP versions and the retrieval of the adequate CP version for a given situation. This solution comprises (1) a meta-model to consider the modeling of the CP versions, (2) an ontology-based approach to model and query the context of use of CP versions, and (3) a framework to provide support for both the modeling of CP versions and the context querying.

DOI: 10.4018/978-1-7998-4891-2.ch002

Copyright © 2021, IGI Global. Copying or distributing in print or electronic forms without written permission of IGI Global is prohibited.

INTRODUCTION

Process flexibility is an active research area in the field of Business Process Management (BPM). It is defined as the ability of processes to respond to both foreseen and unforeseen changes occurring in their operating environment. Change support is important for processes running within a single company (*i.e.*, intra-organizational processes), but also for Collaborative Processes (CP), which are processes crossing the boundaries of companies. More precisely, a CP is defined as a set of independent intra-organizational processes/partners interacting together (Aalst, 2000). BPM tools are convenient to manage CP that do not change over time. However, flexibility of CP, which corresponds to the ability of CP to change over time, has not been deeply investigated and it is still an open issue (Cognini, Corradini, Gnesi, Polini, & Re, 2018). This issue is very important as the strong competition between companies leads them to frequently change and adapt their CP to face new clients' requirements or to benefit from new collaboration opportunities.

In the literature, the version-based approach is largely used to cope with process flexibility, notably in the context of intra-organizational processes. Many research contributions have recommended the version-based approach to address process flexibility (*e.g.*, (Ben Said, Chaâbane, Bouaziz, & Andonoff, 2018; Chaâbane, Bouzguenda, & Bouaziz, 2011; Dadam & Reichert, 2009; Ellouze, Chaâbane, Bouaziz, & Andonoff, 2016; Ekanayake, La Rosa, ter Hofstede, & Fauvet, 2011; Kradolfer & Geppert, 1999; Zhao & Liu, 2013)) for the following reasons. On the one hand, it is the basic reality in companies: new technologies, governmental rules, organizational contexts or the adoption of new standards lead them to define several versions of their processes. On the other hand, it helps address four main needs of process flexibility (Reichert & Weber, 2012): (i) flexibility by variability, since it is possible to model alternative versions depending on the context of their execution, (ii) flexibility by evolution, since the different significant changes on processes are modeled within process versions, (iii) flexibility by looseness, since it is possible to model not completed versions, and (iv) flexibility by adaptation, since it is possible to model versions for occasional situations or anticipated exceptions.

However, BPM practitioners can face difficulties in a multi-version *environment*, mainly when modeling CP versions, due to the proliferation of versions. Therefore, the research question addressed in this paper is "how can we use the version-based approach to easily model flexible CP?" This question leads to another one, which is related to the reuse of (CP) versions, and, which can be summarized by the following question "Does an appropriate version exist for a given situation or is it necessary to create a new one?" This question is of utmost importance in a multi-version environment, where numerous versions co-exist. More precisely, in such an environment, BPM practitioners (*i.e.*, BPM end-users and designers) have to face the problem of selecting, among different versions, the most appropriate one to a given situation/context. This selection is required both at run-time, if BPM practitioners have to select the version of a CP to be executed, and at design-time, if they have to select an existing (CP) version to be used to make up a new (CP) version.

As each version is required in a specific context, it becomes crucial to consider the context to select an appropriate (CP) version. In the BPM area, the notion of context is defined as "the minimum of elements containing all relevant information that impact the design and the execution of a process" (Rosemann, Recker, & Flender, 2008). Actually, several taxonomies have been proposed to classify these context elements (*e.g.*, (Brocke, Zelt, & Schmiedel, 2016; Rosemann *et al.*, 2008; Saidani, Rolland, & Nurcan 2015; Wang, Zhang, Gu & Pung, 2004)). We outline the largest one, described in (Rosemann *et al.*, 2008), which distinguishes four types of context (i) immediate context, which covers elements on process components, namely context of activities, events, and resources, (ii) internal context, which includes elements on the internal environment of an organization that impacts the process (iii) external context, which encompass elements relating to external stakeholders of organizations, and finally (iv) environmental context, which contains elements related to external factors.

We emphasize the requirement of context-awareness in process versioning to define the context of use of (CP) versions and to create context-based queries to select adequate (CP) versions. We recommend an ontology-based approach for context modeling and querying. Indeed, it is worth taking advantage of the ontology to ensure a semantic interoperability between the partners involved in collaboration and to benefit from its reasoning capabilities.

Therefore, the contributions of the paper are as follows. The first contribution is VP2M, a meta-model for modeling CP versions. The second one is onto-VP2M, an ontology-based approach as a solution for context modeling and version querying. The third contribution is the onto-VP2M-Fw framework, which provides support for (i) context version modeling in the BPM area, and (ii) context querying based on reasoning mechanisms of the proposed ontology. Finally, the paper illustrates the modeling of flexible CP using onto-VP2M-Fw and considering a real case study from the maritime area, namely the Subsea Pipeline CP case study.

Accordingly, the remainder of the paper is organized as follows. The next section gives the basis of our solution for modeling flexible CP. In the "VP2M for Modeling Versions of Processes" section, we present the VP2M meta-model for CP versioning. The next section, entitled "Ontology-based Approach to Model and Query Version Context of CP", is devoted to the presentation of Onto-VP2M, the ontology-based approach for context modeling and version querying. In the "Onto-VP2M-Fw Framework" section, we present the framework supporting VP2M and Onto-VP2M, *i.e.*, allowing (i) the modeling of version and underlying context of use and (ii) the querying of version using context. The section entitled "Case Study" introduces the Subsea Pipeline case study, which will be used to illustrate the modeling of flexible CP. In the "Related Work" section, we give an overview of works addressing version modeling, context modeling and context querying in BPM, and compare our approach with that of these works. Finally, the last section concludes the paper and gives some directions for future works.

BASIS OF THE RECOMMENDED SOLUTION FOR MODELING FLEXIBLE CP

To address flexibility of CP, we recommend in this paper a solution that combines (i) the version-based approach to model versions of a CP and its components and (ii) the context-based approach to both describe the context in which versions are used and to facilitate version retrieval according a given situation when modeling flexible collaborative processes. In the following two sub-sections, we explain these two approaches, respectively.

Version-Based Approach

A version corresponds to one of the significant states that an entity (*e.g.,* a process, an activity …) may have during its life cycle. When created, an entity is described by only one version. The definition of every new entity version is done by a derivation from a previous one. Such versions are called derived versions and are organized in derivation hierarchies. As shown in Figure 1(a), the derivation hierarchy of entity E1 is a tree of versions. E1.1 is the first version, which is created from scratch, while E1.2, E1.3 and E1.4 are derived versions.

To support version modeling, Chaâbane *et al.,* (2011) introduced a versioning pattern. As shown in Figure 1(b), this pattern is composed of two classes and two relationships. Each versionable class (*i.e.,* for which versions are handled) is described as a class, called *Versionable.* With each *Versionable* class a new class, called *Version_of_Versionable* is associated. Instances of the latter class are versions of *Versionable* class. Regarding the relationships, (i) the *is_version_of* relationship links each instance of the *Versionable* class with its corresponding instances of the *Version_of_Versionable* class; and (ii) the *derived_from* relationship supports versions derivation hierarchies. This relationship is reflexive and the semantics of both sides are: (1) a version (SV) succeeds another one in the derivation hierarchy and, (2) a version (PV) precedes another one in the derivation hierarchy. Finally, the authors introduced attributes, such as *version_number, creator_name, creation_date* and *state* in the *Version_of_Versionable* class.

In order to specify the flexibility need when defining a new version, we extend the versioning pattern by adding a link attribute, called *Type_Deriv*, to the *derived_from* relationship. More precisely, the type of derivation *Type_Deriv* describes one of the three needs of flexibility: (i) *Variability* if the new derived version constitutes another variant for the PV version, (ii) *Evolution* if the new derived version constitutes an evolution over time comparing with the PV version, and (iii) *Adaptation* if the new derived version constitutes an adaptation of the PV version, which can describe an occasional situation or an anticipated exception.

In the section "VP2M FOR MODELING VERSIONS OF PROCESSES", we will show how we use the versioning pattern to model versions of CPs.

Figure 1. Version Modeling

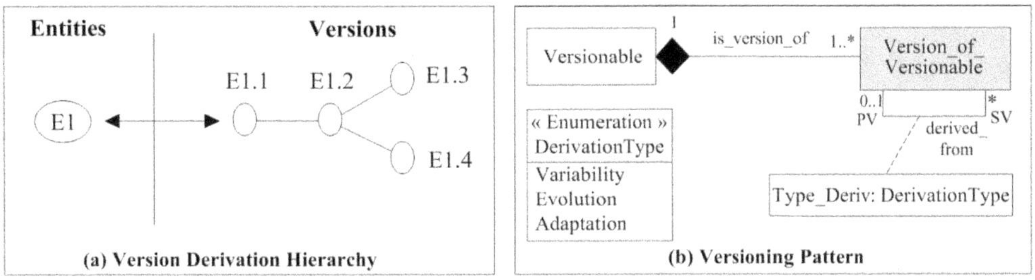

Context-Based Approach

The context plays an important role in several scientific area such as natural language, artificial intelligence, knowledge management, and web systems engineering. In the BPM area, many researchers have recommended a context based approach to configure variants of processes (*e.g.*, (La Rosa *et al.* 2011)) or to adapt processes (*e.g.*, (Saidani *et al.* 2015)).

We believe that context modeling should be used as an integral part of the CP version modeling: it allows specifying the context of use of each version and thus facilitates the retrieval of versions convenient to a given situation This is particularly useful when modeling flexible CPs.

Regarding recommended approaches in contributions addressing context modeling, we distinguish the key/value-based, model-based and ontology-based approaches. The authors of (Strang & Linnhoff-

Popien, 2004) have reported on a comparative study of context modeling approaches based on a set of requirements such as incompleteness, ambiguity, level of formality, reasoning capabilities, and applicability to existing environments, and it has concluded that the ontology-based approach is the most promising for context modeling.

Therefore, we use the ontology-based approach in order to model and to query the context of CP versions. In addition, we adopt this approach to mitigate semantic ambiguity and benefit from its inference capabilities when querying the context of CP versions.

To the best of our knowledge, none of the solutions defining context ontology has fully covered the taxonomy of Rosemann (Rosemann *et al.*, 2008), which is considered as the most convincing taxonomy for process context. Therefore, we have defined a BPM context ontology that supports and details the types of contexts recommended by Rosemann's taxonomy (*i.e.*, immediate, internal, external and environmental context).

To build this ontology, we follow the ontology construction methodology proposed in (Noy & Mcguinness, 2001) since it is the most used and the simplest construction methodologies. This methodology is based on two main stages: (i) determination of the type of ontology, and (ii) enumeration of important terms in the ontology by defining concepts, the hierarchy of these concepts and possible relations and properties. Thus, the type of our ontology is an upper ontology and the enumerations of important terms are given in Figure 4.

Figure 2 is a limited representation of the recommended BPM context ontology. We provide a full OWL copy of this ontology via GitHub[1]. This ontology has been implemented using Protégé 5.1.0[2]. We explain below the different introduced context elements.

Figure 2. BPM-Context-Onto

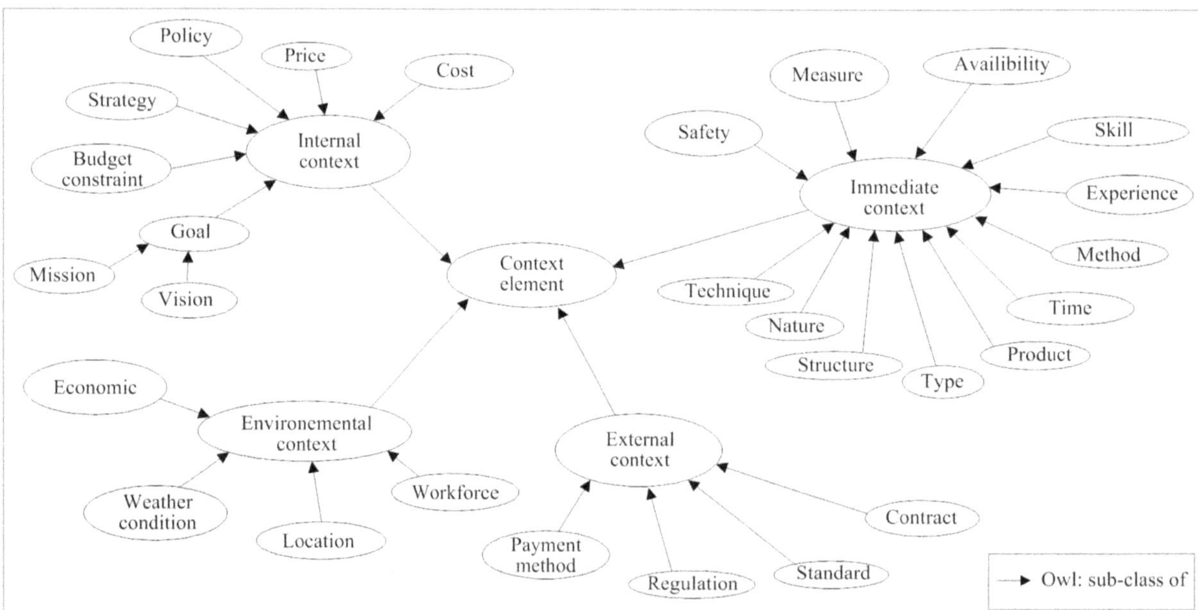

Regarding the immediate context, we define context elements related to processes and their components, *i.e.,* context elements related to the behavioral, informational and organizational dimensions of the processes. In fact, we represent the relevant context elements of processes and activities, such as *Method, Technique, Measure, Time* and *Product*. We also define the relevant immediate context elements of informational resources, such as *Nature* and *Structure*. We also define relevant context elements of organizational units and roles, such as *Availability*, *Skill* and *Experience*. Finally, another important immediate context element is *Safety*. This element can be considered either for a process or for its components as it includes safety of the person or safety of an activity.

The internal context has a less immediate relationship with the process and covers information on the internal environment of an organization that impacts the process. This includes, for example, the corporate *Strategy* and the related process *Goal. Policy* is another important internal context element as it is the main constraining factor on process design activities. Other context elements which are considered as internal are *Budget constraint*, *Cost* and *Price*.

The external context captures the context elements that are beyond the control sphere of an organization but still reside within the business network in which they operate. External context includes what is related to external stakeholders and notably *Contract* and *Payment method*. *Regulation* and *Standard* are also external context elements that have an important impact on the process. They contain directives made and maintained by an authority.

Finally, the environmental context, such as the outermost layer, resides beyond the business network in which the organization is embedded but poses a contingency effect on processes. It includes factors, such as *Weather condition*, *Location*, *Workforce* (*e.g.,* overall worker shortage or strike) and *Economic* environment.

In fact, three advantages can be considered when using the BPM-Context-Onto: first this ontology is dynamic in the sense that new context elements may be added at any time. Second, it is reusable as it is a common ontology regardless of the used domain. Third, it assists the ontologist to define the domain context ontology. Indeed, it acts as a dictionary of abstract elements used by the ontologist to specialize these elements according to a given domain.

VP2M FOR MODELING VERSIONS OF PROCESSES

This section presents VP2M highlighting the core concepts for both intra and collaborative process modeling. VP2M differentiates between two types of processes, (i) intra-organizational process, which is modeled as an individual process, namely a process belonging to a single organization, and (ii) collaborative process, namely a set of individual processes belonging to different organizations and interacting with one another. We first introduce below concepts for intra and collaborative process modeling. Then, we illustrate their versioning. Finally, we propose a taxonomy of operations which allow the creation, derivation, update, validation, and deletion of versions. These operations characterize the dynamic aspects of VP2M.

A UML class diagram of VP2M is given in Figure 2, which adopts the following policies: classes corresponding to versions are visualized in gray, concepts related to individual processes have a blue background, concepts related to collaborative processes have a yellow background and OCL constraints have a green background.

Figure 3. VP2M (adapted from [Ellouze et al., 2016])

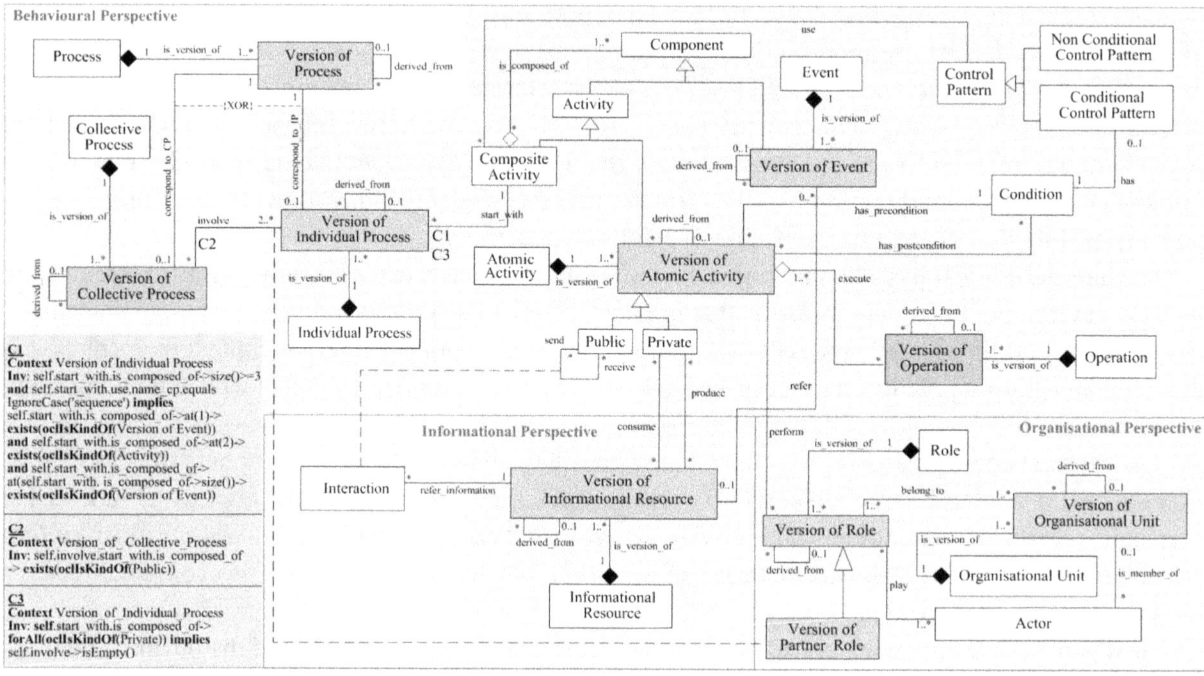

Modeling Collaborative Processes

To model CP, we start by modeling the intra-organizational processes as they are considered as the partners constituting the CP. The main concepts for intra-organizational processes are *Individual Process*, *Activity*, *Control Pattern*, *Event*, *Informational Resource* and *Role*. VP2M differentiates between composite and atomic activities. A composite activity is a set of components (*i.e.,* activities or events) that are coordinated by control patterns while an atomic activity refers to a concrete activity, gathering operations, performed by actors gathered into organizational units or roles and consumes and/or produces informational resources. We note that these concepts support the modeling of the main perspectives of processes, which are known to be essential to have a comprehensive view of how people work in companies (Dumas *et al.,* 2018).

On the other hand, the main concepts for addressing collaborative process modeling are: *Collaborative Process*, *Partner Role*, *Public*, *Private*, *Interaction* and *Process*. A collaborative process defines the set of participating individual processes each of which plays a role, denoted as Partner Role, in the collaborative process. Atomic activities are differentiated between public and private: (i) Public atomic activities correspond to external atomic activities, namely activities supporting the interaction between participating individual processes, and (ii) Private atomic activities correspond to internal activities performed only by individual processes. The notion of Interaction models the exchange of messages between involved individual processes. Finally, the notion of *Process* is introduced to model flexible processes changing from individual to collaborative (or vice-versa). Thus, a process may correspond to an individual or to a collaborative process.

Versioning Collaborative processes

We have used the versioning pattern previously presented in Figure 1(b) to make some classes of VP2M versionable (Ellouze *et al.*, 2016). We differentiate between versionable classes (*i.e.*, classes for which we handle versions) and ordinary classes (*i.e.*, classes for which we do not handle versions). Thus, we manage versions for the following classes: Process, Individual Process, Collaborative Process, Activity, Event, Operation, Role, Partner Role, and Organizational Unit. As a consequence, we have two classes for each versionable concept (*e.g.*, "Collaborative Process and Version of Collaborative Process" model collaborative processes and their corresponding versions). The idea is to keep track of the changes occurring to VP2M's versionable class.

Generally speaking, a new version of an element (*e.g.*, individual process, activity, event, and collaborative process) is defined according to changes occurring to it: these changes may correspond to the addition of information (attribute or relationship) or to the modification or the deletion of existing ones. We have characterized these changes as *dynamic aspects* of VP2M (cf. the following sub-section). For instance, regarding individual processes, we define new versions when there are changes to the involved activities and/or events or in the way these components are synchronized together using control patterns. Regarding collaborative processes, new versions may result, for example, from changes to the involved participants. Therefore, when a participant is added or deleted, it is necessary to define a new version for the collaborative process.

Dynamic Aspects of VP2M

According to Figure 4, a version can be a Working version, a Frozen version or a Disabled version. A working version is a draft version: it can be updated but cannot serve as a support for execution (*i.e.*, it cannot be instantiated). After a series of updates and when it becomes stable, a working version can be validated and therefore it moves to the state Frozen. A frozen version describes a significant and stable state of a version, which cannot undergo changes. A frozen version is enabled and can serve as a support for execution (*i.e.*, it can be instantiated). Note that the validation of a version may trigger the valida-

Figure 4. State Chart for Versions

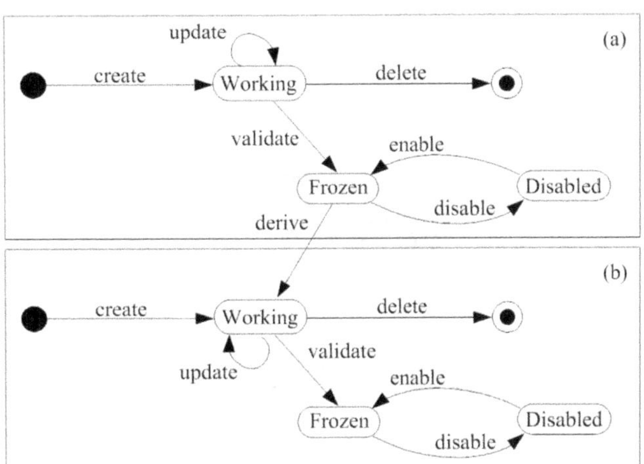

tion of other versions. A working version can be deleted while a frozen version can be disabled. It then moves to the state Disabled. In this state, the version cannot be instantiated and does not serve anymore as a support for execution. Finally, a stable version can serve as a basis for the creation of a new version using the Derive operation. The new created version is a working version. Before being updated, it has the same value as the derived one. Note that the derivation of a version may trigger the derivation of other versions, which are linked to the derived one.

ONTOLOGY-BASED APPROACH TO MODEL AND QUERY COLLABORATIVE PROCESS VERSION CONTEXT

This section addresses the context version modeling to facilitate version querying in the BPM area. It recommends an ontology-based approach, called Onto-VP2M, to model and query versions which are modeled according to VP2M (*i.e.,* versions of individual process, versions of collaborative process,

Figure 5. Synoptic schema of the Onto-VP2M based approach

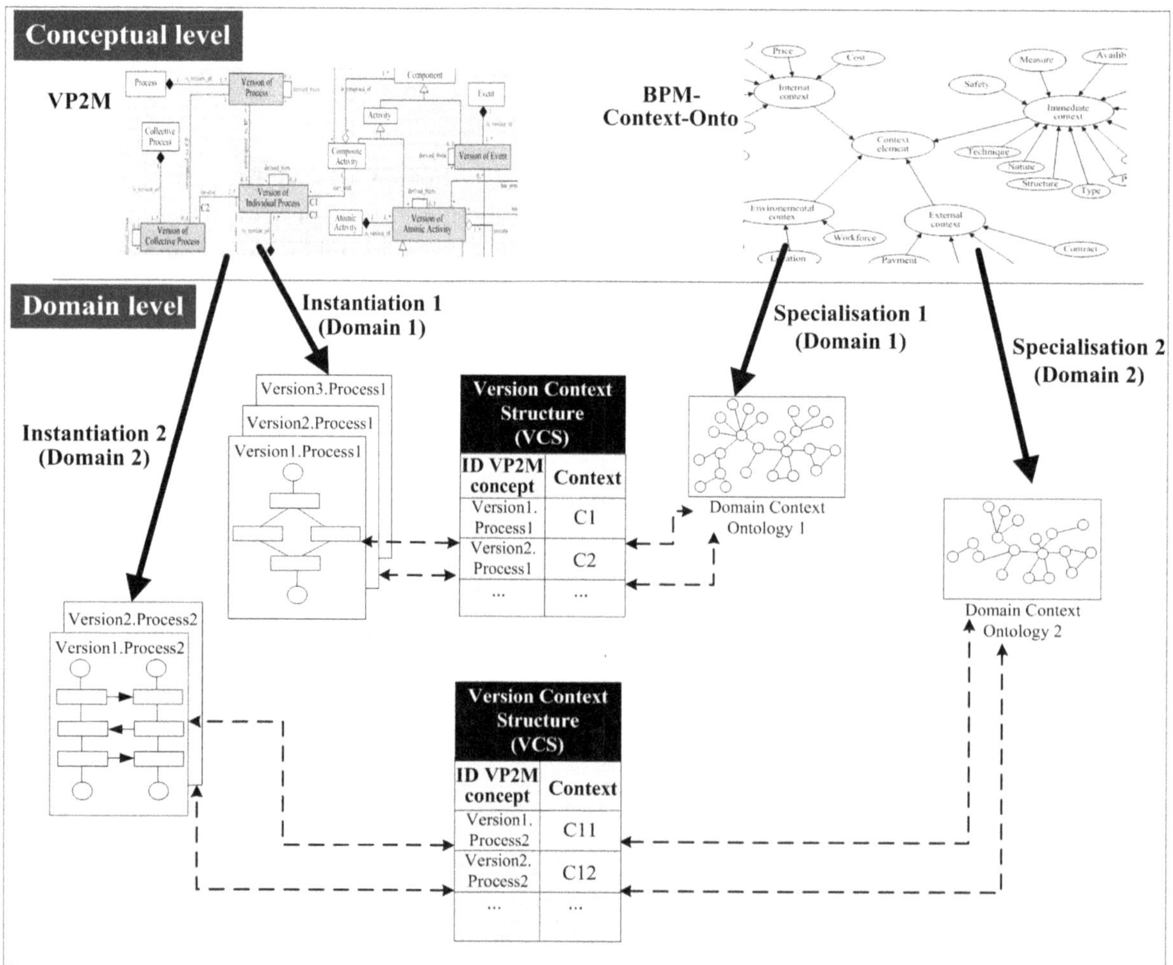

versions of activity, versions of event, versions of role, versions of organizational units and versions of informational resource). Figure 5 shows the synoptic schema of the Onto-VP2M approach. As illustrated in Figure 5, this approach distinguishes two levels, the conceptual level and the domain level:

1. Conceptual level: it includes the VP2M meta-model introducing the necessary concepts for process versioning, and an upper ontology, namely the BPM-Context-Onto which defines abstract concepts for context modeling in BPM.
2. Domain level: it includes process version models as instances of the VP2M according to specific domains, and domain context ontologies, which is defined as a specialization of BPM-Context-Onto. In fact, each process version model shares the same domain of the domain context ontology. In addition, the process version model and its corresponding domain context ontology are merged by a Version Context Structure (VCS) that assigns context information to a process version model.

The following sections detail the domain context ontology and the Version Context Structure linking VP2M' instances to their domain context ontology.

Domain Context Ontology (DCO)

The main characteristic of domain context ontologies (*cf.* Figure 5) is that they are linked by an upper ontology *i.e.,* they share the same context elements of BPM-Context-Onto. However, the difference between them is that each DCO specializes the elements of BPM-Context-Onto in a specific domain. For example, the *Measure* context element of the BPM-Context-Onto can be specialized differently according to each domain. In a Subsea pipeline domain, it is specialized in (i) *pipeline damage severity* in measuring the severity of the subsea pipeline damage, (ii) *pipeline length* for the measurement of the length of the pipeline, and (iii) *sea depth* to measure the depth of the sea in which the pipeline is laid. However, in a bottle production domain, this *Measure* context element could be specialized in (i) *production quantity* to measure the quantity of produced bottles, and (ii) *volume* for the measurement of the volume of the bottle.

Besides specifying the elements of BPM-Context-Onto, each DCO includes a set of rules. We distinguish three types of rules according to their functional capabilities:

Ontology Reasoning: Rules defined in the classes and the properties of the domain context ontology to check the ontology consistency and to achieve inferences using the functions of symmetry, equivalence, subsumption, transitivity, etc. These rules are useful especially to resolve semantic problems. Indeed, in a query setting, the users who submit the query can belong to different organizations where different jargons can co-exist together. Therefore, it is worth taking advantages from ontology reasoning to solve semantic problems.

Domain Rules Reasoning: Domain rules, also called "user-defined rules", support reasoning on the specific domain via SWRL[3]. They are defined in an antecedent-and-consequence implication. An example of SWRL rule in the DCO of the Subsea Pipeline domain can be presented as follows: pipeline_material (?x) ^ transports(?x, ?y) ^ swrlb:stringEqualIgnoreCase(?y, "water") -> HDPE (?x). This rule indicates that if the antecedent is "a pipeline material transports water" then the consequence is "this pipeline material must be HDPE".

At the modeling time, the BP designer specifies the context of a CP version by assigning values to its relevant context elements. This specified context is called *Version Defined Context*$_{designer}$.

Thanks to domain rules, we can enhance the context description of a version by reasoning on *Version Defined Context*$_{designer}$. The new obtained context, which is called *Version Deduced Context*, does not contain elements of *Version Defined Context*$_{designer}$, but contains only other context elements that have been deduced by domain rules.

Deduction Rules: To compensate for Domain Rule Reasoning inability to select and retrieve information, the SQWRL language is adopted to represent complex rules that help reason, query and display messages (O'Connor & Das, 2009). In fact, the deduction rules are useful especially to support context querying (cf., Section "Context Querying of CP Version"). They help to retrieve appropriate versions for a specific context. Each rule has the following form: **If** $\exists$ *Version Defined Context*$_{designer}$ **then return** *VersionID*. Indeed, once the BP designer specifies the context of a version, an SQWRL deduction rule is automatically generated.

Version Context Structure: Linking up VP2M's Instances to Domain Context Ontologies

Version Context Structure (VCS) is a pivot structure that links versions modeled as instances of the VP2M to their corresponding context. More precisely, VCS is organized in the form of context rules each of which corresponds to only one CP version. The context rule of CP version contains its *Version Defined Context*$_{designer}$ and an ID of its SQWRL deduction rule. All the elements defined in the *Version Defined Context*$_{designer}$ refer to the context elements of the corresponding DCO (*cf.* Figure 6).

Figure 6. Example of VCS

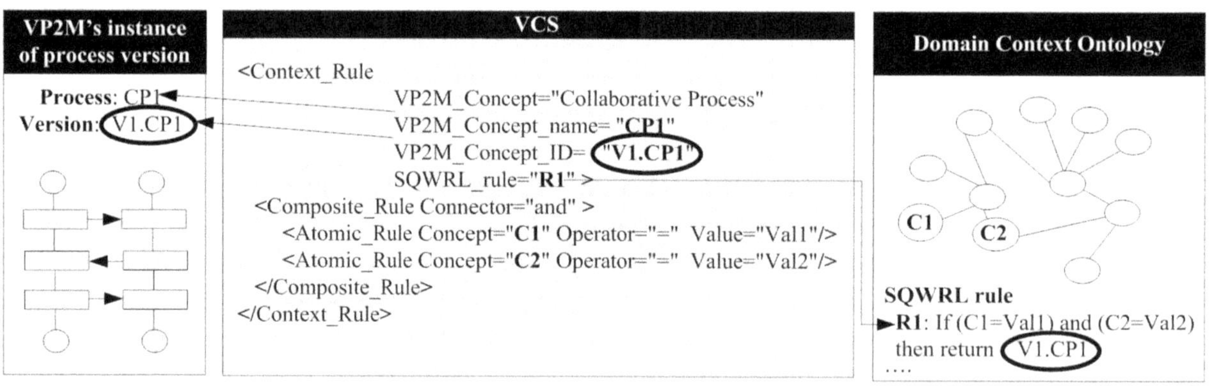

Context rules in the VCS structure are described as follows (*cf.* Figure 7):

More precisely, a context rule can be atomic or composite. Each atomic rule concerns a single context element that is defined by a triplet that describes the context element itself (*i.e.,* a concept of the domain context ontology), an operator and a value. A composite rule is a set of atomic and/or composite context rules connected together by logical operators such as "*and*" and "*or*".

Figure 7. Context Rule description

```
Context-Rule: Atomic_Rule | Composite_Rule
Composite_Rule: Context_Rule Connector Context_Rule Following_Composite_Rule
Following_Composite_Rule: Ø | Connector Context_Rule
Connector: and | or
Atomic_Rule: Concept Operator Value
Operator: > | >= | < | <= | = | <>
```

Context Querying of Version

An Onto-VP2M query is defined as a triplet (*Versionable type*, *Versionable name*, *Situation*). The first element to be specified is a type of the *Versionable* class. The *Versionable type* defines the query target, which can be versions of CP, versions of individual process, versions of activities, versions of informational resources, versions of roles, in short, versions of VP2M versionable components. The *Versionable name* is the second element that indicates the name of the targeted versionable VP2M versionable component. Finally, the last element to be defined is the *Situation i.e.,* the BPM practitioner's current situation in terms of context elements, operators and values.

Once the BPM practitioner submits the query, five major steps are possibly performed (cf. Figure. 8):

Step 1: Query VCS structure: In this step, the VCS structure is queried using XQuery language. Three cases may arise:

Case-1. There is exactly one version that satisfies the BPM practitioner's query (*i.e.,* the *Situation* exactly matches the *Version Defined Context*$_{designer}$ stored according to the VCS). In this case, only steps 2 and 3 are performed.

Case-2. There is no retrieved version: the BPM practitioner may not use the same context elements that are stored in VCS. In this case, step 4 is performed.

Case-3. There are many retrieved versions satisfying the *Situation*. In this case, step 4 is performed.

Step 2: Retrieve version model(s): In this step, the version of CP is retrieved from the version repository.

Step 3: Display results: In this step, the appropriate version (or the appropriate versions from Case-2 and Case-3) of CP is (are) graphically displayed to the BPM practitioner.

Step 4: Context Reasoning: To enhance the query process, this step contains four sub-steps that refer to the context domain ontology. The first sub-step, which solves semantic problems; is of utmost importance, especially, when there is no previously retrieved version (case 2). For example, a BPM practitioner may express a *Situation* using context elements which are synonyms or misnomers to those stored in VCS. This problem can be simply solved thanks to the equivalent class function or to the SKOS annotation (*i.e.,* altLabel) of the domain context ontology. The second sub-step populates the context domain ontology defining individuals Val1, Val2, Val3, respectively, to the corresponding context elements C1, C2, C3 of the domain context ontology (cf. *Situation* in Figure 8). The third sub-step executes the SWRL rules to deduce new knowledge that are stored in *Deduced Context* and enhance *Situation*. The aim of this inference is the gathering of *Version Defined Context*$_{designer}$ of one or more version(s). Finally, the fourth sub-step executes SQWRL rules. Remember that the SQWRL antecedent contains a *Version Defined Context*$_{designer}$ while the

SQWRL consequence contains the *versionID*. If one or more SQWRL rules are activated, then steps 2 and 3 are performed. However, if there is no activated SQWRL rule, step 5 is performed.

Figure 8. Query Principle

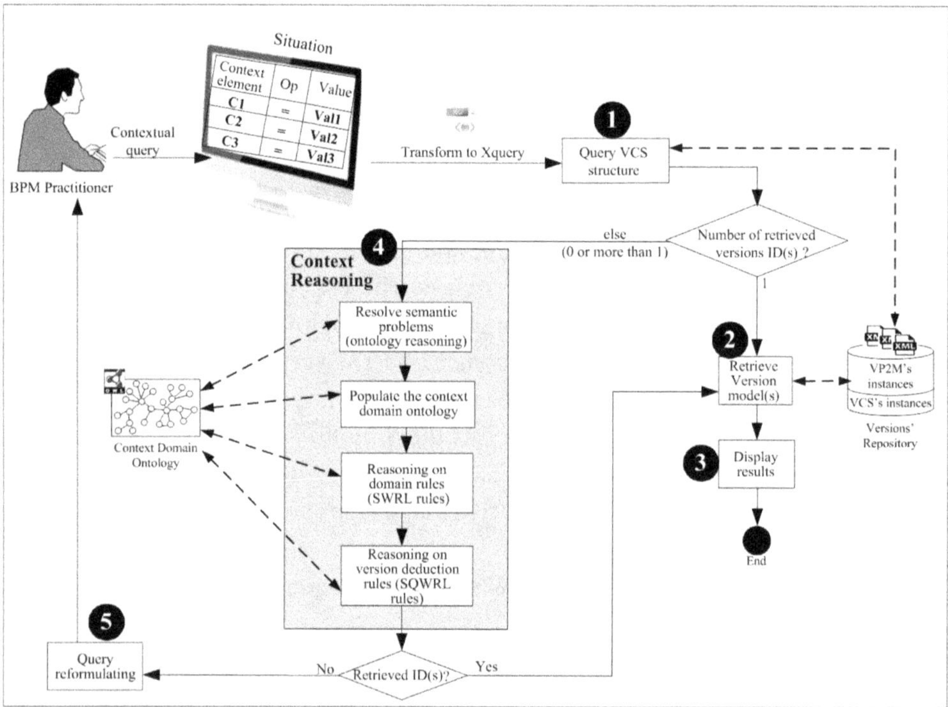

Step 5: Query reformulating: This step notifies the BPM practitioner through a message indicating that there is no version satisfying his/her requirement and requesting him/her to formulate a new query.

It should be noted that the reason for querying the VCS in step 1 is an optimization. The aim is the reduction of the query execution time, especially, when there is no need for the context reasoning (case 1).

ONTO-VP2M FRAMEWORK

Onto-VP2M-Fw is a framework implementing the VP2M meta-model and the onto-VP2M approach. This section presents the architecture of Onto-VP2M-Fw and then introduces as a process the necessary steps for version modeling within the Onto-VP2M-Fw.

Architecture of Onto-VP2M-Fw

Figure 9 below presents the architecture of Onto-VP2M-Fw, which includes:

Figure 9. Architecture of Onto-VP2M-Fw

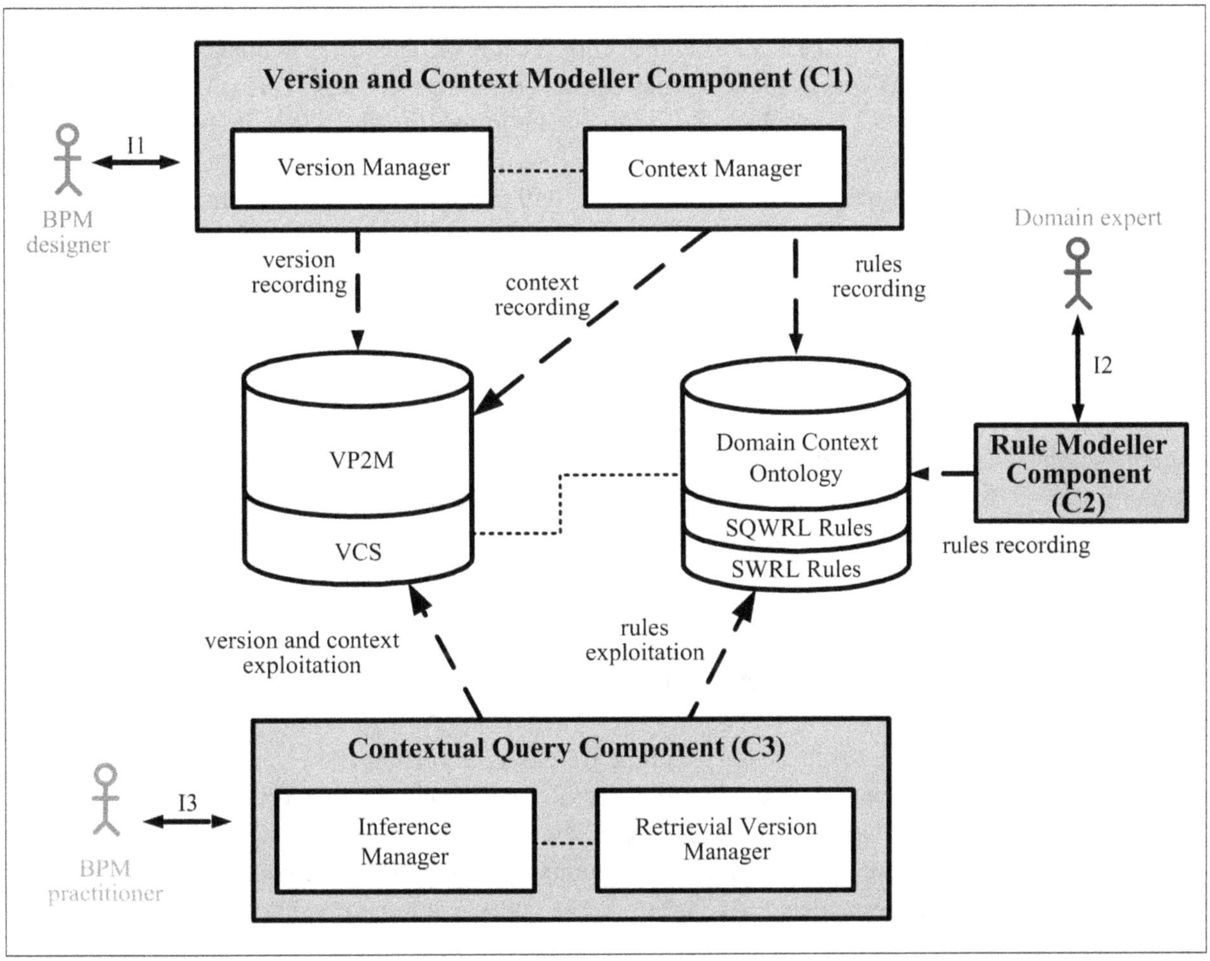

- Two repositories (displayed as cylinders) corresponding to the VP2M repository and to the Domain Context Ontology repository including domain and deduction rules.
- Three functional components (displayed as rectangles) corresponding to version and context modeler component (C1), domain rule modeler component (C2), and contextual query component (C3).
- Three interfaces (displayed as plain arrows) supporting the interaction between the users and the components.

Actions performed by components on repositories are visualized as dotted arrows while thin dotted lines represent connections between the internal elements of components (*i.e.,* (i) between Version Manager and Context Manager, the two sub-components of C1 and (ii) between the Inference Manager and the Retrieval Version Manager, the two sub-component of C3). Finally, the connection between the two repositories is represented with a thin dotted line.

The *Version and Context Modeler* component (C1) supports both the version and context modeling via a unique interface, namely I1. It is a design tool that helps BP designers in the definition, the update, and the storage of versions and contexts. Modeled versions are recorded in the VP2M repository, which is an XML database (implemented with XDB), while their contexts are recorded according to VCS structure via an XML file in the VP2M repository. This XML file refers to context elements of the domain context ontology as well as to the deduction rules (*i.e.,* SQWRL rules). This ontology has been implemented with Protégé 5.1.0 ontology development environment, which is built on top of the OWL API, and which is integrated with the *Drools rule engine* to support the reasoning and inference. We have used OWL formalizations, OWL API and SWRL API to implement the reasoning in the NetBeans IDE 8.1 environment.

The *Rule Modeler* component (C2) supports the management of the domain rules, *i.e.,* the rules defined by domain experts for inference reasons. Domain experts interact with this component via the interface I2.

Finally, the *Contextual Query* component (C3) is the third functional component of the architecture. It supports the contextual querying of the versions stored in the VP2M repository. More precisely, it supports (i) the definition of the BPM practitioner's situation and (ii) the querying of the domain context ontology and VP2M' instances to retrieve the versions satisfying the BPM practitioner. BPM practitioners (*i.e.,* user or BP designer) interact with this component via interface I3.

A complete video demonstrating the Onto-VP2M-Fw is available at: https://www.youtube.com/watch?v=gNOVdznxNdU.

Process for the (CP) Version Modeling

To model a new version, it is first necessary that the BP designer verifies if the version to model already exists or not. Figure 10 indicates the steps to follow by the BP designer for the modeling of a new version.

According to Figure 10, before defining a version, the BP designer ensures that this version does not already exist in the version repository. Thus he/she sends a query in which he/she describes the current situation of the version to be modeled. According to the query result, two scenarios can be met:

(i) only one version is retrieved; thus this version has exactly the same context as the current situation specified by the BP designer in its query: it is well suited to the current situation. So it already exists and it is useless to model a new one,
(ii) none or several versions are retrieved. In this scenario, an enhanced query is submitted thanks to the ontology reasoning (cf. Figure 8). According to the enhanced query's result, two scenarios can be met: (i) there is one or more retrieved version(s); in this case the BP designer has to select one version among them and derive a new version from the selected one, or (ii) there is no retrieved version; in this case, the BP designer creates a new version from scratch. This new version is adequate to the current situation.

To derive a new version from an existing one, the BP designer has to choose the source version which will serve as a basis for the derivation. Once the derivation operation is performed, the BP designer proceeds to update the new version having the state "working" (cf. Figure 4). Note that when updating a derived version, the BP designer may select an existing version component or define a new one to make up the new derived version.

For example, to update a version of an individual process, the BP designer can add or delete a version of activity or version of event. So, the BP designer can send, for example, a query to search for a version

Figure 10. Steps of the version modeling process

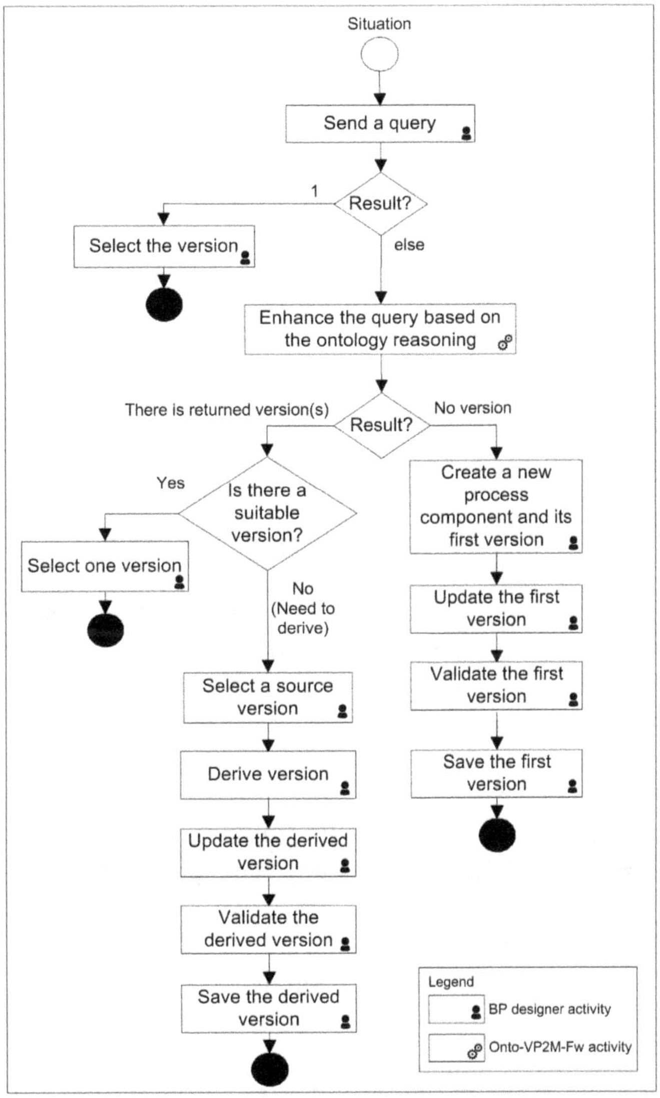

of activity to add it in the new version of the individual process. After a series of updates and when the working version becomes stable, the BP designer can validate it and therefore the version moves to the "Frozen" state. Finally, he/she saves the version to be used henceforth.

On the other hand, when the BP designer chooses to create from scratch a new version, he/she has to model firstly the entity (*e.g.*, the collaborative process, the individual process or the activity) and secondly proceeds to model the entity version. When modeling the new entity version, the BP designer can send queries to select versions useful to make up the new entity version to model.

CASE STUDY: THE SUBSEA PIPELINE INSTALLATION COLLABORATIVE PROCESS

In order to validate Onto-VP2M-Fw, we have conducted an experimentation considering a real case study, namely the collaborative process (CP) of "Subsea Pipeline Installation (SPI)" from SAROST[4], one of the largest Tunisian marine company. This process aims at handling the installation of new subsea pipelines all over the world. This process is collaborative in nature; it involves several partners. In the following, we firstly define the domain context ontology useful for modeling the context of SPI versions. Secondly, we illustrate the modeling of the SPI versions according to VP2M and Onto-VP2M.

Domain Context Ontology

In order to model the context of SPI versions, we have conducted a set of interviews with SAROST domain experts to define the domain context ontology for the Subsea Pipeline. This ontology is an extension of the BPM Context ontology (cf. Figure. 2) with relevant context elements for the Subsea Pipeline domain. Figure 11 shows a partial representation of the obtained domain context ontology. The added context elements are shown in gray. The full OWL copy of this ontology is available via GitHub[5]. In this ontology, we provide additional details to BPM Context ontology using specialization (Owl: Sub-class of), synonymy (Owl: equivalent class) and additional relations (Owl: object property).

We also have defined the domain rules (SWRL rules) for inference mechanisms. For example, five rules are given below in the form of *if-then* statement.

R1: **If** pipeline_length < 5 **then** transported_substance = "water".
R2: **If** transported_substance = "water" **then** pipeline_material = "HDPE".
R3: **If** pipeline_material = "HDPE" **then** (installation_technique = "floating" or "sliding") and (transported_substance = "water").
R4: **If** sea_depth <50 **then** diving_method= "umbilical".
R5: **If** sea_depth <50 **then** Installation technique="sliding" or "floating".

Defining Versions of the Subsea Pipeline Installation CP

In this section, we consider four versions of the SPI CP. We explain respectively these four SPI versions in the following four sub-sections.

Modeling the First Version of SPI

The first version of the collaborative process (identified by SPI.1 in Figure 12a), involves two partners (*i.e.*, two versions of individual process), respectively Client.1 (which refers to the first version of the Client individual process) and SAROST.1 (which refers to the first version of the SAROST individual process). The collaborative process is the following.

The Client Company initiates the process and sends an order describing the requested pipeline installation to SAROST. Once received, SAROST, in its first version SAROST.1, specifies the necessary team and equipments. Then, it proceeds with the assembling and the control of pipes on shore by welders,

Figure 11. Domain Context Ontology for the Subsea Pipeline

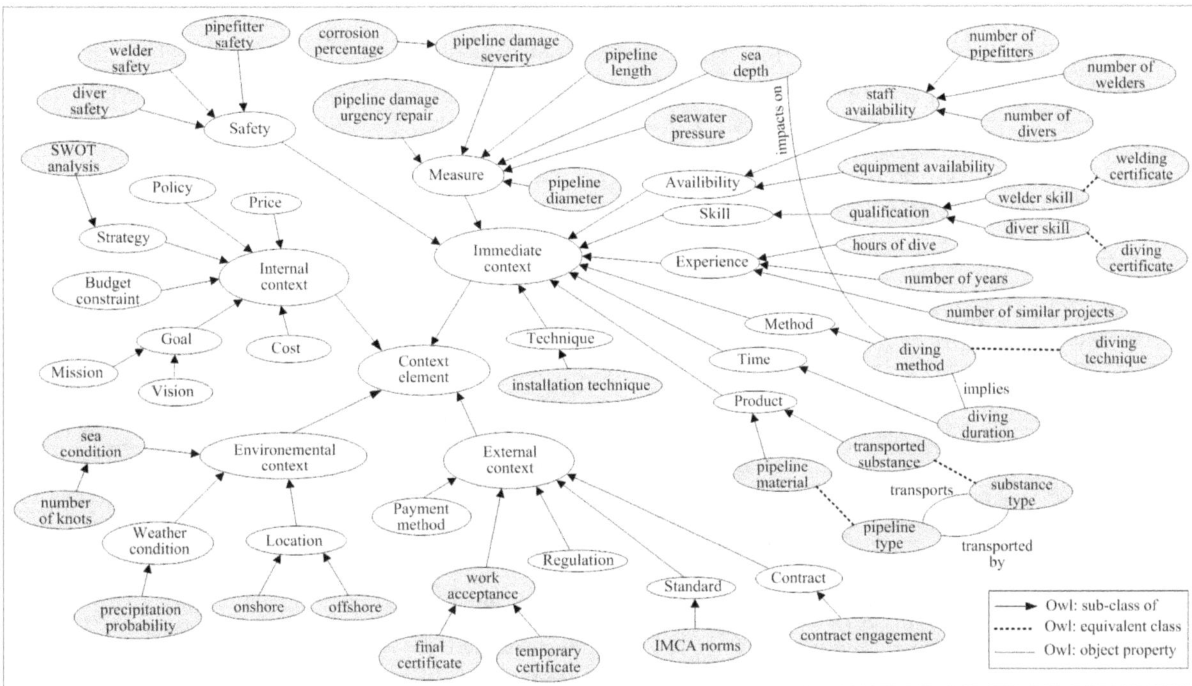

pipefitters and controllers. The next activity is the laying of pipes offshore by the divers. Finally, when the installation is over, a test campaign has to be performed. It should be noted that the assembling, control and laying have to be repeated until reaching the pipeline length. After the test campaign, SAROST prepares an acceptance certificate and sends it to the Client. According to SAROST domain experts, the context of SAROST.1 version is defined for the following context: the sea depth is less than 50 meters, the pipeline length is less than 10 km, the installation technique is floating and the transported substance is water.

In order to model the context of versions, we use four context elements from the Domain Context Ontology for the Subsea Pipeline (*i.e., Sea depth, Pipeline length, Installation technique*, and *Transported substance*) to characterize each version of SAROST and consequently each version of SPI. These elements make up the *Version Defined Context$_{designer}$* of each version. In Table 1, we present 12 versions of SAROST. More precisely, we give, in this table, the values of the sub-elements of both the *Version Defined Context$_{designer}$* and the *Version Deduced Context*. Indeed, this deduced context is obtained thanks to domain rules given by domain experts. An example of domain rule in the Subsea Pipeline domain is as follows: *if Sea depth <50 meters, then Diving method must be "umbilical" and Diver skill must be "class-2"*. It should be noted that the elements constituting the *if and then clauses* are connected by the *and* logical connector. Moreover, for each SAROST version of Table 1, there is an SQWRL rule, stored in the ontology, which deduce versions according to a given context. The SQWRL's antecedent contains the Version Defined Context$_{designer}$ while the SQWRL consequence contains the ID of the corresponding version of the process. For example, the SQWRL rule **RQ1** below is relative to the version SAROST.1.

RQ1: sea_depth(?x) ^ has_value_sea_depth(?x, ?y) ^ swrlb:lessThan(?y, 50) ^ pipeline_length(?z) ^ has_value_pipeline_length(?z, ?a) ^ swrlb:lessThan(?a, 10) ^ installation_technique(?b) ^ has_value_installation_technique(?b, ?c) ^ swrlb:stringEqualIgnoreCase(?c, "floating") ^ transported_substance(?d)^has_value_transported_substance(?d, ?e)^swrlb:stringEqualIgnoreCase(?e, "water") -> sqwrl:**select("SAROST.1"**).

Table 1. Context of SAROST's versions

SAROST Process version's ID	Version Defined Context$_{designer}$				Version Deduced Context			
	Sea depth	**Pipeline length**	**Installation technique**	**Transported substance**	**Pipeline material**	**Diver skill**	**Diving method**	**Number of divers**
SAROST.1	<50	<10	floating	water	HDPE	class-2	umbilical	6 to 8
SAROST.2	<50	<10	sliding	water	HDPE	class-2	umbilical	6 to 8
SAROST.3	<50	<10	floating	gas or oil	steel	class-2	umbilical	6 to 8
SAROST.4	<50	10 to 50	floating	gas or oil	steel	class-2	umbilical	>8
SAROST.5	<50	>50	floating	gas or oil	steel	class-2	umbilical	>14
SAROST.6	>=50	10 to 50	sliding	gas or oil	steel	class-3	wet bell	>8
SAROST.7	>90	10 to 50	sliding	gas or oil	steel	class-3	saturation	>8
SAROST.8	50 to 90	>50	sliding	gas or oil	steel	class-3	wet bell	>14
SAROST.9	>90	>50	sliding	gas or oil	steel	class-3	saturation	>14
SAROST.10	<50	<10	sliding	gas or oil	steel	class-2	umbilical	6 to 8
SAROST.11	<50	10 to 50	sliding	gas or oil	steel	class-2	umbilical	>8
SAROST.12	<50	>50	sliding	gas or oil	steel	class-2	umbilical	>14

Figure 12(b) gives an extract of the instantiation of VP2M according to SPI.1. This instantiation shows one version of SPI (SPI.1), one version of Client (Client.1) and one version of SAROST process (SAROST.1). For clarity reasons, objects of SPI are shown in green, objects of Client are shown in orange and objects of SAROST are shown in yellow. Client.1 starts with a composite activity, CA1, which is a sequence involving the version of Client's start event, the versions of activities to be performed and the version of Client's end event. Because of space limitation and for clarity reasons, we only show the start event SEC.1, along with the two first public activities of TPS: Send Order represented as the version SO.1, and Receive certificate, represented as the version RC.1.

Regarding SAROST.1, it starts with a composite activity. For the same reasons, we only focus on SAROST' start event and the Receive Order and Specify team activities, represented as versions respectively denoted as RO.1 and ST.1. The first version of the collaborative process, SPI.1, involves the two versions of Client's and SAROST's individual processes, Client.1 and SAROST.1, and each of the individual process plays a specific role in the collaborative process (respectively customer and supplier). In addition, the interaction *Order* is exchanged in the receive/send relationship (between SO.1 and RO.1).

Figure 12. SPI's first version

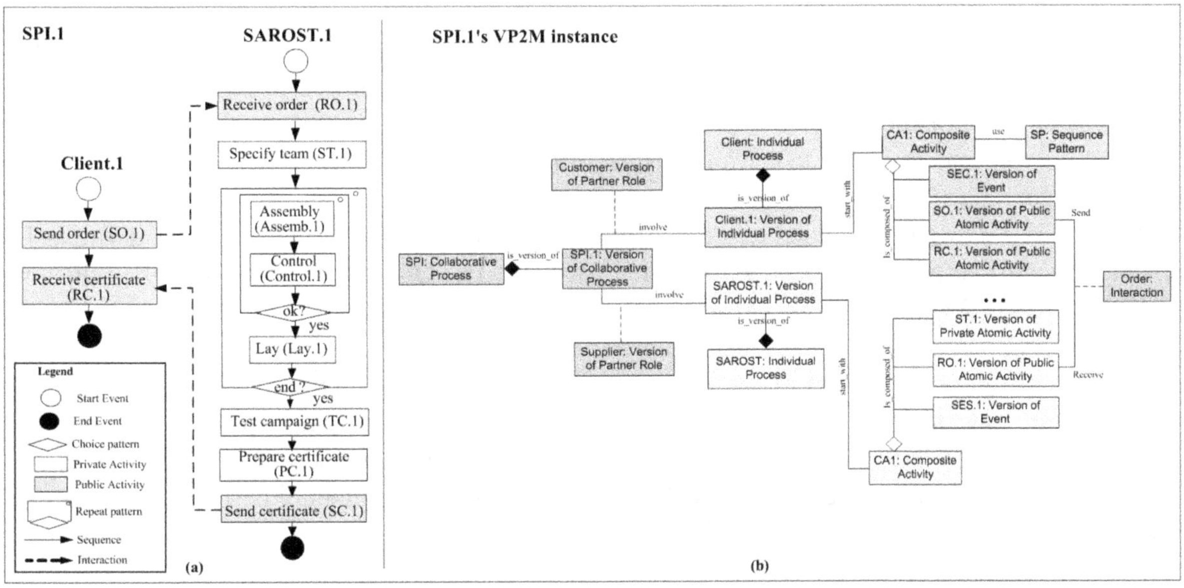

Figure 13. SPI's second version

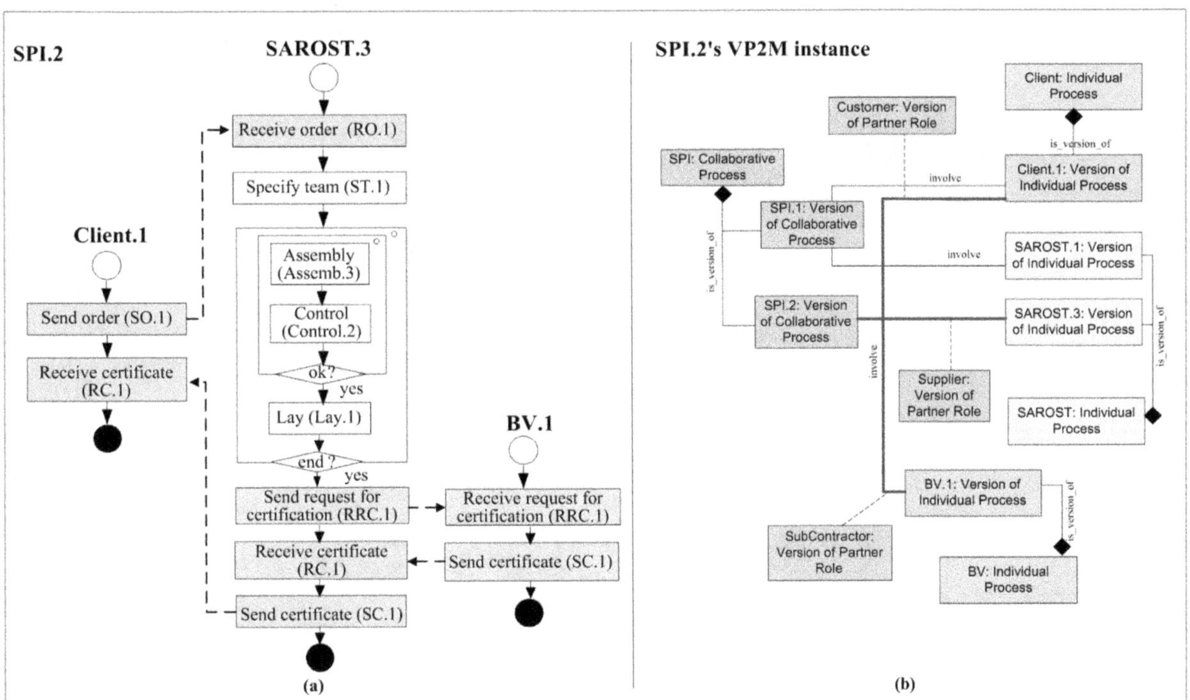

Modeling the Second Version of SPI

For oil or gas transported substance, and when the pipeline length does not exceed 50 km, SAROST only proceeds to the installation without making the test campaign and the certification activities. These two activities will be subcontracted to an external company, such as the Bureau Veritas company. The latter will be contacted by SAROST, which justifies the presence of public activities RRC.1, RC.1, and SC.1 (*cf.* Figure 13(a)).

As there is a new partner added to the collaboration, a new version of the SPI CP is defined. This version is identified by SPI.2 and involves three partners: The Client.1, which is still the initiator of the SPI, SAROST.3 which is a new version used when transporting oil or gas (cf. Table 1) and BV.1 to which SAROST subcontracts the test campaign and the certification activities.

Figure 13(b) gives an extract of the instantiation of VP2M according to SPI.2. This instantiation shows two versions of SPI (SPI.1 and SPI.2), one version of Client individual process (Client.1), two versions of SAROST individual process (SAROST.1 and SAROST.3), and one version of BV (BV.1) individual process. Each individual process plays a specific role in the collaborative process (respectively customer, supplier and subcontractor).

Modeling the Third Version of SPI

In case of big project involving the installation of long and deep-water pipelines, SAROST only proceeds with the installation. Once the installation is over, it sends back a report to the client (*cf.* Figure 14(a)) and ends the process. Then, the Client contact BV to perform the activities of the test campaign and

Figure 14. SPI's third version

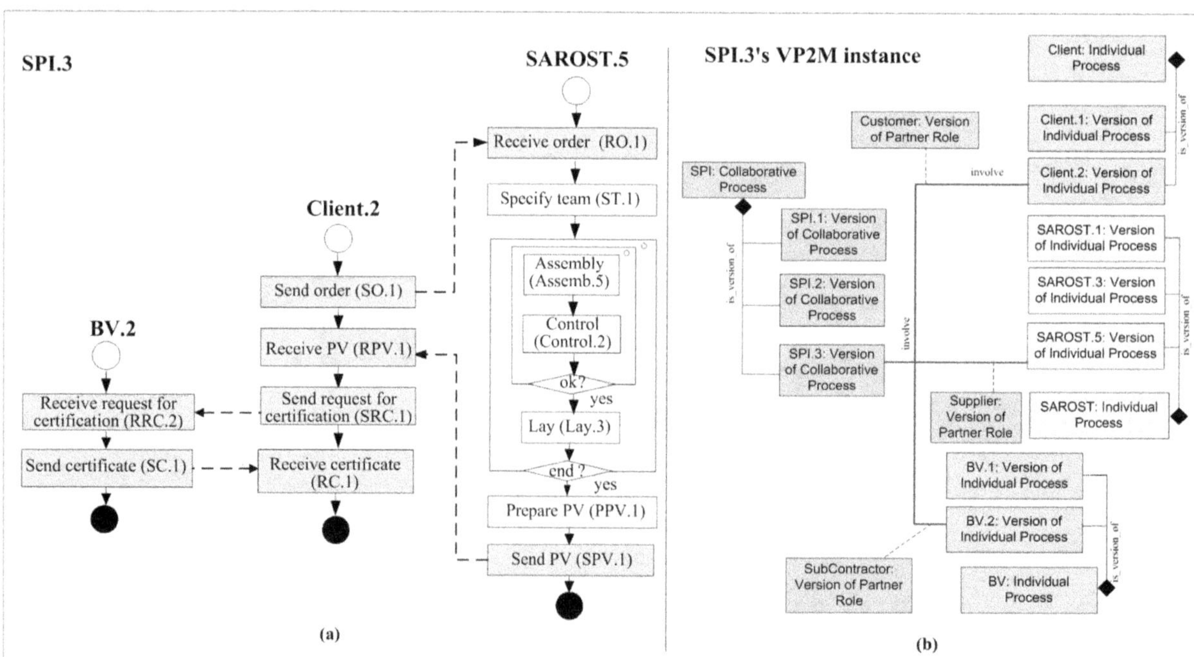

the certification. The changes occurred to Client, SAROST and BV processes lead them to define new versions for their processes. Consequently, a new version of SPI is defined.

Figure 14(b) gives an extract of the instantiation of VP2M according to SPI.3. This instantiation shows three versions of SPI (SPI.1, SPI.2 and SPI.3), two versions of Client individual process (Client.1 and Client.2), three versions of SAROST individual process (SAROST.1, SAROST.3 and SAROST.5), and two versions of BV (BV.1 and BV.2) individual process. As in SPI.1, each individual process plays a specific role in the collaborative process (respectively customer, supplier and subcontractor).

Table 2 summarizes the context of the three versions of SPI.

Table 2. Context of SPI versions

SPI version ID	Version Defined Context$_{designer}$				Version Deduced Context					
	Sea depth	Pipeline length	Installation technique	Transported substance	Pipeline material	Diver skill	Diving method	Number of welders	Number of pipefitters	Number of divers
SPI.1	<50	<10	floating or sliding	water	HDPE	class-2	umbilical	0	6 to 8	6 to 8
SPI.2	<50	<10	floating	gas or oil	steel	class-2	umbilical	6 to 8	6 to 8	6 to 8
SPI.3	<50	>50	floating	gas or oil	steel	class-2	umbilical	>14	>14	>14

SPI Fourth Version: How to Model a New Version of SPI

In this section we show how to model a new version of SPI according to the steps of Figure 10. First of all, let's have the following situation: the BP designer is interested in finding SPI versions appropriate for a 70 kilometres long subsea pipeline, transporting gas at a depth of 47 meters and using the sliding technique for the installation.

According to Figure 10, the first step consists in sending the query (Sea depth=47, Pipeline length=70, Installation technique=Sliding and Transported substance=gas). As shown in Table 2, no version can be retrieved. Thus, Onto-VP2M-Fw's C3 component (cf. Figure 9) proceeds to populate the ontology by creating individuals for "Sea depth", "Pipeline length", "Installation technique" and "Transported substance" context elements of the domain context ontology, having respectively 47, 70, Sliding and gas values (cf. Figure 8).

After an inference mechanism, the *Situation* is enhanced thanks to the above defined SWRL rules of the context domain ontology R1, R2, R3 R4 and R5. Once SWRL inference is done, the domain context ontology is enhanced by new individuals (*e.g.*, executing the above SWRL R4 infers "umbilical" which is a new individual for "diving method" and executing the above SWRL R5 infers "floating" and "sliding" which are two individuals for "Installation technique"). Finally, the SQWRL rules are executed, in order to deduct the appropriate version ID for the user's query.

Given the presence of individuals for "Sea depth", "Pipeline length", "Transported substance", and "Installation technique" along with their respective values "47", "70", "gas", and "floating" "sliding", the SQWRL rule of SPI.3 is activated and consequently executed. Thus, SPI.3 version will be retrieved and displayed to the BP designer.

It should be noted that the SQWRL rules of SPI.1 and SPI.2 couldn't be activated because their SQWRL antecedent values are not stored as domain context ontology individuals (*e.g.*, there is no *water* individual to activate the SQWRL of SPI.1 and there is no *pipeline length inferior than 10* individual to activate the SQWRL of SPI.2 (cf. Table 2).

In this case, the BP designer has to derive a new version from SPI.3 to satisfy his/her needs. This new derived version, identified by SPI.4, contains the same schema of SPI.3. The BP designer proceeds now to update SPI.4 by querying the SAROST process to search for another version suitable to his/her current situation. Thus SAROST.12 is retrieved and consequently selected to replace SAROST.5 (cf. Table 1). Finally, SPI.4 is validated to move from the "working" state to the "frozen" state. Figure 14 shows the SPI.4 as it is defined by the BP designer.

Figure 15. SPI's fourth version

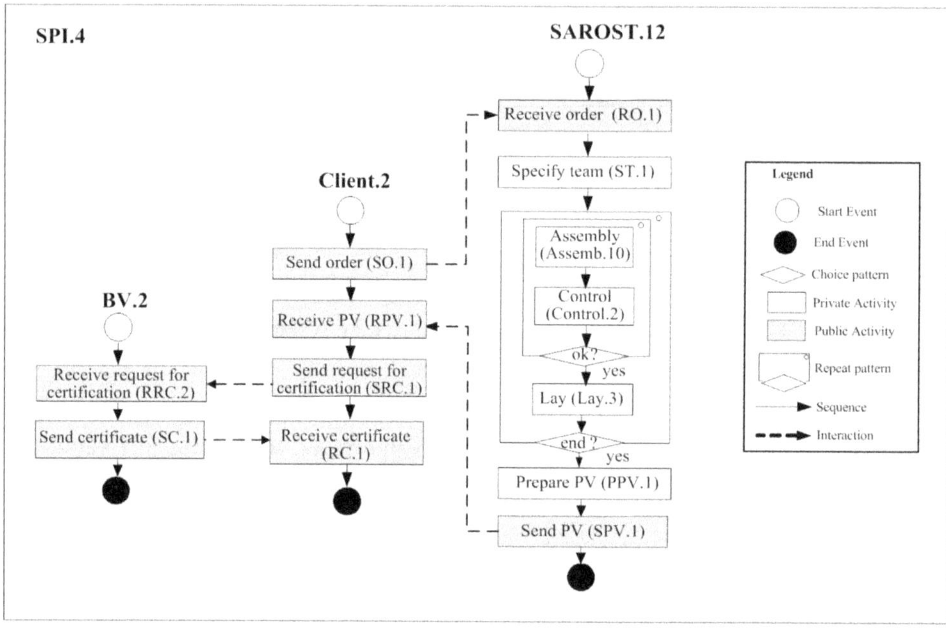

Related Work

This section examines the related work with a focus on the following three questions: How well is the examined contribution capable of modeling versions for collaborative processes? How well is the examined contribution capable of modeling the contexts for the modeled versions? And how well is the examined contribution capable of retrieving the modeled versions based on their context?

The authors of (Ben Said, Chaâbane, Andonoff, & Bouaziz, 2018), (Ekanayake, La Rosa, Ter Hofstede & Fauvet, 2011) and (Zhao & Liu, 2013) introduced specific meta-models to capture the process changes over time using a version-based approach. These version-based meta-models support the modeling of versions for the intra-organizational process. The meta-model, proposed in (Ben Said et al., 2018), supports also the modeling of collaborative processes. However, these authors neither modeled the context for versions nor proposed a solution to retrieve versions.

In (Lassoued, Bouzguenda, & Mahmoud, 2016), the authors addressed context modeling and querying only for versions of the intra-organizational process. Regarding the context, it is modeled by a specific process context meta-model, which focuses only on immediate and internal context of Rosemann's taxonomy. As for context querying, the authors introduced the VBPQL SQL-like language for the definition and the manipulation of intra-organizational process version context. This language helps query the context with the use of a domain ontology. However, this work poorly takes advantage of ontology as the authors do not implement any reasoning strategy as no rules are modeled.

On the other hand, the authors of (Hallerbach, Bauer, & Reichert, 2010) recommended the Provop approach, which helps configure context-aware process configurations. This approach consists on a base process, a set of options and a context model. In Provop, such context model comprises a set of context variables where each represents one specific dimension of the process context, and is defined by a name and a value range. In the configuration phase, each defined option is associated with a context rule, which is evaluated based on the data describing the process context. Although the principle of variant (*i.e.*, alternative version) selection is advocated, there is no query language to facilitate variant retrieval. Indeed, it is necessary to go through the whole process and specify the context in each option.

In (La Rosa & Dumas, 2008), the authors addressed only the problem of the retrieval of versions. They proposed a new solution called Questionnaire which is applied to lead the user to choose a process version based on formal conceptualization of the domain knowledge. This approach considers especially the goal of the version and does not consider the other context types of Rosemann's taxonomy.

Moreover, some existing BPM systems ensure CP versions modeling based on Web technologies. Examples include Aeneis (Aeneis, 2014), Signavio (Signavio, 2015) and BPaaS (Scheer, 2015). However, the major limitation of these tools is that they focus on CP versions modeling without supporting the context modeling of the versions. In addition, these BPM tools focus on process querying using only the metadata that describe each modeled version: CP name, publishing date, author's name, revision comment, etc. They fall short of providing any guideline or help to retrieve the adequate version of CP appropriate for a specified context. In (Janiesch & Kuhlenkamp, 2018), the authors propose a context engine based on business rules to enhance BPM systems' context-awareness. The generic architecture provides the flexibility to adapt running instances at decision gates or during execution due to significant context change. However, the authors did not propose a conceptual solution at the modeling time to keep track of versions modeled to different contexts.

Another attempt for modeling the context in business process modeling is proposed in (Santra & Choudhury, 2018). The authors recommended a context model in terms of a graph to extend the BPMN model. The context model considers all the four types of Rosemann's taxonomy. The designer models the business process model and integrates its context model. Finally, the authors consider that incorporating context-awareness in BPMN model is an enhancement of the modeling technique in terms of process flexibility.

Table 3 lists the comparison between the previous works and our paper's contributions. The evaluation is notified as follows: + (-) means that the feature is supported (not supported), while +/- means that the feature is partially supported. In summary, our contributions contribute to the modeling of flexible collaborative process with the following supports:

CP versioning: the proposed VP2M is an independent meta-model from any language and notation. It is used in business process modeling to address process flexibility; it allows modeling versions of intra and collaborative processes. Likewise, it defines the core concepts both for version modeling and process's dimensions modeling (*i.e.*, behavioral, informational and organizational). The dynamic aspects of VP2M have been also addressed by introducing operations for version management. Finally, the instantiation of VP2M is illustrated using the Subsea Pipeline Installation CP.

Version context modeling: the proposed Onto-VP2M is an ontology-based approach that supports context modeling of CP version modeled using the VP2M meta-model. To model the context, we have recommended the use of a context domain ontology which is a specialization of the BPM-Context-onto ontology. This later is an upper ontology that covers all Rosemann's taxonomy.

Version querying: the proposed Onto-VP2M supports also the version querying based on the context of versions. Although there are recommended contributions for contextual querying in BPM, they do not ensure semantic interoperability in a collaboration setting. Therefore, resolving semantic problems is of a major importance as partners in CP are heterogeneous and different jargons can co-exist. Hence we have recommended the Onto-VP2M ontology-based approach. Note that, version querying can help (i) the BP designer if he/she has to select an old version component to be used to make up a new CP version, and (ii) the user if he/she has to select a version of CP to be executed.

Table 3. Evaluation of examined works and our paper's contributions

	Version Modeling	Context Version Modeling	Version retrieval
(Ben Said et al., 2018)	+	-	-
(Ekanayake et al., 2011) (Zhao & Liu, 2013)	+/- (only for intra-organizational)	-	-
(Lassoued et al., 2016)	+/- (only for intra-organizational)	+	+
(Hallerbach et al., 2010)	-	+	-
(La Rosa & Dumas, 2008)	-	-	+
Aeneis, Signavio, BPaaS	+	-	+/-
(Janiesch & Kuhlenkamp, 2018)	-	+	-
(Santra & Choudhury, 2018)	-	+	-
Our solution	+	+	+

CONCLUSION

This paper has addressed the modeling of collaborative process (CP) versions, which is an important issue in the Business Process Management (BPM) field. The modeling of CP versions has led to another dependent issue namely the reuse of CP versions and more generally the reuse of versions. Indeed, in a multi-version environment in which a large number of versions can co-exist, BPM practitioners have to face the problem of retrieving, among different versions, the most appropriate one to a given situation. In this paper, we claim that the context notion is very helpful for version retrieval as it helps describe the situation in which the versions have to be used. In fact, the problem of retrieving version may arise both at run-time when BPM users have to choose the CP version to be executed, and at design-time when BP designers have to choose a version to participate in the modeling of another version.

To address this issue, we have recommended (i) the VP2M meta-model that adopts the version-based approach to support version modeling in BPM and thus CP version modeling, (ii) the Onto-VP2M approach that provides support for modeling and querying the context of versions, and (iii) the Onto-VP2M-Fw framework that implements both the VP2M meta-model and the Onto-VP2M approach.

The key strengths of our contribution are the following. Firstly, VP2M is comprehensive as it integrates the main dimensions of processes and considers versioning of concepts related to all process dimensions. Secondly, the Onto-VP2M approach is implemented in a comprehensive framework supporting version modeling and their corresponding context of use. Thirdly, version querying is described in terms of context-based queries, which are used to find out the appropriate version for a given situation using an ontology-based approach. Fourthly and lastly, we have illustrated the use of the Onto-VP2M-Fw framework for flexible CP modeling within a case study from the maritime area, namely the Subsea Pipeline installation CP. This case study highlights the real need for context and versions in BPM. Indeed, a big number of versions were modeled for this process, thus arising the challenge of selecting the most appropriate version for a given situation.

Future works shall address the detected weaknesses of our contribution. In fact, researchers and practitioners predict that in the future, technology will be collaborative (de Vreede, Antunes, Vassileva, Gerosa, & Wu, 2016). Thus we have planned to improve the collaborative modeling in Onto-VP2M-Fw framework, as several process designers have to define collaborative process schema in a collaborative way. We have also planned to define a methodology to assist BP designers in the modeling of the CP versions and the retrieval artifacts. This methodology encompasses a modeling language, computer-aided software and modeling processes as guidelines assisting BP designers.

REFERENCES

Aalst, W. (2000). Loosely coupled interorganizational workflows: Modeling and analyzing workflows crossing organizational boundaries. *Journal of International Management*, *37*(2), 67–75.

Aeneis. (2014). *Aeneis Handbuch: intellior AG*. Retrieved from https://www.intellior.ag/wp-content/uploads/Handbuch_Aeneis_Anwender.pdf

Ben Said, I., Chaâbane, M. A., Andonoff, E., & Bouaziz, R. (2018). BPMN4VC-modeller: Easy-handling of versions of collaborative processes using adaptation patterns. *Journal of Information Systems and Change Management*, *10*(2), 140–189. doi:10.1504/IJISCM.2018.094604

Brocke, J., Zelt, S., & Schmiedel, T. (2016). On the role of context in business process management. *Journal of International Management*, *36*(3), 486–495.

Chaâbane, M. A., Bouzguenda, L., & Bouaziz, R. (2011). Towards a Business Process Versions Querying and Manipulating Language. In *The International Conference on Information Technology and e-services* (pp. 12–19). Sousse, Tunisia: Academic Press.

Cognini, R., Corradini, F., Gnesi, S., Polini, A., & Re, B. (2018). Business process flexibility-a systematic literature review with a software systems perspective. *Journal of Information Systems Frontiers*, *20*(2), 343–371. doi:10.100710796-016-9678-2

Dadam, P., & Reichert, M. (2009). The ADEPT project: A decade of research and development for robust and flexible process support. *Journal of Computer Science-Research and Development*, *23*(2), 81–97. doi:10.100700450-009-0068-6 de Vreede, G. J., Antunes, P., Vassileva, J., Gerosa, M. A., & Wu, K. (2016). Collaboration technology in teams and organizations: Introduction to the special issue. *Journal of Information Systems Frontiers*, *18*(1), 1–6. doi:10.100710796-016-9632-3

Dumas, M., La Rosa, M., Mendling, J., & Reijers, H. A. (2018). *Fundamentals of business process management* (2nd ed., Vol. 1). Springer. doi:10.1007/978-3-662-56509-4

Ekanayake, C. C., La Rosa, M., Ter Hofstede, A. H., & Fauvet, M. C. (2011). Fragment-based version management for repositories of business process models. In *Proceedings of the International Conferences OTM Confederated On the Move to Meaningful Internet Systems* (pp. 20-37). Hersonissos, Crete, Greece: Springer. 10.1007/978-3-642-25109-2_3

Ellouze, F., Chaabane, M. A., Bouaziz, R., & Andonoff, E. (2016). Addressing inter-organisational process flexibility using versions: The VP2M approach. In *Proceedings of the International Conference on Research Challenges in Information Science* (pp. 1-12). Grenoble, France: IEEE. 10.1109/RCIS.2016.7549280

Hallerbach, A., Bauer, T., & Reichert, M. (2010). Capturing variability in business process models: The Provop approach. *Journal of Software: Evolution and Process*, *22*(67), 519–546.

Janiesch, C., & Kuhlenkamp, J. (2018). Enhancing business process execution with a context engine. *Journal of Business Process Management*.

Kradolfer, M., & Geppert, A. (1999). Dynamic workflow schema evolution based on workflow type versioning and workflow migration. In *Proceedings of the International Conference on Cooperative Information Systems*, (pp. 104-114). Edinburgh, UK: IEEE. 10.1109/COOPIS.1999.792162

La Rosa, M., & Dumas, M. (2008). Configurable Process Models: How To Adopt Standard Practices In Your How Way? *BPTrends Newsletter*.

Lassoued, Y., Bouzguenda, L., & Mahmoud, T. (2016). Context-aware business process versions management. *International Journal of e-Collaboration*, *12*(3), 7–33. doi:10.4018/IJeC.2016070102

O'Connor, M., & Das, A. (2009). SQWRL: a query language for OWL. In *Proceedings of the 6th International Conference on OWL: Experiences and Directions* (pp. 208-215). Chantilly, VA: Academic Press.

Reichert, M., & Weber, B. (2012). *Enabling flexibility in process-aware information systems: challenges, methods, technologies*. Springer Science & Business Media. doi:10.1007/978-3-642-30409-5

Rosemann, M., Recker, J., & Flender, C. (2008). Contextualisation of business processes. *Journal of Business Process Integration and Management*, *3*(1), 47–60. doi:10.1504/IJBPIM.2008.019347

Saidani, O., Rolland, C., & Nurcan, S. (2015). Towards a generic context model for BPM. In *Proceedings of the 48th Hawaii International Conference on System Sciences* (pp. 4120-4129). Kauai, HI: IEEE. 10.1109/HICSS.2015.494

Santra, D., & Choudhury, S. (2018). *C-BPMN: A Context Aware BPMN for Modeling Complex Business Process*. CoRR abs/1806.01333

Scheer. (2015). *Scheer BPaaS. Scheer*. Retrieved from https://aws-institut.de/wp-content/uploads/2016/02/AWScheer_Whitepaper5_Industrie-4_0.pdf

Signavio. (2015). *Benutzerhandbuch. Signavio*. Retrieved from https://docs.signavio.com/userguide/editor/de/index.html

Strang, T., & Linnhoff-Popien, C. (2004). A context modeling survey. *In Workshop Proceedings of the 1st International Workshop on Advanced Context Modeling, Reasoning And Management*, Nottingham, UK.

Zhao, X., & Liu, C. (2013). Version management for business process schema evolution. *Journal of Information Systems*, *38*(8), 1046–1069.

ENDNOTES

1 https://github.com/Onto-VP2M/context-BPM/blob/master/BPM Context Ontology.owl

2 http://protege.stanford.edu/

3 https://www.w3.org/Submission/SWRL/

4 http://www.sarost-group.com/

5 https://github.com/Onto-VP2M/context-BPM/blob/master/myOnto.owl

Chapter 3
The Impact of E-Collaboration and Traditional Learning Styles on Learning Outcomes and Anxiety

Yu Zhonggen
https://orcid.org/0000-0002-3873-980X
Department of English Studies, Faculty of Foreign Studies, Beijing Language and Culture University, China

ABSTRACT

Nowadays, information technologies are catching growing attention and their application to English language learning is also prospering. Using a Foreign Language Classroom Anxiety Scale and College English Test Band 4, this study explored the different impacts of e-collaborative learning via QQ group and traditional multi-media learning on learning outcomes and anxiety among tertiary students. Around 70 participants were involved in different styles of learning and instruction and received both surveys and tests. The results showed that QQ group-based e-collaborative learning could significantly decrease anxiety but no significant gain was found in learning outcomes compared with traditional multi-media learning. Correlation between learning outcomes and anxiety was also studied, which resulted in no significant findings. Both disadvantages and advantages of this study were discussed, and future research was recommended as well.

INTRODUCTION

Numerous scholars have been committed to online technology assisted learning and teaching (e.g. Yu, Zhu, Yang, & Chen, 2018; Yu, 2018abcd; Yu, 2019ab). QQ is one of the most popular online communicative tools in China. Users can invite friends who share common interests to communicate within one group. QQ group, an instant and heterochronous communication platform established by Tencent Company, to cater for requirements of users can function as a tool to share, store and transfer files, play

DOI: 10.4018/978-1-7998-4891-2.ch003

Copyright © 2021, IGI Global. Copying or distributing in print or electronic forms without written permission of IGI Global is prohibited.

collaborative online games, send and capture messages and pictures, share online music and videos, etc. In addition, Tencent also provides space services, where users can use Bulletin Board System (BBS), photo album, shared files and other means of communication. QQ groups are divided into different levels which can contain different numbers of users. For instance, an ordinary group can often contain 500 people while an advanced one can hold 1000. Users can also make full use of the group and develop e-collaborative learning.

Collaborative learning refers to the learning mode based on interaction among a team of students (Jaime, et al., 2013). The learners collaboratively share experiences playing certain roles and try to accomplish a common task or assignment interdependently (Dillenbourg, 1999; Szewkis et al., 2011). In order to realize e-collaborative learning, peers should share a common goal, conduct cooperatively, and communicate with each other, coupled with individual responsibility, awareness of common efforts and joint rewards (Szewkis et al., 2011). E-collaboration is also referred to as a collaborative activity that involves people from distant geographic locations working together via Internet tools and other resources (Harris, 1999). This activity is related to telecommuting and telework, a working style which is growingly popular, resulting from the fact that many organizations work on projects at various locations and require virtual teams of dispersed members (Cox, 2009). E-collaboration can realize learning or working at different locations and hours. These virtual teams predominantly use information technology tools for coordination and communication (Cramton & Webber, 2005; González-Navarro, Orengo, Zornoza, Ripoll, & Peiró, 2010). Virtual teams offer many benefits to organizations, while at the same time they also present many challenges in the work process for team effectiveness and satisfaction (Szewkis et al., 2011).

LITERATURE REVIEW

QQ group is featured as powerful instant messaging (IM), which consolidates collaborative learning. Farmer (2007) argued that IM was actively used by millions of people who were connected from anywhere such as home, office, mobile, providing increasing collaborative opportunities. IM supported learning could be especially placed in three contexts: workplace, school and home (Deng, 2008).

Numerous studies explored IM. Some studies (Klavins, 2005; Snyder and Field, 2006) addressed how to design an IM, while others focused on how teenagers used IM, (e.g. Ribak et al., 2002; Klavins, 2005; Snyder and Field, 2006) or the use of away messages (Baron et al., 2005). Grinter and Palen aimed to compare the similarities and differences of SMS and IM and the impact of communication technologies on the pursuit of independence (Grinter and Palen et al., 2006). Grinter and Palen (2002) found teenagers dealt with school work with the aid of IM. The frequency of using IM increased as they became more mature. But they did not provide details on how participants finished the assignment with the aid of IM. It could be generally acknowledged that IM, as a feature of QQ group, might facilitate e-collaborative learning.

Traditional learning is operationally defined as the learning style assisted with multi-media projector and blackboard in this study. Students and the teacher are situated in a classroom equipped with multimedia and blackboard, where the teacher presented language points, language notes, and anything related on a blackboard or a large computer screen. The teacher can also prepare slides for lectures and then play slide by slide in class. Students receive the information mainly through blackboard and computer screen, coupled with teacher's face-to-face explanation. This study aimed to identify the differences of both learning styles, coupled with language anxiety in the learning process.

Since 1970s, language anxiety, an important factor influencing language learning, has been discussed by numerous studies (e.g., Bailey, 1983; Horwitz, Horwitz, & Cope, 1986). Earlier studies mainly centered on causes of anxiety. The relationship between learners' competitiveness and self-esteem was considered as a potential reason for anxiety (Bailey, 1983). Bailey (1983) argued that anxiety might be the consequences of the competitive nature of L2 learning, language tests and learners' perceived relationship with their teachers. This argument was supported by Young (1991), who revealed that six potential causes of language anxiety were involved in students' language learning, namely personal and interpersonal learner beliefs about language learning, instructor beliefs about language teaching, instructor-learner interactions, classroom procedures and language tests. It could be easily identified that learners, teachers and instructional practice were three aspects influencing anxiety, with which Bailey's findings were in agreement.

The findings of Horwitz, Horwitz and Cope (1986) produced an influential impact on studies of language anxiety. The participants, 225 language learning beginners at the University of Texas, made a contribution to the scope of foreign language anxiety. Through this study, the researchers designed a well-known research instrument--Foreign Language Classroom Anxiety Scale (FLCAS) including 33 items. Three related components were integrated into this scale, i.e. communication apprehension, test anxiety, and fear of negative evaluation. After numerous experiments via FLCAS, Horwitz (1991: 39) concluded that anxiety in foreign language learning could be validly and reliably measured, which played an important role in language learning (Wang and Wan, 2001). This scale has nowadays been widely used to measure foreign language learners' anxiety and to identify its impact on language learning outcomes in different situations (Cao, 2011). In this study, this scale will also be used to measure learners' anxiety.

It is becoming increasingly difficult to ignore learning outcomes and anxiety by means of e-collaborative and traditional learning. Therefore, it is important to explore the differences in learning outcomes and anxiety between traditional and e-collaborative learning. Research hypotheses in this study are raised as: (1) e-collaborative learning via QQ group can significantly decrease anxiety compared with traditional learning; (2) e-collaborative learning via QQ group can significantly increase learning outcomes compared with traditional learning; (3) there is a negative relationship between learning outcomes and anxiety.

Methods

This study attempts to adopt a quantitative method comparing data of learning outcomes and anxiety respectively obtained from e-collaborative and traditional learning so as to identify if significant differences exist, coupled with correlation between learning outcomes and anxiety.

Participants

Participants were randomly selected from those with similar English proficiency (M=82.30, Std. Deviation=1.40) among freshmen undergraduates in a university in China. 71 undergraduates were finally determined and randomly divided into two classes. Class A, consisting of 35 students (18 males and 17 females; mean age: 18.6 years), received traditional teaching for one semester. Class B, involving 36 students (19 males and 17 females; mean age: 19.2 years), were taught with e-collaborative style.

Instruments

The instruments adopted in this study included: (1) College English Test Band 4 (CET4) in order to identify changes in English proficiency after different styles of learning for one semester, and (2) Foreign Language Classroom Anxiety Scale (FLCAS) including 33 items aiming to determine different degrees of anxiety after different styles of learning for one semester. Attracting more than 6 million examination candidates annually (Wang and Wan, 2001), CET4 is a large-scale standardized test developed by National Ministry Education of China in order to measure students' comprehensive English proficiency and provide feedbacks and recommendations for English teaching and learning. CET4 includes a vast variety of test items such as writing, skimming and scanning, short and long dialogues listening, passage listening, blank fillings, in-depth reading, cloze, error correction, sentence translation and short question answer. Since established in 1987 it has been proved valid and reliable to test students' English proficiency in terms of listening, speaking, reading and writing (Yang, 2003).

FLCAS is made up of demographic information and 33 questions, covering three components concerning anxiety in the classroom, namely communication apprehension, test anxiety and fear of negative evaluation, among which 29 questions deal with typical difficulties in listening, speaking, reading, writing, linguistic memory and processing (Wang and Wan, 2001). The 33 questions are answered on a five-point Likert scales, ranging from *strongly disagree* to *strongly agree* with values 1-5 assigned to them respectively. Questions 2, 5, 8, 11, 14, 18, 22, 28, 32 were negatively indicated, and so the scores were reversely computed. The general rule is: the higher the score is, the more anxiety there will be. "Foreign language" was changed into "English language". All question items produced significant corrected item-total scale correlations. Test-retest reliability reached a satisfactory level ($r=.83$, $p<.001$) (Horwitz et al., 1986).

Procedure

At the preparatory stage, more than 2000 freshmen undergraduates were randomly selected on the basis of their English admission scores. 79 students whose admission English scores ranged from 80 to 85 points were selected, out of whom 8 were unwilling to participate in the experiment. Consequently, 71 were finally enrolled (mean score = 82.34, Std. Error = .17). Participants from both classes finished learning 4 units in one semester. Each unit centered on one text, including (1) cultural background of the text; (2) text comprehension; (3) exercises attached to the text.

In order to check the internal reliability of FLCAS, a pilot study was conducted. Randomly selected 26 students were willing to answer 33 questions. After this, two classes were administered by two English language instructors who experienced specialized training on e-collaborative teaching and traditional instruction respectively. At the end of the semester, both classed were tested by both CET4 of Dec. 2012 and FLCAS. Then all the data obtained from CET4 and FLCAS were entered into SPSS13.0 for computation and analysis.

The e-collaborative instruction was featured as student-centered online instruction via QQ group. The instructor delivered lectures explaining the text and its background each week in QQ group in the form of teaching slides, coupled with movies and voice background etc. After this, participants received assignment online and were required to accomplish the exercises within a certain time. After accomplishing the assignment, they were required to share the answers and questions in QQ group at a set time, and the instructor publicized guidelines. Participants could also discuss related answers and explanations in the group. Participants were reminded of preparation before each virtual class and encouraged to collaborate with peers via QQ group when coming across any difficulty.

The traditional multi-media instruction was conducted in the classroom with the instructor-centered pedagogy. The instructor gave lectures regarding culture, text and exercises face-to-face by showing slides on a large computer screen via multi-media projector or by presenting points on a blackboard. Participants were required to learn in the classroom and to finish the assignment after class. Then they brought the assignment to the instructor for face-to-face feedbacks. They were asked to preview language points before class and encouraged to consult the instructor if they met any question.

RESULTS AND DISCUSSION

The Pilot Study

After checking the data obtained from 26 participants, we found 3 surveys were invalid since the answers were highly homogeneous. Hence the remaining 23 surveys were computed and analyzed. Questions of the survey were shown in Table 1.

As shown in Table 1, means and deviations of 33 questions are provided in the third and fourth columns respectively. Cronbach's alpha is revealed in the last column, which is .90, having arrived at a satisfactory level. This shows FLCAS is internally reliable.

The Study

In this study, participants completed both FLCAS and CET4 of Dec. 2012 after one semester's different styles of English learning. Both results were computed and analyzed below.

The FLCAS

In FLCAS, there are three main components to measure foreign language classroom anxiety: communication apprehension, test anxiety, and fear of negative evaluation. The first component, labeled as communication apprehension, contains 11 items reflecting the communication (Horwitz et al., 1986) which are numbered 1, 4, 9, 14, 15, 18, 24, 27, 29, 30, and 32. The second component, labeled as test anxiety, contains 15 items indicating anxiety relating to test (Horwitz et al., 1986) which are 3, 5, 6, 8, 10, 11, 12, 16, 17, 20, 21, 22, 25, 26, and 28. The third component, labeled as fear of negative evaluation, contains 7 items that show students' fear relating to the evaluation in the foreign language classroom (Horwitz et al., 1986), namely 2, 7, 13, 19, 23, 31, and 33.

The two classes were taught by means of traditional and e-collaborative instruction respectively for one semester. Both teachers for each class were at the same teaching level and were both trained on specific teaching styles. Three components in FLCAS in terms of both learning styles were compared in this study. In the traditional class, 4 surveys were not considered for analysis due to the information missing. In the class where e-collaborative learning style was adopted, there were 3 invalid surveys due to their being highly unanimous. Therefore, there remained 31 valid surveys for traditional style and 33 for e-collaborative one. The results were summarized and analyzed in Table 2.

Table 1. Data of FLCAS in the pilot study

No.	Questions	Mean	SD	α
Q1	I never feel quite sure of myself when I am speaking in my English class.	2.65	.88	
Q2	I don't worry about making mistakes in English class.	3.22	.95	
Q3	I tremble when I know that I'm going to be called on in English class.	3.17	1.07	
Q4	It frightens me when I don't understand what the teacher is saying in English.	2.83	.72	
Q5	It wouldn't bother me at all to take more English classes.	3.17	.94	
Q6	During English class, I find myself thinking about things that have nothing to do with the course.	3.22	.90	
Q7	I keep thinking that the other students are better at languages than I am.	3.17	1.11	
Q8	I am usually at ease during tests in my English class.	3.13	.81	
Q9	I start to panic when I have to speak without preparation in English class.	3.04	.93	
Q10	I worry about the consequences of failing my English class.	3.17	.72	
Q11	I don't understand why some people get so upset over English classes.	2.96	.98	
Q12	In English class, I can get so nervous I forget things I know.	2.91	.95	
Q13	It embarrasses me to volunteer answers in my English class.	2.83	.78	
Q14	I would not be nervous speaking English with native speakers.	3.34	.83	
Q15	I get upset when I don't understand what the teacher is correcting.	2.96	1.07	
Q16	Even if I am well prepared for English class, I feel anxious about it.	3.00	.90	
Q17	I often feel like not going to my English class.	3.04	.98	.9
Q18	I feel confident when I speak in English class.	3.35	1.02	
Q19	I am afraid that my English teacher is ready to correct every mistake I make.	2.87	1.06	
Q20	I can feel my heart pounding when I'm going to be called on in English class.	2.83	.83	
Q21	The more I study for an English test, the more confused I get.	2.65	.935	
Q22	I don't feel pressure to prepare very well for English class.	2.78	.951	
Q23	I always feel that the other students speak English better than I do.	2.96	1.02	
Q24	I feel very self-conscious about speaking English in front of other students.	3.04	.88	
Q25	English class moves so quickly I worry about getting left behind.	2.83	.89	
Q26	I feel more tense and nervous in my English class than in my other classes.	2.70	1.02	
Q27	I get nervous and confused when I am speaking in my English class.	2.96	1.07	
Q28	When I'm on my way to English class, I feel very sure and relaxed.	2.96	1.11	
Q29	I get nervous when I don't understand every word the English teacher says.	2.83	.98	
Q30	I feel overwhelmed by the number of rules you have to learn to speak English.	2.87	.87	
Q31	I am afraid that the other students will laugh at me when I speak English.	2.91	1.04	
Q32	I would probably feel comfortable around native speakers of English.	2.87	.87	
Q33	I get nervous when the English teacher asks questions which I haven't prepared in advance.	2.83	.83	

As shown in Table 2, three components show differences between e-collaborative and traditional learning styles. It is obviously revealed that the mean of communication apprehension of e-collaborative learning (M=27.91) is significantly lower than that of traditional learning (M=33.13) (t=4.81, p=0.00), which indicates that the anxiety of communication apprehension is significantly less in e-collaborative

Table 2. Differences in three components between two learning styles

Components	Learning styles				M.D.	*t*	Sig (2-tailed)
	Traditional		E-collaborative				
	M	S.D.	M	S.D.			
Communication apprehension	33.13	4.49	27.91	4.19	5.22	4.81	.00
Test anxiety	44.06	6.01	38.88	5.09	5.19	3.74	.00
Fear of negative evaluation	20.29	3.65	16.91	2.66	3.38	4.25	.00

Note: M.D. = mean differences; M=mean; S.D. = standard deviation

than in traditional learning. Learners tend to be less anxious when they receive e-collaborative style of instruction than traditional style in terms of communication apprehension.

Reasons for communication apprehension might be various, some of which are summarized and discussed below.

In e-collaborative learning, participants might have felt quite sure of themselves when they were speaking in class because they had abundant online resources to refer to and could adjust themselves to a comfortable mood. On the contrary, in traditional learning, participants had to speak without aid of information from the Internet and had to speak under any condition when required by the instructor. Therefore, it was normal to find more anxiety in traditional style than in e-collaborative learning.

E-collaborative learning could give participants opportunities to communicate with peers or to seek information online when they failed to understand the instructor, while traditional learning seldom provided this chance. Consequently, even when participants came across difficulty in understanding the instructor, they might still be able to find solution through e-collaborative learning style, which was not true of traditional learning.

In case participants were required to speak in class without any preparation, they tended to be panicked. However, they might be less panicked in e-collaborative learning since they could use information technology to facilitate flow of ideas, such as referring to famous speech or sample answers online.

When the instructor was correcting the participants in traditional class and they failed to follow the instructor, they might be worried and anxious. Nevertheless, e-collaborative learning could provide image, picture, word, sound, dialogues, movie and even personal communication online, which was helpful to remove barriers to perception. If participants still felt upset with all of these aids, they could contact peers or the instructor without being detected by others. This could relax them and possibly improve learning outcomes.

Test anxiety, as demonstrated in Table 2, is also significantly decreased in e-collaborative learning (M=38.88) than in the traditional (M=44.06) (t=3.74, p=.00). The reasons why test anxiety decreased in e-collaborative learning might be of various kinds. One of the reasons might be that participants could choose the right place to log onto the QQ group class and make themselves most comfortable. While in traditional learning, they had no other choices than sitting in the prescribed classroom. Even when they were going to be tested, they could save more time to prepare than traditional style since they did not need to waste time traveling and walking to the classroom.

Table 2 also revealed that fear of negative evaluation in the traditional (M=20.29) was significantly larger than in the e-collaborative (M=16.91) (t=4.25, p=0.00). When sitting at their own homes, participants might be able to get better prepared to join the class and perform better in class. They could also contact peers anonymously and retrieve information they desired without being known by peers and the instructor. In this way, the worry about being mocked at silly mistakes and misunderstandings could be minimized. Fear of negative evaluation could thus be decreased.

To sum up, anxiety was globally and specifically decreased when learners received the e-collaborative learning compared with the traditional one. Therefore, the first hypothesis "e-collaborative learning via QQ group can significantly decrease anxiety compared with traditional learning" was accepted.

The CET 4

Both classes took part in CET4 of Dec. 2012 at the end of semester after respectively receiving e-collaborative and traditional instruction. The comparison of differences in results between both learning styles was summarized and analyzed in Table 3.

Table 3. Comparison of differences in CET4 scores between both learning styles

Learning styles	N	Mean	Mean differences	Std. Deviation	F	Sig. (2-tailed)
Traditional	28	73.79	-1.64	4.83	1.85	.18
E-collaborative	26	75.42		3.66		

There were 71 participants joining CET4. However, 17 test papers were invalid since they were carelessly conducted with numerous simplistic errors indicating that the participants were not cautious enough to finish the test. As a result, 54 papers were valid, 28 from traditional class and 26 from e-collaborative class.

As shown in Table 3, there were some differences in CET4 scores (Mean differences = -1.64). The mean of CET4 scores under e-collaborative instruction (M=75.42) was a little higher than that under traditional instruction (M = 73.79). Nevertheless, it was definite that no significant differences were found (F=1.85, p=.18), revealing that participants under either traditional or e-collaborative instruction did not produce significantly different learning outcomes although significant different degrees of anxiety were caused.

The reasons why two styles of learning did not result in significantly different outcomes might be of many kinds. Traditionally instructed participants had to attend the class and finished the assignment both in and outside the class, which might have forced them to learn and understand what the instructor delivered. On the contrary, for those under e-collaborative instruction, compulsory attendance was difficult to abide by. Participants might have evaded the task assigned by the instructor since it was hard for the instructor to identify those who did not accomplish the task. If they were not self-disciplined enough, they might also escape from the QQ group--the online class since it was not so easy for the instructor to spot out the absentees online. Participants might also use QQ group to communicate issues which were not related to learning hence much time was wasted. In a traditional class, such business happened much less frequently. Online learning might also bring about many other attractive engagements such as online gaming, shopping, chatting and surfing, which possibly distracted the learners. The findings echoed some previous studies which claimed there was no influence of virtual collaboration on post-test grades (Solimeno, Mebane, Tomai, & Francescato, 2008; Tutty & Klein, 2008). Nevertheless, some studies noted the positive effects of e-collaboration as opposed to face-to-face collaboration, such as better quality outcomes (Francescato et al., 2006), which was not in conformity with this study. .

As a result, e-collaborative learning failed to produce better learning outcomes than the traditional one because its advantages might have been offset by the disadvantages. Consequently, the second hypothesis "e-collaborative learning via QQ group can significantly increase learning outcomes compared with traditional learning" was rejected.

The last hypothesis "there is a negative relationship between learning outcomes and anxiety" cannot be tested unless a correlation between learning outcomes and anxiety is conducted. Therefore, after the data of CET4 and three components of anxiety were entered into SPSS13.0, a correlation analysis was conducted with the result summarized in Table 4.

Table 4. Correlations between anxiety and learning outcomes

		CA	CET4	TA	FNE
CA	Pearson Correlation	1	.023	.613(**)	.553(**)
	Sig. (2-tailed)		.867	.000	.000
	N	64	54	64	64
CET4	Pearson Correlation	.023	1	.007	-.086
	Sig. (2-tailed)	.867		.961	.537
	N	54	54	54	54
TA	Pearson Correlation	.613(**)	.007	1	.743(**)
	Sig. (2-tailed)	.000	.961		.000
	N	64	54	64	64
FNE	Pearson Correlation	.553(**)	-.086	.743(**)	1
	Sig. (2-tailed)	.000	.537	.000	
	N	64	54	64	64

Notes: CA = communication apprehension; TA = test anxiety; FNE = fear of negative evaluation
**Correlation is significant at the 0.01 level (2-tailed).

As described in Table 4, it was obvious that there were positive relationships between three components, namely communication apprehension, test anxiety, and fear of negative evaluation at the .01 level. This indicated that if there was more communication apprehension, there would be more test anxiety and fear of negative evaluation. More test anxiety would lead to more fear of negative evaluation and communication apprehension and so forth. This proved the consistency of this anxiety measure scale. It was argued that there was a negative relationship between learning outcomes and anxiety, meaning that more anxiety would cause poorer academic performance and less anxiety would give rise to better learning outcomes on the contrary (Wang and Wan, 2001). The relationship between learning outcomes (CET4) and three components, however, was not found significant at the .01 level. This was not in conformity with previous literature.

Previous studies also found that anxiety had something to do with complexity of structures of oral language (Kleinmann, 1977). In addition, after studying French, German and Spanish learners, Young (1986) revealed that there was some relationship between oral Proficiency Interview and measures of anxiety. The conflicts in this study with previous studies might have been caused by disadvantages in e-collaborative learning and advantages in traditional learning. Disadvantages in e-collaborative learning, such as more distracters and absentees, might have become barriers to its facilitation in learning outcomes. So e-collaborative learning did not result in learning outcomes although it could significantly decrease the degree of anxiety. Traditional learning style, however, did not lead to poorer CET 4 scores despite its contribution to anxiety possibly because it had many benefits, e.g. fewer absentees and distracters. Therefore, the last hypothesis "there is a negative relationship between learning outcomes and anxiety" was rejected.

However, e-collaborative learning is possibly advantageous to the traditional style. English learners can also explore language issues and complete assignments e-collaboratively when they stay in their own houses or dorms. This can avoid distant travel and time-consuming seat-finding in the crowded library or classroom. Instead, time can be saved for learning. Learners can communicate and solve academic problems at any time they would like and at any place they want to remain. This mode of learning undoubtedly saves time and energy and thus most likely facilitates learning.

Traditionally, when language learners came across a problem which was difficult to solve, he or she tended to call peers. Sometimes, learners even failed to solve the problem on the phone since they could do nothing but hearing each other. If they failed to understand the pronunciation, then misunderstandings would arise, leaving the problem unsolved. Today, such misunderstandings could be easily resolved through various kinds of presentation of learners' ideas. Through QQ group, they can type words, speak online, see each other, send files, show pictures and make or present movies.

As for English language instructors, they can teach English through QQ group as well. They can show their lecture notes using the program Power Points, assign homework to learners, speak to learners, see learners and even hold a video conference if necessary. Instructors can also check learners' assignment, show some evaluation results, find out frequent mistakes and remind any other potential similar error. Learners have easy access to all of the actions. Traditional blackboard and multimedia projectors will not be needed any more.

CONCLUSION

This part will discuss both advantages and disadvantages of this study, together with future research directions for readers' reference.

Advantages

This study was in possession of some advantages. Applying the well accepted Foreign Language Classroom Anxiety Scale and the durably validated CET4, the study identified the impact of e-collaborative and traditional learning styles on learning outcomes and anxiety. The scale was proved internally reliable and externally valid since its Cronbach's alpha reached a satisfactory level .90 and many scholars certified its effectiveness. CET4 was also considered reliable and valid because it had experienced more than 20 years' revision and perfection. The number of the participants also arrived at a sufficient level. The duration of the study was also appropriate. The comparison between two groups after one semester was also considered proper. However, there were still some findings beyond previous studies. An example was that no negative relationship was found between anxiety and learning outcomes although some literature proved it.

Disadvantages

The abnormal findings might have been caused due to random errors. Two different instructors teaching two classes via different pedagogies might have posed challenges for the learning outcomes and anxiety. It was difficult to ensure their teaching was at an identical level although both of them had received formal training before the study. In collaborative learning, participants might have been distracted by plentiful online information such as news and games. In traditional learning, participants might have not been or have been as anxious as they used to be due to unavoidable bias of the instructor. In addition, the testing environment and participants' mood might also have exerted some influence on the results.

Although QQ group is an excellent tool to carry out e-collaborative learning and teaching, there still exist some defects. A standardized rule is not yet set up to regulate QQ group. Storage of information is not powerful enough because flow of questions in the exchange box is rapid and easily ignored, which may make students feel difficult to catch the specific contents of the information. On the other hand, if the content of the information is too voluminous, it tends to be hard for students to totally take in. The size of files is limited. If users want to transfer or download some files of an excessively large size, the speed may be slow and sometimes downloading is even forbidden due to space limitation. QQ group is also imperfect if too large a class is operated since group members are also limited. The last but not the least, the speed of Internet might be an inescapable factor when conducting e-collaborative instruction via QQ group.

Prospects

With swift improvement of science and technology, increasing kinds of technologies are being applied to English learning and teaching. Among them, QQ group is only presently a popular tool. In the future, it may be no longer well accepted if its technologies remain at the primary stage. Further improvements on QQ group may be needed. Developers should make every effort to make it better for e-collaborative learning. Teachers may need to understand the function and application of QQ group thoroughly in order to organize and operate the class successfully.

In view of limitations of QQ group, breakthroughs will never be considered unnecessary. Pedagogies equipped with high-tech need to be improved constantly in order to keep pace with the fast development of new technologies. E-collaborative learning can be greatly effective if it is integrated into proper technologies and organized and utilized in a proper way. Besides QQ group, other technologies might be also satisfactory media of instruction, which needs effortful exploration. English e-collaborative learning and instruction may be better if it is connected with cognitive sciences, computer technologies, linguistics, and education theories. Cross-disciplinary effort may be able to realize something that otherwise cannot be dreamed about.

ACKNOWLEDGMENT

The author wishes to thank the people who help this study and the projects which financially support this study: Chinese national fund for the humanities and social sciences (Chinese Academic translation) (17WSS005).

REFERENCES

Bailey, K. (1983). Competitiveness and anxiety in adult second language learning: Looking at and through the diary studies. In H. Seliger & M. Long (Eds.), Classroom-oriented research in second language acquisition (pp. 67-102). Rowley: Mass Newbury House.

Baron, N., Squires, L., Trench, S., & Thompson, M. (2005). Tethered or Mobile? Use of Away Messages in Instant Messaging by American College Students. In R. Ling & P. Pedersen (Eds.), *Mobile Communications: Renegotiation of the Social Sphere* (pp. 293–312). Springer. doi:10.1007/1-84628-248-9_20

Cao, Y. (2011). Comparison of Two Models of Foreign Language Classroom Anxiety Scale. *Philippine ESL Journal*, *7*, 73–93.

Cox, W. (2009). Improving quality of life through telecommuting. *The Information Technology & Innovation Foundation*, *1*, 1–22.

Cramton, C. D., & Webber, S. S. (2005). Relationship among geographic dispersion, team process, and effectiveness in software development work teams. *Journal of Business Research*, *58*(6), 758–765. doi:10.1016/j.jbusres.2003.10.006

Deng, H. (2008). A Case study on undergraduates' Informal learning supported by QQ. *2008 International Conference on Computer Science and Software Engineering*, 649-654. 10.1109/CSSE.2008.235

Dillenbourg, P. (1999). Collaborative learning: Cognitive and computational approaches. In *Advances in learning and Instruction Series*. Elsevier Science, Inc.

Farmer, R. (2006). Instant Messaging: Collaborative Tool or Educator's nightmare! *Proceedings of 2003 The Web Learning Conference*. https://www.unb.ca/naweb/proceedings/2003/PaperFarmer.html

Francescato, D., Porcelli, R., Mebane, M., Cuddeta, M., Koblas, J., & Renzi, P. (2006). Evaluation of the efficacy of collaborative learning in face-to-face and computer-supported university contexts. *Computers in Human Behavior*, *22*(2), 163–176. doi:10.1016/j.chb.2005.03.001

González-Navarro, P., Orengo, V., Zornoza, A., Ripoll, P., & Peiró, J. M. (2010). Group interaction styles in a virtual context: The effects on group outcomes. *Computers in Human Behavior*, *26*(6), 1472–1480. doi:10.1016/j.chb.2010.04.026

Grinter, R. E., & Palen, L. (2002). Instant Messaging in Teen Life. *Proceedings of the 2002 ACM conference on Computer supported cooperative work*, 21-30.

Harris, J. (1999). First steps in telecollaboration. *Learning and Leading with Technology*, *27*(3), 54–57.

Horwitz, E., Horwitz, M., & Cope, J. (1986). Foreign language classroom anxiety. *Modern Language Journal*, *70*(2), 125–132. doi:10.1111/j.1540-4781.1986.tb05256.x

Jaime, A., Domínguez, C., Sánchez, A., & Blanco, J. M. (2013). Interuniversity telecollaboration to improve academic results and identify preferred communication tools. *Computers & Education*, *64*, 63–69. doi:10.1016/j.compedu.2013.01.008

Klavins, X. (2005). *Instant Messaging Tool for Collaboration in a Peer to-Peer Network: MyBook Instant Messenger.* Thesis Paper. https://www.ohiolink.edu/etd/sendpdf.cgi/KLAVINS%20AINARS.pdf?acc_num=ucin1109305316

Kleinmann, H. (1977). Avoidance behavior in adult second language acquisition. *Language Learning*, *27*(1), 93–107. doi:10.1111/j.1467-1770.1977.tb00294.x

Ribak, A., & Jacovi, M. (2002). Ask Before You Search "Peer Support and Community Building with ReachOut. In *Proceedings of the 2002 ACM conference on Computer supported cooperative work*. ACM Press.

Snyder, J., & Field, M. (2006). We got the message: creating an instant messenger service point. *User Services Conference*. 10.1145/1181216.1181297

Solimeno, A., Mebane, M. E., Tomai, M., & Francescato, D. (2008). The influence of students and teachers characteristics on the efficacy of face-to-face and computer supported collaborative learning. *Computers & Education*, *51*(1), 109–128. doi:10.1016/j.compedu.2007.04.003

Szewkis, E., Nussbaum, M., Rosen, T., Abalos, J., Denardin, F., Caballero, D., Tagle, A., & Alcoholado, C. (2011). Collaboration within large groups in the classroom. *Computer-Supported Collaborative Learning*, *6*(4), 561–575. doi:10.100711412-011-9123-y

Tutty, J. I., & Klein, J. D. (2008). Computer-mediated instruction: A comparison of online and face-to-face collaboration. *Educational Technology Research and Development*, *56*(2), 101–124. doi:10.100711423-007-9050-9

Wang, Y. Q., & Wan, Y. S. (2001). Anxiety in Foreign Language learning and its impact on foreign language learning. *Foreign Language Teaching and Research*, *33*(2), 122–126.

Yang, H. Z. (2003). Fifteen years review on CET4 and CET6. *Waiguoyu*, *145*(3), 21–29.

Young, D. (1986). The relationship between anxiety and foreign language oral proficiency ratings. *Foreign Language Annals*, *19*(5), 439–445. doi:10.1111/j.1944-9720.1986.tb01032.x

Young, D. J. (1991). Creating a low-anxiety classroom environment: What does language anxiety research suggest? *Modern Language Journal*, *75*(4), 426–439. doi:10.1111/j.1540-4781.1991.tb05378.x

Yu, Z., Zhu, Y., Yang, Z., & Chen, W. (2018). Student satisfaction, learning outcomes, and cognitive loads with a mobile learning platform. *Computer Assisted Language Learning*. Advance online publication. doi:10.1080/09588221.2018.1517093

Yu, Z. (2018a). Differences in serious game-aided and traditional English vocabulary acquisition. *Computers & Education*, *127*, 214–232. doi:10.1016/j.compedu.2018.07.014

Yu, Z. (2018b). Third-Level Digital Divide in English Teaching and Learning. *International Journal of Information and Communication Technology Education*, *14*(3), 68–80. doi:10.4018/IJICTE.2018070106

Yu, Z. (2018c). Comparative effectiveness between game-enhanced and pencil-and-paper English vocabulary learning approaches. *International Journal of Gaming and Computer-Mediated Simulations*, *10*(2), 1–20. doi:10.4018/IJGCMS.2018040101

Yu, Z., & Zhu, Q. (2018d). Schema Theory-based Flipped Classroom Model Assisted with Technologies. *International Journal of Information and Communication Technology Education*, *15*(2), 31–48. doi:10.4018/IJICTE.2019040103

Yu, Z. (2019a). A meta-analysis of use of serious games in education over a decade. *International Journal of Computer Games Technology*, *1*, 1–8. doi:10.1155/2019/4797032

Yu, Z. (2019b). Mobile device- and video-aided flipped English classrooms. *International Journal of Mobile and Blended Learning*, *11*(2), 19–32. doi:10.4018/IJMBL.2019040102

Chapter 4
Factors Influencing Interprofessional Collaboration in Healthcare Environment:
An Empirical Analysis

Ramaraj Palanisamy
St Francis Xavier University, Canada

Nazim Taskin
Massey University, New Zealand

Jacques Verville
École de Management de Normandie, France

ABSTRACT

The increases in complexity of patient care, healthcare costs, and technological advancements shifted the healthcare delivery to interprofessional collaborative care. The study aims for identifying factors influencing the quality of team collaboration. The study examines the impact of trust and technology orientation on collaboration with the mediating effects of communication, coordination, and cooperation. The results of the study validate that (1) collaboration has positive and significant relationship with coordination, and cooperation; (2) trust has positive and significant relationship with communication, coordination, and cooperation; and (3) technology orientation has positive and significant relationship with cooperation but not with communication and coordination. The research and managerial implications of these factors are given in the discussion. The results can be used by healthcare professionals and managers to advance their understanding on the impact of trust and technology on collaboration mediating communication, coordination, and cooperation practices.

DOI: 10.4018/978-1-7998-4891-2.ch004

Copyright © 2021, IGI Global. Copying or distributing in print or electronic forms without written permission of IGI Global is prohibited.

INTRODUCTION

In the modern healthcare system, interprofessional collaboration has become a vital component of an effectively-functioning healthcare system (Karam, Brault, Van Durme, & Macq, 2018). The healthcare provision has shifted from that of autonomous practice to interprofessional team based approach which involves multiple professionals with different educational background, training and expertise, working on behalf of patients, sharing a common goal (Woods, Jackson, Ziglar, & Alston, 2011). In most of the cases, collaborative care is required for a patient care, as there is no single professional can fulfill all the needs of a patient (Matziou, Vlahioti, Perdikaris, Matziou, Megapanou, & Petsios, 2014). Interprofessional team approach enhances healthcare access, efficiency of services, resource utilization, health knowledge, skills and more satisfaction for the patients (Barrett, Curran, Glynn, & Godwin, 2007; Safran, 2003).

Patients receive safer and higher-quality care when healthcare professionals work as a team and collaborate effectively while they practice. The increases in complexity of patient care, healthcare costs for medical specialization and technological advancements shifted the way the healthcare is delivered to interprofessional collaborative care (Gaboury, Bujold, Boon, & Moher, 2009; Smith, Greene, & Meeker., 2002; Welton, Kantner, & Moriber, 1997). The increasing complexity of health problems inevitably makes professionals interdependent in a collaborative manner foregoing a competitive approach (D'Amour, 1999). In the complex healthcare environment, poor collaboration among health professionals significantly increases the possibilities of mistakes occurring in the delivery of patient-care, medication-error-related deaths, wrong-site surgeries and increased staff turnover (Woods et al., 2011). Interprofessional collaborative practice meets current demands of the healthcare system reducing errors and costs and thereby improving quality of patient care (Canadian Health Services Research Foundation, 2006; Lemieux-Charles & McGuire, 2006).

High degree of interprofessional collaboration is essential for team success. The task of improving interprofessional collaboration has received considerable attention as it is a key factor to increase the effectiveness of healthcare services. Nonetheless, effective team functioning in a collaborative manner is challenging and difficult to achieve (Bailey, Jones, & Way, 2006; Sicotte, D'Amour, & Moreault, 2002). The literature provides conceptual definitions and frameworks of interprofessional collaboration and indicates about limited knowledge of this complex phenomenon. Specifically, the vast majority of published work on the influence of determinants of interprofessional collaboration relies on conceptual approaches rather than empirical data (Rodriguez, Beaulieu, D'Amour, & Ferrada-Videla, 2005). The knowledge on the factors influencing quality of team collaboration and the linkages between the elements in the complex interprofessional relationships is limited (Gocan, Laplante, & Woodend, 2014; Baerg, Lake, & Paslawski, 2012; D'Amour, Ferrada-Videla, Rodriguez, & Beaulieu, 2005; Zwarenstein, Reeves & Perrier, 2004). As effective collaboration does not emerge merely by grouping the professionals together, very few studies have investigated the influence of interactional determinants for effective collaboration.

Based on a qualitative study, communication, coordination, cooperation, and trust were found to be the factors for communication-based-collaborative practice (Palanisamy & Verville, 2015). In a review of qualitative articles, the factors such as communication, trust, coordination, and cooperation were found to be commonly influencing interprofessional collaboration (Karam et al., 2018). In general, successful collaborative practice in healthcare requires coordination and cooperation (Williams, Lasky, Dannemiller, Andrei, & Thomas, 2010; Apker, Kathleen, Wendy, & Hofmeister, 2006; Way, Jones, & Busing, 2000). Way et al. (2000) emphasize on communication and coordination mechanisms as they play a key role for developing collaborative relationship among team members. The quality and effective interprofessional cooperation between the healthcare team members is a major concern because it directly affects the healthcare and patient outcomes (Foth, Block, & Stamers, 2015). The complexity of healthcare problems could be addressed by different interprofessional cooperation types (Molleman, Broekhuis, Stoffels, & Jaspers, 2008). The collaboration of healthcare professionals requires mentoring and constantly communicating with team members to clarify the roles and responsibilities of team members, which is an important characteristic of cooperation (Apker et al., 2006). In providing high-quality care to patients, professionals have to interact and collaboratively work together with a number of other healthcare professionals cultivating relationships using best communication practices ensuring better patient outcomes (Haeuser & Preston, 2005; Thomas, Sherwood, Mulhollem, Sexton, & Helmreich, 2004).

The professionals interact in a collaborative environment, which provides opportunities as well as constraints thereby increase in complexities for effective collaboration. In the complex environment, trust is another determinant of collaboration and enables communication, coordination and cooperation of healthcare professionals (Jacobsen, 1999; Mechanic, 1998; Rodriguez et al., 2005). Trust enables communication and enhances the quality of interactions (Jacobsen, 1999); mutual trust is emphasized for coordinated behavior among the team members and using coordination mechanisms (Rodriguez et al., 2005). Furthermore, trust is a facilitator for having smooth cooperative interprofessional relationships (Misztal, 1996). As patient care is provided by multidisciplinary healthcare professionals, the technology orientation facilitates communication among healthcare professionals by improving information flows, coordinates the common goal of enhanced health outcome by caring the patients, and accomplishes cooperation among professionals to seek healthcare solutions (Weaver, Lindsay, & Gitelman, 2012; InfoDev, 2006; Henault, Eugenio, Kelliher, Alexis, & Conlin, 2002).

The study examines the question of what are the factors improving the quality of interprofessional collaboration among healthcare professionals in healthcare industry in North American settings? The paper aims to advance our understanding of current practices of interprofessional collaboration by empirically testing the impact of trust and technology orientation on collaboration in association with communication, coordination and collaboration having mediating effects with trust and collaboration as well as technology orientation and collaboration. In particular, the study aims for empirically examining (i) the impact of trust on communication, coordination and cooperation; (ii) the impact of technology orientation on communication, coordination and cooperation; and (iii) the impact of communication, coordination and cooperation on collaboration. The study results enable to find the factors influencing collaboration and provide guidelines for implementing communication, coordination and cooperation of healthcare practices.

The remaining part of the paper is organized as follows. Section 2 evolves the research model based on a review of literature; Section 3 documents the research methodology followed for this study; Section 4 shows the data analysis and findings; Section 5 discusses the managerial implications of this study followed by areas of future research; and Section 6 gives the limitations and concluding remarks.

RESEARCH MODEL

This section gives the conceptual definitions of the various constructs of the model. The hypotheses are evolved based on a review of literature.

Collaboration

Interprofessional collaboration is defined as "two or more healthcare professionals who have specific roles, perform interdependent tasks, and share a common goal; a negotiated agreement which values expertise and contribution that each individual brings to patient care" (Gagliardi, Dobrow, & Wright, 2011). In the context of healthcare, collaboration is based on the sharing of resources and collective actions for the patient-care in a trusted and harmonious environment. Morgan, Pullon, and McKinlay, (2015) define interprofessional collaboration as a "partnership between people from diverse backgrounds with distinctive professional cultures and possibly representing different organizations or sectors, who work together to solve problems or provide services" (Morgan, Pullon, McKinlay, 2015, p. 1218). The healthcare team is defined as two or more healthcare professionals who are working together for a common goal of caring a patient and the professionals hold themselves accountable for their activities. Collaboration isthe relationships and interactions between professionals, seen as a process comprised of dynamic, interactive, interpersonal, transformational and evolving nature of processes (D'Amour, Ferrada-Videla, San Martin, & Beaulieu, 2005; Hanson, Carr, & Spross, 2000; Sullivan, 1998; D'Amour, Sicotte, & Le´vy, 1999). These professionals may or may not work with the same organization. Collaboration in healthcare is the process by which interdependent professionals structure a collective action towards patient's care (D'Amour, 1997). Working with other professionals in a collaborative manner leads to enhanced healthcare outcomes that are not achievable individually. The two key elements of collaboration are: (i) the team's collective action for addressing the complexity of patient needs; and (ii) integrating the perspectives of each professional into a team in which trusting relationships are built (D'Amour et al., 2005).

Promoting and integrating interprofessional collaboration is a complex process eliminating professional boundaries and overcoming organizational hierarchical factors (Goldsberry, 2018). Interprofessional collaboration is characterized by interdependence between multiple stakeholders including physicians, nurses, pharmacists, clients, community partners and health educators among many other health professionals working side by side in clinical practice to develop a cohesive plan that meets clients' needs (Careau, Vincent, & Swaine, 2011). Way et al. (2000, p3) define collaborative practice as "an inter-professional process for communication and decision making that enables the separate and shared knowledge and skills of care providers to synergistically influence the client/ patient care provided". The effective interprofessional collaboration is the engagement of multiple different professionals working together from different disciplines as a team sharing a common goal (of optimal/ improved patient care), sharing the knowledge/ skills/ expertise of other professionals for creative outcomes by understanding other professionals' roles in a team, having multiple interactions over time by showing symmetrical power, and showing interdependence among professionals in a supportive organizational environment (Broers, Poth, & Medeyes, 2009). The concept of power refers to the professional's power based on knowledge and experience recognized by team members (Henneman, 1995).

The 'collaboration' construct is not yet fully understood and operationalized; in the literature, it is commonly defined through five underlying concepts: sharing, partnership, power, interdependency and process (D'Amour et al., 2005). As collaboration is more likely to occur when professionals share similar interests and the following facets of sharing can be seen in a collaborative undertaking: shared responsibilities, shared decision-making, shared values, shared data, sharing different professional perspective, shared planning and intervention (Wagner, 2004; Arslanian-Engoren, 1995; D'Amour, 1997). In a collaborative learning setting, the influences can be Individual to Group (I-to-G) and Group to Individual

(G-to-I) (Papanikolaou & Gouli, 2013). In collaborative relationships, extensive efforts are taken to avoid conflicts concerning the sharing of tasks and responsibilities. The concept of partnership implies that two or more actors join in a collaborative task characterized by a collegial like relationship that is constructive and authentic (Hanson, Carr, & Spross, 2000). Interdependency implies mutual dependence of professionals who depend on one another for addressing the patient's needs (D'Amour, 1997). The skills required for interprofessional collaboration are: rapport building, effectively communicating skill, leadership, and conflict management (Baerg et al., 2012). For effective collaboration, the professionals should understand their competencies, and should have the capability to share their professional skills and knowledge (Ho et al., 2010).

Communication

Communication is defined as the process of transmitting/ exchanging message(s), formal as well as informal sharing of meaningful and timely information for common understanding between the sender and receiver (Keyton, 2011; Sharma, Qiang, Wenjun, & Qi, 2013; Khan, 2014). The various aspects of communication are share and receive information, express or perceive feelings, define and clarify issues, present or understand views or opinions (Merriman-Webster, 2009). When there is no common understanding, there is no effective communication. The key elements of communication process are sender, receiver, message, medium, noise and feedback (Cheney, 2011). Sender initiates the communication with a desire to convey a(n) idea/ concept/ opinion to receiver to whom the message is sent. The idea is encoded in the form of message by selecting words, symbols, or gestures. The message takes the form of verbal, nonverbal, written or electronic. The message is sent through a medium or channel (say face-to-face, telephone, email, or written document). The receiver gets meaningful information out of decoding the message. Any distortion in the communication process is the noise (say barriers or interruptions). The receiver's response to the message is the feedback, which ensures the receiver understands the sender's intended message. These elements in the communication process determine the effectiveness of communication. The effectiveness is hampered if there is any problem in any one of these elements. Effective communication is a two-way interactive mutual process based on human emotions demanding efforts and skills from both sender and receiver (Alshatnawi, 2014).

Formal communication is motivated by the need to overcome the difference with other professional and to achieve common ground for productive exchange (Lingard, Reznick, Espin, Regehr, & DeVito, 2002). Besides, each professional in the healthcare team needs to clearly articulate his/ her contribution to the team by effectively delegating the work and directing other team members (Suter et al., 2009). Lingard et al. (2006) give two types of formal communicative utilities: informational and functional. In interprofessional communication informational utility occurs when there is a visible improvement of team's awareness or knowledge by exchanging new information, explicit confirmation, reminders and education. Here, the formal communicator makes use of negotiating skills to overcome differences in viewpoints and enhances the team-understanding of the issue. Functional utility occurs when formal communication prompts decision-making, follow-up actions, problem identification, and other work-related connections. Lingard et al. (2008) give examples of variety of communication failures in healthcare settings with and without visible consequences. The key failures are content and occasion (timing or frequency of exchange). When relevant information is not exchanged among the team members, the issues are not resolved resulting in delays in providing healthcare. Late or less frequent information exchange results into inefficiency, tension and repetition of work.

Communication and Collaboration

Collaboration takes place through communication between and among the healthcare professionals within the same or different organizations (Karam et al., 2018). The communication takes place between individual and group of professionals. Formal and informal communications among healthcare professionals are the key to collaborative care (Kripalani et al., 2007). Communication is an interactional element that influences the degree of collaboration and communication skills of health professionals play a key role for developing collaborative relationship among team members (Way et al., 2000). The reasons for communication to be key determinants of collaboration are: to clarify the roles of each professional and to understand the span of professional boundaries (Dugan, 2012); to help the professionals to understand how their work contributes to team goals, allows constructive negotiations with other professionals, and drives other determinants of collaboration, such as trust (Lindeke & Block, 1998; Henneman, Lee, & Cohen, 1995).

Communication is found to be a major key factor for successful collaboration (Mior, Barnsley, Boon, Ashbury, & Haig, 2010). The collaborative practice requires appropriate communication and coordination mechanisms, such as sessions, forums, formal meeting structures involving all team members (Way, Jones & Busing, 2000). The capabilities for collaborative practice include communication of sharing of professional knowledge (mentoring) and reflection (e.g., problem solving, feedback) (Walsh, Gordon, Marshall, & Hunt, 2005). Lack of communication on how each professional contributes to the team, delegating work and directing team members hamper collaboration (Brown, Crawford, & Darongkamas, 2000; Hall, 2005). Improving communication among health professionals can improve collaboration in terms of knowledge sharing and collaborative decision making (Vazirani, Hays, Shapiro, & Cowan, 2005). Stein, Watts, and Howell (1990) noted that more communication makes use of professional's observational and intellectual skills and thereby improves the ability to contribute to patients' care in a collaborative manner. Furthermore, the collaboration aspects include communication in analyzing patient's information for applying to treatment decisions (Hansen, Biros, Delaney & Schug, 1999). For collaborative management of healthcare, the most heavily used communication methods are face-to-face, telephone, electronic communication of which regular meetings (both electronic and non-electronic) improves collaboration and access to information to support decision making (Batt & Purchase, 2004; Safran et al., 1998). In the context of interprofessional family health teams, the research has found that collaboration is nurtured by communication (Gocan et al., 2014). Ineffective communication or miscommunication among the healthcare professionals results into misdiagnosis, delayed treatment, medication errors, or even death (Foronda, MacWilliams, & McArthur, 2016). As professionals have diversity in education, social background and training, their usage of communication media and styles for collaboration are different. "The embracing of true multivocality by a team is the key to its achieving the kind of integrated communication required for effective collaboration" (Clark, 2014, p. 37). The above discussion leads to Hypothesis H1.

Hypothesis 1: The degree of collaboration is positively related with the level of communication.

Coordination

Coordination means the regulation of diverse professionals into an integrated and harmonious operation with a goal and plan to support patient for receiving effective healthcare (Stille, Jerant, Bell, Meltzer,

& Elmore, 2005). Bodenheimer (2007) defined coordination as a function for meeting patient's needs for health services achieving by sharing information across professionals. Alter & Hage (1993) defined coordination as "the articulation of elements in a service delivery system so that comprehensiveness, accessibility and compatibility among elements are maximized". In the context of interprofessional coordination, "comprehensiveness" means the extensive involvement of the team members; "accessibility" means access to information or resources needed for patient care; and "compatibility" means professionals working together in a coherent manner. The studies on healthcare coordination have been grounded on this coordination framework (e.g., Axelsson & Bihari-Axelsson, 2005; Brazil et al., 2004; Gulzar & Henry, 2005). Shortell et al. (1994) defined coordination as "the extent to which functions and activities both within the unit and between units are brought together in a way that promotes cost-effective continuous care". This "bringing together" refers to the coordination of activities of healthcare professionals as a team. In general, coordination is achieved by vertically integrating the team using a management hierarchy (Meyer, 1985). The team coordination results into value added services/ activities for achieving goals and plans for the patient care using complementary expertise and resources that could not be delivered by each professional separately. Starfield et al. (1998) describes coordination in healthcare as "the availability of information about prior problems and services and the recognition of that information as it bears on needs for current care."

Interprofessional coordination is typically established by standardizing healthcare practice so as to avoid conflicts and reducing replicated activities as well as an efficient flow of knowledge and information among team members (Brazil et al., 2004). Team coordination encourages inputs that may be needed to improve planning of patient outcomes (with more knowledge about patients and procedures) from team members and acknowledges them for their contribution and thereby participate in decision making regarding patient care. In a coordinated environment, professionals interact with colleagues with more freedom to be different and to disagree.

Collaboration and Coordination

Collaboration is the act of working together and coordination means regulating the team for higher order functioning (Stille et al., 2005). Team coordination means team members' shared and organized understanding of relevant knowledge for performance (Burtscher & Manser, 2012) and it makes team members to feel "on the same page" with respect to the common task to be performed (Mohammed, Ferzandi, & Hamilton, 2010). Apker et al. (2006) give the following skill set required for collaboration: identifying solutions to problems, participate decision making, actively listening to team members, seeking clarification, solve patient care problems, and presenting information in a precise and concise manner. The skill set for coordination are: collaborative skills regarding patient goals and plans, conflict resolution skills, committing to work together, delegating tasks to team members, sharing updated information, mentoring team members, and serving as liaison between team members who have limited contact with each other (Apker et al., 2006). For patient-centered collaborative practice, competencies most commonly emphasized are communication, understanding roles of other health professionals, effective team working skills including understanding group norms, conflict resolution and the ability to tolerate differences, the ability to contribute to shared care plans and goal setting, a willingness to collaborate with mutual trust and respect (Suter et al., 2009; Canadian Health Services Research Foundation [CHSRF], 2006; Rodriguez et al., 2005). Information sharing which is a characteristic of coordination has been found to be related to collaboration (Williams et al., 2010). Thus, having a shared understanding regarding team member's knowledge and skills facilitates collaboration. Besides, in case of doctor-nurse team work, the effective collaboration depends on the effective coordinated efforts of working together of these professionals (O'Connor et al., 2016). Based on this discussion, this study derives Hypothesis H2.

Hypothesis 2: The degree of collaboration is positively related with the level of coordination.

Cooperation

The Merriam Webster dictionary defines cooperation as "a situation in which people work together to do something". Our particular interest is interprofessional cooperation in healthcare settings. Cooperation is the actions of individuals, committing to work together as a team of healthcare professional in a complementary mode rather than competing mode, which is being helpful by doing what is wanted or asked for improving the care of the patients. The cooperative professional shares a common vision of patient's care that asks and provides opinion from other professionals, who is straightforward when sharing information, who discusses and plans joint strategies for patient-care, who understands (her) his roles and shares decision-making responsibilities. Cooperation in healthcare setting is the assistance provided by different professionals by frequently communicating with colleagues from other disciplines to include their views, to give consistent feedback and thereby fulfilling the expectations of other professionals (Davies, 1996; Krogstad, Hofoss, & Hjortdahl, 2004). In a cooperative environment, the professionals have a good understanding of the distinction between their roles and support the role of other colleagues (Verschuren & Masselink, 1997). This way each professional works to the expectation of the other by often seeking patient information and providing feedback.

The cooperation of professionals varies along a continuum ranging from low to high degree of cooperation (Doherty, 1995). 'Consultation' occurs in the lower end where providing information and support to another on request happens; and in the other extreme, high degree of cooperation refers to 'multidisciplinary teamwork' (MTW), where professionals with different backgrounds, collectively discussing for decision-making and action to enhance the quality of healthcare (Molleman et al., 2008). The team work creates opportunities for more dialogues and creative problem-solving by integrating expertise from different professions. Depending on the complexity of patients' health problems, the degree of cooperation varies. For simple problems, less intensive cooperation, such as 'consultation' is needed and more complex problems require a high degree of cooperation, such as 'multidisciplinary teamwork'.

Cooperation and Collaboration

In the last two decades, the complexity of healthcare problems has increased due to multiple and interrelated problems (Hudson, 2002). On the healthcare provider side, there is a growth in advanced and comprehensive technologies for evidence-based knowledge and treatment. The knowledge expansion has demanded an increased specialization of functions with different professional backgrounds (Heinemann & Zeiss, 2002). Molleman et al. (2008) analyzed the complexity of healthcare problems to cooperation types and concluded that the complexity could be addressed by interprofessional cooperation and collaboration. Barimani & Hylander (2008) explore healthcare professionals' cooperation to conceptualize barriers and facilitators of cooperation to generate a comprehensive theoretical model. The past research emphasize the main barriers as tendency to professional ethnocentricity (Schofield & Amodeo, 1999), ignorance about the other professional's area of competence and a tendency among professionals to regard their profession as superior to the others (Waskett, 1996). In general, the intensity of collaboration depends upon the roles and relationships of healthcare professionals which are the characteristics of cooperation (Hojat, et al., 2001). Healthcare professional (e.g., physician or a nurse) collaborates by serving as team leader/ member who exhibits leadership role, assigns responsibilities, organize team member roles, frequently communicate, providing consistent feedback, support the role of colleagues and serve as the communicative hub of their healthcare teams (Apker et al., 2006). For patient-centered collaborative practice, competencies most commonly emphasized are communication, providing consistent feedback and understanding roles of other health professionals (Suter et al., 2009; Canadian Health Services Research Foundation [CHSRF], 2006; Rodriguez et al., 2005). Collaboration means mentoring and constantly communicating with team members to ensure clarity on individual roles and responsibilities. This discussion provides the basis for Hypothesis H3.

Hypothesis 3: The degree of collaboration is positively related with the level of cooperation.

Trust

Trust is essentially a psychological state seen as important in its own right involving an element of vulnerability where an individual who places trust on other party is vulnerable irrespective of the ability to control over the actions or inactions of the other party. Trust is defined as "the willingness of a party to be vulnerable to the actions of another party based on the expectation that the other will perform a particular action important to the trust or, irrespective of the ability to monitor or control that other party" (Mayer, Davis, & Schoorman, 1995, p.715) or, more briefly, "accepted vulnerability to another's possible but not expected ill will (or lack of good will)" (Baier, 1986, p.235.). Trust is the reliance by one individual, or group, or firm (or trustor) upon a voluntarily or non-voluntarily accepted duty on the part of the other individual, or group, or firm (or trustee) to recognize and protect the rights and interests of all others engaged in a joint endeavor, information exchange or economic exchange (Culnan & Bies, 2003; Hosmer, 1995). In general, trusting someone refers to voluntary action based on expectations of behaviors in relation to oneself. Trust can build up among the healthcare professionals over a period of time and depends on the quality and nature of previous experiences of collaboration (Bradley, Ashcroft, & Noyce, 2012). When the expectations are disappointed, then trust decays and generates negative outcomes (Brockner & Siegel, 1996; Luhmann, 2000). The distrust is formed when a professional starts doubting the motive of the others; feeling of insecurity over the involvement of others and having lack of confidence in other professional's skill (Dey, De Vries, & Bosnic-Anticevich, 2011). Therefore, trust has an element of risk based on trustee's uncertain future actions.

Interprofessional trust characterizes a relationship between two or more professionals known to each other (Goold, 1998). This has been conceptualized with the following overlapping domains: caring for the patients interests and avoiding conflicts of interest; competence for interpersonal skills, decision-making (trusting patient-care decisions), and avoiding mistakes; honesty, avoiding intentional falsehoods by telling the truth; and confidentiality, privacy maintenance of sensitive information (Mechanic & Meyer, 2000). In the early treatment process, interprofessional trust is more likely to build and as the interprofessional relationship continues, results build trust and members learn more about each other keeping informed about events or changes that affect them (Hall, Camacho, Dugan, & Balkrishnan, 2002). Since learning is important to the development of trust, trust decays when interprofessionals do not deliver on their promises and underperform (Berwick, 2003).

Trust enables communication among the professionals to understand how their contribution helps to achieve team goals and thereby drives determinants of collaboration (Henneman et al., 1995). Trust in terms of emotional bonds facilitates repeated interactions in the interprofessional relationships (Newman, 1998). Past experience of each other and communicative behaviors form expectation of trusting behavior. Prevalence of trusted relationship among professionals enhances the quality of their interactions lead to quality decisions in treatment (Mechanic, 1998). Therefore, trust encourages communication and information flows (Jacobsen, 1999). The care decision-making approaches allow engagement and dialogue among health care professionals and thereby facilitate the process of building trust. The above discussion leads to the following Hypothesis H4.

Hypothesis 4: The level of trust is positively related with the level of communication.

Interprofessional interactions take place by using coordination mechanisms, such as sessions, forums, and formal meeting structures where mutual trust is commonly emphasized for collaborative practice (Rodriguez et al., 2005; Cabello, 2002). Trust facilitates smooth interpersonal relationships among team members and thereby enables coordinated behavior. Building trust requires confidence in one's own abilities, coordinated efforts for collaborative practice, patience, and previous positive experiences with others (Henneman et al., 1995). Trust is indispensable for establishing coordinated and collaborative working relationships (Baggs & Schmitt, 1997; D'Amour, 1997). In the context of healthcare settings, the term coordination conveys the idea of sharing (knowledge, tasks and responsibilities) implies collective action oriented towards a common goal in a spirit of trust (D'Amour et al., 2005). Trust facilitates and underpins coordination, which is collective action to achieve common goals and plan quality care of patients (Gilson, 2003). Trust-based coordination makes an important contribution to building value in patient-care and work through conflicts in efforts to resolve them. Continuance in trusted interactions with different professionals creates opportunities for working together with freedom to be different and disagree. This discussion provides the basis for Hypothesis H5.

Hypothesis 5: The level of trust is positively related with the level of coordination.

Trust is a facilitator for smooth running of cooperative interprofessional relationships, helps to reconcile professionals' own interests with others, and secures open communication and dialogue (Misztal, 1996). The types of expected behaviors underlie trust are technical competence, openness, and concern (Davies, 1999; Mechanic, 1996). Trust breaks down the constraints of the cooperative behavior. Trust catalyses cooperative behavior for payoff/ benefits in healthcare, which is rooted in risk and expectations about how another professional will behave in case of uncertainties in healthcare related decisions (Gambetta, 2000). When other professional's future actions are beneficial rather than harmful, cooperation is advantageous outweighing the costs and risks involved in cooperation. Therefore, trust provides a context in which healthcare professionals work cooperatively for setting care objectives and seek ways of achieving them (Perry et al., 1999). Mutual trust between colleagues establishes a platform for knowledge sharing by consistently asking/ giving feedback/ opinion to members of the team, and keeps each other informed about events or changes that affect them by frequent communication (D'Amour et al., 2005). Trust enables frequent communication with colleagues from other disciplines and incorporates views of treatment thereby improves the ability to meet patient needs. Trust protects the interests of professionals for running smooth cooperative relations in caring patients (Misztal, 1996). The above discussion leads to Hypothesis H6.

Hypothesis 6: The level of trust is positively related with the level of cooperation.

Technology Orientation

In general, technology orientation reflects the philosophy of "technology push" where state-of-the-art technology is acquired and applied (Gatignon & Xuereb, 1997). Lee & Meuter (2010, p.357) define technology orientation as "an organizational-wide engagement of technology-oriented practices in developing policies, practices and procedures, and sensing and responding to technology opportunities. These activities will lead to technology adoption and utilization." In the healthcare settings, the technology orientation (adoption and use) transforms the healthcare delivery for improved efficiency and coordination (Senate Finance Committee, 2009). In the healthcare context, technology orientation is the adoption and use of technology in day-to-day operation, which requires healthcare professional's propensity and analytical skills for using it to perform tasks relevant to healthcare. In healthcare, the reliance of individual communication technologies is ever increasing.

Personal technology orientation is how an individual perceives the technology in terms of the details and use by analyzing the technology (Manaikkamakl, 2007). The healthcare professionals with technology orientation perceive the use of sophisticated communication technology for gaining personal productivity, effectiveness and efficiency in healthcare delivery. The technology oriented professional rapidly adopt and use technology for communication advantage among team members for enhancing the work effectiveness.

In general, technology is utilized to lower transaction costs, increase in decision quality and speed of decision making, improved productivity and elimination of routine tasks (Srinivasan, 1985; Byrd, 1992). A variety of models has been applied in the past research for understanding technology usage. IS investigators have suggested models for determinants of technology usage (e.g., the TRA model by Ajzen & Fishbein (1980) and Ajzen's (1991) the planned behavior model). Subsequently, Davis et al. (1989) suggested technology acceptance model (TAM) suggesting two antecedents of technology usage: perceived ease of use (PEOU) and perceived usefulness (PU) of a technology. Perceived usefulness is the user's subjective probability that using a technology will increase his or her job performance. Perceived ease of use is the degree to which the user expects the target technology to be free of efforts. An unused technology provides no value and technology usage is measured by daily use (duration of use), frequency of use, number of applications used, and the number of tasks supported (Igbaria, Guimaraes, & Davis, 1995). Technology adoption by an individual is to be determined by his or her voluntary intentions towards using the technology. The intention is determined by the person's attitude towards using the technology and perception of its usefulness. Attitudes are formed from evaluating beliefs about the use of the technology.

Information and communication technologies (ICT) facilitate communication of information and sharing of knowledge by electronic means. In a broader sense, ICT tools are comprised of the range of digital and analog ICTs, from radio and television to telephones (landline and mobile), computers, Internet, audio-video recording, social networking and web-based communities (GAID, 2010). ICT usage facilitates professionals to work in an innovative manner, positive attitude and commitment for networked environment with global thinking (Open Clinical, 2011). Effective usage of ICT improves information flows and enhances the dissemination of evidence-based knowledge for improving health outcome (InfoDev, 2006).

Technology Orientation and Communication

Usage of electronic communication technologies, such as email, text messaging, and social media are increasing for enhanced outcomes, improving efficiency, decreasing costs and seek solutions in healthcare (Weaver et al., 2012). Email is the e-communication technology used in healthcare, which does not require the presence of both parties at the same time, and allows continuous access and participation (Mann, Lloyyd-Puryear, & Lizer, 2006). Though email communication becomes part of patient's health record, it cannot be used for communicating urgent or time-sensitive information. Text messaging provides one-to-one exchanges of short messages or distributes to a larger audience (Terry, 2008). This type of e-communication is convenient, immediate and can be used for monitoring/ reporting symptoms. Introduction of e-messaging enhances connections among healthcare professionals and made easy access of information (Lyngstad, 2013). The availability of social media tools, such as Facebook, YouTube, Twitter, etc. are used to disseminate health messages and enable the professionals to connect with each other (Fox, 2011).

Information and Communication Technology (ICT) tools can enhance productivity and support interprofessional communication even when the group is multilingual (Aiken, Wang, Gu, & Paolillo, 2011) and virtual (working in a geographically distributed environment) (Duranti & de Almeida, 2012). Early adoption of e-communication technologies increases the flow of information. Methods of e-communications are changing from email to short messaging (SMS) to social networking (Weaver et al., 2012). The use of email facilitates communication among healthcare professionals within the medication system related to care of patients. For electronic communication, the messages are exchanged using personal computers (PC) and many wireless, non-PC options including personal digital assistants (PDAs), pagers, and telephones. The electronic communication among team members is easy, efficient and has several advantages: often less costly, less disruptive than face-to-face communication (Nardi & Whittaker, 2002) has boundary spanning capability to cross geographical and even status boundaries (Sproull & Kiesler, 1991); team members can communicate with a variety of professionals even when members are not able to exchange immediately (Cummings & Ghosh, 2005; Kraut, Fussell, Brennan, & Siegel, 2002). In a group environment, e-brainstorming generates a large number of quality ideas; and e-decision making produces more personal disclosure and uncertainty reduction (Tidwell & Walther, 2002).

In the healthcare settings, the barriers for using technology for communication are: preference of face-to-face communication for richer interaction, privacy/ security concerns, and the potential increase in efforts to learn and use new technologies (Healthcare News, 2001). Specifically, web messaging is preferred to the telephone if the information to be exchanged is not time-sensitive (Liederman, Lee, Baquero, & Seites, 2005); healthcare professionals use secured web-based portals for administrative tasks, such as refill requests and scheduling appointments (Kittler, Carlson, & Harris, 2004). In summary, when the healthcare professionals from different organizations of different locations and time zones or from the same organization but located in different places, the utilization of information and communication technologies enable the professionals for effective communication and thereby for effective collaboration (Shaffer & Speakman, 2014). The above discussion leads to the following Hypothesis H7:

Hypothesis 7: The degree of communication is positively related with the degree of technology orientation.

Technology Orientation for Coordination

E-communication technology creates and sustains interprofessional connections that improve outcomes and accomplishes common goal of patient-care (Weaver, 2012). The electronic communication tools, such as mobile devices are used by healthcare professionals to change prescription, symptom control and so on thereby to achieve the common goal of caring the patients. As patient care is provided by a 'team of care' comprised of multidisciplinary healthcare professionals, communication technology enables coordination among the professionals. The team members work together using e-communication and that use of technology orientation occurs ranging from low to high use for each member (Hinds & Kiesler, 2002). Electronic interaction is often motivated by goals and plans, such as collaboration, conflict resolution, and commitment to work together (Tiegland & Wasko, 2003). Healthcare professionals use email for communication and to better coordinate care of patients (Henault et al., 2002). Technology enables for sharing information across professionals and thereby helps professional coordination. For instance, radiologists in one country may read x-rays, MRIs, or mammograms transmitted from other country (Leonhardt, 2006). Professionals with questions can have audiovisual contact with others to diagnose the problems quickly, to track the use of a variety of medications, and monitor the health conditions (Boden, Sit, & Weinreb, 2006).

Communication tools and technologies, such as PDAs are used routinely by healthcare professionals who are separately responsible for providing care to a patient can share health information, such as drug references, prescriptions and simultaneous view of patient data (Baumgart, 2005). Furthermore, communication technology supports the creation, coordination and management of virtual medical teams for treating patients. Email affords a written record of information exchange and enables professionals to focus on questions to be asked and follow-up questions, which can be reviewed at any time for the purpose of coordination (Ball & Lillis, 2006). Social networks can be a source of learning for health professionals as the social media tools disseminate health messages. This can provide effective forum to interact, share information and concerns, and even manage healthcare. Besides, social media facilitates interactive communication and empower professionals to make decisions. As the network continues to trend upward and provides frequent and topic-specific updates, this can be an excellent source of professional networking and education. In a virtually connected environment enabled by communication technologies, the healthcare professionals get frustrated in case of non-availability or delayed or withheld information about the change of medications, treatment plans or any healthcare event (Jackson, MacKean, Cooke, & Lahtinen, 2017). It validates that the better technology orientation linked with better coordination of care. Technology oriented coordination such as online access to view medical test results, online sharing of information such as diagnoses, expectations on a surgical procedure and post operated treatments medications are vitally important for effective healthcare. The above discussion leads to Hypothesis H8.

Hypothesis 8: The degree of coordination is positively related with the degree of technology orientation.

Technology Orientation for Cooperation

Communication technology enables cooperation of multidisciplinary healthcare professionals by incorporating views of treatment held by colleagues in order to meet patient needs. Electronic communication facilitates the healthcare professionals for consistently giving feedback and for special advice to caring for a patient. For instance, telemedicine networks provide consultations in specialties, such as oncology, radiology, pathology, surgery, pharmacy, psychiatry, and behavioral health (Blanchet, 2005). Health professionals use today's e-communication tools, such as email, invited Facebook groups, text messages, websites and more to effectively manage patients' connection, health and support. In the healthcare environment, providing timely and consistent feedback is important in correcting misunderstandings about the treatment (Armstrong & Cole, 2002). The inconsistency in giving feedback between team members may end up with errors in treatment. Use of communication technology is related with higher levels of message feedback lead to enhanced level of mutual knowledge and ability to meet patient needs (Cramton, 2001).

Providing high quality care demands secure and timely exchange of information in a cooperative manner. Through the usage of communication technology better cooperation is achieved in terms of frequent communication among the professionals; and to understand the distinction between the roles of professionals. Team members are better acquainted with each other's roles and support the roles of colleagues by using electronic communication technology (Bradner, Mark, & Hertel, 2005). Tools, such as Short Message Service (SMS) enables push and pull of data and alerts affecting the entire team of care. The communication technologies, specifically social media tools introduce substantial and ubiquitous changes to communication between individuals replacing face-to-face interactions (Kietzmann, Hermkens, McCarthy, & Silvestre, 2011). Social media technologies facilitate joint interaction with different professionals and establish a communicative environment with open and interoperable systems in which individuals share, discuss, and modify opinions/ contents (Franchi, Poggi, & Tomaiuolo, 2013). Social media tools facilitate conversations among individuals, sharing of information and foster engagement for effectively cooperate in a multidisciplinary work environment (Kaplan & Haenlein, 2010). This discussion provides the basis for Hypothesis H9.

Hypothesis 9: The degree of cooperation is positively related with the degree of technology orientation.

RESEARCH METHODOLOGY

Data was collected through mailing questionnaire survey from Healthcare Professionals located in North America. The survey questions were adopted mainly from previously tested and validated instrument originally developed by Bronstein (2002; 2003). Some questions were modified or designed based on the literature on collaboration in healthcare system as well as through some semi-structured interviews with healthcare professionals while majority of them were used as in the original form. The survey instrument was refined with a small pilot study and a pretest (N=30) that aimed to identify any ambiguities with wording and structure as well as other potential problems with the instrument. Scales adapted five-point Likert.

The finalized questionnaire survey with a cover letter was mailed to a random group of 1800 healthcare professionals working at healthcare companies in North America. The contact information of potential participants was gathered from online databases that the University had access to. In order to enhance the response rate, pre-addresses and pre-stamped envelopes were attached with the questionnaire. The response rate was about 12% with the total returned survey as 216. The responders were from a wide range of areas including medical doctors, nurses, nurse practitioners, etc.

In this study, we utilized SPSS version 20 and WarpPLS 4, an SEM based analysis, for the analysis of the data. There are several reasons of using a Partial Least Squares (PLS) method in this study. PLS, a second generation multivariate method (Fornell, 1987), evaluates both the measurement model and the theoretical or structural model simultaneously (Urbach & Ahlemann, 2010). Other characteristics, such as ability to run with smaller sample sizes (Cassel, Hackl, & Westlund 1999; Urbach & Ahlemann, 2010) unlike covariance based structural equation modeling (SEM) methods and calculate the estimates for each latent variable makes PLS methods are robust and highly used. In addition, PLS can be used for both theory development and confirming a theory (Chin, 1998b; Urbach & Ahlemann, 2010). On the other hand, PLS is considered to be more appropriate for exploratory model analysis. The last but not the least, PLS method does not require normally distributed data.

Non-response bias, to test the representativeness of the selected sample (Rogelberg & Stanton, 2007) in survey-based studies can be tested by comparing the means of early wave of respondents and late wave of respondents (Lambert & Harrington, 1990; Armstrong & Overton, 1977). The reasoning behind this is that late respondents in a study tend to act as non-respondents (Armstrong & Overton, 1977). The sample sizes for the two groups were 175 as early respondents, who returned the survey within 2 weeks and 41 as late respondents, whose data were received between the second and the fourth week. The results on randomly selected variables revealed no significant differences between the two groups of respondents. Therefore, non-response bias was considered not to be an issue in this study.

DATA ANALYSIS AND RESULTS

Tests on measurement model are required before testing the structural model in SEM-PLS analysis. In order to test the measurement model validity and reliability tests were conducted. There are three common tests for validity, namely, content validity, criterion-related validity, and construct validity. Content validity refers to "...the degree to which an instrument has an appropriate sample of items for the construct being measured" (Polit & Beck, 2004, p. 423). Content analysis may include both quantitative and qualitative processes (Haynes, Richard, & Kubany, 1995). Expert opinion is the common way used for testing content validity (Lynn, 1986). Literature provides different approaches for quantifying the expert or judge opinion. These approaches include, but not limited to averaging the experts' ratings and using "pre-established criterion of acceptability" (Polit & Beck, 2006, p.490). Content validity was tested by a group of 4 expert/ judges for this study. The instrument was refined after the first round of expert opinions. In the second round, the required threshold value for scale-level content validity index (S-CVI) (Polit & Beck, 2006) is reached and measured as 0.8.

"Criterion validity is demonstrated by finding a statistically significant relationship between a measure and a criterion" (Nunnally & Bernstein, 1994 as cited by Rubio, Berg-Weger, Tebb, Lee, & Rauch, 2003, p. 95). Correlation is the most common way to test the criterion validity.

Construct validity is "...the degree to which an assessment instrument measures the targeted construct (i.e., the degree to which variance in obtained measures from an assessment instrument is consistent with predictions from the construct targeted by the instrument" (Haynes et al., 1995, p. 239). One way to test the construct validity to use confirmatory factor analysis (CFA) (Rubio et al., 2003). In factor analysis the acceptable values of factor loadings are 0.5 or higher (Hair, Black, Babin, Anderson, & Tatham, 2006). After the first round of analysis, a few indicators were removed or replaced with another indicator if they were cross-loading with another factor. Table 1 shows that all variables in the second round are loading to expected factors and their loading is above 0.5, ranging between 0.519 and 0.886.

Table 1. Factor analysis and loadings

Factors	Coll	Comm	Coord	Coop	Trust	Techn	Alpha	CR
Coll1	0.869	-0.189	0.117	0.110	-0.109	-0.018		
Coll2	0.866	-0.051	-0.114	-0.006	-0.109	-0.002	0.634	0.805
Coll3	0.519	0.402	-0.005	-0.174	0.365	0.034		
Comm1	0.145	0.757	-0.002	-0.079	-0.176	-0.064		
Comm2	-0.035	0.765	0.206	-0.045	-0.054	0.058	0.682	0.808
Comm3	0.079	0.622	-0.369	0.119	0.199	0.006		
Comm4	-0.184	0.715	0.102	0.029	0.071	0.001		
Coord1	0.152	0.094	0.826	0.093	-0.024	-0.073		
Coord2	0.158	-0.255	0.766	-0.007	-0.148	0.063	0.759	0.848
Coord3	-0.087	0.116	0.802	-0.149	0.058	0.061		
Coord4	-0.270	0.038	0.651	0.074	0.133	-0.056		
Coop1	0.276	0.101	-0.213	0.685	-0.141	0.024		
Coop2	-0.211	-0.136	-0.049	0.654	0.338	0.047		
Coop3	-0.162	0.039	0.278	0.584	0.137	0.057	0.724	0.813
Coop4	0.156	-0.141	-0.119	0.698	-0.107	0.078		
Coop5	-0.149	0.117	0.457	0.618	-0.139	-0.161		
Coop6	0.042	0.036	-0.284	0.648	-0.069	-0.054		
Trust1	-0.008	0.100	0.145	-0.101	0.835	0.060		
Trust2	-0.021	-0.092	-0.115	0.243	0.747	-0.036	0.632	0.803
Trust3	0.033	-0.021	-0.051	-0.140	0.693	-0.034		
Tech1	-0.039	-0.126	0.101	-0.040	0.044	0.875		
Tech2	-0.020	-0.031	0.031	0.114	-0.093	0.886	0.807	0.886
Tech3	0.067	0.175	-0.147	-0.084	0.056	0.786		

Notes:
Coll: Collaboration
Comm: Communication
Coord: Coordination
Coop: Cooperation
Trust: Trust
Techn: Technology Orientation

Cronbach's Alpha and composite reliability measures are used for testing reliability and internal consistency of the items. (Fornell & Larcker, 1981; Nunnaly, 1978). Although in general Cronbach's Alpha value of 0.7 is considered as acceptable, values over 0.6 are considered as marginally acceptable (Gliner & Morgan, 2000). The Cronbach's alpha values are 0.634 for collaboration, 0.682 for communication, 0.759 for coordination, 0.724 for cooperation, 0.632 for trust, and 0.807 for technology orientation. Therefore, our results indicate that (see Table 1) all of the constructs are within acceptable or marginally acceptable range in terms of reliability. We also checked whether reliabilities of the constructs are acceptable through composite reliability, especially for those that are in marginally acceptable portion. The composite reliabilities for collaboration, communication, coordination, cooperation, trust, and technology orientation are 0.805, 0.808, 0.848, 0.813, 0.803, and 0.886, respectively. These results indicate that reliabilities of our constructs are acceptable. Because of the criticism on PLS analysis such as bias and consistency issues on the results (Ronkko & Evermann, 2013), factor-based algorithm that provides unbiased results can be used (Kock, 2015b) (see Appendices).

We tested discriminant validity through inter-item correlations. Table 2 reveals the correlations among the constructs as well as square root of average variance extracted (AVE) values in diagonal. Based on these results, the constructs are positively and significantly correlated with each other. One exception for that significant relationship is the one between technology orientation and coordination. In addition, an indication of acceptable discriminant validity is the case where square roots of AVE values are greater than the correlations for that construct with other constructs. In this case, square root of AVEs would have higher scores than the values on the same column and row for that construct. Table 2 indicates that discriminant validity is acceptable for our model. Although AVE values higher than 0.5 is acceptable, AVE for Cooperation was close to but less than this value. This is a limitation of the study, however, considering all other AVEs have higher values and the measures of reliability are acceptable, this does not pose a threat to the study.

Table 2. Correlations and square roots of average variance extracted (AVE) values

Constructs	Collaboration	Communication	Coordination	Cooperation	Trust	Techn
Collaboration	(0.769)					
Communication	0.451**	(0.717)				
Coordination	0.588**	0.700**	(0.764)			
Cooperation	0.569**	0.636**	0.628**	(0.649)		
Trust	0.415**	0.593**	0.675**	0.587**	(0.760)	
Tech.Orientation	0.155*	0.181**	0.077	0.219**	0.170*	(0.850)

*. Correlation is significant at the 0.05 level (2-tailed).
**. Correlation is significant at the 0.01 level (2-tailed).

Variance Inflation Factors (VIF) is a measure for identifying the threat of multicollinearity. VIF values of 5 and above are considered to have risk of multicollinearity. Our results indicate that (see Table 3) multicollinearity may not be a threat for our study since all VIF values are lower than 5, the threshold value. Although there is no globally accepted goodness of fit values for PLS analysis, Average Path Coefficient, and Average block VIF, and Averaged R-Squared are commonly used model fit indices for PLS (Moqbel, Nove, & Kock, 2013). Model fit and quality indices, such as Average Path Coefficient (0.324, $p<0.01$), Average Root Square (0.454, $p<0.01$), and Average Variance Inflation Factors (1.543), show no evidence of problem regarding the fit; therefore, the results indicate that our model has a good fit (see Table 3).

Common method bias (CMB) is considered a type of measurement method problem (Kock, 2015a) for studies collecting data via survey questionnaires (Podsakoff, MacKenzie, Lee, & Podsakoff, 2003). Among different ways to measure CMB, such as Harman's single factor test (Podsakoff & Organ, 1986), marker variable (Lindell & Whitney, 2001), and full collinearity variance inflation factors (VIFs), the last method is considered as a more conservative approach. In addition, VIFs approach is recommended for variance-based SEM analysis (Kock, 2015a; Kock & Lynn, 2012). Therefore, in this study we adopt this approach to test CMB. The results of the study reveals that all of the collinearity VIF values are smaller than the recommended threshold of 3.3 (Kock, 2015a) and varies between 1.086 for Technology Orientation and 2.991 for Coordination as seen in Table 3. Therefore, threat of CMB can be considered minimal for the study.

Table 3. Model fit and quality indices

Constructs	Collab	Commun	Coordi	Cooper	Trust	TechO
Collinearity VIF	1.722	2.314	2.991	2.238	2.064	1.086
Average full collinearity VIF (AFVIF)	2.069			acceptable if <= 5, ideally <= 3.3		
Average path coefficient (APC)	0.324**					

Figure 1 shows the coefficients of paths among the constructs as well as the R square values for the model developed for this study. Results reveal that collaboration has a positive and significant relationship with coordination (β=0.413, p<0.01), and cooperation (β=0.325, p<0.01). As suggested by Figure 1, trust has positive and significant relationship with communication (β=0.582, p<0.01), coordination (β=0.705, p<0.01), and cooperation (β=0.651, p<0.01). Finally, technology has similar relationship with cooperation (β=0.107, p<0.01). However, our results did not indicate any significant relationship between collaboration and communication (β=0.012), as well as between technology orientation and communication (β=0.081) and coordination (β=0.037).

Table 4 shows the hypotheses tested in this study and their status regarding whether they are rejected or not.

DISCUSSION

To advance our understandings of current practices of interprofessional collaboration, this research aims for empirically examining the impact of trust and technology on collaboration in association with mediating effects of communication, coordination and collaboration. In particular, the study finds the factors influencing interprofessional collaboration in healthcare settings. The study results shown in Figure 1 indicate that collaboration has positive and significant relationship with coordination and cooperation but not with communication. On the other hand, the study results validate that trust has positive and significant relationship with communication, coordination, and cooperation. Furthermore, the study results (shown in Figure 1) indicate technology orientation has positive and significant relationship with cooperation but not with communication and coordination. Figure 1 indicates that the constructs are positively and significantly correlated except collaboration-communication, technology-communication, and technology-coordination. These results match the findings of Reeves et al. (2014) which demonstrated the usage of information technology for information exchanges may deteriorate the richer communication such as face-to-face collaboration. Therefore, the study finds coordination and cooperation as the factors significantly influencing interprofessional collaboration. In other words, the study finds positive impact of trust on collaboration with mediating effects of coordination and cooperation; and positive

Figure 1. Estimated parameters in the model (as appeared in Palanisamy et al., 2017)

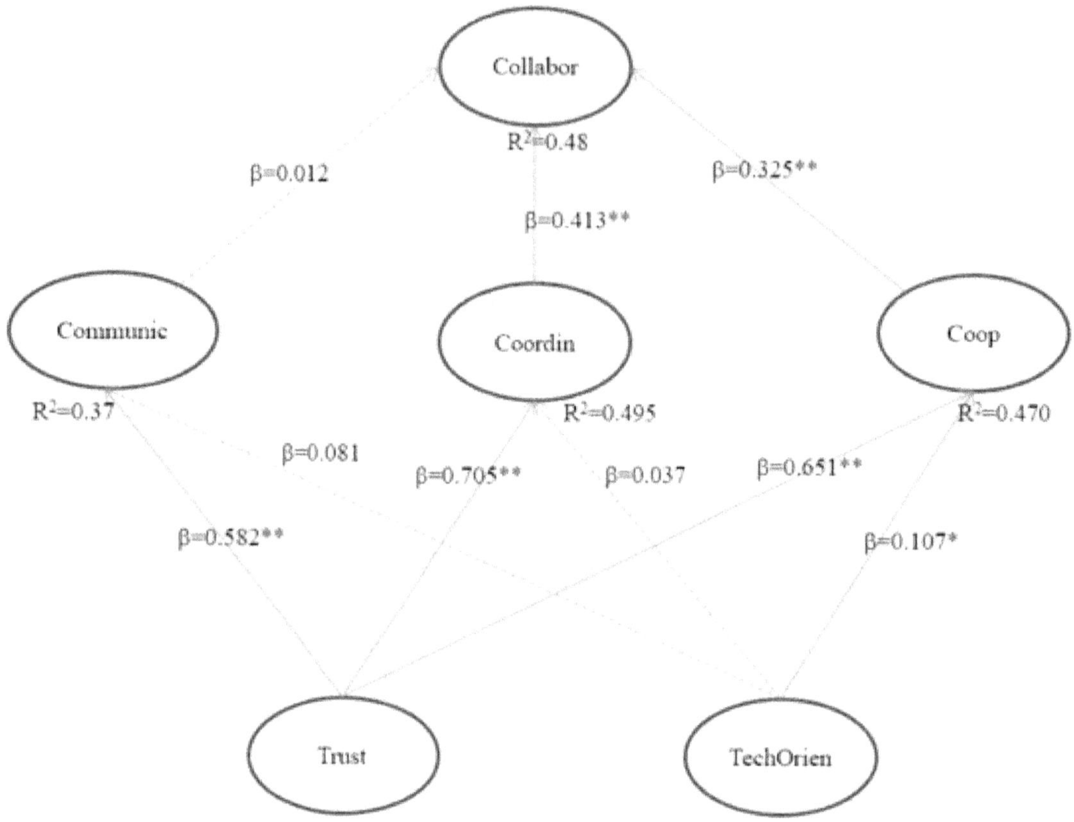

impact of technology orientation on collaboration with mediating effect of cooperation. The discussion on the managerial implications of these findings is given in this section.

Table 4. Hypotheses and their status

Hypotheses	Status
H1: The degree of collaboration is positively related with the level of communication.	Not Supported
H2: The degree of collaboration is positively related with the level of coordination.	Supported
H3: The degree of collaboration is positively related with the level of cooperation.	Supported
H4: The level of trust is positively related with the level of communication.	Supported
H5: The level of trust is positively related with the level of coordination.	Supported
H6: The level of trust is positively related with the level of cooperation.	Supported
H7: The degree of communication is positively related with the degree of technology orientation.	Not Supported
H8: The degree of coordination is positively related with the degree of technology orientation.	Not Supported
H9: The degree of cooperation is positively related with the degree of technology orientation.	Supported

Factors for Collaboration

The primary research question is to find the factors influencing the quality of interprofessional collaboration. The study results indicate coordination and cooperation are the factors influencing interprofessional collaboration but not the communication. Figure 1 shows high degrees of correlations for collaboration with the following constructs: coordination and cooperation.

The findings of collaboration and coordination having positive and significant relationship is consistent with analytical framework of interdisciplinary collaboration developed by Sicotte et al. (2002), in which intensity of collaboration was found to be related with the degree of interprofessional coordination in community health centers. In studying healthcare teamwork behaviors, Williams et al. (2010) found positive relationship between coordination and collaboration. These findings validate the results of the study reported in this paper. D'Amour (1997) developed a model, which has been tested with empirical data to understand interprofessional collaboration (Echaquan, 2003). The key dimension of the model is appropriating a common goal and plan for the patient care. Creative outcomes emerge when multiple different professionals work together sharing a common goal, plan, and decision-making (Woods et al., 2011). Appreciating the workload of other team members, willing to work beyond the boundaries of a professional, willing to help a struggling team member and willing to work as a team enhances the effective coordination. For effective collaboration the interprofessional team efforts are to be coordinated toward a common goal and plan. The significant outcome of coordination is the emergence of creative care and optimal care of patients, which is difficult to achieve individually. Working through conflicts concerning the sharing of tasks and responsibilities is considered to be a key skill for effective interprofessional collaboration (Baerg et al., 2012). As interprofessional collaboration mutually benefits all the parties involved, it needs sharing of authority as well as resources (Green and Johnson, 2015). At the same time, poor or failure of collaboration among the professionals can negatively affect the patient care and health care outcomes (Reeves, Pelone, Harrison, Goldman, & Zwarenstein, 2017). The beliefs and values of diverse professionals foster conflicts and put constraints for effective collaboration. The conflicts are to be approached without hindering the freedom to be different and disagree. Formalizing the tasks and responsibilities offer a collaborative environment for professionals to commit for working together.

Accordingly the healthcare professionals need to effectively coordinate for achieving effective collaboration in patient care delivery. For richer and effective engagement during the interprofessional collaboration, the professionals should have more confidence in individual and group interactions so that safe and effective healthcare can be delivered (Pfaff, Baxter, Jack, Jack, & Ploeg, 2014). For effective coordination of healthcare delivery efforts, the professionals need to function as the communicative hub of their healthcare teams, perform as team leaders, direct/ mentor the team members, assign tasks and responsibilities. Effective collaboration requires processing of needed information for successful delivery of patient care. The effective coordination requires a plan integrating inputs of various professionals toward a common goal of delivering care to the patient. It implies encouraging inputs from other professionals and acknowledging their contributions. Coordination ensures that the patient's needs for health services are met over time. Actively listening to ideas makes the team members feel valued and increases their participation in collaborative decision making for patient care. Similarly, effective coordination requires offering ideas and opinion to others. In general, having a shared understanding of each team member's knowledge and skills facilitate effective coordination and thereby collaboration. The essence of effective coordination requires shared understanding about prior problems and services as it needs for current care, interaction and collaboration. Collaboration through coordination may be challenging when bullying and undermining behavior in the clinical learning environment is frequently experienced (O'Connor et al., 2016).

Franklin, Bernhardt, Lopez, Long-Middleton, and David (2015) have researched the collaboration between interprofessional healthcare team and community healthcare teams. Their research provides evidence for a positive relationship between cooperation and collaboration among the health care team members. The teams develop a common understanding of values, roles, norms, and goals. Though the healthcare professionals realize the need to work in a collaborative manner, they struggle to cope with each other because of heavy clinical workload, imbalances in power relationships, lack of understanding each other's professional boundary, responsibilities, roles, and other organizational constraints (Tang, Zhou, & Liaw, 2018). The cooperation between the health care professionals is often problematic because each professional handles the conflicts in a different way (Foth et al., 2015). For example, between nurses and physicians, physicians may handle the conflicts differently and recognizing the values and skills of all members enhance the interprofessional cooperation. So, working with colleagues in a collaborative practice requires cooperation in terms of frequent communication for sharing knowledge/ skills, incorporating views of others, providing consistent feedback, and clarity of roles influencing creative outcomes in providing quality care to the patients (Barrett et al., 2007; Rodriguez et al., 2005; Way et al., 2000). Frequent communication enables the professionals to understand each other's perspective and one another's contributions so that quality decisions are made for improved patient care. Effective cooperation leads to effective collaboration. In the healthcare team, the professionals need to work in a complementary mode rather than competing mode by understanding each other's role. Valuing the expertise of each team member enhances the cooperation between the professionals. The management needs to upgrade the status of professional (for instance nurses) is paramount to facilitate effective cooperation.

In a review of literature, Supper, et al. (2014) give the facilitators and barriers of interprofessional collaboration in the context of primary health care. The facilitators are: the presence of common and shared interest in collaboration, professionals looking for opportunities to improve quality of healthcare, and to develop emerging professional fields; the major barriers are: lack of awareness of competencies and roles of the team members, lack of information sharing among professionals, and inadequate training. There is a range of barriers for effective collaboration including ignorance or insufficient knowledge about other professional's area of competence, inclination more towards professional ethnocentricity regarding one's profession as superior to others. In general, specialists often may have strong sense of independence, and concerns that they may lose their importance and identities in team environment. This tendency restricts the willingness to participate in cooperative activities. To improve the levels of cooperation aiming at better quality of care, professionals must clarify their position, roles and responsibilities to others in a healthcare team. In general, the complexity of healthcare problems relate to the degree of cooperation. More complex problems need multidisciplinary teamwork (high degree of cooperation) and less complex problems require consultation (low degree of cooperation). The cooperative behaviors of professionals build effective relationships and structure a collective action towards patient care. The intensity of cooperation indicates a positive collaboration resulting in team integration, and joint decision making for enhanced healthcare. Accordingly, interprofessional collaboration requires educating the professionals for developing and nurturing interprofessional team thinking, mutual understanding, acquiring and sharing of information and knowledge (Homeyer, Hoffmann, Hingst, Oppermann, & Dreier-Wolfgramm, 2018).

The study finds that the impact of communication on collaboration is not significant. Frequent and formal communication becomes ineffective and unproductive when the required information is not communicated. As a result, it may not lead to any collaborative outcome. When collaboration takes place, there is an accomplishment of tangible outcomes, such as conflict resolution and creative outcomes. Though the communication enables the professionals' capacity to work together, when the capacity is not effectively utilized, then the professional works on separate silos and the collaborative approach become fragmented.

Impact of Trust

Another research objective is to find the impact of trust on communication, coordination and cooperation. The study results given in Figure 1 shows high degrees of correlations and path coefficients indicating trust has positive and significant impact on communication, coordination and cooperation.

Trust has significant influence on communication. This is convincing as the literature says trust encourages communication and thereby positive information flows (Tyler & Kramer, 1996; Veenstra & Lomas, 1999). Trust keeps the individuals' mind open to ideas and secures more dialogue and communication (Misztal, 1996). The professionals consider the trust beliefs based on their past communication with others and develop a good or bad attitude towards multi-disciplinary team work. When mutual trust between the colleagues is high, building relations in a communicative environment becomes easier. The frequency of information exchange among professionals increases and leads to more formal and informal communication. Trust facilitates more interprofessional communication for both patient understanding and the capacity to work with members of the teams. Overall, trust is positively influencing the quality of health outcomes. Specifically, patients' higher trust in health care professionals bring more satisfaction with the quality of treatment for their health problems (BirkhaÈuer et al., 2017). In the context of patient-physician relationship, trust plays a crucial role and has a positive influence on perceived quality of healthcare services and increases the patient satisfaction on the quality of treatment (Chandra, Mohammednezhad, &Ward, 2018). Mutual trust in healthcare encourages more face-to-face interactions, email communications, messaging, team meetings, interprofessional committees, team retreats, hallway conversations, and mini-conferences for engaging and sharing information for optimized care of patients and decision-making. Building trust is so important for lessening the impact of negative attitude and continuance interactions among professionals. As professionals get more experienced in working with the team in a complex multidisciplinary environment, the risk perception of distrust may change over time. In a multidisciplinary environment, professionals need to keep each other informed about events or changes that affect them. The professionals have to ensure the patient care decisions are always trusted/supported by their colleagues. Thereby, professionals get more confidence in interactions as the communicative experience is positive. Winning trust at the beginning is important as initial trust could be a starting point for continuance participation in interactive decision making aiming quality care of patients.

Trust has significant influence on coordination. Trust facilitates collective action leading to cooperation among professionals to achieve common goal of quality care of patients (D'Amour et al., 2005; Gilson, 2003). As trust protects the professionals' interests in a multi-disciplinary environment, trust-based coordination contributes to build more value in patient-care (Gilson, 2003). Mutual trust between the colleagues enables the professionals to collaborate regarding patient goals and plans. Besides, the existence of trust among professionals keeps each other informed about events or changes that affect them, it provides a basis for their coordination by creating strong personal bonds, conflicts concerning the sharing of responsibilities are resolved without much difficulty. On the contrary, the distrusting environment may create conflicts concerning the sharing of tasks and responsibilities. These conflicts make the professionals to stick rigidly to their job descriptions and generate negative outcomes in delivering patient care. Also, the trusted environment provides more freedom to be different and to disagree, more comfort to ask questions in meetings, and provides ability to express ideas openly without fear of any misunderstandings. When mutual trust between the professionals is high, the element of risk in expected behavior is nullified. As a result, decisions about approaches to treatment are made unilaterally. As a trusted environment keeps the professionals informed about events or changes in the treatment that affect them, it improves their ability to meet patient's needs. When patient care decisions are trusted by other members of the team, the trust facilitates dialogues between professionals from different disciplines. With the mutual trust in the background, professionals accomplish the coordinated activities, such as showing leadership by directing and supervising team members, mentoring others, assigning responsibilities, and delegating tasks to others. Trust facilitates information sharing and organized understanding of relevant knowledge and thereby improves individual's contribution for delivering quality care for patients. Mutual trust between multi-disciplinary professionals underpins the coordination by committing them for working together.

Trust has significant positive impact on cooperation. As trust protects the interests of professionals engaged in a joint endeavor, it can be silent background for running smooth cooperative relations in caring patients (Misztal, 1996). Trust enables the professionals to have autonomy in their own contribution, reconciles their own interests with those of others, and supports cooperative problem solving. Trust establishes a platform for knowledge sharing by consistently asking/ giving feedback/ opinion to members of the team, and for discussing strategies to improve working relationships. As trust is essentially a psychological state rooted in risk, trust or distrust creates expectations of how others will behave (in a cooperative or non-cooperative way). Trust among professionals enables the members better understand the work of other health professionals. In particular, trust plays a key role in distinguishing between roles and responsibilities. In a trusted environment, more support for each other's roles and responsibilities are provided as part of cooperation. As trust is essentially a calculation that the other professional's future action will be beneficial for enhancing the quality of patient-care, in case of necessities, trust motivates the individual to support the tasks outside his/ her job description, which indicates cooperation. Trust breaks down the barriers for cooperative behavior and develops a good understanding of mutual responsibilities.

The collaborative practice comprises of multiple healthcare professionals/ workers with diversified professional backgrounds work together aiming highest quality of care. Lack of collaboration among the professionals can negatively affect the healthcare delivery services and in order to improve the collaboration, interventions are required (Reeves et al., 2017). One of the intervention is to build trust among the professionals. The impact of mutual trust on collaboration mediating coordination and cooperation is emphasized in the literature (D'Amour et al., 2005; Stichler, 1995; Siegler & Whitney, 1994). D'Amour (1997) developed a model for understanding interprofessional collaboration in which 'trusting relationships' among professionals is considered to be a key dimension. Mutual trust is required for two or more professionals to join in a collaborative task, which demands coordination and cooperation among them. For collaboration, professionals are expected to be aware of contributions made by members, develop an understanding of each other's roles/ responsibilities and keep each other informed about events or changes that affect them. This trusted environment is favorable for collaborative undertaking in which members exchange ideas and opinion for delivering quality care for the patients. So, for establishing a collaborative process, professionals have to develop trust among them. On the other hand, simply bringing professionals together in teams will not lead to any sort of collaboration. When mutual trust between professionals is high, collaboration generates creative outcomes as treatment decisions are coordinated and made unilaterally by professionals from other disciplines. Trust enables the professionals to work through conflicts for resolving them through coordination by creating formal procedures/ mechanisms for facilitating dialogue between professionals from different disciplines. In the healthcare, trust means believing the other professional is honest, good or nice and will not harm the performance of the healthcare team. Trust is the unwritten agreement between the professionals to perform certain health related activities without any fear from either side. Accordingly, in a trusted environment, a team member has confidence and reliance expecting other member to be competent, empathic, and behave in a certain way.

Impact of Technology Orientation

The research question associated with technology orientation is to identify the ways in which technology can be used for enhancing communication, coordination and cooperation of healthcare professionals. The study results show positive and significant relationship with cooperation but not with communication and coordination. The impact of technology orientation on collaboration mediating cooperation is significant and positive.

This study suggests that technology orientation plays a large role for cooperation with colleagues in healthcare setting, to incorporate views of treatment of other professionals, to provide consistent feedback to team members, and to support the role of other professionals in the healthcare team. The health professionals use technology for better cooperation. As the healthcare team comprised of diverse backgrounds, experiences, and different perspectives, the patients get an effective healthcare and benefit from the team by getting solutions to the complex health problems. In the patient-centered approach, the members also get opportunities to understand each other's roles, approaches, and responsibilities in a cooperative way for delivering effective healthcare. Thereby the team can respond to complex needs of the patients using a technology-enabled health care. Leonhardt (2006) emphasize the usage of technology beyond communication especially for cooperation. The study findings suggest for professionals to adopt and use technology for enhancing cooperation. As the healthcare team members may not always present in the same location, relying on e-communication technology is increased for information exchange, interaction, and knowledge access for each individual in the team. Technology oriented organizations relying on e-communication technology for accomplishing work is very common and considered to be a substitute for face-to-face interaction (Hinds & Kiesler, 2002). Technology orientation has several advantages including enhanced capability for frequent communication of quality content and resources (Rice & Gattiker, 2001). Furthermore, technology enables the team members to access the expertise of other professional and incorporate views of treatment. Thereby, technology improves the ability of team members to meet patient needs. Of course, the usage of technology for cooperation for each team member occurs along a continuum from low to high use. As an information-seeking activity to understand the distinction between roles, technology enables the team members to engage in information exchange in a timely manner. Encouraging a culture of technology enabled cooperation facilitates improved quality care of patients.

Besides, communication technology is used to bring diverse professionals from areas, such as pathology, oncology, pharmacy, surgery, psychiatry, and behavioral health for frequent communication and consistent feedback. Technology enables the professionals to identify problems quickly and helps to make timely adjustments of therapy. Technology facilitates sharing of personal health information of patients across professionals for providing quality care to a specific patient. Complex and chronic illnesses demands the use of sophisticated technologies by multidisciplinary team of professionals. As the complexity of illness requires providers from diverse areas, technology plays a key role in incorporating views (expertise) of treatment of different professionals and enables for secure, easy and timely exchange of information for the enhanced quality care. Thereby, professionals are powered with e-communication technology as a source of learning to create and maintain cooperation with other professionals. The technology engages them to be better partners in providing care with improved outcomes. Technology enables for more collaborative outcomes as technology contributes for effective cooperation in implementing treatment decisions.

The usage of technology for communication has undergone dramatic changes and continues to evolve over time. Technology facilitates communication among the professionals within a given health care system. Technology enables health professionals to consult with others or can seek "specialty" consults for the benefit of patient care. The communication technology devices allow for "always immediate access" with the exception of out of coverage areas. Though the technology limits face-to-face communication, the usage in terms of daily use (duration), frequency of use, and the number of applications used are ever increasing among healthcare professionals. Since the perceived usefulness and ease of use of these technologies are realized for accomplishing the tasks and the job performance, the acceptance rate of the communication technologies is exponentially increasing. Despite the presence of privacy/ security concerns in using the technology for communication, the usage has increased for communicating sensitive and no time-sensitive issues (Liederman & Morefield, 2003; Liederman et al., 2005).

The study finds that the impact of technology orientation on communication is not significant. This may be because of having more face-to-face communication in healthcare instead of using technology for communication. In the healthcare settings, face-to-face communication has several advantages including richer communication. Non-verbal cues with face-to-face communication make the professional to prefer it compare to the e-communication especially in communicating sensitive information about the patients. Besides, the study finds that the impact of technology orientation on coordination is not significant. This implies that coordinated activities, such as conflict resolution and collaboration regarding patient goals and plans can take place without much use of technology. For instance, face-to-face communication may be more preferred in health-care settings rather than e-communication for coordination especially for handling sensitive, difficult, unanalyzable and non-routine tasks in healthcare.

Example for Implementable Ideas from an Industry Perspective

Healthcare is one of the highest growing industries, in which professionals including physicians, nurses, pharmacists, clients, community partners and health educators' work together to provide medical care to patients. The modern healthcare is divided into several sectors and depends on interdisciplinary teams of trained healthcare professionals to meet healthcare needs of patients. In the industry perspective, the rising cost of healthcare largely from chronic disease is unmanageable. The healthcare providers are committed to address the increasing cost in healthcare spending. Another trend is shared decision making on treatment decisions for which effective inter-professional collaboration becomes necessary. Promoting and achieving interprofessional collaboration is a major challenge due to lack of belongingness among professionals as they mostly come from different corporate cultures (Karam et al., 2018). Vestergaard and Nørgaard (2018) give intervention strategies to implement interprofessional collaboration by promoting coherent practices across the professionals. This section provides an example illustrating how the ideas in the paper could be implemented from an industry perspective.

Consider patients with Diabetes, Heart Disease, Kidney Disease, and other heath related problems. Multi-disciplinary teams of professionals are required for treating such diseases. Each team-member learns from each other's discipline as the disease demands cross-disciplinary knowledge and expertise. The team has to build up the treatment process by knitting and sharing the different pieces from different disciplines and perspectives. Thereby, working with colleagues from other professions becomes necessary as individuals can achieve only limited outcomes. Besides, the collaborative outcomes are more creative and unpredictable compared to that of individuals. The impact of interprofessional teams on patient-reported measures such as satisfaction with care is much more compared to the impact on the direct measures of health outcomes such as visits to the emergency (Gougeon et al., 2017). Bringing the team together to work on may be a challenging task as the members come from varying experience and background. In the practitioner's perspective, for improving the quality of collaboration this research emphasize cooperation and coordination of professionals.

Enhance the Quality of Collaboration

When diverse professionals work together for a common goal, conflicts are common. The health professionals have to work through the conflicts and resolve them to prevent the ongoing impact. Extensive efforts are to be taken to avoid conflicts concerning the sharing of tasks and responsibilities. To cultivate collaborative culture, encourage open communication and allow colleagues openly represent the professional perspectives about patient's healthcare needs. In day-to-day program functioning, collaborative behaviors, such as collaborative treatments are to be encouraged. Contextual strategies/ approaches are to be evolved to bring the team together. Structuring a collective action and joint decision making on treatment enable the team to work in an integrated manner towards patient care. Also, collaboration nurtures the process of sharing knowledge and skills; evolves approaches for engaging multiple different professionals to work together as a team sharing a common goal of improved care for the patients; and creates collaborative culture among the professionals by sharing responsibilities, decision-making, values, data, and intervention.

Understand on How Best to Cooperate

Cooperation creates a work environment in which professionals frequently communicate with colleagues from other professional disciplines. It encourages developments of mechanisms electronically (such as web portal, mobile apps and other electronic access) to incorporate views of treatment held by colleagues from other disciplines. These mechanisms could be used to provide constant feedback to colleagues. Instead of sticking to one's own job description, extending the boundaries by understanding the distinction between each other's roles avoid the professionals to work in silos. In other words, the professionals need to understand that supporting the role of colleagues is also part of their job description. Sometimes, a professional has to sacrifice some degree of his/ her autonomy to support cooperative problem solving. Often, strategies (such as retreats, annual/ semi-annual meetings) are to be discussed to improve working relationships of professionals. These activities usually encourage the colleagues to ask for opinion from other professionals and often refer them for consultations. Hierarchical barriers (if any) are to be removed in these kind of opinion seeking activities (e.g., physicians seeking opinion from nurses). Similarly, work evaluations are to be carried out jointly.

Create a Coordinated Environment

The professionals are to be brought together as a team, which can be achieved by vertically integrating the team using a management hierarchy. Coordination regulates the diverse professionals into an integrated and harmonious operational team with a common goal of providing effective healthcare to patients. It involves the team members by providing access (for both within and between units) to information or resources needed for patient care. A better coordination is achieved when the information about prior problems and treatments (e.g., medical history of patients) are available for current care. Coordination not only standardizes healthcare practices in order to reduce duplicated activities in patient-care, but also emphasizes on the coordinated activities, such as: mentoring the team members, showing leadership by assigning tasks and responsibilities, acknowledging the contribution of other professionals, providing the care in time/ budget, offering/ seeking ideas to/ from others, and developing a shared understanding of the patient's care. Overall, coordination creates a coordinated environment where there is freedom to be different and to disagree.

Effective Communication

Interprofessional communication has to be emphasized for both patient understanding and the capacity to work with members of teams. Most common methods of communication, such as face-to-face, telephone, computer/ mobile (email, social media, or specific mobile app) are to be followed. Education and providing several communication toolkits may enhance effective communication among inter-disciplinary professionals. During formal and informal meetings, each team member should feel free to share his/ her opinions openly without fear of being misunderstood. In other words, participants should feel good comfort level to say what is on their mind (i.e., work related issues, information sharing, etc.). Providing feedback makes communication more effective. The professionals are to be engaged electronically in an interactive manner. For achieving this, an effective web site portal (with access to desktop and mobile) needs to be maintained where announcements, schedules, policies, procedures, and other materials can be posted. Hospitals usually provide the current communication technologies, such as portal, email, phone, blackberry, bulletin board, and specific software systems, which are to be used meaningfully for effective communication.

Build Trust

The professionals have to rely on other colleagues for understanding the treatment decisions. So, creating a trusted environment becomes mandatory where members can recognize and protect the rights and interests of other team members. The trust can be built by caring for the patient's interests, avoiding conflicts of interests, acknowledging patient-care decisions, avoiding mistakes, showing honesty, avoiding intentional falsehoods, and maintaining confidentiality of sensitive information. Continuous learning facilitates the development of trust. Engage the participants with dialogues regarding treatment decisions; thereby, it facilitates the process of building trust among the healthcare professionals. Having confidence in one's own abilities, coordinated efforts, and having previous positive experience with other colleagues establish trusted working relationships. Securing open communication and dialogue, frequent communication, and consistently asking/ giving feedback/ opinion to members of teams build trust among professionals.

Use Technology

Use information and communication technologies for sharing information and knowledge to perform healthcare relevant tasks, to gain personal productivity, to increase decision quality, to eliminate routine tasks, to improve information flows, effectiveness, and efficiency in healthcare delivery. E-communication technologies, such as email, text messaging, social media tools, such as Facebook, YouTube, and Twitter are to be used to disseminate health messages and seek solutions in healthcare. Early adoption of e-communication technologies from e-mail to short messaging to social networking facilitates interprofessional collaboration. Use of technology encourages adopting and using personal communication technologies, such as PDAs, pagers, and mobile devices in an individual environment and use group communication technologies (such as video conferencing) in a group environment. It increases the mobile usage for healthcare such as change prescription, symptom control etc.; and use secured web-based portals for administrative tasks, such as scheduling appointments. Using e-communication tools, such as email, invited Facebook groups, text messages, websites help for effectively managing patients' connection, health and support.

CONCLUSIONS, LIMITATIONS AND AREAS FOR FURTHER RESEARCH

The increases in complexity of patient care, healthcare costs, and technological advancements shifted the healthcare delivery to interprofessional collaborative care. This interdisciplinary team approach inevitably makes professionals interdependent in a collaborative manner by interacting with others cultivating relationships using effective coordination and cooperation. However, collaboration is challenging and difficult to achieve. Though the literature gives conceptual approaches, there is a limited empirical knowledge on factors influencing collaboration.

To fill this gap, the study aimed for understanding current practices of interprofessional collaboration by empirically testing the impact of trust and technology on collaboration in association with communication, coordination and collaboration. Hypotheses were evolved to examine the following: (i) the impact of communication, coordination and cooperation on collaboration (ii) impact of trust on communication, coordination, and cooperation; and (iii) the impact of technology orientation on communication, coordination, and cooperation. Thereby, this research provides insights into the major challenges facing healthcare professionals, managers, policy makers, and other healthcare leaders in promoting, implementing, and assessing interprofessional collaboration.

The results of the study validate that collaboration has positive and significant relationship with coordination and cooperation but not with communication; similarly the study found that trust has positive and significant relationship with communication, coordination, and cooperation. Furthermore, the study results have shown technology orientation has positive and significant relationship with cooperation but not with communication and coordination. Besides, the study finds positive impact of trust on collaboration with mediating effects of coordination and cooperation; and positive impact of technology on collaboration with mediating effect of cooperation. The managerial implications of these findings were discussed.

In considering the study results, interprofessional collaboration can be achieved by creating a trusted relationship among the professionals. The team lead/ manager needs to take efforts to create a positive attitude for each member towards collaboration. Such efforts may include: encouraging members to use several modes of communication (e.g., face-to-face, telephone, email, social media, and digital), frequent exchange of information (which is feasible in the era of social media networking), create opportunities for members to express views/ comments through e-messaging, team meetings, committees, team retreats, hallway conversations, and mini-conferences for effective engagement. In expressing opinion, the team member should be given freedom to be different and to disagree. Electronic maintenance of the past communication on treatment decisions and outcomes (e.g., medical history records) enable the members for building mutual trust with colleagues.

The interprofessional team structure plays a key role for better coordination. A clear definition of roles, tasks, and responsibilities avoid any possible conflicts. A better coordinated collaboration occurs when the professionals are informed about events or changes, latest improvements and conditions in the hospital through a web-portal with an access to all kinds of device including desktop and mobile. This establishes platform for knowledge sharing by asking/ giving feedback/ opinion periodically to team members. This information sharing can happen through several other methods including email, bulletin boards, smaller program meetings (e.g., Diabetes Meeting, Renal Meeting, Cardiovascular Meeting, etc.). As team members may not always be in the same location, it becomes imperative to use technology for enhanced cooperation. Diverse professionals from different fields (e.g., pathology, oncology, pharmacy, surgery, psychiatry, and others) are to be linked by communication technology for sharing their expertise towards patient-care. Though the hospitals usually have adequate technological infrastructure, the team members need to be encouraged for meaningful use of technology. Thus, establishing technological culture facilitates easier and effective way of communication.

Surprisingly, this study has a counterintuitive implication; this research didn't support the impact of technology orientation on collaboration with communication as mediating variable. This is different from what one might expect. This implies that using technology for communication alone does not guarantee any effective collaboration. Besides, leadership is important in teams where generally team members prefer an open door policy where they can discuss any concerns with leaders. When the power and hierarchy of the leader is less, the team members feel more involved in treatment-decision making and this perception leads to a better collaboration.

The previous research contributed conceptual frameworks and this research build upon those conceptual foundations for empirically validating the factors relating to collaboration. The significance of this research is to build collaboration among healthcare professionals, it is imperative to have trust and technology with effectiveness in communication, coordination, and cooperation aiming quality care of the patients. Technology orientation is an important enabler for achieving effective cooperation. There are still many things on collaboration in healthcare setting, which has not been explored. For instance, what are the best practices for coordination and cooperation to achieve effective collaboration? What are the barriers for effective collaboration among healthcare professionals? The future research can design a questionnaire survey to answer these research questions. A descriptive study on trust building strategies for collaboration is a valuable one as trust plays a key role for improved outcomes of healthcare. A case study methodology is suggested to fulfill this objective. Regarding technology orientation, the use of social media for effective collaboration and cooperation has been realized as a key issue. So, a study on acceptance and effective use of social media for collaboration would be an interesting topic for future researchers. Seeing the importance of patient-physician collaboration for enhanced care, another research avenue would be to validate this research model in the context of patient-physician collaboration.

Lack of availability of standard measures for various constructs steered the development of survey questionnaire based on a previous qualitative study and literature on collaboration in healthcare system.

The respondents were asked to indicate their degree of agreement with the statements in the questionnaire. Though we made a concerted effort to include a range of healthcare professionals to participate in the study, their opinion on the degree of agreement is highly subjective. Despite these limitations, however, our study makes a noteworthy contribution to healthcare collaboration.

ACKNOWLEDGMENT

We thank the anonymous reviewers for their suggestion for improving our paper.

This book chapter has been modified from the following published article:

Palanisamy, R., Taskin, N., & Verville, J. (2017). Impact of Trust and Technology on Interprofessional Collaboration in Healthcare Settings: An Empirical Analysis. *International Journal of e-Collaboration* (IJeC), 13(2), 10-44.

REFERENCES

Aiken, M., Wang, J., Gu, L., & Paolillo, J. (2011). An Exploratory Study of How Technology Supports Communication in Multilingual Groups. *International Journal of e-Collaboration, 7*(1), 17–29. doi:10.4018/jec.2011010102

Ajzen, I. (1991). The theory of planned behavior. *Organizational Behavior and Human Decision Processes, 50*(2), 179–211. doi:10.1016/0749-5978(91)90020-T

Ajzen, I., & Fishbein, M. (1980). *Understanding attitudes and predicting social behavior*. Prentice-Hall.

Alshatnawi, E. A. R. (2014). Assessing communication skills among Jordanian tour guides: German tourists' perceptions. ***false***. *Journal of Management Research, 6*(1), 1–11. doi:10.5296/jmr.v6i1.4361

Alter, C., & Hage, J. (1993). *Organizations working together*. Sage Publications, Inc.

Apker, J., Kathleen, M. P., Wendy, S. Z. F., & Hofmeister, N. (2006). Collaboration, credibility, compassion, and coordination: Professional nurse communication. *Journal of Professional Nursing, 22*(3), 180–189. doi:10.1016/j.profnurs.2006.03.002

Armstrong, D., & Cole, P. (2002). Managing distances and differences in geographically distributed work groups. In P. Hinds & S. Kiesler (Ed.), Distributed Work (pp. 167-189). Cambridge, MA: MIT Press.

Armstrong, J. S., & Overton, T. S. (1977). Estimating nonresponse bias in mail surveys. *JMR, Journal of Marketing Research, 14*(3), 396–402. doi:10.1177/002224377701400320

Arslanian-Engoren, C. M. (1995). Lived experiences of CNSs who collaborate with physicians: A phenomenological study. *Clinical Nurse Specialist CNS, 9*(2), 68–74. doi:10.1097/00002800-199503000-00002

Axelsson, R., & Bihari-Axelsson, S. (2005). Intersectoral problems in the Russian organization of public health. *Health Policy (Amsterdam), 73*(3), 285–293. doi:10.1016/j.healthpol.2004.11.020

Baerg, K., Lake, D., & Paslawski, T. (2012). Learning needs and training interest in health professionals, teachers, and students: An exploratory study. *Journal of Research in Interprofessional Practice and Education*, *2*(2), 1–19. doi:10.22230/jripe.2012v2n2a47

Baggs, J. G., & Schmitt, M. H. (1997). Nurses' and resident physicians' perceptions of the process of collaboration in an MICU. *Research in Nursing & Health*, *20*(1), 71–80. doi:10.1002/(SICI)1098-240X(199702)20:1<71::AID-NUR8>3.0.CO;2-R

Baier, A. (1986). Trust and antitrust. *Ethics*, *96*(2), 231–260. doi:10.1086/292745

Bailey, P., Jones, L., & Way, D. (2006). Family physician/nurse practitioner: Stories of collaboration. *Journal of Advanced Nursing*, *53*(4), 381–391. doi:10.1111/j.1365-2648.2006.03734.x

Ball, M. J., & Lillis, J. (2006). E-health: Transforming the physician/patient relationship. *International Journal of Medical Informatics*, *61*(1), 1–10. doi:10.1016/S1386-5056(00)00130-1

Barimani, M., & Hylander, I. (2008). Linkage in the chain of care: A grounded theory of professional cooperation between antenatal care, postpartum care and child health care. *International Journal of Integrated Care*, *8*(4), 1–13. doi:10.5334/ijic.254

Barrett, J., Curran, V., Glynn, L., & Godwin, M. (2007). *CHSRF synthesis: Interprofessional collaboration and quality primary healthcare.* Canadian Health Services Research Foundation.

Batt, P. J., & Purchase, S. (2004). Managing collaboration within networks and relationships. *Industrial Marketing Management*, *33*(3), 169–174. doi:10.1016/j.indmarman.2003.11.004

Baumgart, D. C. (2005). Personal digital assistants in health care: Experienced clinicians in the palm of your hand? *Journal of the American Medical Association*, *366*(9492), 1210–1222.

Berwick, D. M. (2003). Improvement, trust, and the healthcare workforce. *Quality & Safety in Health Care*, *12*(6), 448–452. doi:10.1136/qhc.12.6.448

Birkhäuer, J., Gaab, J., Kossowsky, J., Hasler, S., Krummenacher, P., Werner, C., & Gerger, H. (2017). Trust in the health care professional and health outcome: A meta-analysis. *PLoS One*, *12*(2), e0170988. doi:10.1371/journal.pone.0170988

Blanchet, J. (2005). Innovative programs in telemedicine: The Arizona telemedicine program. *Telemedicine Journal and e-Health*, *11*(2), 116–123. doi:10.1089/tmj.2005.11.116

Boden, C., Sit, A., & Weinreb, R. N. (2006). Accuracy of an electronic monitoring and reminder device for use with travoprost eye drops. *Journal of Glaucoma*, *15*(1), 30–34. doi:10.1097/01.ijg.0000196654.77836.61

Bodenheime, T. (2007). Coordinating care: A perilous journey through the health care system. *The New England Journal of Medicine*, *358*(10), 1064–1071. doi:10.1056/NEJMhpr0706165

Bradley, F., Ashcroft, D.M., & Noyce, P.R. (2012). Integration and differentiation: a conceptual model of general practitioner and community pharmacist collaboration. *Res. Social Adm. Pharm*, *8*(1), 36–46. . 005. doi:10.1016/j.sapharm.2010.12

Bradner, E., Mark, G., & Hertel, T. (2005). Team size and technology fit: Participation, awareness, and rapport in distributed teams. *IEEE Transactions on Professional Communication*, *48*(1), 68–77. doi:10.1109/TPC.2004.843299

Brazil, K., Whelan, T., O'Brien, M. A., Sussman, J., Pyette, N., & Bainbridge, D. (2004). Towards improving the co-ordination of supportive cancer care services in the community. *Health Policy (Amsterdam)*, *70*(1), 125–131. doi:10.1016/j.healthpol.2004.02.007

Brockner, J., & Siegel, P. (1996). Understanding the interaction between procedural and distributive justice: The role of trust. In R. M. Kramer & T. R. Tyler (Eds.), *Trust in organizations: Frontiers of theory and research*. Sage. doi:10.4135/9781452243610.n18

Broers, T., Poth, C., & Medeves, J. (2009). What's in a word? Understanding interprofessional collaboration from the students' perspective. *Journal of Research in Interprofessional Practice and Education*, *1*(1), 3–9. doi:10.22230/jripe.2009v1n1a1

Bronstein, L. R. (2002). Index of interdisciplinary collaboration. *Social Work Research*, *26*(2), 113–126. doi:10.1093wr/26.2.113

Bronstein, L. R. (2003). A model for interdisciplinary collaboration. *Social Work*, *48*(3), 297–306. doi:10.1093w/48.3.297

Brown, B., Crawford, P., & Darongkamas, J. (2000). Blurred roles and permeable boundaries: The experience of multidisciplinary working in community mental health. *Health & Social Care in the Community*, *8*(6), 425–435. doi:10.1046/j.1365-2524.2000.00268.x

Burtscher, M. J., & Manser, T. (2012). Team mental models and their potential to improve teamwork and safety: A review and implications for future research in healthcare. *Safety Science*, *50*(5), 1344–1354. doi:10.1016/j.ssci.2011.12.033

Byrd, T. A. (1992). Implementation and use of expert systems in organizations: Perceptions of knowledge engineers. *Journal of Management Information Systems*, *8*(4), 97–116. doi:10.1080/07421222.1992.11517941

Canadian Health Services Research Foundation. (2006). *Teamwork in healthcare: Promoting effective teamwork in healthcare in Canada. Policy Synthesis and Recommendations.* Ottawa, ON: Canadian Health Services Research Foundation. URL: http://www.chsrf.ca/Migrated/PDF/ResearchReports/CommissionedResearch/teamwork-synthesis-report_e.pdf

Careau, E., Vincent, C., & Swaine, B. R. (2011). Consensus group session of experts to describe interprofessional collaboration processes in team meetings. *Journal of Interprofessional Care*, *25*(4), 299–301. Doi:10.3109/13561820.2011.566649

Cassel, C., Hackl, P., & Westlund, A. H. (1999). Robustness of Partial Least-Squares Method for Estimating Latent Variable Quality Structures. *Journal of Applied Statistics*, *26*(4), 435–446. doi:10.1080/02664769922322

Chandra, S., Mohammadnezhad, M., & Ward, P. (2018). Trust and communication in a doctor-patient relationship: A literature review. *Journal of Health Communication*, *3*(3), 31–36.

Cheney, G. (2011). *Organizational communication in an age of globalization: Issues, reflections, practices*. Waveland Press.

Chin, W. W. (1998). The Partial Least Squares Approach to Structural Equation Modeling. In G. A. Marcoulides (Ed.), *Modern Methods for Business Research* (pp. 1295–1336). Lawrence Erlbaum Associates.

Clark, P. G. (2014). Narrative in interprofessional education and practice: Implications for professional identity, provider patient communication and teamwork. *Journal of Interprofessional Care*, *28*(1), 34–39. doi:10.3109/13561820.2013.853652

Cramton, C. (2001). The mutual knowledge problem and its consequences for dispersed collaborations. *Organization Science*, *12*(3), 346–371. doi:10.1287/orsc.12.3.346.10098

Culnan, M. J., & Bies, J. R. (2003). Consumer privacy: Balancing economic and justice considerations. *The Journal of Social Issues*, *59*(2), 323–342. doi:10.1111/1540-4560.00067

Cummings, J., & Ghosh, T. (2005). *Teams as Networks in a Connected Organization: The Critical Role of Geographic Distance.* Academy of Management Conference, Honolulu, HI.

D'Amour, D. (1997). *Structuration de la collaboration interprofessionnelle dans les services de sante´ de premie`re ligne au Que´bec.* The`se de doctorat. Montre´al: Universite´ de Montre´al.

D'Amour, D., Ferrada-Videla, M., Rodriguez, L. S. M., & Beaulieu, M. D. (2005). The conceptual basis for interprofessional collaboration: Core concepts and theoretical frameworks. *Journal of Interprofessional Care*, *19*(S1), 116 – 131. Doi:10.1080/13561820500082529

D'Amour, D., Sicotte, C., & Le'vy, R. (1999). L'action collective au sein d'e'quipes interprofessionnelles dans les services de sante´. *Sciences Sociales et Sante*, *17*(3), 68–94. doi:10.3406osan.1999.1468

Daneci-Patrau, D. (2011). Formal communication in organisationfalse. *Economics. Management and Financial Markets*, *6*(1), 487–497.

Danermark, B., & Kullberg, C. (1999). *Samverkan: välfärdsstatens nya arbetsform* [Collaboration: The new working methods of the welfare state]. Studentlitteratur.

Davies, C. (1996). The sociology of professions and the sociology of gender. *Sociology*, *30*(4), 661–678. doi:10.1177/0038038596030004003

Davies, H. (1994). Falling public trust in health services: Implications for accountability. *Journal of Health Services and Policy Research*, *4*(4), 193–194. doi:10.1177/135581969900400401

Dey, R. M., De Vries, M. J. W., & Bosnic-Anticevich, S. (2011). Collaboration in chronic care: Unpacking the relationship of pharmacists and general medical practitioners in primary care. *International Journal of Pharmacy Practice*, *19*(1), 21–29. doi:10.1111/j.2042-7174.2010.00070.x

Doherty, W. J. (1995). The whys and the levels of collaboration. *Family Systems Medicine*, *13*(3), 275–281. doi:10.1037/h0089174

Dugan, D. (2012). Interdisciplinary hospice team processes and multidimensional pain: A qualitative study. *Journal of Social Work in End-of-Life & Palliative Care*, *8*(1), 53–76. doi:10.1080/15524256.2011.650673

Duranti, C. M., & de Almeida, F. C. (2012). Is More Technology Better for Communication in International Virtual Teams? *International Journal of e-Collaboration*, *8*(1), 36–52. doi:10.4018/jec.2012010103

Fornell, C. (1987). A Second Generation of Multivariate Analysis: Classification of Methods and Implications for Marketing Research. In M. J. Houston (Ed.), *Review of Marketing* (pp. 1407–1450). American Marketing Association.

Fornell, C., & Larcker, D. F. (1981). Evaluating structural equation models with unobservable variables and measurement error. *JMR, Journal of Marketing Research*, *18*(1), 39–50. doi:10.1177/002224378101800104

Foronda, C., MacWilliams, B., & McArthur, E. (2016). Interprofessional communication in healthcare: An integrative review. *Nurse Education in Practice*, *19*(2), 36–40. doi:10.1016/j.nepr.2016.04.005

Foth, T., Block, K., & Stamers, M. (2015). The long way toward cooperation: nurses and family physicians in northern Germany. *Global Qualitative Nursing Research*, 1–14. Doi:10.1177/2333393614565185

Fox, S. (2011). The social life of health information, 2011. *Pew Internet & American Life Project*. Retrieved from http://pewinternet.org/Reports/2011/Social-Life-of-Health-Info.aspx

Franchi, E., Poggi, A., & Tomaiuolo, M. (2013). Open Social Networking for Online Collaboration. *International Journal of e-Collaboration*, *9*(3), 50–68. doi:10.4018/jec.2013070104

Franklin, C. M., Bernhardt, J. M., Lopez, R. P., Long-Middleton, E. R., & Davis, S. (2015). *Interprofessional Teamwork and Collaboration between Community Health Workers and Healthcare Teams: An Integrative Review. In Health Services Research Management.* doi:10.1177/2333392815573312

Gaboury, I., Bujold, M., Boon, H., & Moher, D. (2009). Interprofessional collaboration within Canadian integrative healthcare clinics: Key components. *Social Science & Medicine*, *69*(5), 707–715. doi:10.1016/j.socscimed.2009.05.048

Gagliardi, A.R., Dobrow, M.J., & Wright, F.C. (2011). How can we improve cancer care? A review of interprofessional collaboration models and their use in clinical management. *Surgical Oncology*, *20*(3), 146–154. .004 doi:10.1016/j.suronc.2011.06

Gambetta, D. (2000). Can we trust trust? In D. Gambetta (Ed.), *Trust: Making and breaking cooperative relations* (pp. 213–237). Department of Sociology, University of Oxford, Retrieved from: http://www.sociology.ox.ac.uk/papers/gambetta213-237.pdf

Gatignon, H., & Jean-Marc, X. (1997). Strategic orientation of the firm and new product performance. *JMR, Journal of Marketing Research*, *34*(2), 77–90. doi:10.1177/002224379703400107

Gilson, L. (2003). Trust and the development of health care as a social institution. *Social Science & Medicine*, *56*(7), 1453–1468. doi:10.1016/S0277-9536(02)00142-9

Gliner, J. A., & Morgan, G. A. (2000). *Research Methods in Applied Settings: An Integrated Approach to Design and Analysis*. Lawrence Erlbaum Associates Publishers. doi:10.4324/9781410605337

Global Alliance for ICT and Development (GAID). (2010). *Information and communication technologies for development: Health.* White Paper. http://www.scribd.com/doc/35120854/GAID-White-Paper-on-ICT4D-Health

Gocan, S., Laplante, M. A., & Woodend, A. K. (2014). Interprofessional collaboration in Ontario's family health teams: A review of the literature. *Journal of Research in Interprofessional Practice and Education*, *3*(3), 1–19. doi:10.22230/jripe.2014v3n3a131

Goldsberry, J. W. (2018). Advanced Practice Nurses Leading the Way: Interprofessional Collaboration. *Nurse Education Today*, *65*(1), 1–3. doi:10.1016/j.nedt.2018.02.024

Goold, S. (1998). Money and trust: Relationships between patients, physicians, and health plans. *Journal of Health Politics, Policy and Law*, *23*(5), 688–695.

Green, B., & Johnson, C. (2015). Interprofessional collaboration in research, education, and clinical practice: Working together for a better future. *The Journal of Chiropractic Education*, *29*(1), 1–10. doi:10.7899/JCE-14-36

Gulzar, L., & Henry, B. (2005). Interorganizational collaboration for health care between nongovernmental organizations (NGOs) in Pakistan. *Social Science & Medicine*, *61*(9), 1930–1943. doi:10.1016/j.socscimed.2005.03.045

Haeuser, J. L., & Preston, P. (2005). Communication strategies for getting the results you want. *Healthcare Executive*, *20*(1), 16–22.

Hair, J. F., Black, W. C., Babin, B. J., Anderson, R. E., & Tatham, R. L. (2006). *Multivariate Data Analysis* (6th ed.). Prentice Hall.

Hall, M. A., Camacho, F., Dugan, E., & Balkrishnan, R. (2002). Trust in the medical profession: Conceptual and measurement issues. HSR. *Health Services Research*, *37*(5), 1419–1439. doi:10.1111/1475-6773.01070

Hall, P. (2005). Interprofessional teamwork: Professional cultures as barriers. *Journal of Interprofessional Care*, *19*(1), 188–196. doi:10.1080/13561820500081745

Hansen, H. E., Biros, M. H., Delaney, N. M., & Schug, V. L. (1999). Research utilization and interdisciplinary collaboration in emergency care. *Academic Emergency Medicine*, *6*(4), 271–279. doi:10.1111/j.1553-2712.1999.tb00388.x

Hanson, C. M., Carr, D. B., & Spross, J. A. (2000). Collaboration. In A. B. Hamric, J. A. Spross, & C. M. Hanson (Eds.), *Advanced nursing practice. An integrative approach* (2nd ed., pp. 315–347). W. B. Saunders.

Haynes, S. N., Richard, D. C. S., & Kubany, E. S. (1995). Content validity in psychological assessment: A functional approach to concepts and methods. *Psychological Assessment*, *8*(3), 238–247. doi:10.1037/1040-3590.7.3.238

Health Care News. (2001). *The increasing impact of eHealth on physician behavior*. Available at: http://www.harrisinteractive.com/news/newsletters/healthnews/HI_HealthCareNews.2001vol1_Iss31.pdf

Heinemann, G. D., & Zeiss, A. M. (Eds.). (2002). *Team performance in health care*. Kluwer Academic Publishers.

Henault, R. G., Eugenio, K. R., Kelliher, A. F., Alexis, G., & Conlin, P. R. (2002). Transmitting clinical recommendations for diabetes care via e-mail. *American Journal of Health-System Pharmacy*, *59*(22), 2166–2169. doi:10.1093/ajhp/59.22.2166

Henneman, E. A. (1995). Nurse-physician collaboration: A poststructuralist view. *Journal of Advanced Nursing*, *22*(2), 359–363. doi:10.1046/j.1365-2648.1995.22020359.x

Henneman, E. A., Lee, J. L., & Cohen, J. I. (1995). Collaboration: A concept analysis. *Journal of Advanced Nursing*, *21*(1), 103–109. doi:10.1046/j.1365-2648.1995.21010103.x

Hinds, P., & Kiesler, S. (2002). *Distributed Work*. MIT Press. doi:10.7551/mitpress/2464.001.0001

Ho, K., Jarvis-Selinger, S., Norman, C., Li, L., Olatunbosun, T., Cressman, C., & Nguyen, A. (2010). Electronic Communities of Practice: Guidelines from a Project. *The Journal of Continuing Education in the Health Professions*, *30*(2), 139–143. doi:10.1002/chp.20071

Hojat, M., Nasca, T. J., Cohen, M., Fields, S. K., Rattner, S. L., Griffiths, M., Ibarra, D., de Gonzalez, A. A.-G., Torres-Ruiz, A., Ibarra, G., & Garcia, A. (2001). Attitudes toward physician-nurse collaboration: A cross-cultural study of male and female physicians and nurses in the United States and Mexico. *Nursing Research*, *50*(1), 123–128. doi:10.1097/00006199-200103000-00008

Homeyer, S., Hoffmann, W., Hingst, P., Oppermann, R., & Dreier-Wolfgramm, A. (2018). Effects of interprofessional education for medical and nursing students: Enablers, barriers andexpectations for optimizing future interprofessional collaboration – a qualitative study. *BMC Nursing*, *17*(1), 13. doi:10.118612912-018-0279-x

Hosmer, L. T. (1995). Trust: The connecting link between organizational theory and philosophical ethics. *Academy of Management Review*, *20*(2), 379–403. doi:10.5465/amr.1995.9507312923

Hudson, B. (2002). Interprofessionality in health and social care: The Achilles' heel of partnership? *Journal of Interprofessional Care*, *16*(1), 7–17. doi:10.1080/13561820220104122

Igbaria, M., Guimaraes, T., & Davis, G. (1995). Testing the determinants of microcomputer usage via a structural equation model. *Journal of Management Information Systems*, *11*(4), 87–114. doi:10.1080/07421222.1995.11518061

infoDev. (2006). *ICT in Health: The Role of ICTs in the Health Sector in Developing Countries*. InfoDev Activity File #1254. Retrieved from: http://www.infodev.org/en/Project.38.html

Jackson, J., MacKean, G., Cooke, T., & Lahtinen, M. (2017). Patient and provider experiences with relationship, information, and management continuity. *Patient Experience Journal*, *4*(3), Article 8. Available at: http://pxjournal.org/journal/vol4/iss3/8

Jacobsen, D. I. (1999). Trust in political administrative relations: The case of local authorities in Norway and Tanzania. *World Development*, *27*(5), 839–853. doi:10.1016/S0305-750X(99)00032-7

Joint Commission on Accreditation of Healthcare Organizations. (2006). *Critical Access Hospital and Hospital National Patient Safety Goals*. Retrieved from: http://www.jcaho.org/accredited+organizations/patient+safety/06_npsg/06_npsg_cah_hap.htm

Kahn, W. A. (1990). Psychological conditions of personal engagement and disengagement at work. *Academy of Management Journal*, *33*(4), 692–724.

Kaplan, A., & Haenlein, M. (2010). Users of the world, unite! The challenges and opportunities of social media. *Business Horizons*, *53*(1), 59–68. doi:10.1016/j.bushor.2009.09.003

Karam, M., Brault, I., Van Durme, T., & Macq, J. (2018). Comparing Interprofessional and Interorganizational Collaboration in Healthcare: A Systematic Review of The Qualitative Research. *International Journal of Nursing Studies*, *79*(2), 70–83. doi:10.1016/j.ijnurstu.2017.11.002

Keyton, J. (2011). *Communication and organizational culture: A key to understanding work experience*. Sage.

Khan, M. T. (2014). Relationship Marketing - Some Aspects (Review). *International Journal of Information. Business and Management*, *6*(2), 108–122.

Kietzmann, J. H., Hermkens, K., McCarthy, I. P., & Silvestre, B. S. (2011). Social media? Get serious! Understanding the functional building blocks of social media. *Business Horizons*, *54*(4), 241–251. doi:10.1016/j.bushor.2011.01.005

Kittler, A. F., Carlson, B. A., & Harris, C. (2004). Primary care physician attitudes towards using a secure web based portal designed to facilitate electronic communication with patients. *Informatics in Primary Care*, *12*(2), 129–138.

Kock, N. (2015a). Common method bias in PLS-SEM: A full collinearity assessment approach. *International Journal of e-Collaboration*, *11*(4), 1–10. doi:10.4018/ijec.2015100101

Kock, N. (2015b). A note on how to conduct a factor-based PLS-SEM analysis. *International Journal of e-Collaboration*, *11*(3), 1–9. doi:10.4018/ijec.2015070101

Kock, N., & Lynn, G. S. (2012). Lateral collinearity and misleading results in variance-based SEM: An illustration and recommendations. *Journal of the Association for Information Systems*, *13*(7), 546–580. doi:10.17705/1jais.00302

Kraut, R. E., Fussell, S. R., Brennan, S. E., & Siegel, J. (2002). Understanding Effects of Proximity on Collaboration: Implications for Technologies to Support Remote Collaborative Work. In P. Hinds & S. Kiesler (Eds.), *Distributed Work* (pp. 139–162). MIT Press.

Kripalani, S., LeFevre, F., Phillips, C. O., Williams, M. V., Basaviah, P., & Baker, D. (2007). Deficits in Communication and Information Transfer between Hospital-Based and Primary Care Physicians Implications for Patient Safety and Continuity of Care Coordination. *Journal of the American Medical Association*, *297*(8), 831–841. doi:10.1001/jama.297.8.831

Krogstad, U., Hofoss, D., & Hjortdahl, P. (2004). Doctor and nurse perception of inter-professional cooperation in hospitals. *International Journal for Quality in Health Care*, *16*(6), 491–497. doi:10.1093/intqhc/mzh082

Lambert, D. M., & Harrington, T. C. (1990). Measuring Nonresponse Bias in Mail Surveys. *Journal of Business Logistics*, *11*(1), 5–25.

Lee, O. F., & Meuter, M. L. (2010). The adoption of technology orientation in healthcare delivery: Case study of a large-scale hospital and healthcare system's electronic health record. *International Journal of Pharmaceutical and Healthcare Marketing*, *4*(4), 355–374. doi:10.1108/17506121011095209

Lemieux-Charles, L., & McGuire, W. (2006). What do we know about heath care team effectiveness? A review of the literature. *Medical Care Research and Review: MCRR*, *63*(3), 263–300. doi:10.1177/1077558706287003

Leonhardt, P. (2006, Apr. 19). Political clout in the age of out sourcing. *The New York Times*.

Liederman, E. M., Lee, J. C., Baquero, V. H., & Seites, P. G. (2005). Patient-physician web messaging: The impact on message volume and satisfaction. *Journal of General Internal Medicine*, *20*(1), 52–57. doi:10.1111/j.1525-1497.2005.40009.x

Liederman, E. M., & Morefield, C. S. (2003). Web messaging: A new tool for patient-physician communication. *Journal of the American Medical Informatics Association*, *10*(3), 263–274. doi:10.1197/jamia.M1259

Lindeke, L. L., & Block, D. E. (1998). Maintaining professional integrity in the midst of interdisciplinary collaboration. *Nursing Outlook*, *46*(5), 213–218. doi:10.1016/S0029-6554(98)90052-5

Lindell, M. K., & Whitney, D. J. (2001). Accounting for Common Method Variance in Cross-Sectional Research Designs. *The Journal of Applied Psychology*, *86*(1), 114–121. doi:10.1037/0021-9010.86.1.114

Lingard, L., Regehr, G., Orser, B., Reznick, R., Baker, G. R., Doran, D., Espin, S., Bohnen, J., & Whyte, S. (2008). Evaluation of a preoperative checklist and team briefing among surgeons, nurses, and anesthesiologists to reduce failures in communication. *Archives of Surgery (Chicago, Ill.)*, *143*(1), 12–17. doi:10.1001/archsurg.2007.21

Lingard, L., Reznick, R., Espin, S., Regehr, G., & DeVito, I. (2002). Team communications in the operating room: Talk patterns, sites of tension, and implications for novices. *Academic Medicine*, *77*(3), 232–237. doi:10.1097/00001888-200203000-00013

Lingard, L., Whyte, S., Espin, S., Baker, G. R., Orser, B., & Doran, D. (2006). Towards safer interprofessional communication: Constructing a model of "utility" from preoperative team briefings. *Journal of Interprofessional Care*, *20*(5), 471–483. doi:10.1080/13561820600921865

Luhmann, N. (2000). Familiarity, confidence, trust: Problems and alternatives. In *Trust: making and breaking cooperative relations* (pp. 94–107). Department of Sociology, University of Oxford. Retrieved from: http://www.sociology.ox.ac.uk/papers/luhmann94-107.pdf

Lyngstad, M., Melby, L., Grimsmo, A., & Hellesø, R. (2013). Toward Increased Patient Safety? Electronic Communication of Medication Information Between Nurses in Home Health Care and General Practitioners. *Home Health Care Management & Practice*, *25*(5), 203–211. doi:10.1177/1084822313480365

Lynn, M. R. (1986). Determination and Quantification of Content Validity. *Nursing Research*, *35*(4), 382–385.

Manaikkamakl, P. (2007). Personal technology orientation in R&D: A tool to intensify organizational learning. *Development and Learning in Organizations*, *21*(6), 18–20. doi:10.1108/14777280710828594

Mann, M. Y., Lloyd-Puryear, M. A., & Lizer, D. (2006). Enhancing communication in the 21st Century. *Pediatrics*, *117*(4, Supplement 3), 315–319. doi:10.1542/peds.2005-2633K

Matziou, V., Vlahioti, E., Perdikaris, P., Matziou, T., Megapanou, E., & Petsios, K. (2014). Physician and nursing perceptions concerning interprofessional communication and collaboration. *Journal of Interprofessional Care*, *28*(6), 526–533. doi:10.3109/13561820.2014.934338

Mayer, R. C., Davis, J. H., & Schoorman, F. D. (1995). An Integrative Model of Organization Trust.'. *Academy of Management Review*, *20*(3), 709–733. doi:10.5465/amr.1995.9508080335

Mechanic, D. (1996). Changing medical organization and the erosion of trust. *The Milbank Quarterly*, *74*(2), 171–189. doi:10.2307/3350245

Mechanic, D. (1998). Trust in the provision of medical care. *Journal of Health Politics, Policy and Law*, *23*(411), 661–686. doi:10.1215/03616878-23-4-661

Mechanic, D., & Meyer, S. (2000). Concepts of trust among patients with serious illness. *Social Science & Medicine*, *51*(5), 657–668. doi:10.1016/S0277-9536(00)00014-9

Merriam-Webster OnLine Dictionary. (n.d.). http://www.merriamwebster.com/dictionary/communication

Meyer, M. W. (1985). *Limits to bureaucratic growth*. De Gruyter. doi:10.1515/9783110865295

Miller, K. (2005). *Communication theories: Perspectives, processes, and contexts* (2nd ed.). McGraw-Hill.

Mior, S., Barnsley, J., Boon, H., Ashbury, F. D., & Haig, R. (2010). Designing a framework for the delivery of collaborative musculoskeletal care involving chiropractors and physicians in community-based primary care. *Journal of Interprofessional Care*, *24*(6), 678–689. doi:10.3109/13561821003608757

Misztal, B. A. (1996). *Trust in modern societies: The search for the bases of moral order*. Polity Press.

Mohammed, S., Ferzandi, L., & Hamilton, K. (2010). Metaphor no more: A 15-year review of the team mental model construct. *Journal of Management*, *36*(4), 876–910. doi:10.1177/0149206309356804

Molleman, E., Broekhuis, M., Stoffels, R., & Jaspers, F. (2008). How health care complexity leads to cooperation and affects the autonomy of health care professionals. Health Care Analysis. An. *International Journal of Health Care Philosophy and Policy*, *16*(4), 329–341. doi:10.100710728-007-0080-6

Moqbel, M., Nevo, S., & Kock, N. (2013). Organizational members' use of social networking sites and job performance. *Information Technology & People*, *26*(3), 240–264. doi:10.1108/ITP-10-2012-0110

Morgan, S., Pullon, S., & McKinlay, E. (2015). Observation of interprofessional collaborative practice in primary care teams: An integrative literature review. *International Journal of Nursing Studies*, *52*(7), 1217–1230. doi:10.1016/j.ijnurstu.2015.03.008

Nardi, B. A., & Whittaker, S. (2002). The Place of Face-to-Face Communication in Distributed Work. In P. Hinds & S. Kiesler (Eds.), *Distributed Work* (pp. 83–110). MIT Press.

Newman, J. (1998). The dynamics of trust. In A. Coulson (Ed.), *Trust and contracts: Relationships in local government, health and public services*. The Polity Press.

Nunnally, J. C., & Bernstein, I. H. (1994). *Psychometric Theory* (3rd ed.). McGraw-Hill.

Nunnaly, J. (1978). *Psychometric Theory*. McGraw Hill.

O'connor, P., O'dea, A., Lydon, S., Offiah, G., Scott, J., Flannery, A., Lang, B., Hoban, A., Armstrong, C., & Byrne, D. (2016). A mixed-methods study of the causes and impact of poor teamwork between junior doctors and nurses. *International Journal for Quality in Health Care*, *28*(3), 339–345. doi:10.1093/intqhc/mzw036

Open Clinical. (2011). eHealth. *Open Clinical: Knowledge Management for Medical Care*. Retrieved from: http://www.openclinical.org/e-Health.html#applications

Palanisamy, R., & Verville, J. (2015). Factors enabling communication based collaboration in interprofessional healthcare practice: A case study. *International Journal of e-Collaboration*, *11*(2), 8–27. doi:10.4018/ijec.2015040102

Papanikolaou, K. A., & Gouli, E. (2013). Investigating Influences among individuals and groups in a collaborative learning setting. *International Journal of e-Collaboration*, *9*(1), 9–25. doi:10.4018/jec.2013010102

Pearce, W. B. (2003). *The coordinated management of meaning (CMM): Theorizing about communication and culture*. Sage.

Perry, H., Robison, N., Chavez, D., Taja, O. O., Hilari, C., Shanklin, D., & Wyon, J. (1999). Attaining health for all through community partnership: Principles of the census based, impact-oriented (CBIO) approach to primary health care developed in Bolivia, South America. *Social Science & Medicine*, *48*(8), 1053–1068. doi:10.1016/S0277-9536(98)00406-7

Pfaff, K. A., Baxter, P. E., Jack, P. E., Jack, S. M., & Ploeg, J. (2014). Exploring new graduate nurse confidence in interprofessional collaboration: A mixed methods. *International Journal of Nursing Studies*, *51*(8), 1142–1152. doi:10.1016/j.ijnurstu.2014.01.001

Podsakoff, P. M., MacKenzie, S. B., Lee, J. Y., & Podsakoff, N. P. (2003). Common Method Biases in Behavioral Research: A Critical Review of the Literature and Recommended Remedies. *The Journal of Applied Psychology*, *88*(5), 879–903. doi:10.1037/0021-9010.88.5.879

Podsakoff, P. M., & Organ, D. W. (1986). Self-reports in Organizational Research: Problems and Prospects. *Journal of Management*, *12*(4), 531–544. doi:10.1177/014920638601200408

Polit, D. F., & Beck, C. T. (2004). *Nursing Research: Principles and Methods* (7th ed.). Lippincott, Williams, & Wilkins.

Polit, D. F., & Beck, C. T. (2006). The Content Validity Index: Are You Sure You Know What's Being Reported? Critique and Recommendations. *Research in Nursing & Health*, *29*(6), 489–497. doi:10.1002/nur.20147

Reeves, S., McMillan, S. E., Kachan, N., Paradis, E., Leslie, M., & Kitto, S. (2014). Interprofessional collaboration and family member involvement in intensive careunits: Emerging themes from a multi-sited ethnography. *Journal of Interprofessional Care*, *29*(3), 230–237. doi:10.3109/13561820.2014.955914

Reeves, S., Pelone, F., Harrison, R., Goldman, J., & Zwarenstein, M. (2017). Interprofessional collaboration to improve professional practice and healthcare outcomes. *Cochrane Database of Systematic Reviews*, 6.

Rice, R. E., & Gattiker, U. E. (2001). New Media and Organizational Structuring. In F. M. Jablin & L. L. Putnam (Eds.), *The New Handbook of Organizational Communication* (pp. 544–584). Sage Publications. doi:10.4135/9781412986243.n14

Rodriguez, L. S., Beaulieu, M., D'Amour, D., & Ferrada-Videla, M. (2005). The determinants of successful collaboration: A review of theoretical and empirical studies. *Journal of Interprofessional Care, 19*(1), 132–147. doi:10.1080/13561820500082677

Rogelberg, S. G., & Stanton, J. M. (2007). Understanding and dealing with organizational survey nonresponse. *Organizational Research Methods, 10*(2), 195–209. doi:10.1177/1094428106294693

Rönkkö, M., & Evermann, J. (2013). A critical examination of common beliefs about partial least squares path modeling. *Organizational Research Methods.*

Rubio, D. M., Berg-Weger, M., Tebb, S. S., Lee, E. S., & Rauch, S. (2003). Objectifying Content Validity: Conducting a Content Validity Study in Social Work Research. *Social Work Research, 27*(2), 94–104. doi:10.1093wr/27.2.94

Safran, C., Jones, P., Rind, D., Bush, B., Cytryn, K., & Patel, V. (1998). Electronic communication and collaboration in a health care practice. *Artificial Intelligence in Medicine, 12*(2), 137–151. doi:10.1016/S0933-3657(97)00047-X

Safran, D. G. (2003). Defining the future of primary care: What can we learn from patients? *Annals of Internal Medicine, 138*(3), 248–255. doi:10.7326/0003-4819-138-3-200302040-00033

Schofield, R. F., & Amodeo, M. (1999). Interdisciplinary teams in health care and human services settings: Are they effective? *Health & Social Work, 24*(3), 210–219. doi:10.1093/hsw/24.3.210

Senate Finance Committee. (2009). *Transforming the health care delivery system: proposals to improve patient care and reduce health care costs.* Retrieved August, 2, 2016, from: http://finance.senate.gov/sitepages/leg/LEG%202009/042809%20Health%20Care%20Description%20of%20Policy%20Option.pdf

Shaffer, K., & Speakman, E. (2014). Using Technology to Enhance Interprofessional Collaborative Practice: Creating Virtual Clinical Opportunities by Implementing Google Doc and Google Hangout in Clinical Rounding. *Collaborative Healthcare: Interprofessional Practice, Education and Evaluation, 5*(1), Article 2. Available at: http://jdc.jefferson.edu/jcipe/vol5/iss1/2

Sharma, G., Qiang, Y., Wenjun,S., & Qi, L. (2013). Communication in virtual world: Second life and business opportunities. *Information Systems Frontiers, 15*(7), 677–694. DOI doi:10.100710796-012-9347-z

Shortell, S. M., Zimmerman, J. E., Rousseau, D. M., Gillies, R. R., Wagner, D. P., Draper, E. A., Knaus, W. A., & Duffy, J. (1994). The performance of intensive care units: Does good management make a difference? *Medical Care, 32*(5), 508–525. doi:10.1097/00005650-199405000-00009

Sicotte, C., D'Amour, D., & Moreault, M. (2002). Interdisciplinary collaboration within Quebec community health care centers. *Social Science & Medicine, 55*(6), 991–1003. doi:10.1016/S0277-9536(01)00232-5

Siegler, E. L., & Whitney, F. W. (1994). *Nurse-Physician collaboration. Care of adults and the elderly.* Stringer Publishing Company.

Smith, M., Greene, B. R., & Meeker, W. (2002). The CAM movement and the integration of quality health care: The case of chiropractic. *The Journal of Ambulatory Care Management*, *25*(2), 1–16. doi:10.1097/00004479-200204000-00003

Sproull, L., & Kiesler, S. (1986). Reducing social context cues: Electronic mail in organizational communication. *Management Science*, *32*(11), 1492–1512. doi:10.1287/mnsc.32.11.1492

Srinivasan, A. (1985). Alternative measures of system effectiveness: Associations and implications. *Management Information Systems Quarterly*, *9*(3), 243–253. doi:10.2307/248951

Starfield, B. (1998). *Primary care: Balancing Health Needs, Services, and Technology*. Oxford University Press.

Stein, L. I., Watts, D. T., & Howell, T. (1990). The doctor-nurse game revisited. *The New England Journal of Medicine*, *322*(6), 536–549.

Stichler, J. F. (1995). Professional interdependence: The art of collaboration. *Advanced Practice Nursing Quarterly*, *1*(1), 53–61.

Stille, C. J., Jerant, A., Bell, D., Meltzer, D., & Elmore, J. G. (2005). Coordinating Care across Diseases, Settings, and.: A Key Role for the Generalist in Practice. *Annals of Internal Medicine*, *142*(7), 700–708. doi:10.7326/0003-4819-142-8-200504190-00038

Supper, I., Catala, O., Lustman, M., Chemla, C., Bourgueil, Y., & Letrilliart, L. (2014). Interprofessional collaboration in primary health care: A Review of facilitators and barriers perceived by involved actors. *Journal of Public Health*, *37*(4), 716–727.

Suter, E., Arndt, J., Arthur, N., Parboosingh, J., Taylor, E., & Deutschlander, S. (2009). Role understanding and effective communication as core competencies for collaborative practice. *Journal of Interprofessional Care*, *23*(1), 41–51. doi:10.1080/13561820802338579

Tang, C. J., Zhou, W. T., & Liaw, S. Y. (2018). Interprofessional collaboration between juniordoctors and nurses in the general ward setting: A qualitative exploratory study. Journal of Nursing Management. *Journal of Nursing Management*, *26*(1), 11–18. doi:10.1111/jonm.12503

Teigland, R., & Wasko, M. (2003). Integrating Knowledge through Information Trading: Examining the Relationship between Boundary Spanning Communication and Individual Performance. *Decision Sciences*, *34*(2), 261–286. doi:10.1111/1540-5915.02341

Terry, M. (2008). Text messaging in healthcare: The elephant knocking at the door. *Telemedicine Journal and e-Health*, *14*(5), 520–524. doi:10.1089/tmj.2008.8495

Thomas, E. J., Sherwood, G. D., Mulhollem, J. L., Sexton, J. B., & Helmreich, R. L. (2004). Working together in the neonatal intensive care unit: Provider perspective. *Journal of Perinatology*, *24*(9), 552–559. doi:10.1038j.jp.7211136

Tidwell, L. C., & Walther, J. B. (2002). Computer-Mediated Communication Effects on Disclosure, Impressions, and Interpersonal Evaluations. *Human Communication Research*, *28*(3), 317–348. doi:10.1111/j.1468-2958.2002.tb00811.x

Tyler, T. R., & Kramer, R. M. (1996). Whither trust? In R. M. Kramer & T. R. Tyler (Eds.), *Trust in organizations: Frontiers of theory and research*. Sage. doi:10.4135/9781452243610.n1

Urbach, N., & Ahlemann, F. (2010). Structural Equation Modeling in Information Systems Research Using Partial Least Squares. *Journal of Information Technology Theory and Application*, *11*(2), 5–40.

Vazirani, S., Hays, R. D., Shapiro, M. F., & Cowan, M. (2005). Effect of a multidisciplinary intervention on communication and collaboration among physicians and nurses. *American Journal of Critical Care*, *14*(1), 71–77. doi:10.4037/ajcc2005.14.1.71

Veenstra, G., & Lomas, J. (1999). Home is where the governing is: Social capital and regional health governance. *Health & Place*, *5*(1), 1–2. doi:10.1016/S1353-8292(98)00037-9

Verschuren, P. J., & Masselink, H. (1997). Role concepts and expectations of physicians and nurses in hospitals. *Social Science & Medicine*, *45*(6), 1135–1138. doi:10.1016/S0277-9536(97)00043-9

Vestergaard, E., & Nørgaard, B. (2018). Interprofessional collaboration: An exploration of possible prerequisites for successful implementation. *Journal of Interprofessional Care*, *32*(2), 185–195. doi:10.1080/13561820.2017.1363725

Wagner, E. H. (2004). Effective teamwork and quality of care. *Medical Care*, *42*(11), 1037–1039. doi:10.1097/01.mlr.0000145875.60036.ed

Walsh, C., Gordon, F., Marshall, M., & Hunt, T. (2005). Interprofessional capability: A developing framework for interprofessional education. *Nurse Education in Practice*, *5*(4), 230–237. doi:10.1016/j.nepr.2004.12.004

Waskett, C. (1996). Multidisciplinary teamwork in primary care: The role of the counsellor. *Counselling Psychology Quarterly*, *9*(4), 243–260. doi:10.1080/09515079608258706

Way, D., Jones, L., & Busing, N. (2000). *Implementation strategies: "Collaboration in primary care – Family doctors & nurse practitioners delivering shared care": Discussion paper written for the Ontario College of Family Physicians*. Ontario College of Family Physicians.

Weaver, B., Lindsay, B., & Gitelman, B. (2012). Communication technology and social media: opportunities and implications for healthcare systems. *OJIN: The Online Journal of Issues in Nursing, 17*(3), 17-24. Advance online publication. doi:10.3912/OJIN.Vol17No03Man03

Welton, W. E., Kantner, T. A., & Moriber, K. S. (1997). Developing tomorrow's Integrated Community Health Systems: A leadership challenge for public health and primary care. *The Milbank Quarterly*, *75*(2), 261–288. doi:10.1111/1468-0009.00054

Williams, A. L., Lasky, R. E., Dannemiller, J. L., Andrei, A. M., & Thomas, E. J. (2010). Teamwork behaviours and errors during neonatal resuscitation. *Quality & Safety in Health Care*, *19*(1), 60–64. doi:10.1136/qshc.2007.025320

Woods, J. A., Jackson, D. J., Ziglar, S., & Alston, G. L. (2011). Interprofessional communication. *Drug Topics*, *155*(8), 42–53.

Ye, J. (2006). *Deliberate Learning in The Frontlines of Service Organizations* (Ph.D. Dissertation). Department of Marketing and Policy Studies, Case Western Reserve University.

Zwarenstein, M., Reeves, S., & Perrier, L. (2004). Effectiveness of pre-licensure interdisciplinary education and post-licensure interprofessional collaboration interventions. In I. Oandasan (Ed.), *Interdisciplinary education for collaborative patient-centred practice* (pp. 38–50). Health Canada.

APPENDIX

Table A1. Correlations and square roots of average variance extracted (AVE) values

Constructs	Collaboration	Communication	Coordination	Cooperation	Trust	Techn
Collaboration	(0.749)					
Communication	0.700**	(0.680)				
Coordination	0.819**	0.940**	0.714			
Cooperation	0.830**	0.894**	0.868**	0.621		
Trust	0.670**	0.919**	0.942**	0.857**	0.703	
Tech.Orientation	0.213**	0.239**	0.106	0.289**	0.234**	0.846

Table A2. Model fit and quality indices

Constructs	Collab	Commun	Coordi	Cooper	Trust	TechO
Collinearity VIF	2760.756	3581.200	14254.568	1733.205	3778.857	231.025
Average full collinearity VIF (AFVIF)	4389.935			acceptable if <= 5, ideally <= 3.3		
Average path coefficient (APC)	0.665**					
Average R-squared (ARS)	1.260**					
Average block VIF (AVIF)	4.032			acceptable if <= 5, ideally <= 3.3		

Table A3. R-Square value, path coefficients and their significances

Constructs	Collab	Commun	Coordi	Cooper	Trust	TechO	R^2	Adj. R^2
Collaboration		1.110**	1.179**	0.803**			2.493	2.515
Communication					0.914**	0.018	0.846	0.844
Coordination					0.961**	0.062	0.920	0.919
Cooperation					0.855**	0.085	0.780	0.778
Trust								
Tech.Orientation								

Chapter 5
Human-AI Collaboration:
Introducing the Virtual Collaborator

Dominik Siemon
https://orcid.org/0000-0002-2945-4167
Technische Universität Braunschweig, Germany

Timo Strohmann
Technische Universität Braunschweig, Germany

ABSTRACT

Continuous increase in computing power and more available data contribute to AI maturing, enabling an efficient and powerful human-AI collaboration. As a result, the nature of work will change, and more and more AI will be involved in joint work. In this study, the authors introduce the so-called Virtual Collaborator (VC), an equal partner in digital collaboration, and report the results of a conducted online study. Based on the results of our study and current research, the concept of a VC was constructed, which consists of potential roles, tasks, level of autonomy, and behavior. This construct can be used as a guideline to design and implement a VC in collaboration scenarios.

INTRODUCTION AND MOTIVATION

New challenges and constantly emerging complex problems, caused by an increasingly networked world, emerging technologies and ambitious customer requirements, require companies to benefit from teamwork and collaboration (Dulebohn & Hoch, 2017; Finkbeiner & Morner, 2015). Information and communication technology (ICT) enables digital collaboration that is location- and time independent. Such digital collaboration is now part of the day-to-day business of many knowledge workers, in which various team members work together using certain systems for communication, information exchange and general collective added value creation (Driskell et al., 2003; Dulebohn & Hoch, 2017; Fiol & O'Connor, 2005). Research in this field has been conducted over the past decades, leading to a variety of guidelines and computer systems that support tasks, like decision making, project and knowledge management or creativity (Resnick et al., 2005; Siemon et al., 2017; Voigt & Bergener, 2013).

DOI: 10.4018/978-1-7998-4891-2.ch005

Copyright © 2021, IGI Global. Copying or distributing in print or electronic forms without written permission of IGI Global is prohibited.

In addition to that, the continuous improvement of computing power and the general development of novel algorithms has significantly matured artificial intelligence (AI) (Russell & Norvig, 2016). This improvement has led to a number of systems and services, like Amazon's Alexa, Apple's Siri or IBM's Watson. With Google's Tensorflow, Facebook's Wit.AI or other services, software developers are now able to implement AI within their products or services more easily. This results in smarter services using AI to interact and even collaborate with customers (Aleksander, 2017; Schwartz et al., 2019; Spinella, 2018). This upswing of AI challenges research and existing theories on collaboration mechanisms, methods and phenomena in group- or teamwork (Aleksander, 2017; Anderson et al., 2018; Schwartz et al., 2019).

The interdisciplinary research field of computer-supported collaborative work (or collaboration technology) has already revealed the various mechanisms required for successful collaboration via information systems (Borghoff & Schlichter, 2000; Grudin, 1994; Siemon et al., 2017). A number of design principles have emerged and been developed from this research, proposing guidelines and different characteristics that support interaction and group dynamics, for example to reduce negative cognitive or social group effects such as production blocking, evaluation apprehension or social loafing (Diehl & Stroebe, 1987; Voigt & Bergener, 2013). Evaluation apprehension for example, or the fear of critics, is a phenomenon that appears when individuals hold back ideas, because they apprehend negative comments and critic. This can lead to ideas and thoughts that are hold back and might be valuable for a beneficial innovation (Diehl & Stroebe, 1987; L. M. Jessup et al., 1990). Using anonymity has been proven to positively impact evaluation apprehension, as users can anonymously contribute and are less or not afraid of criticism. However, anonymity increases social loafing, a phenomenon of individuals exerting less effort in a group (L. M. Jessup et al., 1990). A study from 2015 used an AI-like support system in order to overcome the phenomena of evaluation apprehension in a group setting (Siemon et al., 2015). The researchers implemented a pseudo AI within a creativity support system, examining whether participants fear to contribute when interacting and being supported by an artificial collaborator. The phenomena of evaluation apprehension was not observed within the experiment (Siemon et al., 2015). Even though, the study is limited by virtue of the small number of participants and the results only show a tendency, it shows that novel mechanisms need to be further analyzed.

A study from Strohmann et al. (2018) assessed the requirements for a virtual moderator that is able to conduct Design Thinking workshops and proposed guidelines on the appearance and behavior of the VA. The guidelines involve pro-active behavior and human-like appearance (Strohmann et al., 2018). The qualitative study shows that workshop experts can imagine organizing and conducting a Design Thinking workshop supported by AI in form of a virtual moderator. Furthermore, Seeber et al. (2019) argue that the way IS supports collaboration will change in the next years due to human-machine collaboration. In their paper, they propose a research agenda for a new era of collaboration research and mention AI as one technology that will impact collaboration (Seeber et al., 2019). Based on four different scenarios, technology trends, previous collaboration analysis and a conducted workshop, they define a research model divided into three meta-themes. Adapting these meta-themes by analyzing the many proposed research questions, we argue that an overarching and initial research question needs to be developed and approached, that takes basic principles of collaboration into account and considers how humans conceive a collaboration scenario with AI. Based on these research questions from the Collaboration Sphere and Design Sphere by Seeber et al. (2019) on the understanding of team roles, team behaviors, trust, cognitive, emotional and relationship aspects (Aleksander, 2017; Anderson et al., 2018; Feng & Buxmann, 2020; Randrup et al., 2016; Schwartz et al., 2019; Seeber et al., 2019; Siemon et al., 2017,

2015, 2019), we introduce the concept of the virtual collaborator and aim to shed light on the question, how humans imagine working with AI in a team.

Recent research tries to address this or similar questions by focusing on specific mechanisms and phenomena, like trust, politeness, reciprocity, mindlessness or anthropomorphism (J. Elson et al., 2020; J. S. Elson et al., 2018; Gnewuch et al., 2017; S. Jessup et al., 2020; Nass & Moon, 2000; Saffarizadeh et al., 2017; Schroeder & Schroeder, 2018). Especially trust and reliance are frequently covered topics, as well as privacy concerns and data security when interacting with intelligent systems (J. Elson et al., 2020; S. Jessup et al., 2020; Saffarizadeh et al., 2017). Studies show that trust in intelligent systems is an important aspect that has a major influence on the willingness to share information (Schroeder & Schroeder, 2018) and how users rely upon recommendations from intelligent systems (J. S. Elson et al., 2018). When interacting with computers, data security additionally impacts privacy concerns and overall trust (Saffarizadeh et al., 2017). In summary, the studies underline the importance of trust in computers and subsequently the necessity to consider trust as a major factor within human-machine collaboration. However, the general view of the defined intelligent systems, be it a conversational agent (Gnewuch et al., 2017), an artificial agent (J. S. Elson et al., 2018), a conversational assistant (Saffarizadeh et al., 2017) or simpler, a machine (Schroeder & Schroeder, 2018) reduce the intelligent system to a subordinated partner, that assists the user and is not coequally collaborating with the user. However, the perspective, where the computer is defined as a social actor, was already mentioned in 1996 by Reeves and Nass and further observed by Nass and Moon, who state that humans often apply mindlessly social rules to computers (Nass & Moon, 2000). This highly depends on the perception of computers and their present characteristics. Computers that appear more human-like and act more human, are more likely to be seen coequal (Nass & Moon, 2000). (Gnewuch et al., 2017) address this and state that conversational agents should act more cooperative. The authors mention design principles like reaching a common goal as a major aspect a conversational agent should follow (Siemon et al., 2015). However, the main focus is still on conversational agents that are designed to fulfill customer needs and provide good consultation, not on coequal collaboration. The definition of conversational agents additionally limits the system to conversational-driven interaction, where the input of the agent solely consists of messages aiming to support the user. Autonomously generated content, aiding to contribute to a given problem or task is neglected, thus not being able to coequally collaborative with the user. Even though, many studies already consider trust and reliance and other aspects of cooperation, a comprehensive view on collaboration with machines is missing. 18 years after Reeves and Nass emphasized that humans mindlessly apply social rules to computers, highly depends on the characteristics of computers and needs to be further investigated, especially due to the tremendous improvement in AI, where computers become more human.

THEORETICAL BACKGROUND

Collaboration describes the joint effort of at least two individuals working towards a common goal. It occurs when individual's intent to create value together (Randrup et al., 2016) and it involves various mechanisms and principles (Siemon et al., 2017). With the widespread use of computer technology in the daily working routine, new possibilities to support collaboration emerged. Computer technology enabled a new form of collaboration, where time- and location-independent value creation is possible and specific communication and interaction mechanisms can be facilitated (Briggs et al., 2003). This led to research on how to use ICT to support collaboration and subsequently led to the development of a variety of products and prototypes used to enhance team performance. Terms like Collaboration Technology, Computer Supported Cooperative Work (CSCW), Group Support Systems (GSS) and Groupware were introduced (Borghoff & Schlichter, 2000). Besides of providing various features for shared data storage, shared workspaces and editors, collaboration technology additionally aims to adapt to team behavior and social phenomena in group work (Voigt & Bergener, 2013). A number of frameworks and design guidelines, that take cognitive and social effects into account were published (Resnick et al., 2005; Shneiderman, 2007; Siemon et al., 2017; Voigt & Bergener, 2013). These guidelines discuss the use of specific mechanisms like anonymity, social profiles or evaluation and rating in order to improve social interaction and avoid drawbacks due to negative collective influences (Siemon et al., 2017; Voigt & Bergener, 2013). The integrated framework for creativity support systems by Voigt and Bergener (2013), provide generic components and features like anonymity to overcome evaluation apprehension, social comparison to reduce free-riding or session histories to increase trust in creative team performance. In 2017, an overarching framework for collaboration support systems for teamwork (including collaborative learning, collaborative creativity, collaborative problem-solving and collaborative decision making) proposed guidelines on how to support process gains and reduce process losses within collaboration (Siemon et al., 2017). A specific focus is set on the principles of collaboration, that need to be upheld within a successful team performance. However, with the application of new technologies like AI within collaboration, these guidelines need to be rethought.

With the emergence of new technologies, like virtual reality, augmented reality, AI or robot technology, the way collaboration can be done changes drastically (Aleksander, 2017; Anderson et al., 2018; Schwartz et al., 2019; Seeber et al., 2019). With virtual reality, the sole interaction with a computer screen becomes obsolete and an immersive way of working together emerges in which natural communication and other interaction methods enrich collaboration (Piumsomboon et al., 2017). Methods like, taking your team member's viewpoint (view enhancement), an eye-gaze-based interaction or the virtual awareness of all team members enable new forms of collaboration mechanism that go beyond real face-to-face collaboration and need to be analyzed accordingly (Piumsomboon et al., 2017). With the recent evolution of AI and the application in virtual assistants (VAs) and intelligent agents, the question arises, whether collaboration changes when AI is involved in teamwork.

AI describes software, machines or systems that try to achieve so-called natural intelligence in order to become active in solving tasks or supporting humans (Russell & Norvig, 2016). In computer science, AI is used to mimic cognitive functions that humans possess, such as natural language, learning and reasoning (Nilsson, 2014). Due to the drastic increase of computing power, cloud computing and the improvement of neural networks, AI has developed rapidly over the last few years (Lu et al., 2018). Besides, the various applications in robotics, healthcare, finance and more, AI has become omnipresent (Nilsson, 2014). For all these systems enabling a human conversation between an IS and its user, there is a wide-range of terms, to just name a few: virtual personal assistant (Michael F. McTear, 2004), virtual social agent (Guzman, 2017), digital assistant (Guzman, 2017), voice assistant (M. McTear et al., 2016), social agent (Skalski & Tamborini, 2007), intelligent assistant (Lee et al., 2017), cognitive assistant (Coronado et al., 2018), personal robot (Mondal & Nandi, 2018) and conversational AI (Ram et al., 2018). McTear (2017) shows the relevance and development of this kind of interaction and uses the term conversational interface as a current approach to summarize this variety of terms. He defines a conversational interface as a front-end for a chatbot or VA that allows the user to interact with a system through the use of natural language.

These systems are computer software programs that intelligently perform functions, such as supporting users on their own initiative (Skalski & Tamborini, 2007). Commonly known applications of AI like Apple's Siri or Google Assistant are personal assistants fulfilling everyday tasks for their user (M. McTear et al., 2016; Pearl, 2016). They can carry out tasks and give various information concerning topics like weather, traffic, restaurant information or even make appointments at the user's favorite hairdresser (see Google Duplex[1]) (M. McTear et al., 2016; Zhao, 2006). Hence, these systems are already able to understand natural human language and interact with humans in a social way (Skalski & Tamborini, 2007; Zhao, 2006). According to Maedche et al. (2016), we speak of Advanced User Assistance Systems when amongst other things, the user's context and activities are considered while performing a particular task. They suggest that so-called Anticipating User Assistance Systems are the highest form of user assistance, which include a proactive behavior and self-learning capabilities, adapting to certain contexts and to the user's needs. Maedche et al. (2016) draw attention on this topic and demand future research in this field (Maedche et al., 2016). Seeber et al. (2019) coincide with that and state that technology has the potential to be our smart collaboration partner in the future (Seeber et al., 2019).

This assumption includes, that the support by a smart machine is not solely an assistance, but a coequal value creation between humans and AI. Based on these various definitions of AI that support the user, combined with the theoretical background on collaboration, we define the **Virtual Collaborator (VC)**, a coequal virtual teammate in a collaboration setting. We chose the name virtual collaborator, as it represents a more comprehensive view on existing and especially future applications of AI. Whereas the commonly used term virtual assistant limits the autonomy of the system to assisting functions, neglecting the possibility of systems that act in a coequal way with the user. Thus, applications where AI work in a collaborative manner cannot be allocated and called virtual assistants. The commonly used term conversational interface (Këpuska & Bohouta, 2018; M.F. McTear, 2017), limits the interaction between the system and the user to a conversation. A system that proactively contributes to a given task and autonomously creates content would thus not be a conversational interface. Similar terms like artificial companion (Wilks, 2006), artificial collaborator or artificial agents (Chan, 1995) also encompass physical instantiations, because of the partial term artificial. Therefore, we substitute it with the term virtual to limit the focus on virtual instantiations and focus on cognitive abilities of the system. In doing so, the term virtual collaborator is appropriate for the application of AI within digital and virtual collaboration settings.

METHODOLOGY

To shed light on the newly established term of a virtual collaborator, we conducted an exploratory study for a phenomenon that has not been studied before (Babbie, 2015). In order to understand the conception and in order to identify the influencing factors of team workers towards virtual collaborators, a questionnaire was developed and carried out. The study should tackle new research questions, identify potential focal groups, propose possible experiment settings, bring up rudimentary design guidelines or provide overall guidance for future research (Siemon et al., 2019). In addition, it should provide insights whether team workers expect similar team behavior and group dynamics, when working with a VC and whether collaboration mechanisms are conceived as likewise important as within a solely human team. The study was conducted in form of an online questionnaire and was sent to students and knowledge workers of a large automotive company.

Survey Development

The exploratory questionnaire was designed based on various constructs, theories and recent research questions (Kankanhalli et al., 2005; Randrup et al., 2016; Seeber et al., 2019; Siemon et al., 2017). The first part (**Part I**), consists of demographic questions, like age, sex and profession (or student status). The second part (**Part II**) starts with a definition of a VC as stated in the theoretical background section. This part also asks for previous usage, experience and touchpoints with VAs or similar applications of AI. The following table presents the questions from Part II.

Table 1. Touchpoints and previous experience with VA or similar intelligent services.

Part II: Touchpoints and previous experience
Did you ever use or are you currently using any virtual assistant, voice assistant or similar? *(Apple Siri, Google Assistant, Amazon Alexa, Microsoft Cortana, other)*
If you're not using any virtual assistants, can you imagine to use them in the future? *(Open question)*
In which areas can you imagine the use of virtual assistants? *(Marketing, sales, production, logistics, research & development, human resources, finance, other)*

The third part (**Part III**) asked for possible requirements and a conceptual implementation. Additionally, it consists of open questions for future possible tasks of a VC, whether specific tasks can be fully executed by a VC, how the collaboration with a VC can reduce workload and how a possible VCs could look like. The questions need to be answered on a 5-point Likert scale (1=strongly disagree to 5=strongly agree) or as yes/no answers. The following table presents the questions from Part III.

In the fourth part (**Part IV**), the relevance of certain collaboration principles is asked. The questions aim to further investigate the phenomena of social responses to computers by individuals. Studies show

Table 2. Conception, conceptual implementation and requirements

Part III: Conception, conceptual implementation and requirements
Can you imagine working with a virtual collaborator (VC)?
A VC may also handle sensitive data.
The collaboration should be the same as with human team members.
For successful collaboration, a VC must be subject to stricter rules than human team members.
I expect similar group dynamics as in pure human teams.
A VC can also take on the role of a team leader.
Would you accept instructions from a VC in equal measure as from a human person?
If tasks are shared within a team, a VC should have simpler/less difficult tasks than the other team members.
Which tasks should a VC never take on in any case? *(Open question)*
Can you imagine completely replacing human-made work with a VC?
→ If yes, what kind of tasks. *(Open question)*
In what form should a VC appear to you?

that individuals mindlessly apply social rules and expectations when interacting with computers, even though users know that the computer is not a person (Nass & Moon, 2000). However, when the purpose of the computer is to imitate and act like a human, the application of social rules and responses, as well as the expectations towards the computer's interaction might change. Within collaboration, various social mechanisms and principles exist, which individuals adhere to successfully collaborate, which Part IV of the survey aims to investigate in a human-machine setting. These questions are based on defined principles of collaboration compiled by Siemon et al. (2017), which are reciprocity (Fehr et al., 2002; Kankanhalli et al., 2005), benevolence (Mayer et al., 1995; Riegelsberger et al., 2005; Rusman et al., 2010), trust (J. S. Elson et al., 2018; Riegelsberger et al., 2005; Schroeder & Schroeder, 2018), common goal (Randrup et al., 2016), mutual respect (Kadefors, 2004), commitment (Randrup et al., 2016) and team awareness (Hilliges et al., 2007). The questions need to be answered on a 5-point Likert scale (1=not relevant to 5=very relevant) and are presented in the following table.

Table 3. Relevance of collaboration principles

Part IV: Relevance of collaboration principles	Principle of collaboration
When I share knowledge with a virtual collaborator (VC), I expect to get back knowledge when I need it.	Reciprocity
I expect a VC to work benevolently with me.	Benevolence
I want to be able to trust a VA.	Trust
I expect a VC to treat me with respect.	Respect
I expect a VC to pursue the common goal.	Common goal
I expect a VC to do his tasks conscientiously.	Commitment
I expect a VC to know me and all the team members.	Team awareness

Participants

The survey was carried out to two different target groups, that regularly work in teams. On the one hand, the questionnaire was sent to undergraduate and graduate university students, who collectively learn together to achieve a common learning goal. Collaborative learning means the active engagement of students to solve academic or school tasks in order to improve their individual education (Barkley et al., 2014). On the other hand, the questionnaire was sent to knowledge workers of a large automotive company, where teamwork is a common tool to collectively solve problems and create value (Janz et al., 2006).

Results

Overall 285 people participated in the survey, with 144 fully completing it. From these completed surveys, 103 are male and 41 are female. 78 participants are students (students of computer science, technology-oriented business administration, economics, engineering, or other technological studies) and 59 are working in a company, whereas 7 participants are neither students nor working in a company (e.g. vocational training). The majority of the participants (67 in total) are between the age 25 and 29, whereas 38 participants are between 18-24 and 39 participants are older than 30 (**Part I**). The results show that 42% of the participants did not use any current available VAs like Apple's Siri (used by 38%), Amazon's Alexa (8%), Microsoft's Cortana (6%) or Google Assistant (33%). However, the majority of the participants see potential benefits of VAs in the private sector as well as in marketing, sales, production and logistics. 69% of the participants that did not or are not using any VAs, can imagine using them in the future (**Part II**). The following table shows the results of the third part of the survey about the conception, possible conceptual implementation and requirements of a VC and the fourth part asking whether principles of collaboration are conceived as important when working with a VC.

Table 4. Results of Part III and Part III of the questionnaire

Results Part III:	**1=strongly disagree to 5=strongly agree**
Can you imagine working with a virtual collaborator?	M=3.66 SD=1.11
If tasks are shared within a team, a VC should have simpler/less difficult tasks than the other team members?	M=3.55 SD=1.15
A VC may also handle sensitive data?	M=2.56 SD=1.30
The collaboration should be the same as with human team members.	M=2.39 SD=1.11
For successful collaboration, a VC must be subject to stricter rules than human team members.	M=3.83 SD=1.12
I expect similar group dynamics as in pure human teams.	M=2.45 SD=1.29
A VC can also take on the role of a team leader.	M=1.72 SD=1.09
Would you accept instructions from a VC in equal measure as from a human person?	Yes=31% No=69%
Can you imagine completely replacing human-made work with a VC?	Yes=39% No=61%
Part IV: Results	**1=strongly disagree to 5=strongly agree**
When I share knowledge with a virtual collaborator (VC), I expect to get back knowledge when I need it.	M=4.08 SD=1.09
I expect a VC to work benevolently with me.	M=4.01 SD=1.13
I want to be able to trust a VC.	M=4.23 SD=1.11
I expect a VC to treat me with respect.	M=3.57 SD=1.23
I expect a VC to pursue the common goal.	M=3.98 SD=1.13
I expect a VC to do his tasks conscientiously.	M=4.38 SD=1.04
I expect a VC to know me and all the team members.	M=3.69 SD=1.13

Participants state that with the help of a VC, up to 60% of the workload can be reduced and that the relevance of VCs and AI is drastically increasing. However, most participants only imagine a reduction of workload around 20%. In the next section the results including insightful answers to the open questions are discussed.

DISCUSSION

The results reveal that a substantial part of the participants is not using any VAs in their daily life (42%), because of mistrust ("I prefer to find out the things myself."; "I fear being monitored"; "Skepticism and distrust"), because VAs still don't work as good as needed ("Sometimes doesn't understand what I want") or because they are considered as useless. Apple's Siri and Google Assistant are the most used VAs mentioned by the participants. Overall, Part III reveals a somewhat inconclusive opinion about VCs. Participants can imagine working with a VC, but only when a VC is subject to stricter rules and works on less complex tasks. Whether a VC is allowed to deal with sensitive data, was rated very indecisively, with a mean of 2.56 and the highest standard deviation of the survey (SD=1.3). However, participants do agree on the fact that a VC should not work as a team leader. This leads to the conclusion, that participants do perceive a VC as unequal to other team members, don't conceive a collaboration with a VC the same as with solely human partners, do not completely trust in a VC and would not accept instructions from a VC in equal measure as from a human person. However, the results show, that the answers are close to the mean of the scale (3) and are only distinctive on a few questions. Tasks mentioned by the participants that VCs should not take are executive activities, critical decision making, vital tasks or creative tasks. When it comes to completely replacing human-made work with a VC, only 39% of the participants agree and comment that especially easy tasks can be done by VCs, but "there must always be a last means of human control." Participants name tasks like "Organize appointments", "Write summaries of lecture scripts", "Conduct systematic literature reviews", "Help writing mid-term paper", "Write emails and communicate with clients" or "Secretarial duties" that should and can be done by VCs. Some participants did not answer this question, as they could not imagine any relevant tasks a VC can adopt. The participants state that the workload can be reduced significantly and that a VC can be beneficial in the professional environment as well as in the private sphere. Overall, this part indicates that the conception of a VC is unclear and participants are primarily skeptical towards VCs in a coequal manner. Part IV however, reveals that participants expect a VC to comply to the rules of collaboration. A VC should be reciprocal, trustworthy, respectful, have commitment and work benevolently with all team members towards a common goal. Surprisingly the lowest score is respect, followed by team awareness. This is backed by comments, that a VC should not take tasks involving empathy, personal conflicts or social relationships.

No significant differences between the students and the knowledge worker of the automotive firm could be found in either of the collaboration rules. In summon it can be said, that participants expect a perfect collaboration partner, following the principles of collaboration. However, similar group dynamics are not expected when collaborating with AI and the collaboration setting should be designed differently. These questions are not asked consistently and do not show a substantial tendency. The VC should occur in a realistic form, which is for example a combination of voice and avatar. The participants explicitly decide against a solely text-based or voice-based VC and prefer a more realistic form that has the abilities to talk, write and has a natural appearance.

In summary, it can be said, that the exploratory study provides concrete requirements for a VC. Based on the results, a VC should be a trustworthy collaborator, that rather assists and works on simpler and less relevant tasks. Still, the VC should follow the common goal and conscientiously work to reach it. The appearance should be realistic and the VC should be able to use and understand voice and text at the same time. The VC should not be allowed to make relevant decisions or lead the group and should be subject to stricter rules. Overall, the participants are indecisive considering a conclusive conception of a VC but conceive a VC more like a VA. A possible explanation is that it is still hard to imagine working together with an AI in a coequal manner. Participants stated that "it's difficult to imagine working with an AI" and that "for me, the idea that a robot gives orders is still too far away". Table 5 summarizes the results and presents the artifact of the virtual collaborator as a persona with its tasks, level of autonomy, behavior and appearance.

Table 5. Concept of a virtual collaborator

The Virtual Collaborator		
	Characteristics of a VC	**Not characteristics of a VC**
Tasks and roles	Tasks: Assisting tasks, calculations, research, organization, data acquisition, data processing, evaluation, monitoring, planning Roles: Co-ordinator, resource investigator, expert, mediator	Tasks: Executive activities, critical decision making, vital tasks, creative tasks Roles: team leader, decision maker
Autonomy	Independent work structuring, free resource allocation, independent task selection	Far-reaching decision-making, authorizing power, articulate orders
Behavior	Proactive, supporting, convincing, demanding, challenging, stimulating, reciprocal, trustful, respectful, benevolent, conscientiously	Insisting, manipulating, rude, dominating, irresponsible

CONCLUSION AND OUTLOOK

The aim of this exploratory study was to provide insights about the conception of team workers (students and knowledge workers) on future collaboration, where a VC works in a coequal manner. A questionnaire was designed, carried out and answered by 144 participants who are regularly working in teams (i.e. university students and knowledge worker from a large automotive company). The questionnaire was designed based on various theories and constructs of computer supported collaboration and recent research questions. Even if the results do not reveal any clear conclusions about the exact design and behavior of a VC, it is still possible to set out an essential direction. Based on the results of our study and current research, the concept of a VC was constructed, which consists of potential roles, tasks, level of autonomy and behavior. This construct can be used as a guideline to design and implement a VC in collaboration scenarios. Furthermore, it serves as a basis and first starting point for future research and, in particular, to examine individual aspects more closely.

The conception of the participants that VAs and possible VCs still don't work as satisfying as required, should challenge practice to further develop AI and especially consider collaboration features within their services. Current VAs are limited to features that solely assist the user, like chatbots that are implemented in support or voice assistants like Apple's Siri. Due to the increasing availability of AI services like Facebook Wit.AI, Google TensorFlow, IBM Watson and others, developers and researchers could implement rudimentary VCs and test certain aspects. In the sense of the Design Science Research Paradigm, new artifacts could be tested and new design theories can be evaluated, leading to new insights for collaboration research and technology.

Additionally, our data set could provide further insights by identifying relations or differences between diverse aspects. A correlation analysis for example, could inform, whether there are relations between certain collaboration principles and specific requirements of a VC.

In summary, it can be said, that the novel research endeavor of AI, actively collaborating with humans and working in teams is still in its infancy. With our study, we provided a foundation for future research that can lead to new collaboration theories, mechanisms, artifacts and guidelines.

REFERENCES

Aleksander, I. (2017). Partners of humans: A realistic assessment of the role of robots in the foreseeable future. *Journal of Information Technology*, *32*(1), 1–9. doi:10.105741265-016-0032-4

Anderson, J., Rainie, L., & Luchsinger, A. (2018). *Artificial intelligence and the future of humans*. Pew Research Center.

Babbie, E. (2015). *The practice of social research*. Nelson Education.

Barkley, E. F., Cross, K. P., & Major, C. H. (2014). *Collaborative Learning Techniques: A Handbook for College Faculty*. John Wiley & Sons.

Borghoff, U. M., & Schlichter, J. H. (2000). Computer-Supported Cooperative Work. In *Computer-Supported Cooperative Work* (pp. 87–141). Springer., doi:10.1007/978-3-662-04232-8_2

Briggs, R. O., De Vreede, G.-J., & Nunamaker, J. F. Jr. (2003). Collaboration engineering with ThinkLets to pursue sustained success with group support systems. *Journal of Management Information Systems*, *19*(4), 31–64. doi:10.1080/07421222.2003.11045743

Briggs, R. O., Reinig, B. A., & de Vreede, G.-J. (2006). Meeting satisfaction for technology-supported groups: An empirical validation of a goal-attainment model. *Small Group Research*, *37*(6), 585–611. doi:10.1177/1046496406294320

Chan, T.-W. (1995). Artificial agents in distance learning. *International Journal of Educational Telecommunications*, *1*(2), 263–282.

Coronado, M., Iglesias, C. A., Carrera, Á., & Mardomingo, A. (2018). A cognitive assistant for learning java featuring social dialogue. *International Journal of Human-Computer Studies*, *117*, 55–67. doi:10.1016/j.ijhcs.2018.02.004

Davis, F. D. (1985). *A Technology Acceptance Model for Empirically Testing New End-user Information Systems: Theory and Results*. Massachusetts Institute of Technology.

Dennis, A. R., Valacich, J. S., Connolly, T., & Wynne, B. E. (1996). Process Structuring in Electronic Brainstorming. *Information Systems Research*, *7*(2), 268–277. doi:10.1287/isre.7.2.268

Diehl, M., & Stroebe, W. (1987). Productivity loss in brainstorming groups: Toward the solution of a riddle. *Journal of Personality and Social Psychology*, *53*(3), 497–509. doi:10.1037/0022-3514.53.3.497

Driskell, J. E., Radtke, P. H., & Salas, E. (2003). Virtual Teams: Effects of Technological Mediation on Team Performance. *Group Dynamics*, *7*(4), 297–323. doi:10.1037/1089-2699.7.4.297

Dulebohn, J. H., & Hoch, J. E. (2017). Virtual teams in organizations. *Human Resource Management Review*, *27*(4), 569–574. doi:10.1016/j.hrmr.2016.12.004

Elson, J., Derrick, D., & Ligon, G. (2020, January 7). *Trusting a Humanoid Robot: Exploring Personality and Trusting Effects in a Human-Robot Partnership*. doi:10.24251/HICSS.2020.067

Elson, J. S., Derrick, D., & Ligon, G. (2018). Examining Trust and Reliance in Collaborations between Humans and Automated Agents. *Hawaii International Conference on System Sciences 2018 (HICSS-51)*. https://aisel.aisnet.org/hicss-51/cl/processes_and_technologies_for_team/6

Fehr, E., Fischbacher, U., & Gächter, S. (2002). Strong reciprocity, human cooperation, and the enforcement of social norms. *Human Nature (Hawthorne, N.Y.)*, *13*(1), 1–25. doi:10.100712110-002-1012-7

Feng, S., & Buxmann, P. (2020, January 7). *My Virtual Colleague: A State-of-the-Art Analysis of Conversational Agents for the Workplace*. doi:10.24251/HICSS.2020.020

Finkbeiner, N., & Morner, M. (2015). The Role of Conditional Cooperation in Organizing Change. In *Management of Permanent Change* (pp. 49–64). Springer Gabler. doi:10.1007/978-3-658-05014-6_3

Fiol, C. M., & O'Connor, E. J. (2005). Identification in Face-to-Face, Hybrid, and Pure Virtual Teams: Untangling the Contradictions. *Organization Science*, *16*(1), 19–32. doi:10.1287/orsc.1040.0101

Gnewuch, U., Morana, S., & Maedche, A. (2017). Towards Designing Cooperative and Social Conversational Agents for Customer Service. *ICIS 2017 Proceedings*. https://aisel.aisnet.org/icis2017/HCI/Presentations/1

Grudin, J. (1994). Computer-supported cooperative work: History and focus. *Computer*, *27*(5), 19–26. doi:10.1109/2.291294

Guzman, A. (2017). *Making AI Safe for Humans: A Conversation With Siri*. Academic Press.

Hilliges, O., Terrenghi, L., Boring, S., Kim, D., Richter, H., & Butz, A. (2007). Designing for Collaborative Creative Problem Solving. *Proceedings of the 6th ACM SIGCHI Conference on Creativity & Cognition*, 137–146. 10.1145/1254960.1254980

Janz, B. D., Colquitt, J. A., & Noe, R. A. (2006). Knowledge Worker Team Effectiveness: The Role of Autonomy, Interdependence, Team Development, and Contextual Support Variables. *Personnel Psychology*, *50*(4), 877–904. doi:10.1111/j.1744-6570.1997.tb01486.x

Jessup, L. M., Connolly, T., & Galegher, J. (1990). The Effects of Anonymity on GDSS Group Process with an Idea-Generating Task. *Management Information Systems Quarterly*, *14*(3), 313–321. doi:10.2307/248893

Jessup, S., Gibson, A., Capiola, A., Alarcon, G., & Borders, M. (2020, January 7). *Investigating the Effect of Trust Manipulations on Affect over Time in Human-Human versus Human-Robot Interactions*. doi:10.24251/HICSS.2020.068

Kadefors, A. (2004). Trust in project relationships—Inside the black box. *International Journal of Project Management*, *22*(3), 175–182. doi:10.1016/S0263-7863(03)00031-0

Kankanhalli, A., Tan, B. C. Y., & Wei, K.-K. (2005). Contributing Knowledge to Electronic Knowledge Repositories: An Empirical Investigation. *Management Information Systems Quarterly*, *29*(1), 113–143. doi:10.2307/25148670

Këpuska, V., & Bohouta, G. (2018). Next-generation of virtual personal assistants (Microsoft Cortana, Apple Siri, Amazon Alexa and Google Home). *2018 IEEE 8th Annual Computing and Communication Workshop and Conference (CCWC)*, 99–103. 10.1109/CCWC.2018.8301638

Lee, S., Lee, J., & Lee, K. (2017). Designing Intelligent Assistant Through User Participations. *Proceedings of the 2017 Conference on Designing Interactive Systems*, 173–177. 10.1145/3064663.3064733

Lu, H., Li, Y., Chen, M., Kim, H., & Serikawa, S. (2018). Brain Intelligence: Go beyond Artificial Intelligence. *Mobile Networks and Applications*, *23*(2), 368–375. doi:10.100711036-017-0932-8

Maedche, A., Morana, S., Schacht, S., Werth, D., & Krumeich, J. (2016). Advanced User Assistance Systems. *Business & Information Systems Engineering*, *58*(5), 367–370. doi:10.100712599-016-0444-2

Mayer, R. C., Davis, J. H., & Schoorman, F. D. (1995). An integrative model of organizational trust. *Academy of Management Review*, *20*(3), 709–734. doi:10.5465/amr.1995.9508080335

McTear, M., Callejas, Z., & Griol, D. (2016). The conversational interface. Springer, 6(94), 102.

McTear, M. F. (2004). *Spoken dialogue technology: Toward the conversational user interface*. Springer Science & Business Media. doi:10.1007/978-0-85729-414-2

McTear, M. F. (2017). The rise of the conversational interface: A new kid on the block? Lecture Notes in Computer Science (Including Subseries Lecture Notes in Artificial Intelligence and Lecture Notes in Bioinformatics), 10341, 38–49. Scopus. doi:10.1007/978-3-319-69365-1_3

Mondal, S., & Nandi, G. C. (2018). *Personal robot: Towards developing a complete humanoid robot assistant using the Internet of Things*. Scopus., doi:10.1109/UIC-ATC.2017.8397453

Nass, C., & Moon, Y. (2000). Machines and Mindlessness: Social Responses to Computers. *The Journal of Social Issues*, *56*(1), 81–103. doi:10.1111/0022-4537.00153

Nilsson, N. J. (2014). *Principles of Artificial Intelligence*. Morgan Kaufmann.

Pearl, C. (2016). *Designing Voice User Interfaces: Principles of Conversational Experiences*. O'Reilly Media, Inc.

Piumsomboon, T., Lee, Y., Lee, G., & Billinghurst, M. (2017). CoVAR: A Collaborative Virtual and Augmented Reality System for Remote Collaboration. *SIGGRAPH Asia 2017 Emerging Technologies*, 3:1–3:2. doi:10.1145/3132818.3132822

Ram, A., Prasad, R., Khatri, C., Venkatesh, A., Gabriel, R., Liu, Q., Nunn, J., Hedayatnia, B., Cheng, M., & Nagar, A. (2018). *Conversational ai: The science behind the alexa prize.* ArXiv Preprint ArXiv:1801.03604

Randrup, N., Druckenmiller, D., & Briggs, R. O. (2016). Philosophy of Collaboration. *2016 49th Hawaii International Conference on System Sciences (HICSS).*

Resnick, M., Myers, B., Nakakoji, K., Shneiderman, B., Pausch, R., Selker, T., & Eisenberg, M. (2005). Design Principles for Tools to Support Creative Thinking. *Institute for Software Research.* http://repository.cmu.edu/isr/816

Riegelsberger, J., Sasse, M. A., & McCarthy, J. D. (2005). The mechanics of trust: A framework for research and design. *International Journal of Human-Computer Studies, 62*(3), 381–422. doi:10.1016/j.ijhcs.2005.01.001

Rusman, E., van Bruggen, J., Sloep, P., & Koper, R. (2010). Fostering trust in virtual project teams: Towards a design framework grounded in a TrustWorthiness ANtecedents (TWAN) schema. *International Journal of Human-Computer Studies, 68*(11), 834–850. doi:10.1016/j.ijhcs.2010.07.003

Russell, S. J., & Norvig, P. (2016). *Artificial intelligence: A modern approach.* Pearson Education Limited.

Saffarizadeh, K., Boodraj, M., & Alashoor, T. (2017). Conversational Assistants: Investigating Privacy Concerns, Trust, and Self-Disclosure. *ICIS 2017 Proceedings.* https://aisel.aisnet.org/icis2017/Security/Presentations/19

Schroeder, J., & Schroeder, M. (2018, January 3). Trusting in Machines: How Mode of Interaction Affects Willingness to Share Personal Information with Machines. *Hawaii International Conference on System Sciences.* 10.24251/HICSS.2018.061

Schwartz, J., Hagel, J. III, Wooll, M., & Monahan, K. (2019). Reframing the Future of Work. *MIT Sloan Management Review, 60*(3), 1–6.

Seeber, I., Bittner, E., Briggs, R. O., de Vreede, T., de Vreede, G.-J., Elkins, A., Maier, R., Merz, A. B., Oeste-Reiß, S., Randrup, N., Schwabe, G., & Söllner, M. (2019). Machines as teammates: A research agenda on AI in team collaboration. *Information & Management, 103174.* Advance online publication. doi:10.1016/j.im.2019.103174

Shneiderman, B. (2007). Creativity Support Tools: Accelerating Discovery and Innovation. *Communications of the ACM, 50*(12), 20–32. doi:10.1145/1323688.1323689

Siemon, D., Becker, F., Eckardt, L., & Robra-Bissantz, S. (2017). One for all and all for one—Towards a framework for collaboration support systems. *Education and Information Technologies,* 1–25. doi:10.100710639-017-9651-9

Siemon, D., Eckardt, L., & Robra-Bissantz, S. (2015). Tracking Down the Negative Group Creativity Effects with the Help of an Artificial Intelligence-Like Support System. *2015 48th Hawaii International Conference on System Sciences (HICSS),* 236–243. 10.1109/HICSS.2015.37

Siemon, D., Strohmann, T., & Robra-Bissantz, S. (2019). Towards the Conception of a Virtual Collaborator. *Proceedings of the Workshop on Designing User Assistance in Intelligent Systems,* 7–9.

Skalski, P., & Tamborini, R. (2007). The role of social presence in interactive agent-based persuasion. *Media Psychology*, *10*(3), 385–413. doi:10.1080/15213260701533102

Spinella, L. (2018). *Intelligent Virtual Assistants 101*. Interactions Resource Center. https://resources.interactions.com/library/intelligent-virtual-assistants-101/

Strohmann, T., Fischer, S., Siemon, D., Brachten, F., Lattemann, C., Robra-Bissantz, S., & Stieglitz, S. (2018). Virtual Moderation Assistance: Creating Design Guidelines for Virtual Assistants Supporting Creative Workshops. *Proceedings of the 22nd Pacific Asia Conference on Information Systems.*

Vance, A., Elie-Dit-Cosaque, C., & Straub, D. W. (2008). Examining Trust in Information Technology Artifacts: The Effects of System Quality and Culture. *Journal of Management Information Systems*, *24*(4), 73–100. doi:10.2753/MIS0742-1222240403

Venkatesh, V., Morris, M. G., Davis, G. B., & Davis, F. D. (2003). User Acceptance of Information Technology: Toward a Unified View. *Management Information Systems Quarterly*, *27*(3), 425–478. doi:10.2307/30036540

Voigt, M., & Bergener, K. (2013). Enhancing Creativity in Groups – Proposition of an Integrated Framework for Designing Group Creativity Support Systems. *2013 46th Hawaii International Conference on System Sciences (HICSS)*, 225–234. 10.1109/HICSS.2013.195

Wilks, Y. (2006). *Artificial companions as a new kind of interface to the future internet*. Academic Press.

Zhao, S. (2006). Humanoid social robots as a medium of communication. *New Media & Society*, *8*(3), 401–419. doi:10.1177/1461444806061951

ENDNOTE

1 https://www.youtube.com/watch?v=D5VN56jQMWM

Chapter 6
E-Collaboration in Educational Organizations:
Opportunities and Challenges in Virtual Learning Environments and Learning Spaces

Sofia Th. Papadimitriou
Hellenic Open University, Greece

Spyros Papadakis
Hellenic Open University, Greece

ABSTRACT

The chapter explores the use of virtual learning environments (VLE) to support learning spaces in schools/universities and illustrates their advantages to enhance e-collaboration and its key dimensions. Case studies of learning management systems (LMSs) point out the use of synchronous or asynchronous communication and highlight the advantages, the requirements, and the relevant constraints. In particular, this chapter emphasizes in the development of e-collaborative experiences at schools/universities based on LMSs to support both students and educators in their complex work. VLEs will be presented aiming to e-collaboration and their numerous services to enhance differentiated pedagogy. Case studies of e-collaborating in communities of practice and exemplary LMSs are illustrated in a comparative table highlighting how they support key dimensions of e-collaboration. Finally, the chapter highlights discussion themes raised by e-collaborating in VLEs and generally in learning spaces. Proposals for further development of e-collaboration and conclusions are drawn and commented.

DOI: 10.4018/978-1-7998-4891-2.ch006

Copyright © 2021, IGI Global. Copying or distributing in print or electronic forms without written permission of IGI Global is prohibited.

INTRODUCTION

Today's students, an expression used by Marc Prensky in his paper "*Digital natives, digital immigrants*" back in 2001, represent the Net generation having grown up within digital technology. To use his own words, Prensky said for them *they have spent their entire lives surrounded by and using computers, videogames, digital music players, video cams, cell phones, and all the other toys and tools of the digital age [....] Computer games, email, the Internet, cell phones and instant messaging are integral parts of their lives* (Tapscott 1998, 2009; Prensky 2001; Palfrey and Gasser 2008, Bayne 2011).

Hence, pupils and students of the *Net Generation (Net Gen)* need flexible studies and strongly connected with contemporary technologies. These needs of students today lead to the increasing importance of redefining educational *physical & online space*. On the other hand, all, educational organizations face the challenge to make the shift from in person learning in class or campus to a blended environment of combining face-to-face and online activities. A new teaching and learning blended ecosystem for all educational organizations rises. Collaborating in both physical and virtual spaces (*Learning Spaces*) is a key aspect of that blended ecosystem.

The chapter explores the use of *Virtual Learning Environments (VLE)* to support *Learning Spaces* in Schools/Universities and illustrate their advantages to enhance **e-collaboration** and its key dimensions. VLEs are Web-based platforms that provide teachers with a concrete structure for the creation, storage, and access to online courses which use resources, activities, interactions and different stages of assessments. Case studies of *Learning Management System (LMSs)*, point out the use of various services of synchronous or asynchronous communication and highlight the advantages, the requirements and the relevant constraints. In particular this chapter emphasizes in the development of e-collaborative experiences at Schools/Universities based on LMSs to support both students and educators in their complex work.

This chapter introduces teaching at a distance and the essential need of supporting students in the **first unit**. The **second unit** presents definitions for e-Collaboration and the key dimensions to achieve it. It also focuses on the key aspect of collaborating in both physical and virtual spaces (*Learning Spaces*) aiming to the Net generation learners. The **third unit** approaches the concept of *Communities of Practice (CoP)* and focuses on two case studies, those of "etwinning" and "Teachers for Europe" (T4E) as best practices of educational CoPs which promote e-collaboration and use both virtual and physical spaces to enhance collaborative activities. A special "etwinning" project entitledd "Digital stories" is described thoroughly as an exemplar case study of e-collaboration in a Learning Space.

Virtual Learning Environments which support e-collaboration will be presented in **the fourth unit** and their numerous services to enhance differentiated pedagogy. Exemplary LMSs are illustrated in a comparative table highlighting how their services support key dimensions of e-collaboration. Elaborating LMSs, the *Learning Activity Management System (LAMS)* is proposed as an appropriate open *LMS* which serves e-collaborative activities with a structured way.

Finally, the chapter highlights discussion themes raised by e-collaborating with *Virtual Learning Environments* and generally in *Learning Spaces*. Proposals for further development of e-collaboration and conclusions are drawn and commented.

TEACHING AND LEARNING AT A DISTANCE

Supporting Students at a Distance

The integration of the *Information and Communication Technologies (ICT)* has changed radically learning and transforms education. Advanced technologies support learning in the 21st century following all three generations of pedagogy: behaviorism, constructivism and connectivism. Schools and Universities today approach more and more distance and flexible forms of education since learning is possible to happen in areas outside the traditional Class/Campus, occurring anytime and anywhere.

The Distance Learning methodology aims at activating pupils/students guiding them towards an exploratory approach to knowledge and ensures the maximum possible flexibility in space, time and pace of learning. Most students in Distance Learning (Kokkos, 2001; Hatzilakos, Papadakis & Rossiou, 2007):

- need human support in order to use the educational material,
- cannot approach it critically since they have not cultivated the appropriate study skills,
- are not familiar with the ways of approaching in depth the learning objects and using alternative learning resources,
- are not familiar with writing essays,
- haven't cultivated appropriate self-organization skills and learning autonomy.

These multiple levels of support are provided by educators in Distance Learning (DL). Educators need to combine multiple roles as facilitators, coordinators of learning experiences, developers of pro learning circumstances (Athansoula-Reppa, 2006). Students on their end in DL, expect from educators, coordination, encouragement, counseling, comprehension of concerns, direct response to questions, problem solving, appropriate guidance in activities and exchange of views (Fung & Carr, 2000). In addition, they expect from educators to be clear in describing the goals and the objectives of each activity, having proper administration, sensitivity in individualized needs, new ideas, proposals, DL practices, learning approaches, authentic educational material aimed at their goals, excellent knowledge of their field and the ability to enrich the educational process. The usual reasons for students' failure in e-learning courses are (Jenkins & Vissere, 2001):

- the poor instructional design of the course from not experienced educators,
- technical issues,
- the lack of students' time,
- students' insufficient support in general,
- the lack of supporting students' individualized learning preferences, in particular.

The development of bilateral interactions between educators and students and also among students is most critical for achieving direct or indirect communication. Between face-to-face (f2f) meetings, communication is delivered in asynchronous mode aiming at continuing of discussion and interaction between educators and students. The emerging question is: "*How to instructionally design learning experiences in which students could participate to gain high degrees of interactions and build new knowledge in a common space, in or outside the Class/Campus?*"

Teaching at a Distance

Educators in DL guide and direct students in the learning process and strategies using appropriate instructional design, providing feedback on evaluation of the essays and communicating constantly f2f or through the web. They focus on the significance of metacognitive activities for self-evaluation of the learning process. Furthermore, they highlight the set of competences regarding self-regulation and organization of students. Implementing the essays is the primary way for students in understanding the educational content in the framework of distance studies, whereby students regard themselves as the main responsible for their learning (Vasala, Hatziplis & Lionarakis, 2007).

Evaluating students' essays is one of the most significant features of distance teaching. Educators encourage students' engagement in activities orientated to support metacognitive issues of concern as commenting essays, structuring meta-cognitive exercises, motivating them in exchanging views and in keeping a personal diary recording thoughts regarding their attempts and ongoing progress (Fanariti & Spanaka, 2009).

According DL principles, educators use techniques which enhance the active participation and are based on experiential learning in order to achieve specific learning objectives of the course and to lead in personal goals as well. The convergence of tutor and students' goals leads to eliminate the distance between them. The more effective the convergence is, the smaller the distance remains (Moore, 1973, 1980).

e-Collaboration

Collaboration at a distance supported from advanced learning technologies, is today feasible and effective (*e-Collaboration*) and it also consists a broad field for research and experiment. E-Collaboration can be defined as "*Collaboration among individuals engaged in a common task using modern networking technologies*" according Nagasundaram (2008). Another definition of the researchers Bouras and Tsiatsios (2018) for e-collaboration is "*collaboration, which is conducted without face-to-face interaction among individuals or members of virtual teams engaged in common task using information and communication technologies*".

Both synchronous and asynchronous communication technologies, combined with the development of team dynamics contributes to solve many problems faced today by learners in distance education (Vasala, Hatziplis & Lionarakis, 2007). Pilot studies in the Open University (Freake & Papathanassiou, 2006, Cornelius & Macdonald, 2008) indicate that supporting student tends to be "*the critical factor for successful studies*" therefore educators need to use fluently all means and communication methods and adapt them depending on the case (Papadimitriou & Lionarakis, 2009).

Many LMSs have been developed with a wealth of user-friendly tools, aiming to enhance communication, e-collaboration and co-creativity. Team building cultivates a common sense in the team which is involved in collaborative activities, so it is a fundamental factor through-out a joint project. Key dimensions of e-collaboration which make deeper interactions between members of a team are discussions in forums, interactive videoconferencing, peer assessment and co-creation of digital content. Next units will focus on each one of the aforementioned dimensions (Papadimitriou et. al, 2017).

DISCUSSIONS IN FORUMS

Discussions in forums in VLEs regard course discussions, live seminar discussions, study groups, examinations and technical support. Students create their topics and participate in threads of comments, expressing their arguments, thoughts and questions.

Interactive Videoconference

Interactive Videoconferencing provides opportunities to students to exchange views, share data, and participate actively in a dynamic interactive environment with collaborative construction of knowledge in real time (Anastasiadis, 2007). Pedagogical, technological, administrative and financial issues should be taken into account for designing and implementing an Interactive Videoconference. The proposed pedagogical framework of using videoconferencing is based on:

- Interdisciplinary approach
- Social constructivism theories
- Project based learning
- Distance learning principles by the *American Distance Education Consortium* (ADEC, nd) and
- Evaluation method combining qualitative and quantitative measurements.

Interactive Videoconferencing is not only a tool of synchronous e-learning but it can be exploited afterwards in asynchronous format supporting CoPs. Students who haven't participated in real time are able to view the recording on demand, either in total or partially. Segmented units of videoconferencing aiming to concrete learning objectives could be exploited asynchronously, as "social objects" to enhance interactions in CoPs (Papadimitriou et. al, 2007). Therefore, Interactive Videoconferencing consists an innovative way of building communities beyond spatial constraints.

Peer Assessment

Peer assessment is a learning process whereby students grade assignments or tests for their peers, based on benchmarks provided by the teacher. Rubrics are often used in conjunction with peer-assessment.

This practice is employed to improve students' understanding of the learning materials as well as their meta-cognitive skills. Students can learn from grading their peers' work, understanding the grading process and recognizing their own strengths and weaknesses. By getting involved in this process, they are moving towards a better understanding of how to proceed with their work and also learn better strategies for improving their test results.

Co-Creation

Co-creation is a collaborative process which takes place when many non-pre-defined problems occur. Co-Creation can be understood as a process to deal with real local or global challenges in new ways, addressing difficult and complex problems and delivering fundamental life-changing results. The *Co-creation Methodology* could be implemented following the steps below (Papadimitriou et al, 2017):

- Introduction
    - Exploring the concepts of collaboration and co-creation, pre-defined and non-pre-defined problems.
    - Prototyping problem insights.
    - Approaching the benefits.
- Brainstorming
    - Participants brainstorm and research in small teams on ideas by "solving" the problem-challenge and proposing subjects in their disciplines or combining them.
- Presenting and selecting the ideas

Participants present their ideas to the plenary. The educators pitch the ideas to start their project by:

- Voting for the proposed ideas and selecting a number of them.
- Shaping one group for each idea.
    - Working in groups for each idea

Participants working in groups:

- Define their needs in the synthesis of technical or conceptual materials.
- Plan extensively experimentation in progress.
- Explore "secrets" of successful projects and teams behind them.
- Search and use open educational resources.
- Get mentoring.
- Develop their ideas in projects collaboration.
- Discuss and select platforms to publish their final digital projects.
    - Synthesis - Presentation
- Groups present final versions to other teams – feedback and discussion

Co-creation at a distance can be achieved when participants are far away among them and they are able to deliver digital content or content on the cloud following the previous methodology. Interactions such as brainstorming, presenting and selecting the ideas could be organized using synchronous communication.

Collaborating in Virtual and Physical Spaces

Networks' development, VLEs and modern learning theories compose the new area of *Learning Spaces (LS)* aiming at enhancing interactivity between educators, learners and educational content, opening up new perspectives in DL and also collaboration among students.

Learning Spaces is a broader concept than "classroom/campus" towards the convergence of the *net generation (Net Gen)* students, current learning theories and ICT. The Net Gen students have adopted rapidly and embraced ICT especially the web-based services. "*Therefore, the concept of classroom has both expanded and evolved; virtual space has taken its place alongside the physical space*" (Brown, 2013).

The resources used in education today tend to be digital and delivered via environments on the Web. In addition, internet connectivity is increasingly portable. So, learning is possible to happen, in spaces outside the traditional classroom, occurring anytime and anywhere.

Learning Spaces Aiming to the Net Generation Learners

The Net Gen students are social and team oriented, comfortable with multitasking, and generally positive in their outlook, and have a hands-on, "let's build it" approach—all encouraged by the IT resources at their disposal. Net Gen students have embraced IT, having a mutually influential -almost symbiotic-relationship (Brown, 2013). Universities can offer to digital natives the opportunity of a flexible model in their studies with partial physical or spatial presence.

Information today is plentiful and the student's role is not to memorize or even understand everything, but being able to find and apply knowledge when and where it is needed based on connectivism learning (Anderson & Dron, 2011; Siemens, 2005; Downes, 2007). The ubiquitous networked connections between people, digital artifacts, and content, leads for seeking and defining "social objects" to enhance participation, reflections and interactions in CoPs among students.

According JISC, (2013), *a Learning Space should be able to motivate learners and promote learning as an activity, support collaborative as well as formal practice, provide a personalized and inclusive environment, and be flexible in the face of changing needs.* The design of its individual LS needs to be (JISC, 2013):

- Flexible – to accommodate both current and evolving pedagogies.
- Future-proofed – to enable space to be re-allocated and reconfigured.
- Bold – to look beyond tried and tested technologies and pedagogies.
- Creative – to energies and inspire learners and tutors.
- Supportive – to develop the potential of all learners.
- Enterprising – to make each space capable of supporting different purposes.

Teaching and learning in Learning Spaces is integrated in a continuous blended mode combining *(Table 1)*:

- Face-to-face activities using methods and practices in experiential, situated, active, collaborative problem solving, project-based learning.
- Online activities according personalized, adaptive and collaborative learning.

In this context, pupils/students are able to collaborate asynchronously in the Learning Space "e-Class/Campus" (*e-Class/Campus-LS*):

- participating in forums,
- working in groups for completing specific tasks or assignments,
- creating collaborative projects,
- shaping study groups, discussing and exchanging their thoughts, ideas on key points of their study or asking peer support in their assignments,
- conducting peer evaluation of assignments.

Synchronous mode practices of collaboration in the "e-Class/Campus-LS", include:

- polls, real time interactions,
- interactive videoconferences,
- webinars (Web-based seminars), e-workshops,
- serious games,
- simulations and applications.

Students can use avatars when they log in the Learning Space, navigate e-lessons and engage in immersive conferencing. Activities in Learning Spaces should use *emotional intelligence* theory (Goleman, 2006) to create a sense of belonging in learning communities and enhance interactions in depth and large scale among students and their educators (*team building*). The key human needs are autonomy, belonging and competence. On the other hand every student is worthy of dignity and respect. Diversity is both inevitable and positive. The Class/Campus should reflect the kind of society in which we want are students to live. LS help most students to learn most things that are essential to a given area of study guided by differentiation of instruction in LS. Respectful tasks, flexible grouping, ongoing assessment/ adjustment and differentiate content, process and product for different pupil/students according to learners' readiness, interests and learning profile.

Table 1. Online and f2f activities in e-Class/Campus-LS

online activities in e-Class/Campus-LS	f2f activities in e-Class/Campus-LS
Personalized Learning • courses • educational material • media • self-paced e-experiments • construction of digital artifacts • assignments	Experiential Learning • experiments • problem solving based projects • enquiry and research-based projects
Active and Collaborative Learning • active learning practices, team building • e-collaborative learning practices based on social objects (group work, debates, discussions, role playing, world café)	Active and Collaborative Learning • active learning practices, team building • collaborative learning practices (group work, debates, discussions, role playing, world café)
Connectivism Learning • avatars, polls • joint activities • study groups • e-experiments • webinars, e-workshops • immersive conferencing	Connectivism Learning • team building • polls • joint activities • study groups

LEARNING IN COMMUNITIES OF PRACTICE

Communities of Practice

DL is highly criticized regarding the support of its methodology in collaborative learning (Avouris & Komis, 2003). Collaboration is a basic parameter in fundamental aspects of human activities as working and learning.

Communities of practice (CoP) are groups for exchanging ideas and new practices, sharing a common interest (Lave & Wenger, 1991; Bruckman & Resnick, 1996) and provide resources and peer-support. Lave & Wenger (1998) consider as a CoP, a community of individuals which is united by common goals, interests and practices.

CoPs have an essential role in distance learning (Palloff & Pratt, 1999). Interactions within the community are non-static and continually transforming procedures, therefore each group is characterized by its own potential.

The meta-analysis of Johnson & Johnson (1990) highlights the value of collaboration in the learning process:

- Students working in a collaborative and non-competitive learning environment, have better performance,
- Students participating in groups solve easier problems,
- Students participating in groups, use more methods and metacognitive strategies,
- Collaborative learning cultivates higher level of thinking,
- New ideas and innovative solutions are being produced in working groups.

Collaborating in a virtual place enhances interactions among members of the CoP with discussions, commenting, social networking applications and the co-creation of digital content in knowledge construction spaces.

Some indicative practices of collaboration according to the Toolkit of Maggie Coats (1992) are brainstorming, discussions, debates, role playing, case studies, group working, and simulations. As Rowntree, (1998) mentioned, "*my recent experience taught me that all principles and practices for collaboration in face-t-o face workshops could be applied even if everyone is in different place and time. We are able to split participants in groups, to engage them in activities related with their project, interact testing and cultivating their relevant skills*".

Modern web-based environments can provide students learning sequences designed particularly for differentiated instruction and the DL educators, oriented to different educational goals each time based on individualized needs. Therefore, sequences of learning activities provide personalized, interactive, just-in-time, current and user-centered services. During their implementation they can be adapted in students learning needs and educators' choices so as to be more effective.

The CoP "Teachers for Europe"

The "*Erasmus KA3 Teachers4Europe: Setting up an Agora for Democratic Culture*" (2018-2021) Program "*will exploit, expand and scale up the Teachers4Europe network (T4E) which has proven to be effective at national and local level during the implementation of successful educational projects about EU in*

Greece since 2011" (Teachers4Europe, nd). The T4E' Ambassadors have the key role for the expansion and scaling-up of the network based on their valuable and long-lasting experience. Their role mainly comprises coordination, mediation, but also the enhancement of networking and keeping alive the CoP of *Teachers4Europe (T4E).*

A central aim is to establish partnerships and joint Projects with countries participating in the Program and beyond. Therefore, Program's Ambassadors should emphasize and encourage communication, both internally and externally, through various actions; In addition, these projects should be oriented to the EU and in particular the six thematic areas of the Program.

The T4E Consortium proposes that joint projects could be implemented via:

§ T4E Platform - the technical support is required in order to create collaboration space for the joint project,
§ the e-Twinning platform "Twinspace",
§ any other means known for organizing joint projects such as Web2.0 tools.

T4E proposes flexible and frequent ways of communication considering differentiated ICT knowledge/skills and availability (e.g. Skype, Messenger, Viber, emails etc.). Moreover, it encourages punctuality in meetings and insists that team decisions are respected.

Team building applies to constant interactions and cooperation with Ambassadors T4E and Teachers4Europe in one's country and Ambassadors T4E in partner countries during the supervision of T4E projects, during Joint projects with Ambassadors T4E in partner countries, and after the completion of Joint projects.

Ambassadors T4E support to T4E at all program stages such as to select partners for Joint projects, project topics and teaching/learning methodologies and techniques, to set explicit, reasonable goals, draw curriculum connections, consider teacher/student needs, make and implement coherent lesson plans, solve classroom problems, submit project materials.

For this purpose, the T4E project proposes to all T4E ambassadors to

- Conduct regular online meetings, and make personalized contacts.
- Identify weaknesses and problems, and suggest differentiated lines of action and tailor-made advice.
- Encourage peer collaboration and communication (e.g. regarding project activities, suggested solutions for classroom problems, EU sources, etc.).
- Make the most of social networks for fast and effective communication.
- Make contacts with and request support from EU experts, institutions or other relevant authorities.
- Organize visits to their venues and/or (online/on-site - LS) presentations, and ensure free materials for trainees.
- Remind team members of the team's Organization Calendar in order to be aware of their responsibilities/deadlines.

The table below illustrates the use of virtual and physical spaces in the CoPs of two major EU programs entitled "etwinning" and "T4E".

Table 2. Virtual and physical spaces in the CoPs of etwinning and T4E

	Virtual Space	Physical Space
eTwinning	Twinspace, MOOCs, Webinars	Professional Development, local and European Conferences and events, network of ambassadors in countries/prefectures
Teachers for Europe	T4E Academy, MOOC, Twinspace, Webinars	Professional Development, local and European Conferences and events, network of ambassadors in countries/prefectures

e-Collaborating in the CoP of "Etwinning"

The eTwinning program offers the TwinSpace, which is a platform for staff (teachers, head teachers, librarians, etc.), working in schools of European countries involved, to communicate, collaborate, develop projects, share and, in short, feel and be part of the most exciting learning community in Europe. eTwinning is co-funded by the Erasmus+, the European program for Education, Training, Youth and Sport and has involved so far 797.058 teachers, 205.119 schools and 106.031 projects (2020). Teachers and students of the eTwinning program are an active and sustainable CoP in Europe, which e-collaborates since 2005 presenting essential joint projects.

One of the most important elements of the *eTwinning program* is collaboration among teachers, students, schools, parents, and local authorities. Teachers work together and organize activities for their students having an active role. The eTwinning projects involve the contribution of each member of the team interacting, investigating, making decisions, respecting each other and gaining by that 21st century skills.

Collaboration activities are activities which lead to a tangible result. They can be digital products like movies, e-books, mind maps, slideshows, quizzes, and all Web2.0 constructions. They could also be the results of a forum discussion or an online meeting.

eTwinning projects offer a framework for project-based learning, which includes collaboration between pupils. Groups of pupils in a class create products and share them with partners' class. They express their thoughts/interactions and they both create new content. One step further in the level of collaboration is that students from different class groups directly collaborate on a common product. In the TwinSpace, for instance, web-pages can be assigned to transnational groups of pupils giving a virtual space where they can work together and share outcomes.

Digital Stories: A Learning Space for Greek and Finish Schools

Two schools of primary education in Greece and Finland collaborated via the *Twinspace* and created the joint project "Digital stories". Both schools used physical space (Drama and Language class) and virtual (Twinspace) to exchange, share and work on their common project and developing by that their own *Learning Space.*

In the Greek 1st Primary School of Sparta, 4 teachers and their team explain how they collaborate in creating the digital stories and sharing them with their partner in the following 10 steps:

1. Composing the story during the Drama Class: Brainstorming as a team on a given idea; Choosing collectively the best ideas for the final oral draft; Dividing their story in sections.
2. Painting images by each student during the Arts Class: images are representative of each section of their story. The most imaginative pictures were scanned and sent by snail mail to Finland.
3. Writing down their script based on the final selection of their pictures during the Language Class.
4. Recording by all students the script during the Drama Class: Rehearsing, recording, and listening.
5. Choosing and creating sound effects during the Drama Class.
6. Assembling and combining the scanned pictures, the edited recordings and the sound effects. Photo editing, audio editing and video editing; Reviewing the finalized story in the Drama Class.
7. Subtitling in English.
8. Sharing progress with school from Finland and exchanging videos
9. Receiving and reviewing our partner's stories in the Drama Class.
10. Sharing with school from Finland:
    - Blogging a web-based portfolio in English,
    - 3 actual story books in Greek,
    - A presentation and an arts exhibition of all the students' paintings that were not chosen for our stories' illustrations

Figure 1. Learning Space in an "etwinning" project

VIRTUAL LEARNING ENVIRONMENTS AND LEARNING SPACES SUPPORTING E-COLLABORATION

Learning Technologies

A learning technology is an orchestration of technologies, necessarily including pedagogies, whether implicit or explicit. Technology sets the beat and the timing while pedagogy defines the moves (Anderson, 2009). Trying to design and support such blended learning activities as mentioned in the previous units, we need learning technologies which have the potential:

- to organize sequences of collaborative learning activities with specific learning outcomes, which also can use the wealth of Open Educational Resources (OER),
- to support designing and authoring sequences of learning activities by educators on their own and
- to monitor students' progress providing relevant data aiming to support personalized learning.

Innovative *Learning Spaces* both physical and virtual can emerge then, using sequences of learning activities designed and developed from educators-tutors in order to combine personal online use and face-to-face support. We present in the following units *VLEs* as learning technologies which support e-collaboration and we explore the various needs of those to enhance differentiated pedagogy.

Moodle

Moodle is a learning platform designed to provide educators, administrators and learners with a single robust, secure and integrated system to create personalized learning environments. Moodle provides a flexible tool-set to support both blended learning and full online courses. The configuration of Moodle integrates easily everything needed for a course using its complete range of built-in features, including external collaborative tools such as forums, wikis, chats and blogs (Moodle, 2020).

Because it is open-source, Moodle can be customized in any way and tailored to individual needs. Its modular set up and interoperable design allows developers to create plugins and integrate external applications to achieve specific functionalities. Extend what Moodle does by using freely available plugins and add-ons, the possibilities are endless.

From a few students to millions of users, Moodle can be scaled to support the needs of both small classes and large organizations. Because of its flexibility and scalability, Moodle has been adapted for use across education, business, non-profit, government, and community contexts.

Supporting a Social Constructionist View by Moodle

Pedagogy and software design are closely intertwined in online learning; therefore the "shape" of the software can help or hinder the teacher in what they are trying to do.

In a true collaborative environment, all are both potential teachers as well as learners. Many of the activities in Moodle are designed to allow students to control common content, such as forums, wikis, glossaries, databases, messaging and so on. This encourages students to add to the total course experience for others.

The Moodle allows administrators and teachers to create new roles with any mix of capabilities they like, for example, students to be allowed to facilitate forums, create quiz questions or even control the course layout. Allowing students more flexibility to do things that were previously thought of as something teachers should do is a huge experiment for Moodle courses (Moodle, 2020).

Progression

Moodle needs to be flexible to cater for a wide variety of needs while remaining simple enough for ordinary teachers to start making good use of the power of the internet for community building and collaborative learning.

Moodle can be seen as a toolbox where teachers can start simply and naturally, and then progress to more and more advanced community facilitation over time. A key objective is teachers being involved with and supported by a community of their peers. A typical progression that a teacher might go through as they learn to use the Moodle tools, is the following:

1. Putting up the handouts (Resources, SCORM)
2. Providing a passive Forum (unfacilitated)
3. Using Quizzes and Assignments (less management)
4. Using the Wiki, Glossary and Database tools (interactive content)
5. Facilitate discussions in Forums, asking questions, guiding
6. Combining activities into sequences, where results feed later activities
7. Introduce external activities and games (internet resources)
8. Using the Survey module to study and reflect on course activity
9. Using peer-review modules like Workshop, giving students more control over grading and even structuring the course in some ways
10. Conducting active research on oneself, sharing ideas in a community of peers

Role-Playing and Scenario Simulations

A popular and effective technique in face-to-face teaching is that of role-playing in scenarios, and this is difficult to be implemented online. For example, an Environmental Science course run a role-playing simulation where some students play the government, some as members of an NGO, some as personnel of an industry for a particular scenario.

Developing role-playing and scenario simulations are between future plans for Moodle developers. New modules are in process where people can be assigned roles within a simulated situation and appear to others anonymously in those roles, interacting in forums, wikis, and all the other tools in Moodle according to the rules of the simulation.

Blackboard Collaborate

Today's learners want new ways to engage and collaborate. Virtual classrooms and online professional development deliver new opportunities to meet learners where they are. Using the Blackboard Collaborate, educators can (Blackboard Collaborate, 2020):

- Inspire and engage learners with the easy to use online collaborative solutions they crave.
- Easily reach students, wherever they are.
- Give students more options to stay engaged with collaborative learning tools for their mobile-enabled lives.
- Organize and make easily Web conferencing with full featured collaboration
- Create mobile-friendly flipped lessons.

Moreover, using the Blackboard Collaborate, students can:

- Learn on demand: pause, rewind, or fast-forward lessons.
- Be in charge of his/her learning experience.
- Participate in class or study groups remotely
- Better collaborate for effective learning

The e-me Digital Educational Platform

The **e-me** Digital Educational Platform for pupils and teachers, implements a safe integrated digital environment for learning, collaboration, communication and networking of all members of the school community. The e-me Platform was developed by CTI Diophantus in Greece (CTI, 2020), to become:

- the personal working environment for every pupil and teacher,
- a safe place for collaboration, communication, sharing of files and utilization of digital content,
- a space for the social networking of pupils and teachers,
- a framework for the integration and operation of external apps,
- a space where the work of pupils, teachers and schools can be made public and showcased.

The e-me features include the creation of collaboration spaces (Hives). Teachers and students communicate in Hives through wall posts and comments, in particular:

- participate in collaborative Hives' blogs or create new ones, create your personal blog and publish posts containing e-me content objects,
- create your e-portfolio and showcase your projects,
- create your own interactive learning objects and interactive educational resources in general (via e-me content app) and share them with other members on the Hive wall,
- participate in collaborative Hives' blogs or create new ones, create your personal blog and publish posts containing e-me content objects,

Additional features of the e-me are "e-me assignments" aiming to create and assign tasks to Hive members and also communication features such as video calls and send real-time personal messages to your contacts.

Table 3. LMSs supporting various dimensions of e-collaboration

	Discussion in forums	Interactive Videoconference	Peer Assessment	Co-creation
Moodle	X Facilitate discussions in Forums, asking questions, guiding	X	Assessment and feedback tools Using the Survey module to study and reflect on course activity Using peer-review modules like Workshop, giving students more control over grading and even structuring the course in some ways	Quizzes slideshows, assignments Wiki, Glossary and Database tools (interactive content) Combining activities into sequences, where results feed later activities Introduce external activities and games (internet resources)
Blackboard Collaborate	X	X	Assessment and feedback tools	Wikis, shared workspace / Work in teams on breakout rooms
e-me	X		Assessment and feedback tools	Hives, blogs, e-portfolio, e-me content, assignments
Open e-class	X	X	Assessment quizzes and online tests Receive feedback for polls and surveys Grading book Attendance Book Statistics	Create, manage and grade online assignments. Create polls and surveys and receive feedback
TwinSpace	X	X Live Events	Assessment and feedback tools	Teacher Bulletin, Pages, Project journal, Live Events, Polls, slideshows, quizzes, brainstorming tools padlet, voki, Journal, Web2.0,
LAMS	X	X	Questions & Answers, Survey, Poll, File Submission, Evaluation, Multiple Choice Questions	Chat and Scribe, Discussion forum, building groups, Branches for individual or group work

Open eclass

The Open eClass platform (Open eClass, 2020) is an integrated *Course Management System (CMS)*. It is the solution offered by *the Greek University Network (GUnet)* to support asynchronous eLearning services. Open eClass has been designed to enhance the learning process; it is distributed for free as open-source software and is actively supported by GUnet. Its main goal lies in the integration and constructive use of the Internet and web technologies in the teaching and learning process.

The enhancement and support of educational activities, for both instructors and students, through a high-quality learning environment remains the *GUnet*'s main goal. In particular the GUnet continues to develop and offer advanced education and training facilities, eliminating the spatial and time constraints of conventional teaching, by exploiting the latest improvements of ICTs and web technologies (GUnet, 2020).

Furthermore, the *GUnet* focuses on flexibility, usability, scalability, free distribution not requiring licenses and maintenance, small functional requirements, independence from the underlying Operating Systems, the use of open standards, the possibility of integration with other network services, clear functional structures (registration, access, course development, management, etc.), interoperability and security as well as ongoing support.

Information, Communication and Collaboration Tools of the Open eClass are the following:

- Announcements: an online announcement board.
- Calendar: basic course events presented in a chronological order.
- Messages: Message exchange between students and instructors.
- Notifications: Alerts for course updates.
- Forum: Unlimited asynchronous conversations.
- Web-conference: real-time communication and collaboration.
- Groups: online collaboration via a shared workspace and a private forum.
- Wiki: Collaborative writing.

Assessment and feedback tools of the Open eClass are the following:

- Exercises: create assessment quizzes and online tests.
- Assignments: Create, manage and grade online assignments.
- Questionnaires: Create polls and surveys and receive feedback.
- Grading book: Keep track of learners' performance.
- Attendance Book: Monitor who attends the course.
- Statistics: View course and user statistics, track learners' participation and progress and create reports

TwinSpace

The TwinSpace is a feature offered by the eTwinning programme, aiming to enhance ways of collaboration. It supports schools, teachers and pupils throughout the overall process of their project which means that TwinSpace helps finding partners in Europe and other participating countries in Asia or Africa, supports all types of interactions, provides the virtual place for joint projects, organizes live-events, and finally disseminates co-creation projects.

Communication tools of the platform for all members of the project are the Twin mail, the twin chat, forums, videoconferences and live-events. *Teacher Bulletin* is a communication tool only visible to teachers. The Twinspace offers 2 ways of communication with anyone who is not taking part in the project. Public *Pages* and the *Project Journal* are two available options to select and share information with different stakeholders like parents and other members of the school community. Giving visibility to the eTwinning project is very important and valuable for the participants.

The option *Pages* are used to tell the story of an etwinning project. Uploaded materials like pictures, videos, presentations and other project outcomes can be presented in a coherent context. *Forum* is a tool to involve participants in an ongoing a-synchronous discussion. Only members with administrator's rights can setup forums.

Non-verbal communication is important for an eTwinning project. Teachers and pupils can create stand-alone albums with e.g. videos and pictures of activities in the options of Pages, Forum posts or Journal posts in order to make the Twinspace more attractive.

In an eTwinning project many teachers and pupils make use of additional tools to create content, than those provided in the Twinspace: e.g. a poll, a slideshow, a quiz, a brainstorming tool padlet, voki, and various Web2.0 tools. Furthermore, teachers can set up *Live Events* for the members of the Twinspace.

The Learning Activities Management System (LAMS)

The LMS *Learning Activity Management System (LAMS)* (Dalziel, 2003) is an open source freely available web-based *Learning Management System* 'inspired' by the *Learning Design model* for designing and delivering online and offline collaborative learning activities. LAMS creates a visual 'drag-and-drop' authoring platform in which the formation, supervision, distribution, storing, sharing and remixing/ repurposing1 of a wide range of offline and online educational activities is possible. These activities can include a range of individual tasks, pair or small group work and whole class activities based on learning objects (content) and collaboration. It functions as an autonomous LMS, or integrated in *Course & Content Management Systems, CMSs* as *Sakai, Blackboard, WebCT, Moodle*, etc.

Figure 2. The LessonLAMS Learning Space

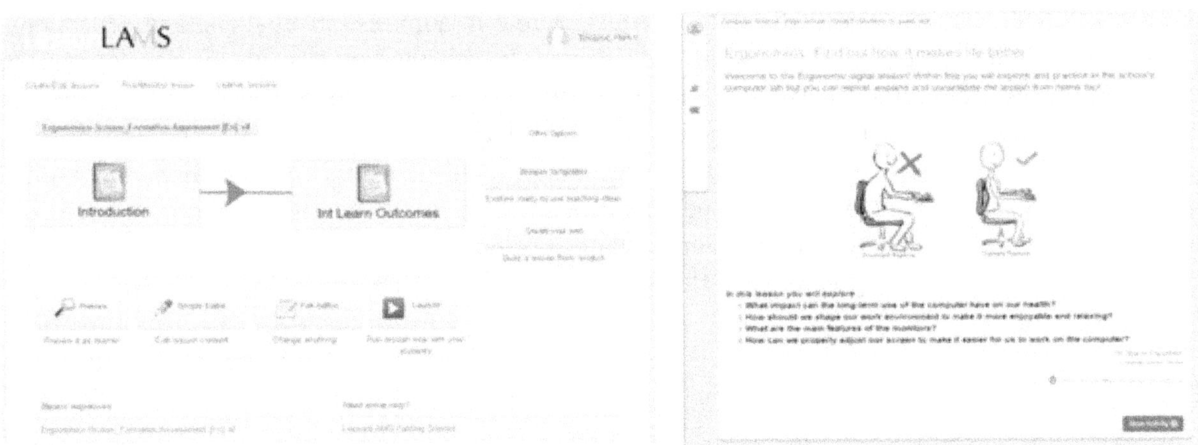

The LessonLAMS Service

In the international Repository, communities of educators can upload and share their own sequences and reuse existing ones freely available with *Creative Commons* licenses or other. Furthermore, an educator can *embed* LAMS lessons in his/her Learning Space as his/her personal blog and also, she/he can create accounts for her/his students. Students execute the sequences and the educator supports them through *LessonLAMS* service (LessonLAMS, nd).

The *LessonLAMS* service disposes also a *LAMS Pedagogical Planner*, a feature which helps course's design based on prior pedagogy strategies and educational techniques by providing exemplary lessons as *templates, ready-to-use teaching ideas*.

LAMS provides a set of tools for authoring activities facilitating:

1. Information (*Notice board, Share Resources, Task list*)
2. Collaboration (*Chat and Scribe, Discussion forum, building groups*)
3. Feedback (*Questions & Answers, Survey, Poll)*
4. Evaluation (*File Submission, Evaluation, Multiple Choice Questions*).
5. Co-creation (*Chat and Scribe, Discussion forum, building groups*)

Activities tools are presented in the authoring area in a simple and comprehensive mode, so as a common user using the familiar technique *drag & drop* can place and combine them to build the modules of her/his learning sequences. The basic rationale behind the *learning design standard* is enhancing collaboration between the learner, the educator, and content and also within learners themselves. It is implemented in synchronous and asynchronous distance activities. Modern collaborative methods and teaching techniques as *Jigsaw* can be designed and implemented easily (Kordaki & Siempos, 2010; Papadakis, Kordaki, & Hadzilacos, 2007) even at a distance using LAMS.

Learning Spaces and Team Based Learning Using LAMS

In this unit, the use of *(LAMS)* is proposed to approach the concept of *Learning Spaces* at Universities/Schools and illustrate a guide to design and develop sequences of collaborative learning activities as a catalyst to enhance the learning process at a distance. Educators in distance education can be supported too and that will contribute critically to their effective role in administrative, social and educational context. The *LAMS* is a proposal according the *learning design standard* towards the development of learning sequences aiming to support both tutor's work and students' progress based in sequences of collaborative online and offline learning activities with different teaching strategies.

For instance, *Team Based Learning (TBL)* is a teaching strategy that uses a combination of individual and small group assessment tasks combined with group debate about chosen answers, combined with whole class discussion. While TBL has been conducted using paper for several decades, LAMS is the first Learning Design system to provide a flexible online toolset for implementing TBL.

Figure 3. Learning Space based on LAMS, Team Based Learning Example

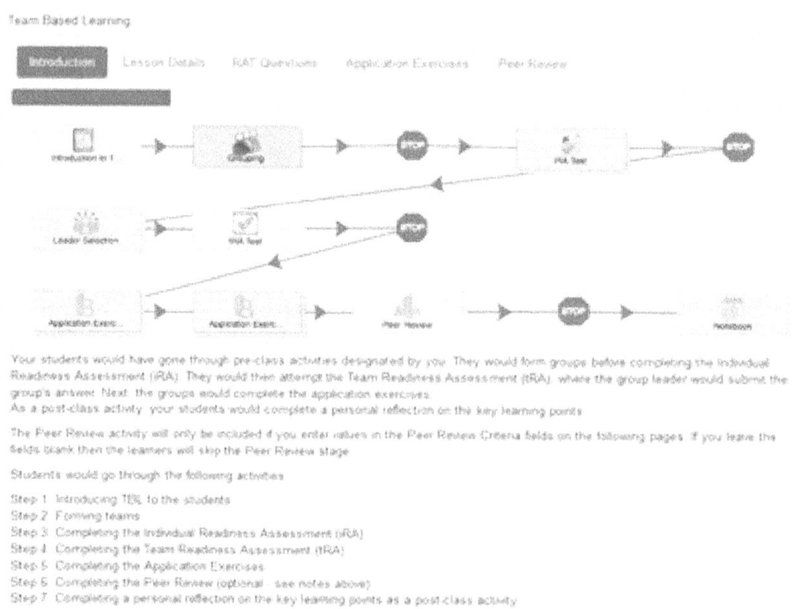

A *Learning Space* could be developed using LAMS sequences providing innovative and flexible learning experiences. LAMS sequences can support essentially e-collaborative experiences among students and therefore they lead in getting higher performances and also decreasing students drop out from their studies. The goal is not to do away with the traditional campus, but rather to reinvent and to integrate it within the *Learning Spaces*, moving towards a single united learning environment (*LAMS-LS*). So, the proposed "LAMS-LS" consists of a Repository of sequences of learning activities in LAMS *(Figure 2)* aiming at:

- supporting students' study and collaboration outside the campus,
- monitoring students' progress and engagement by their educators, using collaborative sequences,
- providing an authoring environment for educators in order to design and develop sequences of learning activities.
- supporting differentiated teaching by providing *learning analytics* to the educators for the monitoring of their students' progress.

Each student shapes his own learning profile, following specific steps in order to accomplish specific learning outcomes and create his own environment "My-Campus" including his work and outcomes in an e-portfolio.

Students implementing the LAMS sequences *(Figure 3)* at Learning Spaces are encouraged to interact with their peers in specifically designed reflective activities and accomplish educational goals in a flexible educational setting. The design of the sequences aims to enhance cognitive process and concept construction, and activate also critical and creative thinking.

Furthermore, each educator is able to design and develop his own learning sequences following specific steps and contribute by that in a common Repository. Building a Repository of learning sequences supports the work of educators and affects critically to their effective role in social and educational context.

The Pedagogical Framework of the Learning Sequences

LAMS learning sequences are based on the pedagogical framework of *experiential* and *active learning*. Experiential learning was proposed as learning theory from the American psychologist Bruner (1966) and its fundamental principle is that learners discover knowledge and develop skills via interactive learning environments experimentation and practice. Students build practical virtual and real symbolic representations through relevant software in order to understand information and develop their cognitive skills. In parallel, emphasis is given in the social context which influences the cognitive processes using technology. Students using LAMS learning sequences participate in *Online CoP* engaging in interactions and approaching socio-constructive theories of learning. Combining pedagogies of behaviorism, constructivism and connectivism is crucial for the development of *Learning Spaces* and could achieve flexibility.

Students' use of LAMS sequences contributes actively in their own learning (*active learning*). Following them step by step, students participate in activities related to teaching goals and objectives, encouraging reflective and self-reflective activities. Cognitive process and concept construction are enhanced, critical and creative thinking are activated and learning engages higher order thinking skills (Fragaki, Reynolds, & Vanbuel, 2009; Matsagouras, 2005: 84-95).

LAMS sequences are based on an educational framework of approaching quality and use a variety of means and tools towards *Polymorphic education* (Lionarakis, 1998). LAMS uses activity tools allowing easily the implementation of three sets of educational material which is supported by the taxonomy of West (1996, in Lionarakis 2001). In addition, it provides diverse learning opportunities for students and relevant feedback throughout their overall study and exploitation.

DISCUSSION AND CONCLUSIONS

According European Union policies "*There is a strong need for flexible, innovative learning approaches and delivery methods: to improve quality and relevance while expanding student numbers, to widen participation to diverse groups of learners, and to combat drop-out. One key way of achieving this, in line with the EU Digital Agenda (European Union, 2010), is to exploit the transformational benefits of ICTs and other new technologies to enrich teaching, improve learning experiences, support personalized learning, facilitate access through distance learning, and virtual mobility, streamline administration and create new opportunities for research*".

The transformational benefits of ICTs provide new challenges and opportunities of e-collaboration in *Virtual Learning Environments* and *Learning Spaces*. Six LMSs (*Moodle, Blackboard Collaboration, e-me, Open e-class, TwinSpace, LAMS*) were presented in the chapter and their key features to support key dimensions of e-collaboration. LMSs could provide flexibility and reconfiguration of e-collaboration and further more in LS step by step in an extensively transformative environment. Nevertheless, transforming the educational processes presupposes two basic components: a time horizon and a new shaping culture within the School/University.

Two active and strong CoPs in European education were highlighted and the ways with which they enhance e-collaboration via the virtual space "Twinspace" and also collaboration in LS. An awarded case study of the etwinning project entitled "Digital stories" showed the blended environment of LS which combines collaboration locally and e-collaboration through virtual environment.

The chapter proposed an alternative case study in LMS LAMS promoting learning sequences of collaborative online learning activities and highlighting *Team Based Learning*. *Learning Spaces* could be created using LAMS sequences providing innovative and flexible personalized or e-collaborative learning experiences. LAMS sequences can contribute essentially in achieving real autonomous and personalized distance learning and prevent students from dropping out their studies. They also can achieve better performances for those students who implement them successfully benefited by group work.

Prerequisite of designing and developing LAMS sequences is the familiarization of educators with online learning environments and also a positive attitude towards blended learning. This could be a possible drawback of using LAMS since the majority of educators prefer to use their traditional teaching methodologies. Educational organizations need to organize training courses so as to familiarize their academic stuff with VLEs and also to achieve authoring new sequences by tutors themselves.

A learning sequence in LAMS illustrates a guide to design and develop collaborative sequences of learning activities as a catalyst to enhance the learning process. Students implementing the sequences on their own or in Class/Campus supporting by facilitators can accomplish specific educational goals in a flexible educational setting. A Repository of LAMS-sequences has the potential to become an innovative Learning Space combining students' work inside and outside the Campus.

VLEs can provide to students, learning sequences designed particularly from their educators, oriented to different educational goals each time based on individualized needs. On the other hand, educators usually are not aware of the new emerging landscape, and moreover not so positive to integrate all these changes in their daily educational practice. They need continuous professional development so as to re-design all aspects of the educational process. However, next steps of this study are recommended to move toward on a large scale aiming to verify the findings from case studies.

The Unesco's proposed learning environments in 2002 are still active today, which means that educators use the same fundamental principles to create meaningful, collaborative and situated in real life, environments. Advanced learning technologies could support their work fostering students' e-collaboration and creativity. All three generations of pedagogy, behaviorism, constructivism and connectivism are necessary to cover the whole spectrum of educational needs of the Net generation' students in the 21st century. Combining pedagogies is crucial for the development of e-collaboration and Learning Spaces and could achieve the design of flexible learning sequences.

Educators are always needed to ignite the fire of learning to their students. The learning context is merely common with the previous generation; however, educators are able to author, use and reuse e-collaborative experiences based on VLEs and Learning Spaces in many rich and meaningful ways (Papadimitriou, 2013).

REFERENCES

American Distance Education Consortium (ADEC). (n.d.). *ADEC EdFuture 2014 Presentations*. Retrieved December 12, 2014 from http://www.adec.edu/conference/edfuture-2014/presentations

Anastasiadis, P. (2007). Advanced Learning Technologies of synchronous and asynchronous transmission serving ODL (in Greek). In A. Lionarakis, (Ed.), *Proceedings of 4th International Conference of Open and Distance Learning, Issue B*. Athens: Propompos.

Anderson, T. (2009). The dance of technology and pedagogy in self-paced distance education. *Proceedings of the 17th ICDE World Congress, Maastricht*. Retrieved November 8, 2013 from http://auspace.athabascau.ca:8080/dspace/bitstream/2149/2210/1/The%20Dance%20of%20technology%20and%20Pedagogy%20in%20Self%20Paced%20Instructions.docx

Anderson, T., & Dron, J. (2011). Three Generations of Distance Education Pedagogy. *International Review of Research in Open and Distance Learning*, *12*(3), 80-97.

Athanasoula-Reppa, A. (2006). Tutor-counselor's role in Open and Distance Learning Lionarakis. In A. Lionarakis (Ed.), *Elements of theory and action*. Propompos. (in Greek)

Avouris, N., & Komis, B. (2003). Synchronous collaboration at a distance: community and interaction issues, (in Greek). In A. Lionarakis (Ed.), *2nd Hellenic Conference of Open and Distance Learning*. Patra: Hellenic Open University.

Bayne, S., & Ross, J. (2011). 'Digital Native' and 'Digital Immigrant' Discourses. In R. Land & S. Bayne (Eds.), *Digital Difference. Educational Futures Rethinking Theory and Practice* (Vol. 50). SensePublishers.

Blackboard, (2020). *Blackboard Collaborate*. Retrieved April 28, 2020 from https://www.blackboard.com/teaching-learning/collaboration-web-conferencing/blackboard-collaborate

Bouras, C., Giannaka. E., & Tsiatsos, T. (2008). *E-Collaboration Concepts, Systems, and Applications*. Retrieved April 28, 2020 from https://www.igi-global.com/chapter/collaboration-concepts-systems-applications/16849

Brown, M. (2013). Learning Spaces. In D. G. Oblinger & J. L. Oblinger (Eds.), *Educating the net generation*. Retrieved August 20, 2013 from https://net.educause.edu/ir/library/pdf/pub7101l.pdf

Bruckman, A., & Resnick, M. (1995). The MediaMOO Project: Constructionism and Professional Community. *Convergence*, *1*(1), 94–109. doi:10.1177/135485659500100110

Bruner, J. (1966). *Toward a theory of instruction*. Belknap Press of Harvard University.

Cameron, L. (2007). Scaffolding Effective Learning Design with Pre-Service Teachers. In C. Montgomerie, & J. Seale (Eds.), *Proceedings of World Conference on Educational Multimedia, Hypermedia and Telecommunications 2007* (pp. 195-202). Chesapeake, VA: AACE.

Coats, M. (1992). *Open Teaching Toolkit – Effective Tutorials*. The Open University. Retrieved August 20, 2012 from http://labspace.open.ac.uk/file.php/5718/LDT_12_Intro.pdf

Cornelius, S., & Macdonald, J. (2008). Online informal professional development for distance tutors: Experiences from The Open University in Scotland. *Open Learning*, *23*(1), 43–55. doi:10.1080/02680510701815319

CTI. (n.d.). *CTI Diophantus*. Retrieved April 28, 2020 from www.cti.gr

Dalziel, J. (2010). *Practical e-Teaching Strategies for Predict – Observe – Explain, Problem-Based Learning and Role Plays*. Sydney: LAMS International. Retrieved October 13, 2014, from http://www.practicaleteachingstrategies.com/

Downes, S. (2007). An introduction to connective knowledge. *The International Conference on Media, knowledge & education—exploring new spaces, relations and dynamics in digital media ecologies*. Retrieved May 10, 2013 from https://www.downes.ca/post/3303

E-me. (2020). *E-me*. Retrieved April 28, 2020 from https://auth.e-me.edu.gr/?eme=https://e-me.edu.gr/&cause=no-token&eat=a6d5e70e1fad5db9975afe235d2c85fb&lang=en_US

etwinning program. (n.d.a). *The etwinning program*. Retrieved April 28, 2020 from https://www.etwinning.net/en/pub/index.htm

etwinning program. (n.d.b). *etwinning projects*. Retrieved April 28, 2020 from https://www.etwinning.net/en/pub/get-inspired/projects.cfm

etwinning program. (n.d.c). *Digital stories*. Retrieved April 28, 2020 from https://digitalstories2014.wordpress.com/making-of/

European Union. (2010). *A Digital Agenda for Europe. Digital Agenda COM 245 final*. Retrieved April 29, 2015 from http://europa.eu/legislation_summaries/information_society/strategies/si0016_en.htm

Fanariti, M., & Spanaka, Ad. (2010, November). Metacognition and learning autonomy during the implementation of essays (in Greek). In the *Open. Education Journal*, *6*(1), 138–151. Retrieved June 2, 2011, from http://journal.openet.gr/index.php/openjournal/article/view/105

Fragaki, M., Reynolds, S., & Vanbuel, M. (2009). A pedagogical framework for the effective use of video in class & Exemplary video- based educational scenarios. In *D6.1- A pedagogical framework for the effective use of video in class / Exemplary video-based educational scenarios, EduTubePlus -A European Curriculum Related Video Library and Hybrid e- services for the Pedagogical Exploitation of Video in Class*. Research Academic Computer Technology Institute.

Freake, St., & Papathanassiou, H. (2006). *Tutorial support for a Level 3 Electromagnetism course - using a blended approach.* Department of Physics and Astronomy, The Open University. Retrieved May 3, 2009 from http://www.open.ac.uk/picetl/activities/details/detail.php?itemId=4612257d02466&themeId=460d2aa4d3c48

Fung, Y., & Carr, R. (2000). Face-to-Face Tutorials in a Distance Learning System: Meeting student needs. *Open Learning*, *15*(1), 35–46. doi:10.1080/026805100115452

Goleman, D. (2006). *Social Intelligence*. Ellinika Grammata. (in Greek)

Gunet. (2020). *The Greek University Network (GUnet)*. Retrieved April 28, 2020 from https://www.gunet.gr/el/

Hadzilakos, T., Papadakis, S., & Rossiou, E. (2007). Group Counseling Conferences (in Greek). *Open Education*. Athens: Propompos.

Jekins, J., & Vissere, G. (2001). *E-learning-Everybody's Business*. Retrieved May 10, 2011 from www.imaginal.nl

JISC. (2013*). Designing Spaces for Effective Learning - A guide to 21st century learning space design.* Retrieved July 20, 2013, from https://www.jisc.ac.uk/uploaded_documents/JISClearningspaces.pdf

Johnson, D. W., & Johnson, R. T. (1996). Cooperation and the use of technology. In D. H. Jonassen (Ed.), *Handbook of research for educational communications and technology* (pp. 170–198). Simon & Schuster Macmillan.

Jonassen, D. (2000). Revisiting Activity Theory as a Framework for Designing Student- Centered Learning Environments. In D. Jonassen & S. Land (Eds.), *Theoretical foundations of Learning Environments*. LEA.

Keegan, D. (1986). *The foundations of distance education* (2nd ed.). Routledge.

Kokkos, A. (2001). Tutor-counselor's role in Open and Distance Learning: the case of Hellenic Open University (in Greek). In *Proceedings of 1st International Conference of Open and Distance Learning, issue A*. Patra: Hellenic Open University.

Kordaki, M., & Siempos, H. (2010). The JiGSAW Collaborative Method within the online computer science classroom. In *The 2nd International Conference on Computer Supported Education*, (pp. 65-74). Academic Press.

LAMS. (n.d.). *What is LAMS?* Retrieved from http://www.lamsfoundation.org/

LAMS Community. (n.d.). *LAMS community*. Retrieved from www.lamscommunity.org

Lave, J., & Wenger, E. (1991). *Situated Learning: Legitimate Peripheral Participation*. Cambridge University Press. doi:10.1017/CBO9780511815355

Lave, J., & Wenger, E. (1998). *Communities of Practice: Learning, Meaning, and Identity*. Cambridge University Press.

LessonLAMS. (n.d.). *LessonLAMS*. Retrieved from https://lessonlams.com/lams/

Lionarakis, A. (1998). Polymorphic Education: A pedagogical framework for open and distance learning. In A. Szucs & A. Wagner (Eds.), *Transformation, Innovation and Tradition Roles and Perspectives of Open and Distance Learning* (pp. 499–504). University of Bologna, Universities in a Digital Era.

Lionarakis, A. (2001). Open and Distance polymorphic education: considerations on a qualitative approach of designing educational material (in Greek). In Views and considerations on ODL. Athens: Propompos.

Matralis, Ch. (1998). Goal and Objectives (in Greek). In The educational material and new technologies, Open and Distance Learning (vol. C). Patra: Hellenic Open University.

Matsagouras, E. (2002). *Critical thinking in teaching*. Gutenberg. (in Greek)

Moodle. (2020). *Moodle*. Retrieved April 28, 2020 from https://docs.moodle.org/38/en/About_Moodle

Moore, M. G. (1973). Toward a theory of Independent Learning and Teaching. *The Journal of Higher Education*, *44*(9), 661–679. doi:10.2307/1980599

Moore, M. G. (1980). Independent study. In R. Boyd & J. Apps (Eds.), *Redefining the Discipline of Adult Education* (pp. 16–31). Jossey-Bass.

Murli Nagasundaram. (2008). E-Collaboration Through Blogging. Boise State University. Doi:10.4018/978-1-59904-000-4.ch031

Open eClass platform. (2020). *The Open eClass platform*. Retrieved April 28, 2020 from https://www.openeclass.org/en/about/

Palfrey, J., & Gasser, U. (2008). *Born digital: Understanding the first generation of Digital Natives*. Basic Books.

Palloff, R., & Pratt, K. (1999). *Building Learning Communities in Cyberspace: effective strategies for the online classroom*. Jossey-Bass.

Papadakis, S., Kordaki, M., & Hadzilacos, T. (2007). Learning Design: the views of Prospective Computer Professionals. In *Proceedings of Informatics Education Europe II Conference*, (pp. 2-11). Academic Press.

Papadimitriou, S. (2013). Open Educational Resources and Practices Unfold a Brand New World Towards an Open Higher Education. In *Open Education 2030 Contribution to the JRC-IPTS Call for Vision Papers Part III: Higher Education*. Retrieved August 20, 2013 from http://is.jrc.ec.europa.eu/pages/EAP/documents/All_OE2030_HE_v%204_author%20revised_OK.pdf

Papadimitriou, S., Lampropoulou, N., & Kampylis, P. (2007). The multiple use of videoconference in distance learning of Greek teachers via Greek School Network. (in Greek). In A. Lionarakis (Ed.), *Proceedings of the 4th International Conference Open and Distance Learning*. Athens: Propompos.

Papadimitriou, S., & Lionarakis, A. (2009). Tutor-counselor's role in Open and Distance Learning and the development of his support mechanism in ODL (in Greek). *The Open Education Journal*, *6*(1), 106-122. Retrieved on June 2, 2011 from: http://journal.openet.gr/index.php/openjournal/article/view/103

Papadimitriou, S., Papadakis, S., & Lionarakis, A. (2017). Supporting Electronic Collaborative Experiences at Universities based on Learning Spaces and LAMS in IGI Global. *Proceedings International Journal of e-Collaboration (IJeC)*. Retrieved June 2, 2020 from https://www.igi-global.com/journal/international-journal-collaboration-ijec/1090

Papadimitriou, S., Papadakis, S., Lionarakis, A., & Kameas, A. (2011). A proposal of using Learning Activities Management System (LAMS) to support the work of Educators in HOU. In A. Lionarakis (Ed.), *Proceedings of the 6th International Conference in Open & Distance Learning - November 2011*. Retrieved March 21, 2012 from http://icodl.openet.gr/index.php/icodl/2011/paper/view/51

Prensky, M. (2001). Digital natives, digital immigrants. The Horizon, 9(5), 1-6.

Rowntree, D. (1998). Workshops role in Staff development. In C. Latsem & F. Lockwood (Eds.), *Staff development in open and flexible learning*. Routledge.

Siemens, G. (2005). A learning theory for the digital age. *Instructional Technology and Distance Education*, *2*(1), 3–10. Retrieved May 15, 2012 from http://www.elearnspace.org/Articles/connectivism.htm

Tapscott, D. (1998). *Growing up digital: The rise of the Net Generation*. McGraw-Hill.

Tapscott, D. (2009). *Grown up digital: How the Net Generation is changing your world*. McGraw-Hill.

UNESCO. (2002). *How students learn* (in Greek). International Bureau of Education. Retrieved November 2, 2010 from http://www.ibe.unesco.org/fileadmin/user_upload/archive/publications/EducationalPracticesSeriesPdf/prac07gr.pdf

Vasala, P., Hatziplis, P., & Lionarakis, A. (2007). Views of undergraduate and postgraduate students at Hellenic Open University on essays: a comparative study of two courses, (in Greek). In A. Lionarakis (Ed), *Proceedings of 4th International Conference of Open and Distance Learning*, (pp. 296-308). Athens: Propompos.

Wenger, E. (1998). *Communities of practice, Learning, meaning and identity*. Cambridge University Press. doi:10.1017/CBO9780511803932

KEY TERMS AND DEFINITIONS

Adaptive Personalized Learning: A category of learning, based on the dynamic adaptation of teaching practices aiming to achieve special learning needs and personal goals for each student.

Co-Creation: A collaborative process which takes place when complex non-pre-defined problems occur and serve as challenges to implement common work in small teams proposing and optimising solutions.

Interactive Videoconference: A synchronous e-learning tool which provides opportunities to students to exchange views, share data, and participate actively in a dynamic interactive environment with collaborative construction of knowledge in real time.

LAMS LMS: An open source freely available web-based *Learning Management System* 'inspired' by the *Learning Design model* for designing and delivering online and offline sequences of learning activities.

Learning Analytics: The measurement, collection, analysis, and reporting of data about learners and their contexts, for purposes of understanding and optimizing learning and the environments in which it occurs. Educators can use learning analytics from advanced learning systems to monitor and intervene in students' performance depending on their individual progress.

Learning Sequence: A guide of learning activities which serves as a catalyst to enhance the learning process. Students accomplish concrete educational goals in a flexible educational setting, implementing the sequences on their own or in *Campus* supporting by facilitators.

Learning Spaces: A combination of virtual and physical spaces aiming at enhancing learning experiences, interactivity, and collaboration between learners of the net generation, educators and educational content, opening up new perspectives in DL.

Peer Assessment: A learning process whereby students grade assignments or tests of their peers, based on benchmarks provided by their teacher. Rubrics are often used in conjunction with peer-assessment. This practice is addressed to improve students' understanding on the learning material and also enhance meta-cognitive skills.

Chapter 7
An Investigation of Collaborative Consumption Engagement and the Interaction With Self-Identity

Youngkeun Choi
Sangmyung University, South Korea

ABSTRACT

The purpose of this study was to investigate the relationships between motivation factors and collaborative consumption engagement and explore the moderating effect of self-identity on that relationship. For this, the present study collected data from 228 college students in South Korean through a survey method. In the results, first, the more sustainability or economic benefits participants perceive in collaborative consumption platforms, the more they are engaged in collaborative consumption. Second, a positive relationship between perceived sustainability and collaborative consumption engagement is stronger for participants in collaborative consumption platforms high rather than low in interdependent self-view. However, interdependent self-view was found to have no significance in the relationship between perceived economic benefits and collaborative consumption engagement.

1. INTRODUCTION

Recently, consumer attitudes have changed, and concerns have risen over ecological, social, and developmental impacts (Albinsson & Perera, 2012; Hosta & Zabkar, 2020). Indeed, public awareness of the environmental and ethical implications of mass consumption contributed to the emergence of the sustainable consumption concept around the beginning of the new millennium (OCSC, 2000). The Oxford Commission for Sustainable Consumption (OCSC) defines the concept as, consumption that supports the ability of current and future generations to meet their material and other needs, without causing irreversible damage to the environment or loss of function in natural systems. In pursuit of this ideal, diverse stakeholders (e.g., businesses, government agencies, and consumer advocates) have begun

DOI: 10.4018/978-1-7998-4891-2.ch007

Copyright © 2021, IGI Global. Copying or distributing in print or electronic forms without written permission of IGI Global is prohibited.

to develop initiatives to produce consumer goods that lower environmental impacts and, subsequently, provide positive social impacts (Cho, Gupta & Kim, 2015). Among the evolving examples of initiatives to promote sustainable consumption, collaborative consumption (CC) has emerged as a promising initiative for reducing consumer waste among diverse product categories. Collaborative consumption represents a range of business models that are fundamentally based on deviations from the concept of traditional ownership, including examples such as renting, lending, bartering and swapping products and services (Johnson, Mun & Chae, 2016).

One outcome of recent hyper-connectivity, in concert with the higher levels of efficiency and trust, has been people willing to engage in all kinds of social and economic exchange with members of their extended digital networks. Technology, and the applications that come with it, has changed the nature of activities ranging from dating (Tinder) to referencing (Wikipedia) to traveling (Airbnb); our connectedness is changing how humans interact. In particular, more people are open to sharing. Whether it is photos or statuses or breaking news, people are offering up more to their networks than ever before.

Despite growing practical importance, there is a lack of quantitative studies on motivational factors that affect participants' attitudes and intentions towards CC. This article explores people's motivations to participate in CC. For this, the article is structured as follows. The next section presents the theoretical framework and background for the hypotheses. This study adopts the lens of intrinsic and extrinsic motivations in attitude formation and uses intentions related to CC (Lindenberg, 2001). The context is of especially great interest since participation in CC communities and services is generally characterized as driven by obligation to do good for other people and for the environment, such as sharing, helping others, and engaging in sustainable behavior (Prothero et al., 2011). However, CC may also provide economic benefits (saving money, facilitating access to resources, and free-riding), which constitute more individualistic reasons for participating. For these reasons, there exists a real practical problem of how CC could become more widespread. In particular, the possible discrepancy between motivations and their effect on attitudes and behavior warrants an exciting context for research (Bray et al., 2011). The relevant studies on self-identity have suggested that the sharing of an object is associated with closer perceived social distances (Belk, 1988). Belk's (1988) work on the extended self-established idea that people expand their concept of who they are to include their possessions and objects they consume. This study applies ideas on the extended self to P2P collaborative consumption. It proposes that by sharing a personal object of consumption, perceived social distances would be closer, vis-à-vis B2C exchange. And, the subsequent section then outlines data and methods, followed by the results. The article concludes with a discussion on implications and avenues for future research.

2. THEORETICAL BACKGROUND AND HYPOTHESIS DEVELOPMENT

2.1 Collaborative Consumption

A collaborative economy is defined as a network of distributed groups of people that come together to use products, skills, etc. via internet technologies. That is, individuals share items and skills among a group instead of solely owning them. For instance, in the United States, Canada, and Western Europe, an average car is used only eight percent of its lifetime (Sacks, 2011). Further, in the US, an average woman does not wear sixty percent of her closet, and the retail value of the unworn clothes in the closet accounts for about 220 billion US dollars (ThredUP, 2017). Hence, sharing such products could be beneficial to the consumers from both financial and practical perspectives, and positively influence the society and environment (Belk, 2014).

A group of similar consumption practices described as 'sharing' Belk (2010), 'Collaborative Consumption' (Botsman & Rogers, 2011), 'access-based consumption' (Bardhi & Eckhardt, 2012), and 'commercial sharing systems' (Lamberton & Rose, 2012) have gained attention in the recent years (Belk, 2014). Collaborative consumption is a business model based on the sharing of certain kinds of products that offer ways to either delay or avoid waste by bartering, borrowing, lending, renting, and swapping underused or unwanted used goods between groups of individuals. Furthermore, CC is an alternative ecological mode of consumption (Botsman & Rogers, 2011). Botsman and Rogers (2010) described CC as "a socioeconomic groundswell that will transform the way companies think about their value propositions - and the way people fulfill their needs" (p.30). Besides, the authors also discussed that CC could be as significant as the Industrial Revolution in terms of transition of thoughts to ownership (Botsman & Rogers, 2011).

Felson and Spaeth initially introduced the term collaborative consumption from a consumer behavior perspective in 1978. The following definitions have presented the various meanings of CC over the years. CCs are regarded as those events in which one or more persons consume economic goods or services in the process of engaging in joint activities with one or more others (Felson & Spaeth, 1978). Botsman and Rogers (2011) suggest that CC means traditional sharing, bartering, lending, trading, renting, gifting, and swapping, redefined through technology and peer communities. Ertz, Durif, and Arcand (2016) argue that CC is the set of resource circulation systems that enable consumers to both obtain and provide, temporarily or permanently, valuable resources or services through direct interaction with other consumers or through a mediator.

Bike-sharing is the fastest-growing CC service in the world (Botsman & Rogers, 2011). One example of this service is LimeBike. Launched in 2017, LimeBike, a US-based bike-sharing service, has revolutionized urban transportation in major US cities affordably and conveniently while eliminating carbon footprint. Forbes reported LimeBike has a value of $225 million and has acquired about 300,000 users (Carson, 2017). Mohlmann (2015) discussed that in recent years, an increasing number of people use car-sharing services such as car2go and Zipcar. Zipcar promotes itself as 'Green Brand' by inspiring car sharing as a sustainable driving practice and making members eligible for tax reduction in certain states in the United States (Bradhi & Eckhardt, 2012). In 2017 alone, car2go, reported having operations in 26 international locations and predicted a fivefold increase in their users to about 36.7 million by the year 2025 worldwide (Saunders, 2017). Thus, CC is no longer a niche trend. Specifically, CC services such as bike and car-sharing illustrate the phenomenal growth of CC in recent years.

2.2 Hypothesis Development

Self-determination theory (Deci & Ryan, 1985) assumes that motivation can be intrinsically or intrinsically distinguishable. The former derives from intrinsic values associated with a given activity, whereas external motivation relates to external pressures such as monetary gain. Participation in CC is generally expected to be highly ecologically sustainable (Sacks, 2011). Such motives generally relate to the ideology and norms conceptualized as intrinsic motivation in this theoretical framework and related research (Lindenberg, 2001). Recent developments suggest that the CC platform is used to foster a sustainable market that optimizes environmental, social, and economic outcomes to meet the needs of both present and future generations (Luchs et al., 2011; Phipps et al., 2013). Also, open-source software development and participation in peer production (e.g., Wikipedia) are driven by altruistic motives such as openness and freedom of information, as argued by Oreg and Nov (2008). Thus, participation and collaboration in online platforms may be influenced by attitudes shaped by ideology and socio-economic concerns, such as anti-establishment sentiments (Hennig-Thurau et al., 2007) or a preference for greener consumption, which this study believes to be a particularly important factor in the context of CC. Therefore, this study operationalizes the intrinsic motivation related to norms as ecological sustainability. And, this study hypothesizes that sustainability is a major predictor for attitude formation and behavioral intentions towards CC.

H1: Perceived sustainability of CC positively influences engagement in CC

Financial motivation positively influences participants' willingness to take part in various CC services, including buying, selling, renting, lending, and swapping among Dutch consumers (Van de Glind, 2013). Cost savings have a positive effect on the satisfaction and future likelihood of using sharing services (Mohlmann, 2015). The economic benefits of peer-to-peer accommodation positively influence travelers to increase travel frequency, stay longer, and participate in more activities (Tussyadiah & Pesonen, 2016). Investigation on the intrinsic and extrinsic motivations for participation in CC among the users of Sharetribe, online CC service package showed economic gains are a strong motivator for participation in CC services (Hamari et al., 2016). A Delphi study with 25 experts involved with sharing economy to identify the key drivers and inhibitors of the CC showed economic gains as the most significant factor. Prominent benefits identified in the study include cheaper transaction costs through the internet, availability of cheaper alternatives, getting more for less money, and lack of ownership costs (Barnes & Mattson, 2016). Further, empirical analysis of participants' motivations for using a car-sharing service showed intention to both rents and recommend to others is positively driven by economic benefits (Barnes & Mattson, 2017). Therefore, this study hypothesizes that economic benefit is a major predictor for attitude formation and behavioral intentions towards CC.

H2: Perceived economic benefits positively influence engagement in CC.

Previous work has used the terms independent and interdependent to describe how individuals derive their self-identity (Markus & Kitayama, 1991). Interdependent individuals and groups tend to put an emphasis on the needs of others, of fitting in with a harmonious group, whereas people from independent cultures tend to value expressing unique inner attributes (Markus & Kitayama, 1991). The more an individual is dependent on the group, the more they will attend to the group cues for the development of their own self-identity (Triandis, 1989). Independent and interdependent self-views have been found to be associated with abstract and concrete representations, respectively. Spassova and Lee (2013) saw that when asked to describe future events, those with independent self-views responded with more abstract descriptions and with a perception that that even was even farther in the future than did those who were interdependent. It may suggest that those described as having higher levels of interdependent self-views are more sensitive to environmental cues and have a propensity to see things in more concrete ways. An in-group boundary is an extent to which an individual sees others as being part of their own social group. The definitions of such boundaries keep adjusting along with situational factors, i.e., things such as common fates, common outside threats, and proximity (Triandis, 1989). So, even though someone with an interdependent self-view does not just indiscriminately subordinate themselves to the needs or goals of others (Markus & Kitayama, 1991), the other people would represent a much more important role and be more of a focal point of one's actions. Given the more central nature of the in-group for an interdependent-self, inclusion may be a more discerning process, and the subjective boundary of an individuals in-group may, on average, be narrower for the interdependent selves than for those with independent selves (Triandis, 1989). However, although individuals with strongly interdependent self-views may be much more selective about in-group membership, they are also much more sensitive to social cues. Therefore, those with an interdependent self-view would be more sensitive to social cues for perceptions of social distances (such cues are expected to be more present in a P2P collaborative consumption context). Also, P2P collaborative consumption reflects more of an exchange-relationship as opposed to a communal-relationship (Triandis, 1989), so the exchange would lack the richly detailed information that collectivists might need to expand their in-group boundary. Yet, in the context of P2P exchange, the relationships between the collaborators need not exhibit and interpersonal trust as would exchange defined as sharing or gifting.

Therefore, people with a high level of interdependent view can have a high level of trust in those participating in the collaborative consumption platform. These people can show enhanced participants' behavior during the collaborative consumption process. In other words, sustainability defined as an intrinsic motivator in the collaborative consumption process may not be achieved by the participant alone, so it is necessary to trust that those who participate in the collaborative consumption platform will think the same way. Therefore, the higher the level of interdependent self-view, the more participants will engage in collaborative consumption because they think that other people will participate in collaborative consumption as they consider ecological sustainability as important.

And, the economic benefits defined as extrinsic motivators in the process of collaborative consumption will not be achievable if other participants are involved in fraud, so trust in those involved in the collaborative consumption platform will be needed. Therefore, the higher the level of interdependent self-view, the more participants will engage in collaborative consumption because they will participate in the collaborative consumption process so that others will do honest transactions. Therefore, this study hypothesizes that interdependent self-view is a major moderator for the relationship between two predictors and engagement in CC.

H3: Interdependent self-view positively influences the relationship between sustainability and engagement in CC.
H4: Interdependent self-view positively influences the relationship between economic benefits and engagement in CC.

3. METHODOLOGY

3.1 Sample

The sample for this study consists of 228 college students with previous experience engaging in online CC platforms (i.e., those who bought, sold, or rented a product using an online CC service). The sample consists of undergraduate and graduate students in programs related to business, social science and engineering in Korea. The criteria for participation in the study includes past engagement in CC and a minimum age of 18 years. Though the sample is considered as one of convenience, college students represent a significant subset of a major participants segment that is the focus of global marketers (Dobbs et al., 2016).

3.2 Data Collection and Instrumentation

The objective of the study was to identify the factors of psychological behaviors related to CC engagement based on empirical analysis. These factors can be identified by measuring the participants' perceptions of CC platforms. The survey research method is very useful in collecting data from a large number of individuals in a relatively short period of time and at a lower cost. Hence, for the current study, the questionnaire survey was used for data collection. All participants received a paper-and-pencil questionnaire with an accompanying letter that explained the purpose of the survey, emphasized voluntary participation, and guaranteed confidently. Participants were asked to fill out the questionnaire and put it back into an envelope that was collected by the researcher.

The questionnaire employed psychometric measurement (Nunnally, 1978). This study measured each construct with four or five items that were all on a 5-point Likert scale. Perceived sustainability was measured using five items from the scale developed by Hamari et al. (2016). For example, "Collaborative consumption helps save natural resources." Perceived economic benefits were measured using four items from the scale developed by Bock et al. (2016). For example, "I can save money if I participate in collaborative consumption." Interdependent self-view was measured using twelve items from the Singelis Interdependent Self-view Construal Scale (Singelis, 1994). CC engagement employs four items (Hamari et al., 2016). For example, "All things considered, I expect to continue CC in the future."

4. ANALYSIS RESULT

4.1 Verification of Reliability and Validity

The validity of variables was verified through the principal components method and factor analysis with the varimax method. The criteria for determining the number of factors is defined as a 1.0 eigenvalue. I applied factors for analysis only if the factor loading was greater than 0.5 (factor loading represents the correlation scale between a factor and other variables). The reliability of variables was judged by internal consistency, as assessed by Cronbach's alpha. I used surveys and regarded each as one measure only if their Cronbach's alpha values were 0.7 or higher.

4.2 Common Method Bias

As with all self-reported data, there is the potential for the occurrence of common method variance (CMV) (MacKenzie & Podsakoff, 2012; Podsakoff et al., 2003). To alleviate and assess the magnitude of common method bias, I adopted several procedural and statistical remedies that Podsakoff et al. (2003) suggest. First, during the survey, respondents were guaranteed anonymity and confidentiality to reduce the evaluation apprehension. Further, we paid careful attention to the wording of the items and developed our questionnaire carefully to reduce the item ambiguity. These procedures would make them less likely to edit their responses to be more socially desirable, acquiescent, and consistent with how they think the researcher wants them to respond when answering the questionnaire (Podsakoff et al., 2003; Tourangeau, Rips, & Rasinski, 2000). Second, I conducted a Harman's one-factor test on all of the items. A principal component factor analysis revealed that the first factor only explained 34.1 percent of the variance. Thus, no single factor emerged, nor did one-factor account for most of the variance. Furthermore, the measurement model was reassessed with the addition of a latent common method variance factor (Podsakoff et al., 2003). All indicator variables in the measurement model were loaded on this factor. The addition of the common variance factor did not improve the fit over the measurement model without that factor, with all indicators still remaining significant. These results do suggest that common method variance is not of great concern in this study.

4.3 Relationship Between Variables

Table 1 summarizes the Pearson correlation test results between variables and reports the degree of multi-collinearity between independent variables. The minimum tolerance of 0.821 and the maximum variance inflation factor of 1.218 show that the statistical significance of the data analysis was not compromised by multi-collinearity.

Table 1. Variables' correlation coefficient

	1	2	3	4
Perceived sustainability	1			
Perceived economic benefits	-.092	1		
Interdependent self-view	.071	.103	1	
CC engagement	.024**	.012**	.014*	1

$p < .05, p < .01$

4.4 Hypothesis Testing

This study used hierarchical multiple regression analyses with three-steps to test the hypotheses. In the first step, demographic variables were controlled. Motivation factors were entered in the second step. In the final step the multiplicative interaction terms between motivation factors and interdependent self-view were entered to directly test the current hypothesis about the moderating effect. Table 2 shows the results. First, only sex among the control variables has a positive relationship with CC engagement. This means that women are more likely to be engaged in CC than men. Second, to analyze the relationship between motivation factors and CC engagement, model 2 in Table 2 shows that all of the motivation factors have statistical significance with CC engagement. Perceived sustainability is positively related with CC engagement ($\beta = .089$, $p < .01$) and perceived economic benefits has positive relationships with CC engagement ($\beta = .039$, $p < .01$). Therefore, hypotheses 1 and 2 are supported.

Lastly, the model 3, consisting of moderators, shows the interactions between motivation factors and interdependent self-view on CC engagement. Interdependent self-view was found to have a positive effect on the relationship between perceived sustainability and CC engagement ($\beta = .101$, $p < .01$). Interdependent self-view was found to have no significance in the relationship between perceived economic benefits and CC engagement. Based on these results, when participants in CC platforms have

Table 2. Analysis 1

	CC engagement		
	Model 1	**Model 2**	**Model 3**
Sex	.028*	.019*	.016*
Age	-.011	-.010	-.009
Educational level	.081	.071	.069
Perceived sustainability		.089**	.079**
Perceived economic benefits		.039**	.031**
Interdependent self-view			.018**
Perceived sustainability * Interdependent self-view			.101**
Perceived economic benefits * Interdependent self-view			.013
Adj. R^2	.101	.141	.179
F	4.641**	8.991**	11.241**

$p < .05, p < .01$

higher interdependent self-view in CC platforms, perceived sustainability has a stronger impact on their engagement in CC, which is expected in H3 (see Figure 1).

Figure 1. Interaction effect

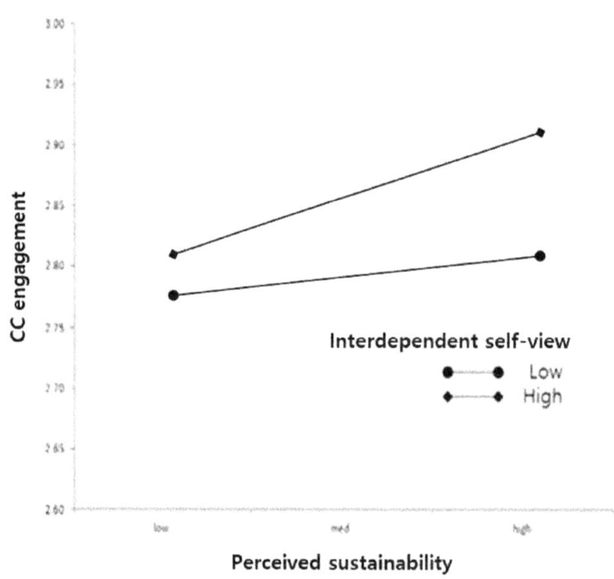

5. CONCLUSION

5.1 Discussion

The purpose of the present study was to examine the relationships between motivation factors and CC engagement and explore the moderating effect of self-identity on that relationship. The results show that the more sustainability or economic benefits participants perceive in CC platforms, the more they are engaged in CC. And in the results, positive relationship between perceived sustainability and CC engagement is stronger for participants in CC platforms high rather than low in interdependent self-view. However, interdependent self-view was found to have no significance in the relationship between perceived economic benefits and CC engagement. This study suggests that people with a high level of interdependent view can have a high level of trust in those participating in the collaborative consumption platform. Based on this suggestion, this study anticipates that these people can show enhanced participants' behavior during the collaborative consumption process. Therefore, the results show that the higher the level of interdependent self-view, the more participants engage in collaborative consumption because they think that other people will participate in collaborative consumption as they consider ecological sustainability as important. And, this study anticipates that the higher the level of interdependent self-view, the more participants will engage in collaborative consumption because they will participate in the collaborative consumption process so that others will do the honest transactions. However, the results that economic benefits that participants expect in CC platforms do not depend on honest transactions. In other words, unlike perceived sustainability, which is an intrinsic motivation factor, perceived economic benefits, which is an external motivation factor, is not realized through the trust among the people participating in the CC platform but is pursued by the individual behaviors of the participants.

5.2 Research Contributions and Practical Implications

For research contribution, first, this study is the first one to examine the integral model of motivation factors of engagement in CC platform. Despite a growing practical importance, there are few quantitative studies on motivational factors that affect participants' attitudes and intentions towards CC. However, this study focused on the motivations of participants directly and especially, proposed a model that integrates intrinsic and extrinsic factors rather than identifying fragmentary factors. Although intrinsic and extrinsic motivations may not coexist or even show conflicts, this study showed that intrinsic and extrinsic motivators could coexist in the CC process. This study shows that people who participate in CC share the philosophy related to CC, unlike general motives of commerce. Second, this study is the first one to investigate the moderating effect of self-identity in CC process. Especially, this study shows that those who participate in the CC process think that the sustainability of CC is possible through trusting others. Therefore, this study extends the scope of the CC study by suggesting the study of the factors of the moderating effect on the relationship between motivation factors and CC engagement.

For practical implications, first, the results of this study show that extrinsic factors such as economic benefits are important to enhance CC participation, but also intrinsic factors such as CC sustainability are important. Therefore, CC platform managers need to make the participants in CC perceive that they can not only get economic benefits, but the platform will also sustain. For example, it would be a good idea to disclose in real-time about the performance of the CC platform (increase in participants, trends in transactions, expansion of items handled, etc.). Second, the results of this study show that the self-identity of the participants enhances the impact of intrinsic motivation, such as perceived persistence on CC participation, but does not affect the impact of external factors such as economic benefits on CC participation. Therefore, CC platform managers need to be aware of their propensity through transaction records of participants. For example, participants in risky transactions on the CC platform will have an interdependent self-view that trusts other participants, so it will not be necessary to recommend a transaction that maximizes economic benefits to them in CC process.

5.3 Limitations and Future Research Directions

By this research results, the present study could have several insights into the motivation of participants in CC. However, it should also acknowledge the following limitations in this research. First, the present study collected the responses from university students in South Korea. There may exist some nation cultural issues in the research context. Future studies should re-test this in other countries in order to assure this results' reliability. Second, as the variables were all measured at the same time, it cannot be sure that their relationships are constant. Although the survey questions occurred in reverse order of the analysis model to prevent additional issues, the existence of causal relationships between variables is a possibility. Therefore, future studies need to consider longitudinal studies. Finally, this study uses perceived sustainability and perceived economic benefits as motivation factors and explore self-identity as a moderator. However, considering the characteristics of CC, future studies may find other motivators and other regulatory factors. For example, as an intrinsic motivation factor, the reputation of the CC platform or extrinsic motivation factors may be considered for enjoyment. In addition, the social distance felt by the participants of the platform can be considered as the control factor.

REFERENCES

Albinsson, P. A., & Perera, B. Y. (2012). Alternative marketplaces in the 21st century: Building community through sharing events. *Journal of Consumer Behaviour, 11*(4), 303–315. doi:10.1002/cb.1389

Bardhi, F., & Eckhardt, G. M. (2012). Access-based consumption: The case of car sharing. *The Journal of Consumer Research, 39*(4), 881–898. doi:10.1086/666376

Barnes, S. J., & Mattson, J. (2016). Understanding current and future issues in collaborative Consumption: A four-stage Delphi study. *Technological Forecasting and Social Change, 104*, 200–211. doi:10.1016/j.techfore.2016.01.006

Barnes, S. J., & Mattson, J. (2017). Understanding collaborative consumption: Test of a theoretical model. *Technological Forecasting and Social Change, 118*, 281–292. doi:10.1016/j.techfore.2017.02.029

Belk, R. (1988). Possessions and the extended self. *The Journal of Consumer Research, 15*(2), 139–168. doi:10.1086/209154

Belk, R. (2010). Sharing. *The Journal of Consumer Research, 36*(5), 715–734. doi:10.1086/612649

Belk, R. (2014). You are what you can access: Sharing and collaborative consumption online. *Journal of Business Research, 67*(8), 1595–1600. doi:10.1016/j.jbusres.2013.10.001

Botsman, R., & Rogers, R. (2011). *What's mine is yours: How collaborative consumption is changing the way we live*. HarperCollins.

Bray, J., Johns, N., & Kilburn, D. (2011). An exploratory study into the factors impeding ethical consumption. *Journal of Business Ethics, 98*(4), 597–608. doi:10.100710551-010-0640-9

Carson, B. (2017, October 16). *Lime Bike Now Valued At $225 Million After Investors Go All In On Bike-Sharing Craze*. Retrieved from https://www.forbes.com/sites/bizcarson /2017/10/16/limebike-now-valued-at-225-illionafterinvestors-go-all-in-on-bike-sharing-craze /#4af3736d4a12

Cho, E., Gupta, S., & Kim, Y. (2015). Style consumption: Its drivers and role in sustainable apparel consumption. *International Journal of Consumer Studies, 39*(6), 661–669. doi:10.1111/ijcs.12185

Deci, E. L., & Ryan, R. M. (1985). *Intrinsic motivation and selfdetermination in human behaviour*. Plenum. doi:10.1007/978-1-4899-2271-7

Dobbs, R., Manyika, J., Woetzel, J., Remes, J., Perry, J., Kelly, G., & Sharma, H. (2016). *Urban world: The global consumers to watch*. Retrieved from https://www.mckinsey.com/global-themes/urbanization/urban-world-the-global-consumerstowatch

Ertz, M., Durif, F., & Arcand, M. (2016). Collaborative Consumption: Conceptual Snapshot at a Buzzword. *Journal of Entrepreneurship Education, 19*(2), 1–23.

Felson, M., & Spaeth, J. L. (1978). Community structure and collaborative consumption: A routine activity approach. *The American Behavioral Scientist, 21*(4), 614–624. doi:10.1177/000276427802100411

Hamari, J., Sjöklint, M., & Ukkonen, A. (2016). The sharing economy: Why people participate in collaborative consumption. *Journal of the Association for Information Science and Technology, 67*(9), 2047–2059. doi:10.1002/asi.23552

Hennig-Thurau, T., Henning, V., & Sattler, H. (2007). Consumer file sharing of motion pictures. *Journal of Marketing, 71*(4), 1–18. doi:10.1509/jmkg.71.4.001

Hosta, M., & Zabkar, V. (2020). Antecedents of Environmentally and Socially Responsible Sustainable Consumer Behavior. *Journal of Business Ethics*. Advance online publication. doi:10.100710551-019-04416-0

Johnson, K. K., Mun, J. M., & Chae, Y. (2016). Antecedents to internet use to collaboratively consume apparel. *Journal of Fashion Marketing and Management: An International Journal, 20*(4), 370–382. doi:10.1108/JFMM-12-2015-0092

Lamberton, C. P., & Rose, R. L. (2012). When is ours better than mine? A framework for understanding and altering participation in commercial sharing systems. *Journal of Marketing, 76*(4), 109–125. doi:10.1509/jm.10.0368

Lindenberg, S. (2001). Intrinsic motivation in a new light. *Kyklos, 54*(2–3), 317–342. doi:10.1111/1467-6435.00156

Luchs, M. G., Naylor, R. W., Rose, R. L., Catlin, J. R., Gau, R., & Kapitan, S. (2011). Toward a sustainable marketplace: Expanding options and benefits for consumers. *Journal of Research for Consumers, 19*(1), 1–12.

MacKenzie, S. B., & Podsakoff, P. M. (2012). Common method bias in marketing: Causes, mechanisms, and procedural remedies. *Journal of Retailing, 88*(4), 542–555. doi:10.1016/j.jretai.2012.08.001

Markus, H., & Kitayama, S. (1991). Culture and the self: Implications for cognition, emotion, and motivation. *Psychological Review, 98*(2), 224–253. doi:10.1037/0033-295X.98.2.224

Mohlmann, M. (2015). Collaborative consumption: Determinants of satisfaction and the likelihood of using a sharing economy option again. *Journal of Consumer Behaviour, 14*(3), 193–207. doi:10.1002/cb.1512

Nunnally, J. (1978). *Psychometric methods*. McGraw-Hill.

Oreg, S., & Nov, O. (2008). Exploring motivations for contributing to open source initiatives: The roles of contribution context and personal values. *Computers in Human Behavior, 24*(5), 2055–2073. doi:10.1016/j.chb.2007.09.007

Phipps, M., Ozanne, L., Luchs, M., Subrahmanyan, S., Kapitan, S., Catlin, J., Gau, R., Naylor, R. W., Rose, R. L., Simpson, B., & Weaver, T. (2013). Understanding the inherent complexity of sustainable consumption: A social cognitive framework. *Journal of Business Research, 66*(8), 1227–1234. doi:10.1016/j.jbusres.2012.08.016

Podsakoff, P. M., MacKensie, S. B., Lee, J.-Y., & Podsakoff, N. P. (2003). Common method biases in behavioral research: A critical review of the literature and recommended remedies. *The Journal of Applied Psychology, 88*(5), 879–903. doi:10.1037/0021-9010.88.5.879

Prothero, A., Dobscha, S., Freund, J., Kilbourne, W. E., Luchs, M. G., Ozanne, L. K., & Thøgersen, J. (2011). Sustainable consumption: Opportunities for consumer research and public policy. *Journal of Public Policy & Marketing, 30*(1), 31–38. doi:10.1509/jppm.30.1.31

Sacks, D. (2011). The sharing economy. *Fast Company, 155*, 88-93.

Saunders, A. (2017, May 3). *Proud to Share! – The New Brand Claim Sums Up the car2Go*. Academic Press.

Singelis, T. M. (1994). The measurement of independent and interdependent self-construals. *Personality and Social Psychology Bulletin, 20*(5), 580–591. doi:10.1177/0146167294205014

Spassova, G., & Lee, A. Y. (2013). Looking into the future: A match between self-view and temporal distance. *The Journal of Consumer Research, 40*(1), 159–171. doi:10.1086/669145

Thred, U. P. (2017). *ThredUP Annual Re-sale Report 2017*. Retrieved from https://www.thredup. com/re-sale/full

Tourangeau, R., Rips, L. J., & Rasinski, K. (2000). *The Psychology of Survey Response*. Cambridge University Press. doi:10.1017/CBO9780511819322

Triandis, H. (1989). The self and social behavior in differing cultural contexts. *Psychological Review, 96*(3), 506–520. doi:10.1037/0033-295X.96.3.506

Tussyadiah, I. P., & Pesonen, J. (2016). Impacts of peer-to-peer accommodation use on travel patterns. *Journal of Travel Research, 55*(8), 1022–1040. doi:10.1177/0047287515608505

Van de Glind, P. B. (2013). *The consumer potential of Collaborative Consumption: Identifying the motives of Dutch Collaborative Consumers & Measuring the consumer potential of Collaborative Consumption within the municipality of Amsterdam* (Master's thesis). Retrieved from https://scholar.google.com/scholar?hl=en&as_sdt=0%2C34&q=Van+de+Glind++2013+collaborative+consumption&btnG

Chapter 8
Impact of COVID-19 Lockdown on Digital Banking:
E-Collaboration Between Banks and FinTech in the Indian Economy

Narinder Kumar Bhasin
https://orcid.org/0000-0001-7167-8730
Amity University, Noida, India

Anupama Rajesh
https://orcid.org/0000-0002-8421-473X
Amity University, Noida, India

ABSTRACT

The COVID-19 outbreak has drastically changed the life of every person and has infected people in 185 countries. Since no vaccine has been developed for this disease so far, lockdown, work from home, and social distancing and only a few essential services were allowed to open. Lockdown and restricted movement of people was the only solution to control this crisis. These steps taken by all the countries have stopped all the commercial activities which left all businesses, banks, and financial institutions to count losses and cost. The big question which has emerged that whether e-collaboration between banks and technology continues to be the key to success for finding solutions to the problems in this new environment which COVID-19 has created. This chapter examines the way the digital banking collaboration between banks and Fintech can resolve the problems provided by the COVID-19 pandemic and control the impending economic fallout in India and across the world.

DOI: 10.4018/978-1-7998-4891-2.ch008

Copyright © 2021, IGI Global. Copying or distributing in print or electronic forms without written permission of IGI Global is prohibited.

INTRODUCTION

It's a time to forget the Fintech Definition that technology meets finance as the banks join their physical hands with virtual banking, virtual currencies, artificial intelligence, block chain, chat bots, big data and robotic process automation. The boundaries between the technology and finance is blurring across the globe resulting in E Collaboration, mergers and amalgamation between traditional banks and technology companies. Banking technology which started with computerization evolved to the revolution in E commerce, digital finance, Insuretech, wealth management as well as non-financial services becoming Fintech. The COVID 19 outbreak has drastically change the life of every person and has infected people in 185 countries. Since no vaccine has been developed for this disease so far, lockdown, work from home and social distancing and only few essential services were allowed to open. Lockdown and restricted movement of people was only solution to control this crisis. These steps taken by all the countries has stopped all the commercial activities which left all businesses, banks and financial institutions to count losses and cost.

The big question which has emerged that whether E Collaboration between banks and technology continues to be the key to success for finding solutions to the problems in this new environment which Covid 19 has created. As cases of the virus spread, the business effect might be equally as far-reaching, causing earnings warnings, shop closures as well as recognition defaults among businesses that depend heavily on China's great usage power. In order to control the ongoing spread Covid 19 pandemic many countries around the globe including India has taken steps like national lockdown, social distancing shutting down public transports, shutting manufacturing units, and restriction in movement. The movement of the people was restricted due to suspension of use of personal conveyance, trains, domestic and travel through airlines both on the domestic and international front. This pandemic has created severe impacts on the financial markets like bond, stock and commodity markets like gold and crude oil. Adverse economic impact was witnessed in the global financial markets like USA. U.K China as well as India.

The essential services which continue to remain open in India during four lockdowns and Unlock 1 were the hospitals, medical shops, diagnostic centres, local grocery / vegetable fruit shops, banks, post office etc. Digital Banking through Internet and mobile banking emerged as an important way of banking transactions as retail banks were working with partial staff strength. As per Indian Bank`s Association`s guidelines the important transactions like cash, clearing, Funds Transfer like RTGS, NEFT were allowed, in case of emergency. Work from home was advised from corporate, regional, circle offices and sales and relationship managers. This has adversely impacted digital banking in major sectors like aviation, manufacturing, retail and hospitality whereas few sectors reflect increase in digital banking like online grocery shopping, Internet and mobile banking and recharges etc. The World Retail Banking Report 2020 survey has revealed 57% of people are using internet and 47% mobile banking instead of visit to bank`s branch.

This particular paper examines the way the digital banking collaboration between banks and Fintech can resolve the problems provided by the Covid 19 pandemic and control the impending economic fallout in India and across the world. The paper also focus on how Banks and Fintech will emerge as agent of change in the challenging times of post COVID 19 in the new normal innovations System.

THEORETICAL BACKGROUND OF THE STUDY

Collaboration between the traditional banks and Fintech companies in Indian Economy were increasing since last five years . Various initiatives were taken by Reserve Bank of India, Government of India and National Payment Corporation of India to promote digital banking for financial inclusion and connecting rural India through mobile and internet banking . **KPMG, NASSCOM, 2015** report Fintech in India – A global growth story reported the Indian Fintech software industry to be worth USD 2.4 billion by 2020 . Indian economy was moving fast towards a digital economy with 886 Mn payment cards and 5 Mn point of sales machines . Various digital solutions and contactless virtual payment modes like Unified Payment Interface (UPI), digital wallets and FastTags adaptation and usage by the customers were increasing . In Q1, 2020 due to the Covid 19 pandemic and lockdown interrupted the Fintech Boom and, Overall volume and value of digital payment transactions sharply fall by 10% to 12% . **(Bhasin, 2019)** in his research paper on the study of Increasing digital banking & Financial Technology trends explain the various new emerging financial technology trends and E collaboration in Indian payment system .With this theatrical back ground of the growth story of Indian digital banking and Fintech, this research study was conducted with the following objectives to analyse the impact of Covid 19 and analyse how the collaboration banks and Fintech can emerge as a successful model and turning point during these difficult and uncertain times.

Objectives of the Study

1. To understand the impact of Covid 19 and challenged faced by Banking System and Digital Payments sector and payment category wise
2. To analyse impact of coronavirus pandemic on various Fintech Sectors across the Globe and in Indian Economy.
3. To evaluate the way, the digital banking collaboration between banks and Fintech can resolve the problems provided by the Covid 19 pandemic and control the impending economic fallout.
4. To study few cases where Banks, Fintech and Digital Payment Vendors in India has emerge as agent of change in the challenging times of post COVID 19 in the new normal innovations System

RESEARCH METHODOLOGY

To understand the role and impact COVID-19 lockdown on banking and Fintech through digital banking and collaboration, we used secondary online sources. The following sections were analysed on the basis of this to identify the Research problem. They are as follows:

- Impact of Covid 19 on Digital Payments and Actions for Digital Payment Enhancement
- Positive and Negative Impact on Fintech stat ups sector and payment category wise.
- Innovative Role of Collaboration between banks and Fintech

The Secondary sources that we used were Online Article, Journals, and Issued Public Interest Booklets.

Literature Review

1. **Pwc, April, 2020 Report "Impact of Covid 19 outbreaks on digital payments**" explains the economic growth and GDP of all the countries will severely hit all the sectors including the digital payment and banking sector. The report focus on the impact on sectoral business, payment categories and suggests short term and long term measures to be taken by Banks, Government, National Payment Corporation of India (NPCI) and Reserve Bank of India. (RBI)
2. **Pwc & FICCI, June, 2020 Report "Redefining the Fintech Experience: Impact of Covid 19"** explains overview of The Fintech sector prior to the COVID 19 Crisis, the impact of COVID 19 on the Indian Fintech sector and funding. The report focus on the response by the Fintech ecosystem and innovation initiatives taken by various Fintech start-ups in India. Report highlights the biggest challenge of sharp decline in Fintech funding due to COVID 19 impact which has restricted global mobility, tourism, trade and customer sentiment.
3. **Pagaria, 2020 in his blog on The Fallout of Covid 19 on the Banking, Financial Services and Insurance (BFSI) Sector reports** the banks and financial institutions are exposed to the risk of deteriorating environment, pressure on capitalization and increasing asset risk as asset growth is likely to replace internal generation of capital. Detailed analysis of impact of pandemic on various services, manufacturing, asset quality and three month waivers on loans moratorium were presented in the report.
4. **John, 2020 in his Trade Finance Global Article** states that Banks, Vendors, Fintech Collaboration plays an Important role post Covid 19 as a lifeline for economic revival to support communities. Since the World Trade Union (WTO) has forecasted 13-32% slippages in the world trade in the year 2020, Banks and Fintech has to collaborate to arrange emergency funding to revive the economy through long term and short term strategies.
5. **Shah, 2020 in his paper in ET BFSI .com newsletter from The Economic Times** states that most of the Fintech and Vendors are adversely impacted with the shocks of Covid 19 pandemic and making efforts to survive though new innovative ways. In this uncertain times where the slump in digital transactions was observed by 30% owing to Lockdown, Zaggle, a prepaid card services Fintech Company has found a sweet spot by launching virtual cards where the human touch or passwords is removed from the systems.
6. **Moneycontrol.com, 2020 Website** in their news article "Fintechs, banks play a vital role in engaging customers amidst the Covid 10 Spread." state that the traditional banks must collaborate with Fintechs as they do not not have the capabilities to support a new payment order. Fintechs are more equipped with advance digital technology having capability of satisfying the changing digital needs of the customer in more effective, transparent, smooth and with speed.
7. **Fincash.com, 2020 on** their website updated Coronavirus guide to investors on the future of Fintech industry. The report reflects the downward funding trends in the global financing activities is expected to similar to as low as in 2017. Fintechs involved in digital lending, digital investment services, digital technology providers and digital deposits and savings will continue to experience growth as the market fluctuations start experience stability once the Covid 19 outbreak settled down as the people, leaders and business across the world able to tackle this coronavirus outbreak.
8. **Shahrawat, Shah 2020** – in their viewpoint series on Fintech Bulletin, 2020 in their perspective "The Impact of COVID 19 on different fintech sectors "explain the impact of Covid 19 on different

fintech sectors like Challenger Banks, Online Lending, Robo advisors / digital wealth managers, payments / transactions processing, institutional capital markets, and Insurtechs.

9. **S&P Global Ratings, 2020** in their Covid 19 Macro & Credit Research tiled Caronavirus Impact explained three important key takeaways. First, tremendous variance across corporate sectors as the credit downturn due to COVID 19 was sudden and severe. Second, the ratings of many sectors will improve once the pandemic slowed down but few sectors where incremental debt was used to finance operations and strengthen the capital base, may face recovery of revenue up to 2022 or beyond. Third, Sectors like telecom, pharmaceuticals, essential retail are less affected as compared to segments like hotels, airlines and non-essential goods.
10. **Marous, 2020** in his Financial Brand Newsletter Article How will the Coronavirus Impact the Banking System highlights the shifts in Fintech Valuations due to Covid 19 Outbreak. The article explains both the positive and negative impact of Coronavirus on Fintech. Fintech, Advanced Data, Regtech and Analytic Firms are expected to attract venture funding if they are capable of facing the challenges and face the current storm of coronavirus.
11. **Nigam, 2020** in his blog in The Times of India on "The Future of Fintech in a Post Covid 19 "writes that as hygiene and sanitization is important for every individual, Fintech will ensure to provide digital lead financial mechanism through contactless and virtual payments with no risk of contracting virus. Various contactless, affordable and new age products like contactless bio metric authentication, dynamic QR Codes and contactless card payments will be more preferred instead of physical contact environment.
12. Appaya, Gradstein, Abdrew, 2020 on their World Bank Blogs "Fintech can help in response to COVID 19 . But where should Policymakers start" give a detailed explanation on the four regulatory approaches solely or in combination for innovation and efficiency. The four categories are wait and see, test and learn, innovation facilitators and regulatory laws and reform.
13. **Dubey, 2019** in his article " Fintech innovations in Digital Banking " published in International Journal of Engineering and technology focus on increase in mobile payments by the customers as a preferred mode of funds transfer and emergence of digital Neo banks collaboration as well as additional competition with the traditional banks . The paper also explain the benefits and use of cognitive banking, Block chain and artificial intelligence for better customer service and satisfaction.
14. **Bhasin, 2019** in his research paper **"** Study of Increasing digital banking & Financial Technology Trends, Challenges and Opportunities in Indian Banking System " published in Bank Quest Journal of Indian Institute of Banking and Finance explains the evolution, digital disruptions, increasing trends and new merging innovative financial funds transfer products in Indian banking and payment system. The study further focus on Digital Banking four stages from 1.0 to 4.0 from the period 1998 to till date and as well as comparative study of increasing digital and Fintech adaptation trends between the period 2015-16 and 2018 -2019.
15. **Rajesh, Bhasin 2019** in their research paper " Increasing digital banking adoption and usage trends in India and its impact on Financial Inclusion studied the trends of growth of digital banking and initiatives taken by the various stake holders for implementation in India .The paper also analyse and examine the sustainability impact of digitalisation and Fintech in achieving the greater financial inclusion . The paper also explain the three most important trends for Retail banking in India in 2018 – Customer Centricity, Vision of the banks for adoption of big data, data analytics, machine learning and robotic process automation.

16. **Singh, Bodla, 2020** in their chapter " Covid 19 Pandemic and Lockdown Impact on India`s Banking Sector: A Systematic Literature Review " attempt to assess the impact of this pandemic on Banks and NBFCs due to lockdown which has resulted into closure of all commercial organisations, educational institutions, public and private offices, suspension of means of transportation, etc. The conclusion in this regard is based on the views expressed by several groups including economists, financial institutions like IMF, World Bank and consulting firms. Secondary sources of information are used to collect the required information. The article has indicated a very severe effect of lockdown on banks and NBFCs in case it prolongs beyond July 2020.
17. **Sharma, 2020 in his article " Voice 3 emerging Robo trends Amid Covid 19 market craziness "** explains that the economic shock created by Covid 19 focus on the power of gaols based strategic planning via Robo advisors . The higher priority and new term goals will lower risk allocation and leading to minimize the short term economic impact.

SECTION 1: IMPACT OF COVID 19 ON BANKING AND DIGITAL PAYMENTS

Challenges for Banks During Covid 19

The banking business, additionally to facing the own difficulties of its, is anticipated to assist clients of this particular hour of need. While banks have well defined business continuity plans, they could be insufficient in managing a crisis of this particular scale as well as influence or maybe address the great number of different problems emanating from the circumstances. Provided banks' important proposition to clients is actually reputation and loyalty, the present crisis is actually a grave challenge, the reaction to which can have a long lasting influence on the long-range performance of theirs, success, and sector positioning. The Coronavirus pandemic has left many banks with the challenges of withdrawl of deposits in lock down and transferred to public sector banks as private sector banks are in losses. **(Singh, Bodla 2020)**

The crisis has given rise to several key macro concerns; to handle the complicated as well as fast changing scenario, banks have to map the problems throughout two important dimensions- stakeholders as well as time period. Problems experienced by the three most prominent stakeholder groups -- clients, regulators and employees have to be mapped throughout three -time period immediate, medium and short-term.

Transmission of Virus Through Coins as well as Banknotes

The COVID 19 pandemic has resulted in unprecedented public concerns regarding viral transmission by money. Core banks claim a sizable rise in queries by the media on the safety of utilizing money. The number of online searches pertaining to both money along with the virus is actually at record highs. You will find sizable cross country differences in these issues. Searches seem to be a lot more common where more small denomination banknotes the style used for everyday transactions are actually in circulation relative to GDP (Graph one, right hand panel). General, Australia, France, Singapore, Switzerland, Ireland, the United Kingdom, Canada, the United States, Kenya and Jamaica have had probably the highest the latest search interest.

Research in microbiology examines if pathogenic agents, which includes viruses, bacteria, parasites and fungi are able to endure on coins and banknotes. A researcher discovers that a number of viruses, including man flu, could persist for days or hours on banknotes, especially when diluted in mucus. A researcher find that non-porous surfaces have greater transfer effectiveness, which means that they are able to transmit bacteria and viruses a bit more easily. The COVID 19 virus may also endure on surfaces. A report by **Van Doremalen et al (2020)** finds that COVID 19 is able to persist for 3 hours of the air, twenty-four hours on cardboard as well as more time on other hard surfaces. (**Basu, 2020**) in his report suggest that though there is limited research on transmission of coronavirus through dirty currency notes or news paper as they exchange many hands, its better people move to digital payments .

Figure 1. Survival time of Covid-19 on different surfaces

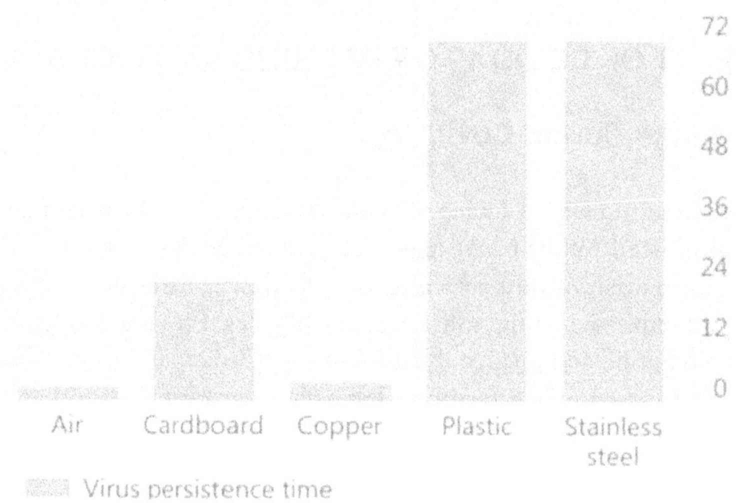

Which said, scientists remember that the likelihood of transmission by banknotes is very low when in contrast to other frequently touched items. To date, there aren't any known instances of COVID 19 transmission by coins or perhaps banknotes. Furthermore, it's not clear if that transmission is actually material in contrast to person to person transmission or maybe transmission through various items or maybe bodily proximity. The simple fact that the virus survives best on nonporous substances, like stainless or plastic steel, suggests that debit or maybe charge card terminals or maybe PIN pads might transmit the virus as well. The head of the German public health institute notes that (viral) transmission through banknotes does not have specific significance, as airborne droplets from infected people are the primary illness risk. Moreover, specialists note that washing hands after touching other items or money might make it possible to decrease the danger of transmission. (**SBI Research 2020**) has suggested Government of India that instead of currency notes, RBI to consider the possibility of polymer currency notes.

Covid 19 pandemic has adversely affected the faster growing digital payment systems in the Indian Economy due to travel bans, shut shops, cancelled air tickets, low consumer spends on dining out in restaurants, movies, tourism etc. The low revenues in the major sectors like auto, retail, hospitality, aviation, E commerce have resulted in the job losses and business failures. Digital payments in India registered a decline of 30% in transaction value during lockdown period both in online and offline. (Shrivastava, Manakadan 2020) ET Bureau reports that the major decline in digital payments were observed in the metro cities like New Delhi, Mumbai, Kolkatta. Chennai and not pan Indian wide. However, the number of transactions continues to be high and value of transactions have declined. Figure 1 reflects the Digital Payment Contributions in value terms in different sectors of Indian Economy. Air lines and E Commerce have shown reduction in Digital Payment up to 30% and 40% for the reason that March to May months attracts highest travel and retail consumers item due to school holidays and annual closing of various business houses.

Views of various online payment solution service provider regarding reduction in online spends and its impact on various sectors involving Banks and Digital Payments are summarised below in Table 1.

Figure 2. Digital Payments Sector Wise Contributions in Value Terms
Source. The Economic Times dated 17th May, 2020 – Digital Payment slip 30% on Covid 19 Curbs

On the other hand, Paytm, Indian E Commerce Payment System and Fintech Company have reported 20% growth in their digital payment as compared to regular business of the day. Customers preferring offline payments i.e. Paytm over cash have also increased by 12%. Repeat transactions were also observed for utility bills payments electricity, water, insurance premiums, fuel stations and school fees. In the last three months from March to May 2020 the coronavirus has changed the consumer's behaviour and attitude towards spending, safety and shift from cash to digital payments. PWC in their report Impact of Covid 19 outbreaks on digital payments studies in detail the business impact sectoral as well as payment categories wide in Indian economy.

Table 1. Reduction in Digital Payments on online platform Source: The Economic Times

S No	Banks, Fintech, Vendor	Type of Digital Payment	Segment	Accounts for Online Spends	Reduction in Digital Payments
1	Rajorpay	Online Payment Solution Provider	Travel	25%	35% to 40%
2	CC Avenue	Payment Gateway Platform	Travel	25%	35% to 40%
3	Bharat Pe	QR Code based	Retail	Not Available	10% - 15%
4	Pine Labs	Offline Aggregators	Service providers	Not Available	10%

SECTION 2: IMPACT OF COVID 19 ON DIFFERENT FINTECH SECTORS ACROSS THE GLOBE AND IN INDIAN ECONOMY

FinTech or Financial Technology has been defined and understood based on financial inclusion, financial literacy, adoption and usage of digital payment systems. In India, there are multiple issues in adoption, usage and access of banking and financial services because there is various type of payment systems from physical paper based to electronic funds transfer and users are located in remote rural, semi urban and metro. Fintech can be defined as a payment service providers or business which offers affordable financial services through advanced technology. **Shahrwatat, Shah (2020)** explain the impact of Covid 19 on different Fintech sector in brief are as below:

Challenger Banks or Neo Banks

The term Challenger Banks or Neo Banks are used interchangeably for convenience of operating banking transactions, opening accounts, funds transfer, on line payments and alternative payment solutions to unbanked or underbanked or MSME sector. One major difference in Digital Bank and Neo Bank is exist online without any physical branches or in partnership with traditional banks where digital bank is in form of on line subsidiary of regulated player in the banking sector. Neo Banks need not required banking license but they have partnership tie up with licensed banks for offering online wallet or bank to bank services. Few examples of NEO Banks across the globe are Webank, Yolt, Lunarway and Moven and in India –NIYO, PayZello, Yelo, Instantpay and Open. Neo bank raised $ 116 million in 2019 as more than 190 million Indians are still unbanked. (**PWC India, 2020**) report on " Neo Banks and the next banking revolution " suggests that with the changing expectations and behaviours of the customers in digital era, the banking value chain, operational and business models to be more innovative. The report also explain the case study of private sector bank partnered with Neo Bank to offer digital wallet, mobile application and multi pocket card based on regulatory IndiaStack principles.

Declining business activity, tight new funding and a weakening economy will especially have a negative impact on challenger banks. India has a big opportunity for Fintech start-ups for MSME sector as more than 40% of borrowers under MSME borrow from the informal sector. Indian MSME has a gap of USD 380 billion in spite of the fact that MSME Sector contribute 31% of India`s GDP. NEO Banks will face low negative impact as in these uncertain times as on boarding of new customers is stopped or reduced, customer may again start routing their deposits and lending transactions through traditional banks and MSME / merchants facing funding issues. The positive impact of Covid 19 will be observed only slight increase in value added services in digital platforms for SME and digital customer acceptance.

Short term negative impact of Payment Fintech sector is low POS transactions as shopping malls and big markets were shut down, less physical delivery of POS terminals, EMI collections by banks and NBFC were deferred due to interest loan moratorium waiver, and low digital payment transactions for e commerce, hospitality and travel sectors. The positive impact on payments are rise in digital payments in Tier2 and Tier3 cities in India for p2p payments and grocery shopping, utility payments, recharges and other essential goods.

Online and Alternative Lending

Digital lenders could be facing various issues of low profitability, lower net interest margins, reduction in fresh lending, EMI default and increasing non-performance assets. The 3.6% YoY growth in 2019 for all loan balances at US banks (FDIC data) will almost certainly flatten due to the economic lockdown. Lenders that had begun serving subprime and small/medium businesses (SMB) due to competition for prime borrowers may see default rates rising and discover they have inadequate reserves. Merchant lending and Consumer lending are the two important segments of lending. Alternative lenders play an important role of meeting the credit needs of financially excluded, unserved segments of economy through on line and digital lending. The negative impact of Covid 19 on online and alternative lending are banks and NBFC restricted unsecured retail loans and new disbursements because default in EMI, decrease in physical collections and reduce spends on discretionary expenses resulting fall in demand. Positive impact will be increase in lending digital start-ups, on line education, pharma, new product launches and expand lending by sufficient capitalized Fintech in mergers and acquisitions.

Robo Advisors / Wealthtechs

Wealth investors and millennials avail the services of robo advisor's Severe volatility and the lack of recovery in public stocks may scare away all investors, especially millennials, who are the biggest customer segment for robo advisors. Self-directed investors using robo advisors and online trading platforms may gravitate away towards established wealth management shops (Charles Schwab, Fidelity Investments, Morgan Stanley) who have matched the "zero commission" model of e-brokers, financial consultants and investment advisors as well as human consultancy advice. Over time, robo advisors have shifted business models from earning revenue from transactions to AUM-based fee models that will suffer as markets remain soft. Robin hood's technical problems have dented investor confidence at the most ill-opportune time and will shake the trust of customers in all robo advisors. Wealth Tech Fintech segment have few positive impact like increase in account opening by new investors and dormant accounts will be live and active for long term wealth creation. Digital or Video KYC process have been adopted by many banks in India with scanned documents uploaded and Shred through E mail or what sup images. Increase usage and adoption of wealth money market instruments will increase.(**Sharma, Zhang, Horne, Steiner, 2020**) in their report " Impact of Coronavirus (Covid 19) on Robo advisors suggests three themes emerging on the impact on Robo advisors – Goal based planning will show benefits, short term asset allocation dn long term perspective and communication with clients will be the key.

Payments/ Transaction Processing

Payment and transaction processing Fintechs will face a mixed picture. A paralyzed global economy with consumers and corporations curtailing travel and entertainment will have a profound impact on consumption in the short term. This will result in a fall-off in transactions, which are the lifeblood for payment Fintechs. Visa and MasterCard's warning that sales will fall short of expectations in the current quarter by 2-4% and a sharp contraction in cross-border flows will hit money transfer Fintechs and other payment providers, especially hard. The one positive trends that in growing digital and mobile transactions is that it is not adversely impacted by the lockdown and restricted travel movements of people during Covid 19.

Short term negative impact of Payment Fintech sector is low POS transactions as shopping malls and big markets were shut down, less physical delivery of POS terminals, EMI collections by banks and NBFC were deferred due to interest loan moratorium waiver, and low digital payment transactions for e commerce, hospitality and travel sectors. The positive impact on payments are rise in digital payments in Tier2 and Tier3 cities in India for p2p payments and grocery shopping, utility payments, recharges and other essential goods.

Institutional Capital Markets / Enabling Tech

Institutional brokers, exchanges, clearing firms are benefitting from the current elevated volatility, though runaway volatility for an extended period of time could have the opposite effect of freezing up trading. Fintechs providing trading infrastructure may benefit from this short-term volatility-driven euphoria, but their future depends on how their institutional clients fare as the market downturn continues. Sectors like Alternate Data may suffer as institutional investors become conservative and gravitate towards traditional investment methodology and practices. Capital markets Fintechs focused on better managing risk and lowering costs (outsourced trading, cloud-based delivery) will gain favor as brokers and asset managers cut costs to maintain margins. Regtech and compliance Fintechs will remain popular as a market dislocation doesn't impact demand for their services. Investors may double down on these investments, boosting their valuations. Enabling technology Fintech will have short as well as medium term positive impact on digital technology platforms like ekyc, voice boats, chatbots, CRM tools, compliance, sandbox for customer engagement, adoption of internal employees and new demand for eco system enablers. However, decrease in IT Budgets and cost optimisation will leads to differed innovative projects

Insurtechs

Usually, massive calamities spell bad news for insurance carriers. But we don't expect large claims from COVID-19 as most insurers most often exclude pandemics or infectious diseases from their coverage. But the virus could boost demand for certain types of insurance by increasing awareness and demand for greater life, health and business disruption coverage. The P&C (Property & Casualty -Insurance) sector insurtechs will not have any negative or downfall trends as an event like COVID-19 doesn't impact that sector. In other insurance segments that address unconventional risks (cybersecurity, climate change, social disruption), investors have been keenly funding insurtechs, so the demand for start-ups in these segments will continue to attract investor interest. The positive impact on insure tech will be rise in health insurance policy, favourable change in customer behaviour towards health and life insurance policy.

negative impact will be observed in increase in claim settlement, reduced travel and vehicle insurance policy and physical visits for claim processing will not be possible. **(ET Online, 2020)** report explain the impact of covid 19 on motor insurance industry that due to lack of demand of purchase of new vehicles will dicrease in the number of motor insurance policy . Unavailability of independent surveyors during lockdown to survey the accidental vehicle upto Rs. 75000 /- which will impact claim surveying .

SECTION 3: COLLABORATION BETWEEN BANKS AND FINTECH DURING COVID 19

After understanding and analysing the challenges, positive and negative impact on Banks and Fintech, the big question at this stage is to analyse that whether Digital Collaboration between banks and Fintech will emerge as a winner to meet the specific fall out of Covid 19. Downwards trends in the customer spending behaviour on non-essential goods were one of the reason as people are working from home and less movement from their homes to buying groceries and other essential goods. As a result, positive impact was observed with rise in payments through on line applications and proportion of payments have shifted from cash to digital payments. **(Makhija, 2020)** in her report Covid 19: An opportune time for Fintech to grow expressed her views that as the world economies are moving from respond to recover to resurrect, economic crisis will shift to the new opportunities created for Fintech . The report focus on concerted push for virtual and contactless to replace paper money with digital payments, customer interactions through online channels and innovation of touch less technology between machine and humans .

Disruptions, Innovation and Collaboration

Fintech may disrupt, innovate, enable, create or collaborate through partnerships and tie ups with the traditional banks. The global impact of COVID-19 would also lead banks to rethink how they interface with consumers and fast track digital innovation efforts. Banks are looking to potentially do more with technology, not less. Several banks would now look to modernize payments infrastructure by working with FinTechs. Traditional banks which have a brick and mortar structure with various bankers interacting with customer along with digital payments limited to Internet and Mobile banking must collaborate with FinTechs new payment systems. Fintech or neo Banks are flexible and have advanced technology based products which are capable of satisfying digital needs of the end customer effectively and quickly.

SaaS-based models and the cloud will play a vital role as banks work to ensure services are available and accessible by all consumers. Fintech collaborating with banks through cloud computing and SaaS Software offers interoperability, 24 by 7 uptime, web based platforms and safe storage, Financial technology companies with strong underlying fundamentals that can help business speed the transition to digital and offer innovative pay-as-you-grow business models will be able to successfully navigate the current crisis. On the positive side, digital payments could transition from a high-value, low-volume business to a low-value, high-volume business, with customers adopting digital modes for small-ticket transactions. As customers self-quarantine, e-commerce traffic will register growth. We foresee a significant uptick in doorstep deliveries of food, groceries and pharmacy. Large retail chains will invest in their own online stores to take advantage of the trend. Local retailers and stores selling the daily essentials needs require to change the sales strategy of accepting orders on phone and shift to QR CODE, PAYTM or electronic payments. This could be a real opportunity to address India's long tail by aggregating small and medium merchants as well as smaller corporates and bringing them into the digital fold. Online bill payments could also show a strong growth trajectory, as consumers increasingly move away from manual touch points.

India's digital economic surge is well under way, with the digital payments market in India expected to become a USD 1T market by 2023. The government push and a favourable regulatory environment has made India the third largest Fintech Hub globally. In India, the FinTech start-up ecosystem is experiencing rapid growth in collaboration with banks, supported by a large market base in a landscape that is driven by innovation. According to Medici, mobile, digital wallets, gateways, POS, mobile POS sub-segments account for over 50 percent of the payment start-ups in India. Indian payment systems have moved on to digital platform through National Payment Corporation of India (NPCI) – Retail payment operator though innovative products UPI, Aadhaar for eKYC, BharatQR for QR-based payments, biometric payments (AEPS), e-wallets and sound-wave-based payments for rural engagements, and last-mile connectivity.

The world after coronavirus will be different from the one that entered the Covid-era. This transformation will be marked by the persistence of social distancing-codes and other health & hygiene-focused lifestyle adjustments across all spheres that have already become a norm since the onset of the pandemic. As renowned Israeli Historian and author Yuval Noah Harari points out, "The decisions people and governments take in the next few weeks will probably shape the world for years to come."

New-age Fintech players that will rise to the occasion on the back of relevant, high-impact financial solutions will earn a leading edge over their peers in the post-Covid-19 market. Neo and Challenger banks in the country's Fintech space are provide support to traditional banks through digital wallets and linking the accounts of the quarantined population – individuals and enterprises alike – in the lockdown-battered scheme of things. Amidst the ongoing lockdown, people are relying on online payments and other digital-led financial mechanisms such as credit/debit cards, e-Wallets, UPI etc. Why? Because digital-first systems enable people to meet their financial obligations without moving out from their home, thereby enabling them to observe mandated social distancing-protocols to prevent the spread of Covid-19. As a result, various digital payments companies registered a transactional surge in online payment volumes since nationwide lockdown was announced near the end of March. In order to follow social distancing norms to minimise one's physical contact and use on line payments, digital-based Fintech services prevent users from engaging in the exchange of cash which can function as a potential Covid-19 carrier. These benefits enable Fintech companies the key to success to unlock a safer and more financial inclusive future in the post-pandemic landscape.

SECTION 4: THE FINTECH ECOSYSTEM OF THE FUTURE AND CASE STUDIES

The Fintech Ecosystem of the Future

The mission of the Fintech sector is to leverage technology to deliver both existing and emerging banking services to the maximum number of people in the most convenient format. In the post-Covid-19 future, sanitization and hygiene will comprise the priority for every individual. Therefore, Fintechs will step into this picture by making payment services contact-less and more accessible so that the maximum number of people can use new-age financial services at the minimum risk of contracting the virus. In other words, the Fintech services of the future will be tasked with transforming the financial landscape to make it safer besides more efficient, accessible, and affordable.

To achieve this, Fintech service providers will need to adopt new-age, contactless features and make them available to the masses. These include dynamic QR codes, contactless biometric authentication, and contactless card payment solutions, among other things. UPI is another existing technology which has already gained significant traction in India, especially since the onset of the lockdown. With time, all contact-based payment models such as PoS machines will get replaced with the aforementioned contactless, mobile-based solutions.

However, the country is home to a large chunk of people who are not only underprivileged, unbanked, and underserved but also lack access to a smartphone as well as the prerequisite knack for technology essential for using such tech-based services. Against this backdrop, Fintechs face the challenge of coming up with relevant solutions specifically designed for this target group. AePS & mATM comprises one such solution that has the potential to thread through all of these requirements.

In a country such as India, the hassle-free financial services offered by AePS delivers a robust channel to reach out to and uplift the underprovided and underserved segment. Since a large majority of people, including those from remote regions, are already linked with Aadhaar, AePS can play an instrumental role in enabling the much-needed paradigm shift towards a new, critical transactional routine in the post-lockdown, post-pandemic financial ecosystem.

According to a recent study, India is home to more than 504 million active internet users, making it the second-biggest internet market after China. Interestingly, 2019 became the year when the digital divide went for a toss when the number of rural users surpassed urban internet users by a margin of 10%. This number has only grown in 2020. Hence, the country's rural space is ripe for disruption by new-age Fintech players and the future will see them capturing this market segment on the back of effective digital-first solutions specifically designed for the rural consumers.

The futuristic Fintech landscape will also see the emergence of innovations that will facilitate holistic financial services over a single mobile interface for Indian users across geographies. The shift in user sensibilities will encourage service providers to collate and deliver their offerings to enable cross-selling of services over one platform. New-age Fintech platforms are already offering consolidated Fintech solutions to users, enabling them to carry out a range of operations such as spending, lending, investing, fund transfer, etc. Assisted e-commerce on existing B2B2C platforms is another feature that new-age Fintechs will provide to Indian users in the post-lockdown, post-pandemic future. Innovation-focused players are committed to resolving all the bottlenecks inhibiting a seamless positive transformation within the country's financial ecosystem. Their progress-oriented vision will see the emergence of. And considering present trends, unlocking a safer, more accessible, and inclusive Fintech ecosystem is no longer a matter of possibility, but merely that of time. Figure: reflects various leading Fintech Start-ups in India and will study the success story of five Fintech in India.

Fintech Case Studies from India

1. **Paytm & Paytm Money**
2. **PhonePe**
3. **MobiKwik**
4. **ETMoney**
5. **Policy Bazar**

Figure 3: Fintech Start-ups
Source: Warpcore, 2020; Building Super App: How Paytm is leading Fintech Revolution

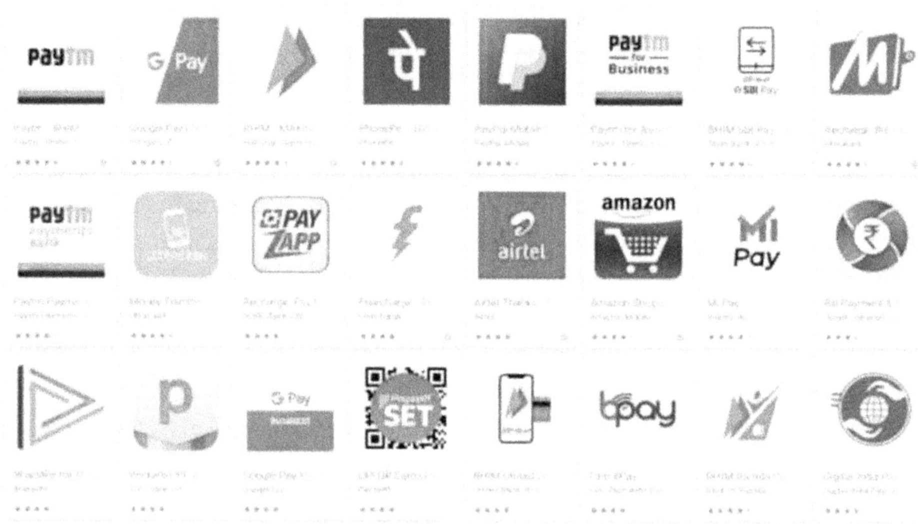

1. Paytm

Paytm was Launched as digital payments and investments category company and holding company One 9 Communications in 2010 by Mr Vijay Shekhar Sharmawith. Paytm headquarters is in Delhi /NCR. Paytm and it early days it focussed on processing online DTH / telecom / post-paid services. Paytm Fintech is a visionary company which in 2013 was early to enter into digitalisation and smart phone penetration and played an important role in Financial Inclusion. Paytm enters into digital wallet services, utility bill payments, investments, payment gateway, payment bank and tie up with Uber became popular with the users. Key Investors in PAYTM are Softbank, Japan with 20%, Alibaba 42% China and became a company worth1. more than $10 Bn) and total funding till date was $ 2.5 Bn in 2019. Paytm also tie up with Bill desk, CC Avenue, small vendors as the users just need to tap Wallet icon linked with Paytm gateway.

Paytm's revolutionary and phenomenal success came with the Financial Inclusion PMJDY Scheme in 2014 and demonetisation replacing high value notes of Rs. 1000/- and Ras. 500 /- in November 2016. Users moved from cash payments to Paytm digital wallet. With 4G and Jio, data cost became affordable for customers. Smartphone brands like Xiaomi enable Indian users to start using internet and mobile. The company also launched an investment, Paytm bank account opening, trading platform, ecommerce, Paytm money and Paytm Mall. This company became largest Fintech payments apps with Customer base grew to 185 Mn from125 Mn . Since then, Paytm grow to 300 Mn mark in 2018 and in 2019 its valuation touched US$ 16 billion. with 140 million monthly user base.

2. PhonePe

PhonePe, Fintech Company with headquarter in Bengalaru, India was launched in 2015 by Rahul Chari, Sameer Nigam, Burzin Engineer and offers payment application based on UPI (Unified Payments Interface) platform regulated by National Payment Corporation of India. (NPCI). PhonePe offered various digital payments services and support utility bills, mobile and phone recharges, online and e commerce services. In August 2019, as per data released by NPCI, PhonePe was the top user's acceptance leading application for UPI digital payments in India. Various services offered by PhonePe are funds transfer for receiving or sending funds, DTH or mobile recharge, credit card payments, shopping offline or online, insurance premiums, travelling and wallets. It's very simple to download and easy to use by customers by linking their bank accounts and registered mobile number to UPI platform. Key Investors of PhonePe is Flipkart.

3. MobiKwik

MobiKwik is a Fintech launched in 2009 by Bipin Preet Singh, Upasana Taku, providing digital wallets and financial services which are an issuer-independent. Its headquarter is in Gurgaon, India and the services offered by Mobikwik relates to various segments of the fintech ecosystem. Mobikwik have received total funding $162 Mn and main investors of Mobikwik are Sequoia Capital India, GMO Payment Gateway and Net 1 UEPS Technologies Inc, . The services offered includes digital wallets, mobile and other payments, wealth management, money transfers, insurance, shopping, utility bills like electricity and tax payments. The success of Mobikwik was first Lending Fintech in India to quickly disburse loans in 90 seconds and do online Kyc verification, checking customer credit score with low customer acquisition cost.

Mobikwik also offers three important products -One Partnership with other Fintech as business partners and customers to reach 100 million users for digital payments. Mobikwik has 30 lakhs business partner and have collaborations with banks and IT Vendors. Second, Mobikwik offers on line payment gateway solutions having diverse payment options, mobile friendly, seamless integration, secure, best conversion rates, secure and analytics. Third, Mobikwik offers support in finding suitable mutual funds to customers for investment in regular plans without any fees and charges.

4. EtMoney

ETMONEY was launched in 2015 as Fintech Company with Times Internet as a main investor. ET MONEY has its headquarters in Gurgaon, India' and founded by Mr. Mukesh P Kalra. ET money offers various services like investments in top mutual funds, personal loans, instant disbursement of loans, term life insurance, health insurance, car insurance, bike insurance. ETMoney has become the largest Fintech services application which help customer on financial advising on saving income tax as well as provides credit scoring tools. ETMONEY also offers Equity Linked Savings Scheme (ELSS) Mutual funds, Credit cards and Pension schemes without any commission. ETMoney growth rate is 340% year on year basis with 7 Mn users and with non payment annual $ 500 Mn transaction volumes.

REFERENCES

Belgavi, V., & Gandhi, M. (2020, April). *PWC India report - Impact of the Covid 19 outbreak on Digital Payments*. https://www.pwc.in/assets/pdfs/consulting/financial-services/fintech/point-of-view/pov-downloads/impact-of-the-covid-19-outbreak-on-digital-payments.pdf

Bhasin, N. K. (2019). Study of Increasing Digital banking & Financial Technology Trends, Challenges and Opportunities in Indian Banking System. *Bank Quest, 90*(4), 33–44.

Bhasin, N. K., & Rajesh, A. (2019). *Increasing Digital Banking Adoption and Usage Trends in India and its Impact on Financial Inclusion. International Journal of Recent Technology and Engineering.*

Biji Kurian John. (2020, June 10). *Bank and Fintech Collaboration –Lifeline for Economic Revival Post Covid 19.* Trade Finance Global Articles. https://www.tradefinanceglobal.com/posts/bank-and-fintech-collaboration-lifeline-for-economic-revival-post-covid19/

Dubey. (2019). FinTech Innovations in Digital Banking. *International Journal of Engineering and Research & Technology, 8*(10).

Fincash. (2020, July 12*). Impact of Covid 19 on the Future of Fintech Industry*. Academic Press.

Money Control News. (2020, April 2). *Fintech: Banks play a vital role in engaging customers amidst the COVID 19 spread.* https://www.moneycontrol.com/news/technology/fintechs-banks-play-a-vital-role-in-engaging-customers-amidst-the-covid-19-spread-5101931.html

Nigam, A. (2020). *Future of Fintech in a Post Covid world.* https://timesofindia.indiatimes.com/blogs/voices/future-of-fintech-in-a-post-covid-world/

Online, E. T. (2020, June 17). *Coronavirus impact on motor insurance, health and life insurance*. PWC Report. https://economictimes.indiatimes.com/wealth/personal-finance-news/coronavirus-impact-on-motor-health-and-life-insurance-pwc-report/articleshow/76418575.cms?from=mdr

Pagaria, V. (2020, April 16). *The Fallout of Covid 19 on the BFSI Sector, ET BFSI.Com.* https://bfsi.economictimes.indiatimes.com/blog/the-fallout-of-covid-19-on-the-bfsi-sector/4170

PwC India Report. (2020, June). *Redefining the Fintech Experience: Impact of Covid 19.* https://www.pwc.in/assets/pdfs/services/crisis-management/covid-19/redefining-the-fintech-experience-impact-of-covid-19.pdf

Shah, I. (2020, March 8). *ET BFSI.Com. Covid 19 is a turning point for this Fintech.* https://bfsi.economictimes.indiatimes.com/news/fintech/covid-19-is-a-turning-point-for-this-fintech/74861775

Shahrawat, D., & Shah, V. (2020, March 3). *The Impact of COVID 19 on different Fintech Sectors*. Fintech.

Sharma, N. (2020, March 25). *Voices 3 emerging Robo trends amid Covid 19 market craziness*. Financial Planning.com. https://www.financial-planning.com/opinion/3-emerging-robo-trends-amid-coronavirus-stock-market-volatility

Singh, J., & Bodla, B. S. (2020). COVID-19 pandemic and lockdown impact on India's banking sector: A systemic literature review. In *COVID-19 Pandemic: A Global Challenge* (pp. 21–32). New Delhi: Aryan Publications.

Chapter 9
The Challenge of Building Communities About PBL Supervision:
From Networks of Practice to Communities of Practice

Hans Hüttel
Department of Computer Science, Aalborg University, Denmark

Dorina Gnaur
https://orcid.org/0000-0001-5508-5011
Department of Culture and Learning, Aalborg University, Denmark

ABSTRACT

Problem-based learning (PBL) is central to the degree programmes at Aalborg University (AAU), but if one is a member of the teaching faculty with a degree from another institution, it is unlikely that one is familiar with PBL. In this chapter, the authors describe the development of an ongoing experiences with PBL Exchange, a web-based platform whose goal is to facilitate the transfer and development of knowledge and skills within PBL project supervision by means of a web-based crowdsourcing approach that makes it easy to exchange and discuss one's specific problems and experience with project supervision. The goal was to build a new community of practice from a network of practice, but this has turned out to be difficult. The authors discuss and analyze their experiences and suggest technical and social developments that may be able to facilitate the creation of community of practice.

DOI: 10.4018/978-1-7998-4891-2.ch009

Copyright © 2021, IGI Global. Copying or distributing in print or electronic forms without written permission of IGI Global is prohibited.

1. INTRODUCTION

A major challenge in providing high-quality learning at universities is that of developing professional competence for the teaching staff involved. It is essential to be able to capture and maintain the expertise that evolves through teaching practice.

At Aalborg University, problem-based learning (PBL) is central to all degree programmes offered. However, the teaching competences needed in the PBL model differ from those used at many other institutions of higher education and are not widely known. This means that members of the teaching staff that have their background from other academic institutions are likely not to have any experience with supervising PBL projects, that each comprise 15 ECTS or more. While there are now formal programmes at Aalborg University that are intended to provide qualifications in supervising PBL projects, there appears to be a chasm between the formal competence development carried out and the informal communities of practice that also exist. Moreover, these informal communities can be highly divergent in their interpretations of PBL and the informal, collective understanding of what constitutes good PBL practice does not get written down.

Crowdsourcing is now advocated as a powerful strategy for mobilizing creative knowledge development and problem solving (Howe, 2006), and as an approach to peer learning (Stonebraker and Zhang, 2015). So far there has been little research on how to apply this approach in the area of competence development. Albors et al. (2008) have built a taxonomy of networking platforms that considers the interplay of social and informational connectivity based on work by Bernard (2006). In this taxonomy, crowdsourced platforms appear at the high end of social connectivity and at a medium-high level with regard to the potential for creating knowledge as compared to merely sharing information. On one hand, crowdsourcing has a stronger emphasis on knowledge creation than that of other social networking platforms. On the other hand, crowdsourcing has a stronger emphasis on the social negotiation aspect as compared to other social platforms for creating knowledge. Moreover, knowledge occurs most effectively among people with a common frame of reference and a common field of practices (Contu, A. and Willmott, H., 2003). This combination makes crowdsourcing interesting in the context of informal competence development within a knowledge-oriented social community set-up in an academic professional context.

In this paper we describe the development of, and ongoing experiences with PBL Exchange, a web-based platform whose goal is to facilitate the transfer and development of knowledge and skills within the field of PBL project supervision by means of a web-based crowdsourcing approach that makes it easy to exchange and discuss one's specific problems and experience with project supervision.

Following the social knowledge creation argument, PBL Exchange has been conceived as a *closed expert crowdsourcing* forum in the sense of (Stonebraker and Zhang, 2016), where practitioners guide colleagues within the same field of reference towards solving problems that arise in their daily practice: the users of the system are project supervisors at Aalborg University.

The development of PBL Exchange is an example of *design-based research (DBR);* this is an approach that has attracted both researchers and various layman groups, mostly within the area of technological interventions to improve learning outcomes (Anderson and Shattuck 2012). DBR is driven by a double aim, which is that of conducting an intervention addressing a problem in practice together with an empirical examination that can further theoretical conceptualization in the domain and inform future actions. DBR commits to mixed methods that are used widely in educational research (McKenney and Reeves 2012) and leans onto learning design principles (Gravemeijer and Cobb, 2006) with the purpose of furthering both research and practice. The framework adopted is often one of practitioner-researcher partnerships, similar to those used in action research (Ørngreen 2015). DBR claims its raison d'être from its dual aim, to advance both theory and practice in novel areas of potential interest to both parties, e.g. technology and learning.

However, there are inherent limitations in DBR when it comes to carrying out the design interventions, as these are often developed in lab-like environments detached from the messiness of real learning ecologies (Jackson 2012). This may impair the transfer process (McKenney and Reeves 2013; Ørngreen 2015). Similarly, it can be difficult to assess the real value of the theoretical outcomes of DBR. This is partly due to the ongoing, iterative pattern of design interventions that makes it difficult to report on the impact on practice. It is also due to the fact that there are relatively few studies that report actual theoretical deliberations as a result of design-based interventions. The value of DBR rests perhaps not with concluding, but with opening up the field by means of novel interventions and initiating theoretical discussions based on preliminary findings and ongoing analysis. In this vein, this paper presents preliminary theoretical reflections on the basis of an ongoing intervention in its third iteration.

In Section 2 we give an overview of problem-based learning as it is intended to be practiced at Aalborg University and of the challenges associated with teaching within this format and with developing the teaching competences of PBL supervision. Next, in Section 3 we describe the design of the PBL Exchange platform. A particularly important notion is that of a network of practice and how it relates to communities of practice. Section 4 gives an account of the experiences that users had with the first version of the platform. Section 5 contains our reflections on attempting to build a community of practice, and in Section 6 we describe how our reflections can shape a new version of PBL Exchange.

2. PBL AND THE CHALLENGES OF PBL SUPERVISION

The design of the PBL Exchange platform has as its outset our observations of the existing practice concerning the supervision of PBL projects at Aalborg University and of how and to what extent the experience associated with this practice is disseminated. In this section we give an account of our observations and of the challenges that exist.

2.1 Problem-Based Learning at Aalborg University is Collaborative and Project-Based

At Aalborg University problem-based learning (PBL) has been the foundational learning philosophy of all degree programmes since the university was founded in 1974. Most often, PBL at Aalborg University is carried out using a project-based format in which content knowledge is created and expanded in the process of attending to real-life problems based on scientific methodology. Aalborg University (2015) describes an ideal version of PBL as that of project work based on authentic problems, self-governed group work and collaboration. Students work in groups, usually comprised of at most 6 students, and the project consists in analyzing and solving (or trying to solve) a problem within a semester theme related to the subject area. Each project group is assigned a supervisor that is supposed to facilitate the project process and contribute with knowledge within the subject area. Typically, a project will last a semester and constitutes at least half of the teaching load of the semester. The outcome of a project is usually a report written by the participants of the group and the assessment is most often done in the form of an oral exam that involves all students participating in a project.

The Aalborg model of PBL provides students with tools for independent acquisition of knowledge, skills and competences at an advanced academic level. At the same time, the model supports students in developing communication and cooperation competences, and in acquiring the skills required when taking an analytical and result-oriented approach.

About 50% of the total of teaching at AAU is devised as project work, with teaching in the form of PBL supervision and facilitation. However, this also requires that members of teaching staff must be able to support the development of all of the competences associated with this: A supervisor must act as a facilitator for the problem analysis, must be able to provide advice for the process of academic writing and must also be able to facilitate the process-oriented, collaborative aspects of a project such as planning and knowledge-sharing. In some cases, supervisors will have to help resolve conflicts within a group of students. These competences are important and by no means trivial; it takes time and effort to develop them.

2.2 Developing and Maintaining Teaching Competences in PBL

Problem based learning (PBL) is not a new learning philosophy, nor is it universally accepted. New members of academic staff at universities that adopt PBL usually have little or no experience with this pedagogical approach, and even if they do, it is important to develop a systematic approach to PBL practices and help their understanding grow. There are several challenges here.

2.2.1 External Change Makes the PBL Model Vulnerable

The first challenge is that the body of competence is vulnerable in the presence of external change. An illustrative example of this is that of the changes that occurred to the examination of projects at Aalborg University. From the inception of the university in 1974 to 2007, projects were assessed via group-based oral exams. However, this form of oral exam was explicitly banned by the Danish government in 2007. When the ban was lifted in 2012 and group-based project exams re-introduced, a generation of students and teaching staff had emerged with no knowledge of and a large amount of scepticism towards an examination practice that had been at the core of PBL practice for a long time (Dahl and Kolmos, 2016). It became a major task to re-create good project exam practice and to ensure that it would be maintained.

2.2.2 Teaching Staff is Transient

Another form of external challenge is the result of the lack of permanent positions in modern-day academia. This has led to a large throughput of temporary teaching staff and external lecturers with short academic careers and little teaching experience. Many temporary members of staff come to see the role as project supervisor as an isolated one and end up thinking that the problems that they face are theirs alone. Moreover, an increasing percentage of temporary teaching staff (as well as a sizeable fraction of the permanent staff) will have no previous exposure to PBL in general and the AAU-model in particular, not to mention the many discipline specific elements of PBL work, which are often tacitly taken for granted. Project-based teaching formats are not particular to Aalborg University, but PBL is a student-centered pedagogy according to which students learn best when applying theory and research based knowledge on open-ended problems. In degree programmes at other universities projects will often take the form of large, closed-form assignments with little or no problem analysis being carried out by students. Supervisors familiar with this latter format are not always aware of how PBL projects are different or why the PBL approach to projects is essential.

2.2.3 Formal vs. Informal Understandings of PBL

Finally, there is the challenge of how formal competence development and informal practice are separate and sometimes at odds with each other.

Since PBL project work is central to degree programmes, Aalborg University now has a formal competence development strategy in the form of courses for teaching staff on developing competence in PBL supervision. If supervisors are to develop their PBL competences and connect them to practical experience, and in particular to avail themselves of assistance in the specific situations and types of problems that they encounter, they will have to share and reflect on their experiences. This can take the form of collegial supervision. Following work by Lauvås, Lycke and Handal (2004), the notion of colleagues that challenge each other and help each other develop their competences within teaching is widely embraced in various educational contexts in the Nordic countries. Consequently, in courses on competence development at Aalborg University there will often be some degree of collegial supervision involved. However, this kind of supervision is only carried out as part of such courses; it is not an ongoing practice.

There is also a large body of literature on PBL practice available from the local PBL Academy (PBL Academy, 2019) that is being used for competence development in courses on competence development. However, the sources are often not based in current experience but are either normative descriptions of how PBL should be carried out or retrospective studies.

3. THE DESIGN OF THE PBL EXCHANGE PLATFORM

In this section we describe the external aspects of the design of PBL Exchange. Later, in Section 6, we outline the ideas behind the system architecture of the new version of PBL Exchange.

3.1 Networks and Communities

A central notion in our approach is that of a *network of practice.* A network is any set of individuals that are connected through social relationships that can be strong or weak. The notion of a network of practice originates in the work by Brown and Duguid (2000) and denotes the collection of informal, emergent social networks that facilitate information exchange between individuals that share practice-related goals. Networks of practice can range from communities of practice, where learning takes place, to virtual or electronic communities such as PBL Exchange.

The notion is related to that of *Communities of Practice (CoP),* which is a concept that was introduced in 1991 (Lave and Wenger) and significantly expanded by Wenger (1998) to signify formal and informal groups of people that engage socially in a common endeavour through processes of collective learning, helping each other to perform in the interest of the common practice. A community of practice relies on strong social relationships, so every community of practice is a network of practice, but the converse does not hold.

At an institution of higher education many small, informal communities of practice exist both within research and teaching. At Aalborg University, our own experience is that teaching staff will often discuss their experience with PBL supervision in informal settings, such as during breaks, and that less experienced supervisors sometimes ask their more experienced colleagues for advice. Very occasionally, some form of informal collegial supervision may even take place.

However, there are several risks here. One is that the informal communities within the university, become isolated and diverge in their views of PBL. Another is that the informality does not guarantee that those that have a need for developing their competences will actually seek or get any support. It is not always the case that the norms for PBL supervision found in informal communities are made explicit, let alone challenged – for they may not necessarily be good norms. In fact, a criticism that is often voiced when learning in CoPs is concerned, is that this kind of learning has a risk of simply reproducing what is already known and taken for granted in the community and is less inclined to be innovative. This may be particularly true of the norms held by the dominant members of a community (Contu, 2014; Wenger, 2010). And finally, whatever advice is given, is only passed on in the form of word-of-mouth advice and is not preserved for posterity. No systematic or structured base of knowledge gets developed based on practice.

3.2 Crowdsourcing for Building a Community of Practice

The intention of PBL Exchange system has been to use a form of crowdsourcing to build an online community of practice and to preserve, structure and reflect on the experience that PBL supervisors have. The collection of questions and answers is a searchable knowledge base built by the interactions by the teaching staff.

Others have attempted to develop an integrated definition of crowdsourcing by indicating certain characteristics, such as the presence of a task with a clear goal; the recompense received by the crowd; the crowdsourcer and the benefit it receives; the participative nature of the task; and the existence of an open call (Estellés-Arolas and González-Ladrón-De-Guevara, 2012). When confined to a single institution, the term 'crowd' can be debated as per how many active participants it should involve. However, it has been argued that crowdsourcing is increasingly associated with certain forms of participatory activities that tap into collective intelligence and is widely applied to almost any Internet-based collaborative activity (Estellés-Arolas and González-Ladrón-De-Guevara, 2012).

It is important to understand what generates the motivation for this type of participation and how it can be stimulated when initiating projects such as the present one. The authors reckon that PBL Exchange relies upon social engagement as a way of making individuals work collaboratively towards a common purpose, which is to develop PBL skills through addressing specific issues as encountered in one's current practice. Gradually, the exchanges generated by practice related issues will stimulate knowledge creation through processes of meaning negotiation and learning from more experienced members of the wider PBL community at AAU.

3.2 The Use and Usefulness of Questions and Answers in Crowdsourcing

The fundamental form of contributing to PBL Exchange is that of asking questions and providing answers and comments. A screenshot of PBL Exchange showing this can be seen in Figure 1. Any member of the teaching staff can ask a question, and any of their colleagues at the university can then contribute with answers to the question. This is directly inspired by StackExchange (StackExchange, 2019). StackExchange fora are open and expert-based and cover a wide variety of topics. Since its inception, StackExchange has become increasingly popular with students in higher education as well as with professionals (Keller, 2010).

Moreover, PBL Exchange integrates specific gamification elements directly inspired by StackExchange: Questions and answers can receive upvotes and downvotes from users, and in this way the users accumulate points. In this sense, the system will be self-regulating: Content judged to be of high quality will become prominent, while content that the community considers to be of low quality will sink to the bottom. However, for this to be a viable model, the user base must be sufficiently large and sufficiently active. It is therefore very important to take steps that facility the emergence and continued existence of a community of users.

The PBL Exchange platform is therefore meant to extend and supplement collegial supervision by using interactive, written format that enables insights to be preserved and structured. Moreover, and importantly, because of the nature of a web platform that can be shared by the entire teaching staff, this makes it possible to share experience across departments and degree programmes in a way that collegial supervision often does not allow for.

Figure 1. Screenshot of the PBL Exchange platform

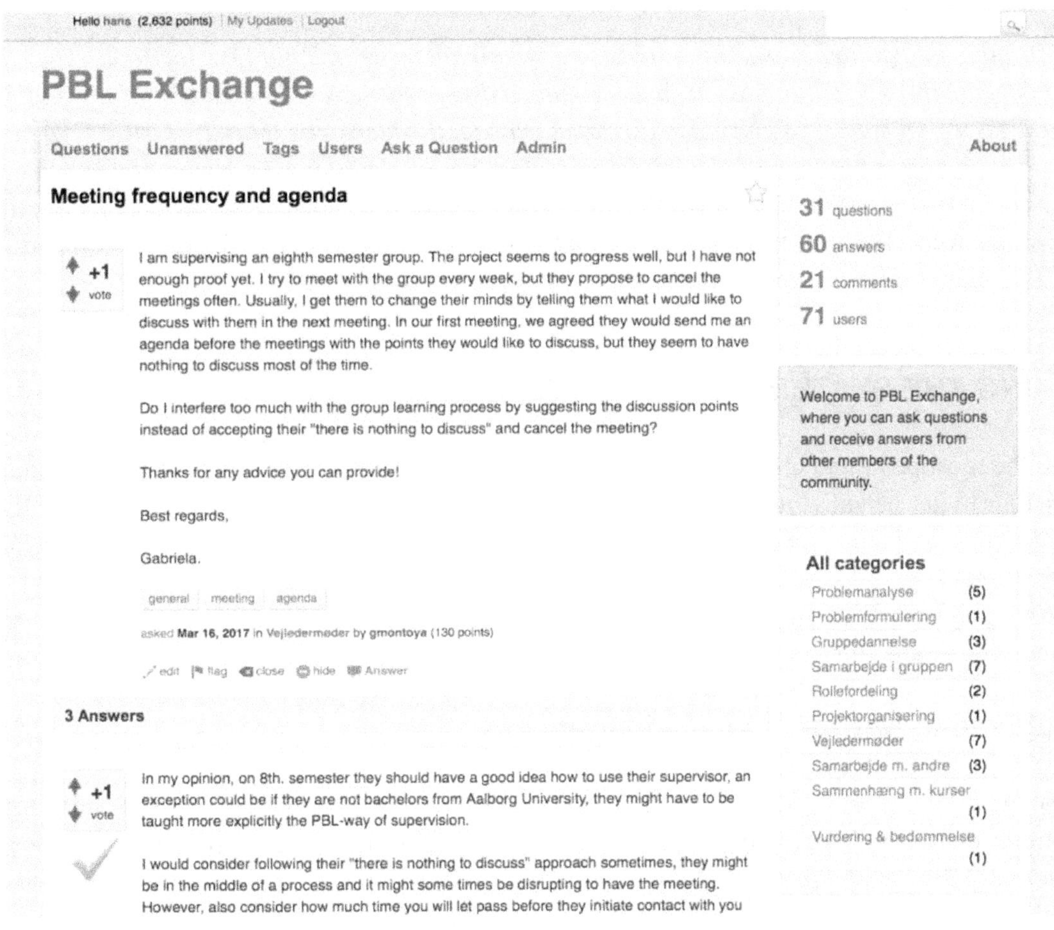

4. USER EXPERIENCE

The first version of PBL Exchange was rolled out to a small community across Aalborg University that was deemed to be receptive, and the next version, to be introduced to a much larger community of teaching staff and described in Section 6, takes the initial user experience into account.

4.1 A Survey of the First Version

During the initial phase we involved a total of 40 test users and asked them to evaluate their experience with PBL Exchange in the form a mixed quantitative/qualitative survey. The authors sought to involve a diverse set of users from several faculties with both experienced and less experienced supervisors. In particular, the participants of the pedagogical course that is mandatory for junior lecturers at Aalborg University were targeted.

A major concern was whether or not PBL Exchange is at all useful. The replies reveal that this is indeed the case. One user writes

Of cause [sic] the answers are nice and I have tried to implement several answers into my supervision. Besides, it's nice to know that other people are having the same questions, challenges etc.

The question *How could we get more people to contribute to PBL Exchange?* gave rise to the following reply in the survey, which is typical.

Maybe through integration in existing systems, e.g. notifications when logging onto Moodle. [. . .] When a new system is introduced, it must fit in as seamlessly as possible (i.e. limited disturbance of existing work processes and habits), it must also be stated from up the hierarchy that this system is to be used.

It turns out that a particular concern that we did not foresee, was one of anonymity for questions as well as for answers. This may be related to the fact that there seems to be a particular interest in problems related to collaboration, as these will often involve person-sensitive issues.

5. TAKING THE SYSTEM TO THE LOCAL USERS

Overall, the most persistent challenge has been to introduce PBL Exchange to a larger community, and in particular to get potential users interested and to make them engaged as well as remain active. Using the terminology introduced above, our intent was to foster a community of practice by means of a network of practice.

In 2017 and early 2018 the authors have tried to address these issues by presenting PBL Exchange to the individual departments at Aalborg University in a series of local seminars.

5.1 Cultivating Networks and Communities

The goal of building a network of practice is a challenge in itself. Within various types of online mediated interactions, there is now a growing understanding of the importance of network building in the general setting of crowdsourcing. Among the work in this area is that of Hossain (2012) who studies the factors that will influence whether users will participate in a crowdsourcing effort and distinguishes between *intrinsic* and *extrinsic* factors. According to Hossain, intrinsic incentives are a dominant motivational factor in a crowdsourcing setting: the task itself of participating and contributing is enough for satisfaction.

The interest in community building and community maintenance in the setting of professional development within a smaller, well-defined community is fairly recent.

In the setting of competence development, Hur and Hara (2007) analyzed the challenges faced when developing an online community for professional development among K-12 teachers in Korea. They found that intrinsic factors, such as a sense of ownership and autonomy and that of the organization acknowledging the value of participating in the community, were important.

Since the motivational factors are non-commercial, participation must be driven intrinsically by personal interests, or by inherently engaging tasks. When it comes to professional competence development in the context of PBL pedagogy, one may well be able to identify intrinsically motivated people, driven by the PBL philosophy as such. Their presence is presumably consistent within various university settings and they are active in many ways, both formally and informally. The task is then to expand their engagement spectrum to include digital activism. As for the nature of the tasks, one should count on participants' interest in clarifying and refining PBL practice to novices and colleagues, as well as renegotiating certain aspects of PBL with like-minded experts. However, for this to happen, the option of asking online questions should be known to novices and more peripherally connected staff (e.g. temporarily employed or external lecturers); and they should then be willing to and confident in asking questions and thereby expose their presumed lack of knowledge, as it were.

5.2 Formal and Informal Networks in Further Community Development

There are several considerations regarding the next iteration of the project with designing a collaborative interface for the development and consolidation of PBL practice at AAU, in the form of PBL Exchange. One of them is to outline a more systematic approach to creating a network of practice that can become a new community of practice.

The seminars that presented PBL Exchange gave an insight into why introducing the platform was going to be difficult.

An obstacle that has often been mentioned by those attending presentations of the system is that of the predominance of existing informal communities concerning PBL supervision – the word-of-mouth transfer of competence is comparatively well-established and well understood.

The role of existing networks should not be underestimated. Landqvist and Teigland (2005) studied what they called electronic networks of practice and found that

"...the most successful effort to create an electronic network of practice was within education and that one contributing factor was the site's ability to leverage existing offline networks of practice to create a relational structure of stronger social ties between members."

Another obstacle that has been pointed out by colleagues attending the seminars is that PBL Exchange runs the risk of being seen as "yet another system". At Aalborg University there is already a plethora of web services, and while most of the services rely on the same authentication service (we return to this in Section 6), the lack of interoperability has become a common complaint: while most of the services use the same authentication front-end, most of the existing services are not well-integrated with each other and have very different user interfaces.

Among various frameworks to build online communities, one finds Wang et al. (2008) and their three principles for growing a successful CoP. The first is that of removing barriers to individual participation. The second consists in providing support and enriching the development of each individual's uniqueness within the context of the community. The third concerns the linking of that uniqueness with the community's purpose. The PBL Exchange system has already removed barriers to individual participation by assigning a single sign-on directly accessible from the university LMS. The authors believe that encouraging participants to enter with personally encountered problems and observations makes the exchange personal and unique to each individual. In order for this to work as intended, members need to know of this possibility, and to be willing to engage. Following the dynamics of CoP's there are three interdependent terms to be observed, i.e. *mutual engagement*, *joint enterprise* and *shared repertoire* (Wenger, 1998).

The shared repertoire in a community is larger than one of issues that are strictly related to work. Mattson and Davidson (2018) have investigated if it is the case that off-topic networks of practice would serve to stimulate discussions of work-related issues in a network of practice. A paradoxical observation that they make is that off-topic discussions distract members from participating in the domain-specific forums, but that it is also the case that off-topic discussions are socializing mechanisms that have a function similar to breaks from work: likeminded members meet each other and create social bonds and attachments with each other.

A related reflection is that of Abdallah (2020) who has studied the types of interactions that occur in an electronic network of practice in software engineering field and finds that narrative posts can allow for better social learning and interaction in network discussion forums.

PBL supervision and the teaching of courses are the main teaching responsibilities of teaching staff; moreover, the intent is often that projects and courses contribute to related learning goals. It may therefore be beneficial to think of a wider forum for sharing the experience of teaching staff beyond that of PBL supervision.

Theoretical and empirical research investigating the effect of IT-based enhancers for online community interaction is limited (Agarwal, 2007). We are particularly inspired by the notion of a *sense of virtual community* to monitor the degree of involvement of members in a community. This is a taxonomy of members' feelings of belonging toward the community. When a sense of virtual community is present, the members of the community give mutual support, contribute with knowledge to the community and reinforce its norms. The feeling of belonging is assumed to increase by growing into the purpose and the activities of the community.

Any further development of the platform should make use of these findings and opt for becoming a more encompassing medium for teaching staff with a wider selection of topics, including other aspects of teaching and topics, beyond teaching, and drawing on existing networks.

6 REFLECTIONS ON A NEW VERSION OF PBL EXCHANGE

The next version of PBL Exchange addressed the concerns that arose from the pilot version. In this section we describe the technical issues that we have sought to address in the new version and still need to be addressed.

6.1 Some Technical Considerations

Some aspects of the internal design of PBL Exchange merit further attention.

6.1.1 Modularity Issues

A main motivation behind the development of PBL Exchange version 2 was that of creating an extendable platform. The original system described in (Gnaur and Hüttel, 2017) uses Question2Answer (2019), an open source system implemented in PHP and using a mySQL database. However, the codebase of Question2Answer is poorly structured and uses programming styles that are at best dubious. As a result, it is very difficult to reuse the existing work on Question2Answer in new settings, where extensibility is necessary.

An early prototype of the system based on Question2Answer has been operational since September 2016 with a small user base of 40 members of the teaching staff across campus. In February 2017 a survey was conducted of this initial user base, and other extensions were suggested by the participants – notably that of mail notifications (see Section 3.4).

As a consequence, PBL Exchange was re-implemented in the Django framework (Django, 2019) in order to create a modular system that can be easily extended and that can support further features. The Django framework is written in Python and uses Python throughout; the framework was chosen because it can help ensure pluggability and ease of reusability of code. Using the Django framework allowed for a modular structure, where one for modules such as authentication could use existing modules that have already been tested.

6.1.2 The Need for Authentication

The intention of PBL Exchange is that teaching staff can discuss their practice (including person-sensitive issues) without interference from students. One of the challenges has therefore been that of setting up authentication. Most web services provided at Aalborg University rely on a Central Authentication Service (CAS), and in order to make PBL Exchange easily accessible to new users and to enable integration with other, already existing services, it was chosen to use CAS.

PBL Exchange uses the CAS of Aalborg University together with the default Django user model. By using CAS in conjunction with the default Django user model one can attain a high degree of extensibility. Another benefit from using CAS is that a user's information, such as the user's name or alias, is consistent with other institutional web services also using CAS. Moreover, CAS can be replaced without affecting the functionality of PBL Exchange.

Consequently, the authentication module ensures that the site is inaccessible to students. When a user attempts to log in, her/his email address is checked against two lists, namely disallowed domains and exempt users; if the user's email is in the disallowed domains list and not in the exempt users list, access to PBL Exchange is denied.

6.2 Technical Approaches to Strengthening Networks of Practice

Some other issues of a technical nature are external in that they can strengthen networks of practice.

6.2.1 A Truly Multilingual Platform

Another important requirement of PBL Exchange has been that it should address the diversity at Aalborg University and in particular it should accommodate the large number of non-Danish speaking members of the teaching staff. As these colleagues have an academic background that is almost always from outside Aalborg University, this means that they are a particularly important target group. At the same time, there is a well-established Danish terminology within the local PBL practice, and most degree programmes are taught mostly (or wholly) in Danish.

For these reasons, it is important that PBL Exchange can support multiple languages and allow the user to view the content in her language of change. Original content is shown in the chosen language whenever possible, while all other content is translated by means of the Google Translate API (Google, 2019).

6.2.2 Mail Notifications

The Question2Answer system used for the initial prototype of PBL Exchange supports a simple form of mail notification: users that have asked a question will be alerted to any further activity (answers or comments) for this particular question. However, social media allow for a much more fine-grained form of mail notifications that can be used to alert users to activity of any kind that matches the profile of the individual user. This is an important technique for community building.

As a consequence, PBL Exchange supports mail notifications in the form of weekly digests of new content as well as specialized digests.

From the initial prototype of PBL Exchange both email notifications and digests remained options, while extending the customizability of the emailing feature such that a user can decide if she/he wants to receive notifications and/or digests, and what specific users, categories and tags to receive digests from.

7. CONCLUSIONS AND FURTHER WORK

This paper has presented the PBL Exchange platform, which is the result of a design-based project that aims to change and extend existing communities of practice among supervisors of PBL projects in the degree programmes at Aalborg University. The PBL Exchange platform itself is a potential new infrastructure for communication within and between existing CoP's for PBL project supervisors, but making this become reality is an ongoing challenge.

7.1 Discussion of Our Experiences So Far

The theoretical contributions of the present project relate to new ways of building communities of practices by creating a network of practice built on crowdsourcing. In the direct interactions with existing CoP's within departments the authors have captured diverse perspectives regarding the need for a question-based, readily accessible online CoP.

Senior PBL practitioners often see existing CoP's as satisfactory ways of providing informal professional exchanges and practice development, while younger staff members are visibly more open to the idea of having and making use of such a forum. One therefore has to tread carefully the terrains of existing CoP's and create incentives for members of diverse motivations to participate as well as to make use of the informal networks of practice that exist.

The gamification aspects of PBL Exchange, and in particular the challenge and bounty feature, were intended as a main incentive. Challenges can nudge more experienced PBL practitioners to participate by discussing core aspects and potentially developmental aspects of PBL. Bounties can empower other members of the emerging community to advance issues of importance to their personally defined learning. But it remains to be seen if incentives of this kind fit well with the norms that are found in the informal networks that already exist.

Design-based research offers many ways to cross the boundaries between educational design experiments and theory development. PBL Exchange came about as a well-defined project designed and advanced by the project team, and it can therefore fall under the criticism of being what proponents of DBR would call a lab-like intervention. In the project the authors have dealt with this by interacting with the user base and by gathering feedback that could be used in further iterations of the design. However, more efforts need to be made in order to make PBL Exchange become part of the shared repertoire of the PBL community at AAU.

Systems such as PBL Exchange aim to extend existing CoP's to a larger online community, and this requires careful attention. In this case it led to the design of further technology enhancers such as anonymity in order to address the orientations of both experienced supervisors and newcomers to the practice of PBL.

In general, however, CoP-based approaches to learning stress the need to orchestrate 'thinking-together' processes, and under these circumstances an online medium, which is socially facilitative in nature, such as crowdsourcing, can be a vehicle for these processes.

In an ongoing design process such as the one behind PBL Exchange, the conclusions concerning the design and its usefulness are necessarily only partial, but still enough to inform further iterations of the design. From the authors' experience, it is clear that particular attention needs to be given to facilitate community building and enliven the community spirit, since this can support PBL-related exchanges as part of an online forum for CPD. If a network of practice is to succeed in the sense that it will create and uphold a community of practice, further attention should be given to the role of informal communities and their rôle in establishing a common practice.

Moreover, and importantly, the COVID-19 pandemic in 2020 has led to a shift towards online communities in the setting of teaching; there is less physical interaction with students but also much less physical interaction with colleagues. This shift may mean that there may eventually be a new role for a semi-formal online network of practice that involves discussions of teaching practice and is in line with the informal professional exchanges that usually take place at work.

7.2 Further Work

PBL Exchange contains the potential for supporting an online community of practice. There are two aspects to the further work on PBL Exchange.

At the technical level, there is still a challenge concerning the use of multiple languages. The Google Translate API for translation of content is not free, costing $100 for the translation of a million words. Moreover, efficiency is also an issue. For these reasons, a future version of PBL Exchange will use a local cache to store local copies of the translations of both questions, answers, and comments; the translation cache should only updated if answers are updated or a translation that did not previously exist is requested by a user.

Another technical issue to be dealt with is that of incorporating a community wiki that will allow for a structured presentation of the content in the system similar to the wiki used by StackExchange (2019). The technical issue here is that of finding and integrating an appropriate codebase for the wikiware; a more substantial challenge at the social level is to ensure that the wiki is continually maintained, as the use of a wiki will introduce a new form of crowdsourcing with new practices into the community that is to be built

At the social level, further efforts are going to incorporate the informal communities more systematically. Faraj et al. (2011) describe the dynamics of online communities as fluid, i.e. flowing with participants' need for, interest and will to invest in knowledge building. It is therefore important to investigate how this fluid nature of online communities can be exploited. As a consequence of the COVID-19 lockdown, social institutions such as universities have been forced to rethink their practice to rely more on online communication. This may be particularly challenging when it comes to informal professional exchanges. This might arguably create a novel need to rely on semi-formal online collaboration. PBL Exchange may provide such a medium, given that one can make use of existing informal and semi-formal structures (e.g. the PBL Academy at AAU and semester coordinators that are responsible for coordinating PBL supervision at specific semesters) to reach out and find early adapters that can be influential. The ongoing need for online communication in academia resulting from the COVID-19 lockdown makes this even more important. While contact with local communities in the form of information activities directed at the departmental level is still part of ongoing efforts, two further strategies will be important.

One is to develop the platform such that it can include a broader variety of discussions and exchange of information, such as discussions of lecturing and of general academic practice. Another is to identify a group of dedicated users that can be explicitly nursed and become a permanent core of the community. Here, it will be important to identify key members of the informal communities and get them interested in participating in this resilient core such that the informal communities can support the new networks of practice instead of seeing them as an unwelcome replacement. It is also important to ensure support at the management level in order to create a sense of legitimacy among the user base. The outcome of further efforts will contribute to a concrete, evidence-based strategy for building new communities around existing, informal ones.

REFERENCES

Aalborg University. (2015). *Problem-based Learning. November 2015.* https://www.pbl.aau.dk/digitalAssets/269/269243_148025_pbl-aalborg-model_uk.pdf

Abdallah, S. (2020). Social Interactions in Electronic Networks of Practice: A Model for Effective Knowledge Construction, Problem Solving, and Learning. *International Journal of e-Collaboration (IJeC), 16*(2), 27-44. doi:10.4018/IJeC.2020040103

Academy, P. B. L. (2019). *The Problem-Based Learning Academy at Aalborg University.* http://www.pbl.aau.dk

Albors, J., Ramos, J. C., & Hervas, J. L. (2008). New learning network paradigms: Communities of objectives, crowdsourcing, wikis and open source. *International Journal of Information Management, 28*(3), 194–202. doi:10.1016/j.ijinfomgt.2007.09.006

Anderson, T., & Shattuck, J. (2012). Design-Based Research: A Decade of Progress in Education Research? *Educational Researcher, 41*(1), 16–25. doi:10.3102/0013189X11428813

Bernard, P. E., Chautemps, M. L., & Galaup, X. (2006). *Le rôle de réseaux sociaux dans la création et la structuration de l'information sur Internet, Initiation à la recherche*. École Nationale Supérieure des Sciences de l'Information et des bibliotheques. Working paper no DCB, 15, 6.

Blanchard, A. L., & Markus, M. L. (2004). The experienced sense of a virtual community: Characteristics and processes. *ACM Sigmis Database, 35*(1), 64–79. doi:10.1145/968464.968470

Brabham, D. C. (2008). Crowdsourcing as a model for problem solving: An introduction and cases. *Convergence (London), 14*(1), 75–90. doi:10.1177/1354856507084420

Brown, J. S., & Duguid, P. (2000). *The Social Life of Information*. Harvard University Press.

Butler, B. S., Bateman, P. J., Gray, P. H., & Diamant, E. I. (2014). An attraction-selection-attrition theory of online community size and resilience. *MIS Quarterly, 38*(3), 699-728. /2014/38.3.04doi:10.25300/MISQ

Chotto, M. & Dirckinck-Holmfeld, L. (2008). *Facilitating Communities of Practice in Teacher Professional Development* (Vol. 1). Lancaster University.

Clegg, S. (2003). Problematising ourselves: Continuing professional development in higher education. *The International Journal for Academic Development, 8*(1-2), 37–50. doi:10.1080/1360144042000277928

Contu, A. (2014). On boundaries and difference: Communities of practice and power relations in creative work. *Management Learning, 45*(3), 289–316. doi:10.1177/1350507612471926

Contu, A., & Willmott, H. (2003). Re-embedding situatedness: The importance of power relations in learning theory. *Organization Science, 14*(3), 283–296. doi:10.1287/orsc.14.3.283.15167

Crawford, K. (2008). Continuing professional development in higher education: The academic perspective. *The International Journal for Academic Development, 13*(2), 141–146. doi:10.1080/13601440802076657

Dahl, B., & Kolmos, A. (2016). Students' attitudes towards group based project exams in two engineering programmes. *Journal of Problem Based Learning in Higher Education, 3*(2).

Django. (2019). https://www.djangoproject.com

Eraut, M. (2000). Non-formal learning and tacit knowledge in professional work. *British Journal of Educational Psychology, 70*, 113–136. doi:10.1348/000709900158001

Estellés-Arolas, E., & González-Ladrón-De-Guevara, F. (2012). Towards an integrated crowdsourcing definition. *Journal of Information Science, 38*(2), 189–200. doi:10.1177/0165551512437638

Faraj, S., Jarvenpaa, S. L., & Majchrzak, A. (2011). Knowledge collaboration in online communities. *Organization Science, 22*(5), 1224–1239. doi:10.1287/orsc.1100.0614

Gnaur, D., & Hüttel, H. (2017). A Platform for Developing and Maintaining Competences in PBL Supervision. In *Emerging Technologies for Education - Second International Symposium, SETE 2017*. Springer. 10.1007/978-3-319-71084-6_33

Google. (2019). *Cloud Translate documentation*. https://cloud.google.com/translate/docs/

Gravemeijer, K., & Cobb, P. (2006). Design research from a learning design perspective. In *Educational design research* (pp. 29–63). Routledge.

Hossain, M. (2012). Users' motivation to participate in online crowdsourcing platforms. In *2012 International Conference on Innovation Management and Technology Research*, pp. 310-315. IEEE. 10.1109/ICIMTR.2012.6236409

Howe, J. (2006) The rise of crowdsourcing. *Wired, 14*(6). https://www.wired.com/wired/archive/14.06/crowds.html

Hur, J. W., & Hara, N. (2007). Factors Cultivating Sustainable Online Communities for K-12 Teacher Professional Development. *Journal of Educational Computing Research, 36*(3), 245–268. doi:10.2190/37H8-7GU7-5704-K470

Illeris, L. (2012). *International Perspectives on Competence Development: Developing Skills and Capabilities*. Routledge. doi:10.4324/9780203523032

Jackson, N. (2012). *Exploring learning ecologies*. https://www.lulu.com/shop/norman-jackson/exploring-learning-ecologies/paperback/product-24288878.html.

Keller, J. (2010, November). Stack Overflow's crowdsourcing model guarantees success. *Atlantic (Boston, Mass.)*, 18.

King, K. (2011). Professional learning in unlikely spaces: Social media and virtual communities as professional development. *Intenational Journal of Emerging Technologies in Learning, 6*(4), 40–46. doi:10.3991/ijet.v6i4.1765

Knight, P. T., & Trowler, P. R. (2001). *Departmental leadership in higher education*. Society for Research into Higher Education and Open University Press.

Landqvist, F., & Teigland, R. (2005). Collective Action in Electronic Networks of Practice: An Empirical Study of Three Online Social Structures. In P. Van Den Besselaar, G. De Michelis, J. Preece, & C. Simone (Eds.), *Communities and Technologies 2005*. Springer. doi:10.1007/1-4020-3591-8_19

Lauvås, P., Hofgaard Lycke, K., & Handal, G. (2004). *Kollegaveiledning i skolen (Professional guidance in schools)*. Cappelen Akademisk Forlag.

Lave, J., & Wenger, E. (1991). *Situated learning: Legitimate peripheral participation*. Cambridge University Press. doi:10.1017/CBO9780511815355

Mathematics Educators. (2018). *Mathematics Educators. StackExchange Forum*. https://matheducators.stackexchange.com

Mattson, T., & Davidson, E. (2018). Promoting Domain-specific Forum Participation via Off-topic Forum Participation in Electronic Networks of Practice. *Communications of the Association for Information Systems, 43*, 35. Advance online publication. doi:10.17705/1CAIS.04335

McKenney, S., & Reeves, T. (2012). *Conducting educational design research*. Routledge.

McKenney, S., & Reeves, T. (2013). Systematic Review of Design-Based Research Progress: Is a Little Knowledge a Dangerous Thing? *Educational Researcher, 42*(2), 97–100. doi:10.3102/0013189X12463781

Media, T. (2018). *Teaching Media*. http://www.teachingmedia.org

Moodle. https://moodle.org

Ørngreen, R. (2015). *Reflections on Design-Based Research In Online Educational and Competence Development Projects*. Paper presented at Human Work Interaction Design (HWID), Denmark.

PBL Development Projects at Aalborg University. (2017). https://www.strategi.aau.dk/ AAU+strategy/Handleplaner+Viden+for+verden/Problem+based+learning/Problem+based+learning/

Pendry, L. F., & Salvatore, J. (2015, September). Individual and social benefits of online discussion forums. *Computers in Human Behavior, 50*(C), 211–220. doi:10.1016/j.chb.2015.03.067

Pyrko, I., Dörfler, V., & Eden, C. (2016). Thinking together: What makes Communities of Practice work? *Human Relations, 70*(4), 389–409. doi:10.1177/0018726716661040 PMID:28232754

Question2Answer. (2019). *Free Open Source Q&A Software for PHP.* https://www.question2answer.org/

Rice, S., & Gregor, M. N. (2016). *E-Learning and the Academic Library: Essays on Innovative Initiatives*. McFarland, Incorporated Publishers.

StackExchange. (2019). http://www.stackexchange.com

Stonebraker, I. & Zhang, T. (2015). *Crowdsourcing reference help: using technology to help users help each other*. Libraries Faculty and Staff Scholarship and Research.

Stonebraker, I. & Zhang, T. (2016). Participatory culture and e-learning. In E-Learning and the Academic Library: Essays on Innovative Initiatives, (pp. 201–213). McFarland.

Vasilescu, B., Capiluppi, A., & Serebrenik, A. (2012). Gender, Representation and Online Partici- pation: A Quantitative Study of StackOverflow. *2012 International Conference on Social Informatics*, 332–338. 10.1109/SocialInformatics.2012.81

Velasco, P. J., Learreta, B., Kober, C., & Tan, I. (2014). *Faculty Perspective on Competency Development in Higher Education: An International Study. Higher Learning Research Communications, December 2014*. Laureate Education, Inc. doi:10.18870/hlrc.v4i4.223

VIA University College. (2017). *VIA Connect*. https://challenges.dk/da/challenges

Wang, C. Y., Yang, H. Y., & Sengcho, T. C. (2008). Using peer-to-peer technology for knowledge sharing in communities of practices. *Decision Support Systems, 45*(3), 528–540. doi:10.1016/j.dss.2007.06.012

Wenger, E. (1998). *Communities of Practice: Learning, Meaning, and Identity*. Cambridge University Press. doi:10.1017/CBO9780511803932

Wenger, E. (2010). *Communities of practice and social learning systems 1: Communities of practice and social learning systems: the career of a concept*. Springer Publishing.

Wikipedia. (2017). https://www.wikipedia.org/

Chapter 10
Teacher Networking, Professional Development, and Motivation Within EU Platforms and the Erasmus Plus Program:
Teacher Networking Dynamics in the Knowledge Society

Salvatore Nizzolino
https://orcid.org/0000-0002-3008-2890
Sapienza University of Rome, Italy

ABSTRACT

This chapter deals with the continuous professional development required in the teaching profession with a focus on the European Union, embracing the education sector as a whole socio-anthropological structure with similar needs and expectations. In particular, the topic of professional networking and mobilities, analyzed under the effect of the Erasmus Plus program, emphasizes the need for a new perspective. Social network analysis improves the understanding of particular behavioral patterns promoted by the implementation of European education policies in public education networking. The chapter contributes to policymakers in the field of education and training in the education sector.

INTRODUCTION

The first part of this chapter offers a bird's eye view of the role of social networking in the professional development of teachers and the relevance of this subject within some research approaches. The second part focuses on the EU's strategies and surveys to analyze the top-down policies implemented nationally and locally to foster the exchange of best practices among EU teachers in the digital and networking contexts. Lastly, the third section presents some reflections on research performed by professors and

DOI: 10.4018/978-1-7998-4891-2.ch010

Copyright © 2021, IGI Global. Copying or distributing in print or electronic forms without written permission of IGI Global is prohibited.

scholars affiliated with the MTA-PE Budapest Ranking Research Group and the Hungarian Academy of Science (Gadár et al., 2020). The investigation presents a spacial analysis of an Erasmus mobility network, promoting a line of research that applies Social Network Analysis (SNA) to education networking in the EU, in particular to University students' mobilities. This research perspective is what should be promoted to better understand the behavioral patterns generated by the implementation of the European education policies in public school networking. These self-organizing education networks can reach high levels of complexity and reveal recurrent patterns that may appear from the international and local interactions, thus, disclosing unknown elements that contribute to these systems. Notwithstanding the great peculiarities emerging from the different education grades, this investigation shows the potential of SNA when applied to education networking. Thus, this third section offers the opportunity to reflect on a promising line of investigation with a growing interest due to the cross-disciplinary teams and collaborations that may be formed around this specific research topic.

ABOUT TEACHERS' AWARENESS OF THEIR SOCIAL ROLE IN THE EU

Worldwide, only 26% of teachers in OECD countries and economies that participate in TALIS surveys (OECD, 2020) think their profession is valued by society. Moreover, senior teachers are more likely than their younger colleagues to perceive their profession as undervalued, suggesting a gradual degree of professional disillusionment throughout their careers: "14% of teachers aged 50 years or less express a desire to leave teaching within the next five years, i.e., well before they reach retirement age" (OECD, 2020, p. 13).

Despite the need for improving the awareness of their social role, there are some encouraging signs of a growing attitude toward sharing and mutual collaboration, as the TALIS report declares:

Teachers in OECD countries and economies in TALIS are quite likely to employ basic collaborative practices like discussing the development of specific students with colleagues (61% of teachers on average do this) and, to a lesser extent, exchanging teaching materials with colleagues (47%). However, far fewer teachers engage in the deeper forms of professional collaboration... with only 9% of teachers saying they provide observation-based feedback to colleagues, and 21% engaging in collaborative professional learning at least once a month. (OECD, 2020, p. 14)

Concerning public school policies in the European Union, notwithstanding the common frameworks and strategies aiming to harmonize the socio-economic and educational discrepancies among all member states (Commission of the European Communities, 2000; European Commission 2013; 2020; European Council, 2010, 2017; Redecker & Punie, 2017), the EU national education system is still a mosaic with profound differentiations (European Commission/Eurydice, 2018a, 2018b, 2018c). In addition, the European Commission surveys show that the teaching profession is going through a problematic stage since it does not always receive high social recognition in many EU countries, and salaries are not rewarding according to the level of responsibility and work efforts. Thus, "the teaching profession is becoming less attractive as a career choice" (European Commission/EACEA/Eurydice, 2018a, p. 17). Also, the notorious annual report *Global Teacher Status Index* provides a view showing EU countries not ranking at the top of the list for teachers' recognition and social reputation, and the surveys performed explicitly reveal that "in the majority of countries, actual teacher wages were lower than what was perceived to be fair by respondents" (Dolton et al., 2018, p. 79).

According to several EU statements, the education system in Europe should undergo a set of improvements and modifications to improve the attractiveness of the teaching profession. The decision whether to consider an improvement of the attractiveness of the teaching profession as a central objective depends more on the importance attached to the quality of teachers as a strategic factor in improving the effectiveness and equity of education systems (European Commission, 2013, pp. 24–25).

Remuneration is a key element in making teaching an attractive profession. Along with other factors such as working conditions, career prospects, professional development opportunities and recognition, it plays an important role in drawing people into the profession as well as ensuring that serving teachers are satisfied and sufficiently motivated to continue to provide high quality teaching. (European Commission/EACEA/Eurydice, 2018b, p. 11)

In the EU, the range of elements that vary from one national school system to another counts dozens of dimensions: school cycles, recruitment process, induction programs, mentoring and support processes, employment contracts, career systems, salaries, working hours, students-teacher ratio, workload besides teaching, evaluation of performances, national teacher mobility, continuous professional development, professional status, and reputation (Dolton et al., 2018; European Commission/Eurydice, 2018a, 2018b, 2018c). Nevertheless, there are elements in common among all the 28 Members States, and one of them is the shared official perspective of teachers as lifelong learning professionals. The following excerpt from the EU policy platform declares this common view in favor of continuous training:

They play a critical role in achieving high-quality education for all learners and, therefore, need to continuously develop their competences. Initial education and continuous professional development need to be of the highest quality, and access to professional support throughout their careers is essential.[1]

Some researches demonstrated that teachers' awareness of themselves in terms of social capital also affects their perception about side-associated phenomena as innovation, professional learning communities, and performances affecting students' results (Fox & Wilson, 2015; Pil & Leana, 2009; Van Waes et al., 2018; Vouriaky et al., 2012). One key element in this process of self-recognition is the role of communities of practices and networking, perceived as a complex dimension to catalyze the growth of a professional community that can support the theoretical and empirical aspects of teaching (Fox & Wilson, 2015; Parlar et al., 2019; Pil & Leana, 2009; Van Waes et al., 2018). Social relationship networks in schools and between schools enhance the sense of shared identity and facilitate the sharing of new ideas and the production of knowledge as it happens, while every other professional field undergoes profound transformations related to the knowledge management age (Boisot & Child, 1999; Bollinger & Smith, 2001; Bucher & Helmond, 2018; Mansour et al., 2013; Von Krogh, 2012). Numerous investigations on social dilemmas of knowledge sharing have found how a sense of group identity can positively influence the contributions to a public good, and especially once groups were shown to have a common identity, individuals began to share information more frequently (Cabrera & Cabrera, 2015). In addition, the interactions of social networks and participation from school stakeholders have the potential to positively affect the flow of information in education establishments and can improve work engagement (Cheng, 2012, 2013, 2017; Lin et al., 2008; Song et al., 2014; Parlar et al., 2019; Zhao, 2010) and even prevent teacher burnout. Moreover, it can engender a sense of accomplishment and a more fully developed professional identity (Wood, 2002). Communities of practice generate transformations at all levels when those teachers acting as change agents are networked and formally established (Kools & Stoll, 2016). Thus, a stronger formal recognition by school communities and/or other authorities may be a relevant aspect to enhance motivation and results.

In addition, a decent professional wage is substantially linked to teachers' perceptions of their working time and other formal obligations. Despite the timetables and the weekly and monthly schedules, working hours are often experienced as a "multifaceted, dynamic and nonlinear" (Collinson & Cook; 2000, p. 23). This heavily affects the objective of school knowledge management, which should instead set up a "school learning system to facilitate teachers' learning so as to improve teacher professional development" (Zhao, 2010, p. 174) and demands teachers, tutors, and school managers' awareness (Corredato Periotto & Wessellenns, 2018; Kools & Stoll, 2016). Conversely, the more a school system relies on non-formal channels and teachers' self-motivation to upgrade professional profiles, the more teachers are demanded to invest their extracurricular time (their free time), often with no overtime compensation or extra benefits, and this is what is currently happening in several national school systems in the EU[2]. The continuous professional updating is often perceived as an implied corollary (the matter is explored in the next sections). As a consequence of more formal training procedures, "it seems that the formalized plans for knowledge-sharing activities facilitated teachers' conversion of knowledge" (Rismark & Sølvberg, 2011, p. 157).

Notwithstanding the steps already taken to exchange good practices and innovations among school partnerships in the EU, mostly through the Erasmus Plus program, school curriculum development is still one step behind. The curriculum is expected to respond to the developments and changing contexts of a digital network society perspective (Volungevičienė et al., 2020). On the one hand, this theme should have a huge impact on European policies, but since the curriculum is still a matter of national education policies, teacher networks are often centered on these specific areas and on experiences performed in the frame of teaching autonomy and school organizational autonomy (European Commission/Eurydice, 2018a, 2018b, 2018c).

TEACHERS' COMMUNITIES OF PRACTICE IN THE NETWORK SOCIETY

"As people participate in a system, they change it, and the system changes them" (Trust et al., 2016, p. 17). Educators can experiment with this axiom when participating in professional learning networks or personal learning networks. An aspect that offers a common ground on the international level would compare research and surveys (inside and outside the EU) and is the growing dimension of professional networking in every field (Boisot & Child, 1999; Bollinger & Smith, 2001; Bucher & Helmond, 2018; Castells, 2014; Cheng, 2012, 2013, 2017; Linares Pons et al., 2014; Lin, F.; Lin, S. & Huang, 2008; Nonaka & Konno, 1998; Song et al., 2014; Parlar et al., 2019; Von Krogh, 2012; Zhao, 2010). Most recent results show that within personal development plans, teachers' willingness to take part in connections and networks have been growing (Van Waes et al., 2014), and there is evidence that teachers have a more general disposition toward patterns related to the questioning of the nature of learning, to the design of the teaching/learning experience, to the ways of organizing knowledge, and to enable and assess the classroom practice (Pateraki, 2018; Song, 2014; Volungevičienė et al., 2020; Zhao, 2010). Currently, in the EU, teachers' continuous upskilling seems to have been assigned mainly to non-formal and informal systems, since these type of professional learning spaces can support the holistic needs of teachers since informal learning opportunities allow educators to activate the process of co-constructed knowledge, involving collaborations with peers (Trust et al., 2016).

Thus, the assumption that teachers' everyday work cannot be observed outside their networks of direct and indirect contacts is gaining more and more attention at every level of education, from early childhood to advanced tertiary education. A teacher's behavior, performance, and experience always affect the overall efficiency of an entire educational environment (proximity network). On a digital level, it can trigger complex network dynamics related to co-learning and communities of practice on an international level (Avalos, 2011; Granovetter, 1973; Van Waes et al., 2018; Zhao, 2010). As Manuel Castells, the father of the term "network society," points out, the basis of any network community is the sharing of common values, interests, and/or attitudes. The main characteristics of a teacher's network are not only recognizable in a mass of individuals lumped together by the same profession, but they also act as a community of like-minded people. This represents a powerful social structure that can give a great autonomous contribution to the molding of the knowledge society.

The key to the process of individuation is the construction of autonomy by social actors, who become subjects in the process. They do so by defining their specific projects in interaction with, but not submission to, the institutions of society. This is the case for a minority of individuals, but because of their capacity to lead and mobilize they introduce a new culture in every domain of social life: in work (entrepreneurship), in the media (the active audience), on the Internet (the creative user), in the market (the informed and proactive consumer), in education (students as informed critical thinkers, making possible the new frontier of e-learning and m-learning pedagogy), in health (the patient-centered health management system) in e-government (the informed, participatory citizen), in social movements (cultural change from the grassroots, as in feminism or environmentalism), and in politics (the independent-minded citizen able to participate in self-generated political networks). (Castells, 2014, p. 138)

Thus, educators and teachers are part of those minorities of individuals representing a class of social capital and can actively mobilize forces capable of fostering knowledge dynamics inside their immediate work environment and, thanks to the digital technology, they can generate factual revolutions "regardless of the barriers of rigid social organizations" (Castells, 2014, p. 139).

There is a common-sense idea about the fact that when teachers have gained a lot of practical work experience, they need to find new challenges and motivate themselves if they do not want to fall into a routine. Knowledge management in schools is a process too often left to individual initiatives, while personal development plans are carried out by top-level authorities or local bodies. On the other hand, in many Eastern European countries, there is no specific forward planning at all (European Commission, 2018a). Since KM is a process involving tangible and intangible assets in school, it requires strategies, standards, and coordination. Teaching networks cannot be considered a side effect anymore, in particular, when they build a path of continuous development practice. Many scholars point out the benefit for teachers of participating in professional networks locally and internationally through digital tools (Cachia et al., 2012; Kolls & Stoll, 2016; Nizzolino, 2020; Klamma et al., 2009; Lin et al., 2008; Moolenaar, 2012; Parlar et al., 2019; Pateraki, 2018; Trust et al., 2016; Volungevičienė et al., 2020, Vuorikari et al., 2012; 2015; Zhao, 2010). If national policies do not always specify clear references to the appropriate set of skills required to foster digital networking, the education environment is already permeated by a non-formal and informal set of tools, routines, and processes that support this social-digital practice. Teachers regularly put strategies in practice to create and facilitate learning processes, knowledge retrieval, storage and sharing through professional and personal social networks, not only through person-to-person contacts, but with increasing frequency participating in teams and groups of practice (Cheng, 2012, 2017; Cheng & Chu, 2018; Cheng et al., 2017; Klamma et al., 2009; Fox & Wilson, 2015; Pil & Leana, 2009; Trust et al., 2016; Van Waes et al., 2018; Vuorikari et al; 2012; Zhao, 2010). Even though the literature exploring the effectiveness and self-conception of teachers as network-users is not substantial yet (Trust et al., 2016; Van Waes et al., 2018) it is not disputed that the digital age is characterized by the knowledge society and is the new dimension for any form of continuous education, training, cooperation, knowledge creation and co-construction, innovation, and sharing (Boisot & Child, 1999; Bollinger & Smith, 2001; Bucher & Helmond, 2018; Castells, 2014; Cheng, 2012, 2013, 2017; Linares Pons et al., 2014; Lin et al., 2008; Nonaka & Konno, 1998; Song et al., 2014; Parlar et al., 2019; Von Krogh, 2012; Zhao, 2010). The EU offers an ideal ground to start large-scale investigations on the efficiency of teaching networking due to common frameworks, international exchange schemes, fund mobility programs, and e-platforms.

One of the most popular and effective tools to catalyze teacher personal development plans on a regular basis is the eTwinning Platform, the online community of schools in Europe. Launched in 2005, it is a web-based exchange space offering a great range of activities, debate opportunities, training, and professional development. According to the real-time detection of the platform, the current number of members exceeds 817,000 individual users, and more than 208,000 schools are involved in more than 107,000 projects activated since its launch in 2005[3]. The platform contents are available in 28 languages, and it periodically disseminates newsletters and reports. It is possible to access as a registered member on condition that personal details are associated with a public school (or recognized as equivalent) in the EU. Therefore, users are all teachers, headteachers, and librarians who, through projects, exchanges, and events, have been involved with more than 4 million national and international students.

The eTwinning platform was created to detect and manage the relational complexity of a very specific segment: School Education in the EU. Despite the great number of reports available, the usual focus highlights the accomplishments or the experiences related to specific projects, sharing content, and professional development plans. Usually, teachers from different school levels register in the eTwinning platform to access new challenges and opportunities for their personal growth and professional development. On-line partnerships and collaborations benefit their local environment, help to experiment with new strategies, and motivate students through international peer-to-peer digital exchanges. The Erasmus Plus program, in synergy with the platform, is a key part of the eTwinning experience. Therefore teachers also have the opportunity to practice complex collaborations with other European schools during an Erasmus Plus international exchange. The Erasmus Plus *Key Action 2* can innovate education strategies through synchronous and asynchronous experiences, which also include mobilities abroad.

MOTIVATION AND NETWORKING THROUGH THE ETWINNING PLATFORM

Vouriaky et al. (2012) is the most relevant research applying SNA to explore the eTwinning dynamics and was published six years after the platform was launched and two years before the official establishment of the Erasmus Plus program, which was fully integrated with the platform.

Over time, the teacher network may form a network topology that features a strongly connected core group of teachers that is connected to other smaller groups (focused stage). Alternatively, the network may develop towards an interdisciplinary typology where several groups are connected via some gatekeepers, but where there is no core group. It may also develop towards a hierarchical topology in which some "super gatekeepers" connect a hierarchy of groups together. (Vouriaky et al., 2012, p. 42).

This analysis focused on teacher digital networking on the internal eTwinning aggregation-features (mostly the eTwinning projects) and highlighted the main two forms of social capital recognizable in eTwinning, the gatekeepers (individuals) and closures (dense groups), observing that "gatekeepers with high degree possess high betweenness and low clustering coefficient" (Vouriaky et al., 2012, p. 46).

Lying on the border of different communities has an advantage: teachers in this position have more control and power over the network as well as more sources for new information. This form of social capital is that of the gatekeeper, and it can be studied through the calculation of node and network properties. (Vouriaky et al., 2012, p. 50).

The three dimensions of teacher knowledge identified by Cochran and Lytle (1999) are knowledge-for-practice, knowledge-in-practice, and knowledge-of-practice. These are not always easily unshelled when a complex environment like an interconnected digital multitude of networks provides the opportunity to develop all of them at the same time. For this reason, one of the key sources used to extract useful data in this section is the Eurydice report *Teaching Careers in Europe*:

The Eurydice report Teaching Careers in Europe: Access, Progression and Support provides a comparative overview of national policies on teacher careers across Europe. It maps existing regulations and policy recommendations at primary and general secondary levels, and covers all the countries of the European Union as well as Albania, Bosnia and Herzegovina, the Former Yugoslav Republic of Macedonia, Switzerland, Iceland, Liechtenstein, Montenegro, Norway, Serbia and Turkey. (Teaching Careers in Europe, 2018a, p. 132)

The first comparison is the possible relation between the chance of career improvements and the motivation to be involved in networking projects with other schools, both on national and European levels. Generally, a teacher's career does not develop or see a radical change in professional status or environment. A promotion usually implies an extension of responsibilities, along with a salary increase and/or other allowances.

The next step is to calculate a conversion rate for the project to teachers to cluster those countries with higher values and consider the career opportunities in those national contexts. This comparison is the first attempt to find teachers' personal motivation to increase with their skills and experiences useful for career progression.

It is worth noticing that 13 countries with multi-level career structures, out of a total of 20 (65%), show a conversion rate higher than 0.500, while 7 countries with flat career structures emerge out of 15 (46,6%). Thus, the multi-level career structure may indicate a stronger professional motivation to participate in recognized networks and international online projects. Further data confirms this trend; the incentive-policy defined by top-level authorities encourages teachers to participate in continuous personal development. Thanks to the Eurydice report (European Commission/EACEA/Eurydice, 2018a),

Table 1. Comparison between eTwinning Platform numbers[4] and Types of Career Structure for fully qualified teachers as defined by the top-level education authority, primary and general secondary education

Country	Projects	Teachers	Schools	Multi-Level Career Structure	Flat Career Structure	No Top-Level Regulations
Albania	3700	5269	1484	●		
Austria	2138	5195	1880	●		
Belgium	3696	8412	2338		●	
Bosnia and Herzegovina	1201	1694	539		●	
Bulgaria	7140	9584	2854	●		
Cyprus	2107	3001	714	●		
Croatia	6437	13686	2337	●		
Czech Republic	9021	11367	4121	●		
Denmark	2626	8502	2010		●	
Estonia	3245	4974	953	●		
Finland	4085	8109	2429		●	
France	24209	61499	20349	●		
Germany	11833	27113	9586		●	
Greece	17018	29168	9074		●	
Hungary	2791	5482	2246	●		
Iceland	1043	1660	307		●	
Italy	29810	84662	11059		●	
Ireland	1691	3439	1774	●		
Latvia	4134	7110	1152	●		
Lichtenstein	15	40	17		●	
Lithuania	8003	9454	1085	●		
Luxembourg	355	651	142		●	
Malta	1833	3653	287	●		
Netherlands	3303	8525	2408			●
North Macedonia	2758	2082	480		●	
Norway	2772	5926	1719		●	
Poland	32976	71521	18263	●		
Portugal	12624	17553	1957		●	
Romania	21284	31047	9414	●		
Serbia	3157	3671	1192	●		
Slovenia	3790	4724	874	●		
Spain	26766	68535	15508		●	
Slovakia	9442	10689	2786	●		
Sweden	3760	11679	3393	●		
Turkey	40329	226134	50733		●	
United Kingdom	12282	29736	14980	●		

Note. (ISCED 1-3), 2016/17 (European Commission/EACEA/Eurydice, 2018a). The eTwinning portal includes 44 countries, but the Eurydice analysis only reports 36. Thus, the following countries are not in this chart: Armenia; Azerbaijan; Georgia; Jordan; Lebanon; Republic of Moldova; Tunisia; Ukraine. (Personal elaboration from European Commission/EACEA/Eurydice, 2018a)

*Table 2. Comparison between eTwinning Countries with Multilevel Career Structure (marked with *) and project to teacher conversion rate.*

Country	Projects	Teachers	Schools	*Conversion rate projects: teachers*
*Albania	3700	5269	1484	**0,702**
*Austria	2138	5195	1880	0,411
Belgium	3696	8412	2338	0,439
Bosnia and Herzegovina	1201	1694	539	**0,708**
*Bulgaria	7140	9584	2854	**0,744**
*Cyprus	2107	3001	714	**0,702**
*Croatia	6437	13686	2337	0,470
*Czech Republic	9021	11367	4121	**0,793**
Denmark	2626	8502	2010	0,308
*Estonia	3245	4974	953	**0,652**
Finland	4085	8109	2429	**0,503**
*France	24209	61499	20349	0,393
Germany	11833	27113	9586	0,436
Greece	17018	29168	9074	**0,503**
*Hungary	2791	5482	2246	**0,509**
Iceland	1043	1660	307	**0,628**
Italy	29810	84662	11059	0,352
*Ireland	1691	3439	1774	0,491
*Latvia	4134	7110	1152	**0,581**
Lichtenstein	15	40	17	0,375
*Lithuania	8003	9454	1085	**0,846**
Luxembourg	355	651	142	**0,545**
*Malta	1833	3653	287	**0,501**
**Netherlands	3303	8525	2408	0,387
North Macedonia	2758	2082	480	**1,324**
Norway	2772	5926	1719	0,467
*Poland	32976	71521	18263	0,461
Portugal	12624	17553	1957	**0,719**
*Romania	21284	31047	9414	**0,685**
*Serbia	3157	3671	1192	**0,859**
*Slovenia	3790	4724	874	**0,802**
Spain	26766	68535	15508	0,390
*Slovakia	9442	10689	2786	**0,883**
*Sweden	3760	11679	3393	0,321
Turkey	40329	226118	50733	0,178
*United Kingdom	12282	29736	14980	0,413

Note: The Netherlands is the only country with No Top-Level Regulations (marked with **). All other countries follow a Flat career Structure. The values above 0,500 appear in bold since they are the object of further observations. (Personal elaboration from European Commission/Eurydice report 2018a and eTwinning official numbers.)

an interesting correspondence between those school systems where continuous training is required for a promotion (multi-level career systems) and those countries with the highest eTwinning project to teacher ratio (minimum of 0.500 or higher). Thus, it is possible to group the following countries where the high eTwinning project to teachers conversion rate (Table 2) matches the career promotion based on professional development: Bulgaria, France, Hungary, Cyprus, Latvia, Lithuania, Malta, Romania, Slovenia, Slovakia, Albania, and Serbia (13 out of 20; Cfr. Tables 1 and 2). Among those countries with a lower entry-salary and require a salary progression based on results and training, it is possible to find many in the same cluster.

At the lower secondary level, 20 education systems have a starting salary that is below the EU average even when the Luxembourg outlier is removed (Bulgaria, the Czech Republic, Estonia, Greece, Latvia, Lithuania, Hungary, Malta, Poland, Romania, Slovenia, Slovakia, the United Kingdom – England, Wales, Northern Ireland, Bosnia and Herzegovina, Montenegro, Serbia, Turkey and the former Yugoslav Republic of Macedonia). In seven countries (Latvia, Hungary, Poland, Slovakia, Bosnia and Herzegovina, Serbia and the former Yugoslav Republic of Macedonia), the starting salary is less than half the EU average, ranging between 10 000 PPS and 14 000 PPS. In Bulgaria and Romania, it is even lower. At 8 493 and 8 538 PPS respectively, the starting salary amounts to approximately one-third of the EU average. (European Commission/Eurydice, 2018c, 15)

It is worth noticing that, among the other countries with a flat career structure (Table 1), Portugal stands out with a remarkable conversion rate. Not surprisingly, the Portuguese directorate-general for education of the Ministry of Education uses the DigCompEdu framework for professional development courses for teachers since 2016 (Vouriaky et al., 2016). North Macedonia has the highest conversion rate among those countries with a flat career structure (Table 2). More research about the implementation of the National Program for Development of Education through the Program for Quality Assurance and Control in Education[5] is needed to investigate high performance related to eTwinning's popularity.

The EU frameworks provide theoretical approaches that stimulate further evolution of methodologies grounded on practical teaching/learning experiences to "facilitate reflection on the integration of new technologies into their everyday teaching practices" (Michos & Hernandez-Leo, 2020, p. 20). The need to redefine teachers as professionals involves innovation and has been a matter of widespread and increasing interest over the past decade (Avalos, 2011; Cheng 2012, 2013, 2018; Cochran-Smith & Lytle, 1999; Harris & Jones, 2018; Rismark & Sølvberg, 2011; Vuorikari et al., 2016; Zhao, 2010). This topic is expected to receive even further attention. The pervasive expansion of knowledge management approaches is also influencing the educational sector even in lower grades. Although this effect is not yet declared and visible in the same manner in all countries, the nature of teaching is increasingly less routine and more prone to knowledge sharing, collaborative re-contextualization, and experimentation (Avalos, 2011; Cheng 2012, 2013, 2018; Cheng et al., 2017; Cheng & Chu, 2018; Cochran-Smith & Lytle, 1999; Corredato Periotto & Wessellenns, 2018; Fox & Wilson, 2015; Harris & Jones, 2018; Michos & Hernandez-Leo; Rismark & Sølvberg, 2011; Vuorikari et al., 2016; 2020; Zhao, 2009). There is a broad literature spreading the general recognition of the complexity of teacher training and how professional development is a continuous process that can benefit co-learning and knowledge sharing (Avalos, 2010; Cachia et al. 2012; Cheng 2013, 2018; Cochran-Smith & Lytle, 1999; Kolls & Stoll, 2016; Klamma et al. 2009; Lin et al., 2008; Moolenaar, 2012; Parlar et al., 2019; Pateraki, 2018; Rismark & Sølvberg, 2011; Trust et al., 2016; Volungevičienė et al., 2020, Vuorikari et al., 2012, 2015; Zhao, 2010). There are multiple contexts where it is possible to highlight this professional transformation and are clearly promoted by institutional regulations and national or international policies. It is also emerging as innovative impulses that are justified by the new skills required for global citizenship. To better focus on this collective process, it is appropriate to observe some implications of the Erasmus Plus program, which is one of the fundamental strategies for innovating education in Europe.

NETWORKING SAVVY IN THE ERASMUS PLUS PROGRAM

Erasmus Plus is the main EU program to support and foster education, training, youth, and sport among the member states, and it extends its actions to a number of non-EU countries[6]. The Lifelong Learning Programme of the EU (cycle 2007–2013) replaced the previous Socrates program, and the current denomination Erasmus Plus includes a range of programs operating since 2007. The first Erasmus Plus cycle was from 2014 to 2020, and on 30 May 2018, the European Commission launched the next cycle of the program, which doubled the total budget to 30 billion euros for the period 2021–2027[7]. The program aims to provide exchange opportunities for over 4 million European students and teachers (all ISCED grades) to study, train, and gain experience in an international context. Erasmus Plus offers a range of actions opened to many individuals, public, and private organizations. The specific actions are modulated according to National Agencies, which implement the top EU guidelines through a variety of actions according to the specific needs that can vary from one country to another.

Erasmus (without the attribute PLUS) was originally a University student exchange program, where a student could apply to spend a few months at a European university. Alternatively, the student could complete an internship at a European country. Erasmus Mundus was a further evolution of the program that provided scholarships for studies in European universities through joint programs (Masters Courses and Joint Doctorates) operated by a group of universities. Both of these programs have now been combined under the umbrella of Erasmus Plus. Each approved project proposal always implies an organization acting as a lead coordinator, responsible for the whole partnership, and the other subjects as partner organizations with the responsibility of focusing more on local coordination. There are some limitations in terms of roles, budget, and actions for the selected group of non-EU members:

Eligible countries are divided into two groups, Programme countries and Partners countries. Although Programme countries are eligible for all actions of Erasmus+, Partner countries can only take part in some, and are subject to specific conditions.[8]

Each project under the Erasmus Plus guidelines must have between two and six partner organizations (under Key Action 2, *Cooperation for Innovation and Exchange of Good Practices*). In addition to this, it always demands a focus on further networking to foster the dissemination of results to involve and inspire more users. In other words, the program boosts networking on different layers through an ecosystem of platforms and good practices[9].

As one of the key-strategic programs for education in the EU, Erasmus Plus tests teachers' innovation skills and their ability to build effective networks of schools and individuals, exchange good educational practices, and disseminate effectiveness. According to the EU perspective, teacher learning is strongly linked to continuous educational change and innovation in schooling. EU member states express different conceptions of the teacher/learning experience through their national school systems, although

Figure 1. Previous EU Programmes and Actions subsequently merged under Erasmus Plus

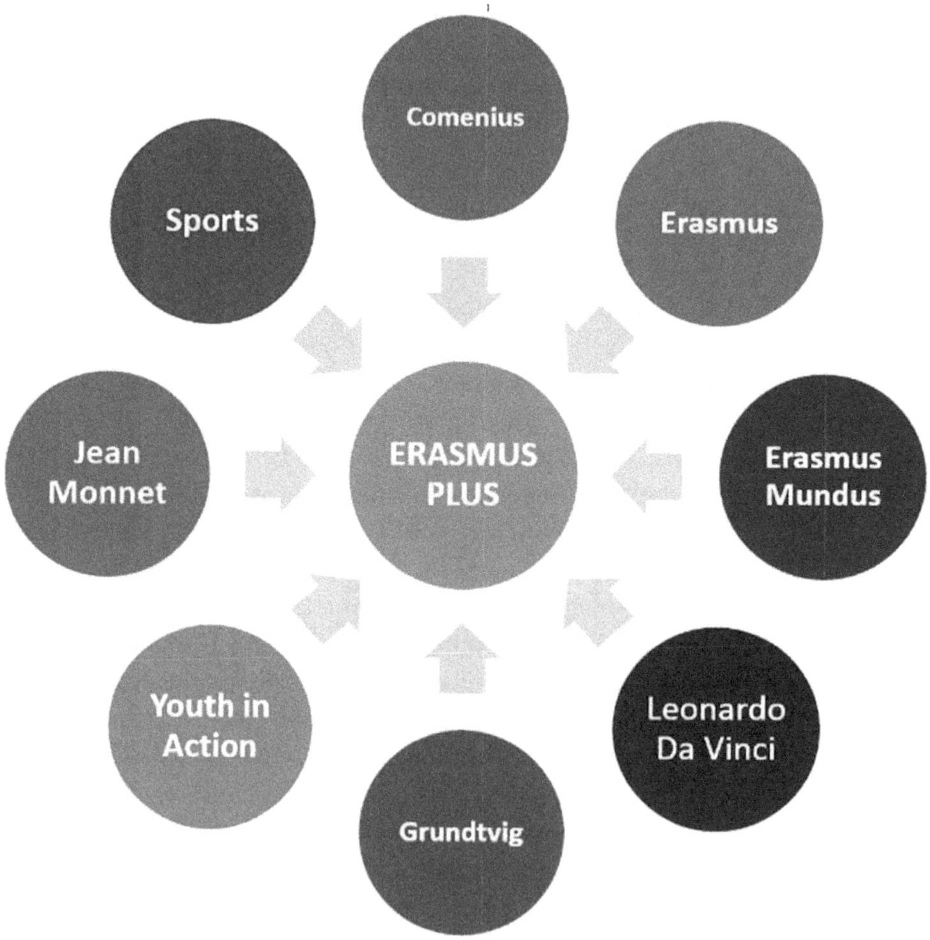

this diversity is not always made explicitly. The different approaches and ideas can meet and create exchanges to share a common ground of professional development. Thanks to the Erasmus Plus frame and guidelines, different school environments from different EU countries can codify that wisdom of practice under the process of shared consolidation in other geopolitical regions.

A common problem reveals that teachers need more expertise to develop and implement projects at an international level, and the evaluation of many project proposals reveals prevalent weaknesses linked to an overly narrow interpretation of the program requirements. This is because the school system perspective is dominated by routine processes and not by benchmarking, measurement indexes, and results[10]. This could be a paradox since schools are places for excellence devoted to evaluation. Indeed, these aspects are related to a different set of abilities, more concomitant with networking skills and networking awareness, which in turn are always inter-linked to ICT and social skills. According to the official statistics published by the European Commission, comparing the approval project rates related to school partnerships, in 2017 and 2018, the following results show that the success rate for the school partnership sector (ISCED 0 to 4 excluding Vocational schools) did not improve in the two-year-period.

Table 3. Statistics from the Erasmus Plus Annual Report (2017).

Action Type	Projects Received	Project Contracted	Success Rate
Strategic Partnerships for school education (KA201)	1184	367	31%
Strategic Partnerships for Schools Only (KA219)	2530	1086	43%
Strategic Partnerships for vocational education and training (KA202)	1683	469	28%
Strategic Partnerships for higher education (KA203)	748	201	35%
Strategic Partnerships for youth (KA205)	1874	318	17%

Note. Adult education projects have not been included.

Frequently, a school center decides to approach the Erasmus Plus program under the influence of a shared idea enthusiastically grown and nurtured in a few months, often by a certain teacher who kept it stored in the bottom drawer. Thus, a frequent scenario implies a group of teachers who elaborate an abstract and, afterward, seek other potential partner schools through specific platforms as eTwinning, OTLAS, or EuropartnerSearch, while still handling their day-to-day workload. In other cases, the project idea starts from a real needs analysis or a school development plan, revealing strong awareness about beneficiaries, stakeholders, implementation process, and improvements to be accomplished through the project activities. Indeed, Erasmus Plus can be considered a real professional development plan that includes job shadowing through mobilities, which can be one of the most rewarding ways of improving professional development by shadowing colleagues in another European school. In an Erasmus Plus project with six schools, for example, one partner organization generally hosts the other five partner delegations (students and teachers or only teachers), then the planned mobility calendar schedules that another partner school to be the next host. The exchange experience can benefit from formal recognition and schemas (certifications) to increase the transparency of qualifications and mobility of citizens in Europe, through the European Curriculum Vitae, Language Passport, Europass Mobility, Certificate Supplement, and Diploma Supplement. These tools are all available on the Europass Platform[11], and they require a process of recognition between the two school establishments involved in the mobility. "Two partner organizations involved in the mobility project, the first in the country of origin and the second in the host country. The partners may be universities, schools, training centers, companies, NGOs, etc."[12]

Indeed, according to the Lisbon Treaty, Erasmus Plus promotes networking as one of the greatest priorities of the program to facilitate cross-European exchanges:

Table 4. Statistics from the Erasmus Plus Annual Report (2018). Adult education projects have not been included. (Personal elaboration)

Action Type	Projects Received	Project Contracted	Success Rate
Strategic Partnerships for school education (KA201)	1253	390	31%
Strategic Partnerships for Schools Only (KA229)	2530	1086	43%
Strategic Partnerships for vocational education and training (KA202)	1523	453	42%
Strategic Partnerships for higher education (KA203)	740	225	34%
Strategic Partnerships for youth (KA205)	1972	353	18%

The program promotes the creation and development of European networks, providing opportunities for cooperation among stakeholders and the exchange and transfer of knowledge and know-how in different areas relating to sport and physical activity. This reinforced cooperation will notably have positive effects on developing the potential of Europe's human capital by helping reduce the social and economic costs of physical inactivity. (European Commission, 2020, p. 5)

One of the strengths of the program is the networking setting, which does not end with the partnership itself, but requires all involved to increase the number of beneficiaries, outside the partnership, through dissemination and exploitation activities of their project results. This can be obtained through the related web-based ecosystem: eTwinning, School Education Gateway, and the Erasmus Project Results platform. As a matter of good practice, a project partnership always starts a web site, blog, forum, or web platform to enhance visibility and reach local school communities who do not have access to the platforms. Thus, the involved school communities need to develop a strong awareness regarding social network creation and continue to evolve. Moreover, dissemination through digital media is a strict requirement in the Erasmus Plus guidelines.

In recent years, the EU has put increased attention toward the digital competencies in the education sector. The DigCompEdu (European Framework for the Digital Competence of Educators; Redecker & Punie, 2017) is an official framework that describes a set of skills and abilities needed to have a digitally competent teacher. It aims to provide a general frame of reference to support the professional development of teachers and educators in the EU at all levels: vocational education and training, special needs education, and non-formal learning. In this framework, the expression "social network" only is mentioned twice, and there is no direct reference to a specific set of skills that are needed to create, maintain, and develop a personal education network. This may suggest that teacher networking is still perceived as a side effect in their digital development, a kind of natural mere-exposure-effect produced by continuous contact with ICTs and social interactions. Regrettably, this area requires a much more complex interaction of abilities, motivations, and a marked digital social dexterity.

Nowadays, the concept of innovation is irretrievably and compulsorily associated with the praxis that can generate effectiveness through ICTs. The category of efficiency comes from a socio-cultural legacy tied to technological progress, which has gone through three industrial revolutions, and now with the fourth (Industry 4.0), digitalization represents one of the leading indexes of efficiency. Even though schools have their feet firmly on the evaluation ground, when elaborating on an Erasmus Plus project, they seem to struggle with the aspects of assessment criteria not directly linked to the student performance. Indeed, complex project management performance does not belong to the average education environment, but the peer-to-peer exchange and networking help teachers getting familiar with concepts like direct and indirect impact, benchmarking, stakeholders support and engagement, budget control, GANTT charts, and WBS (work breakdown structure). This lexicon is not part of the everyday teaching language and knowledge, but thanks to the interactions flowing through the project-network, which also implies mediation and mutual training, these unusual nomenclatures become more familiar and enter the customary language of the participants. As a matter of fact, they are all related to the networking skills and operations in the frame of a successful Erasmus Plus.

Another element for the successful introduction and dissemination of project results is the creation and sharing of OER (Open Educational Resources). The channel began to spread Creative Commons open licenses in European partnerships between schools. Indeed, open-access projects are one of the key features of the program to support learning, and generally, an Erasmus Plus generates original contents, materials, tangible and intangible outputs to document the experiences. Generally, in the EU, teachers of technical disciplines had been known for using open-access licenses, such as the Creative Commons, drawn from the Gnu/GPL licenses of the Free Software Foundation. Thanks to the Erasmus Plus propagation, this free editorial communication tool is growing in popularity at all school levels and among teachers of non-technical disciplines.

RESEARCH ON ERASMUS MOBILITIES WITHIN THE PERSPECTIVE OF SOCIAL NETWORK ANALYSIS

Social network analysis (SNA) is the process of investigating and representing social structures through the use of networks and graph theory. Relations between subjects are all described as networks with the nodes being the actors (i.e., an individual, a certain group, a profession, a department, a project) and the relationships being described as edges or arrows, which indicate the direction of interactions between the nodes (Barbási et al., 2012; Granovetter, 2001; Wasserman & Faust, 1994). Notwithstanding its growing role in the digital age, the potential of an SNA-approach has not yet been extensively exploited to reveal structures and patterns in public education networking. For this reason, the potential impact of a systematic SNA-methodology in light of the results generated by specific research about Erasmus Mobility in the University sector is explored.

A team of professors and scholars affiliated with the MTA-PE Budapest Ranking Research Group and the Hungarian Academy of Science (Gadár et al., 2020) investigated the flow of students, teachers, and staff between European Higher Education Institutions between 2008 and 2014 (before Erasmus become Erasmus Plus). They enriched the merged database with elements from four areas and previous existing databases (whose data they manually improved): (1) type of participants, (2) institutions' profiles according to their main activity, (3) institution's orientation in academic researches, and (4) points of interest (e.g., bars, pubs, restaurants, fast foods, museums, theatres, parks, and other elements that help enrich university life). The spacial projections represent the flow of students, teachers, and staff as well as the weighted networks that connect institutions, regions, and countries. The network data were manually enriched with institutional socio-economic data from the European Tertiary Education Register[13] and the Global Research Identifier Database[14]. All the institution headquarters were geocoded and characterized according to the attractiveness and quality of their contexts and environments based on the point of interest data. The inter-linked datasets offered relevant information to increase the understanding of the mobility patterns and attractiveness of education institutions. The investigation also used the Erasmus official and accessible reports, since the mobility databases were published every year until 2014 in the EU Open Data Portal[15] using different formats. These factsheets indicated the type of participants (i.e., students, teachers, or staff), and they followed three separate mobility datasets.

The mobility networks with different subject dimensions during the 2011–2012 academic year are presented in the following three visual maps. The size and color intensity of the nodes are related to the number of incoming students, while the size and color intensity of the edges are related to the number of students traveling between the linked institutions, including the number of incoming students and lecturers (Gadár et al., 2020).

The understanding of the mechanisms, patterns, and driving forces behind mobilities is a significant area of research as the development of integrated higher education is one of the focuses of the European Union, and most of the higher education ranking systems.

(Gadár et al., 2020, p. 1)

Figure 2. Network visualization through Gephi software, showing the mobility flow under the filter of Humanities and Arts.
(Figure from: Gadár et al., 2020, p. 9)

Mobility networks can be represented as multidimensional environments where the edge-weights originates from classified variables (e.g., subject area, education level of students, type of participants) of the mobility database (Gadár et al., 2020). The power of nodes (their degree of attractiveness) can

Figure 3. Network visualization through Gephi software, showing the mobility flow under the filter of Engineering, Manufacturing, and Construction.
(Figure from: Gadár et al., 2020, p. 9)

Figure 4. Network visualization through Gephi software, showing the mobility flow under the filter of Agriculture and Veterinary.
(Figure from: Gadár et al., 2020, p. 9)

be expressed and determined through socioeconomic indicators. Then, the geographic location of the institutions helps construct the analysis of spatial networks.

CONCLUSIONS AND POTENTIAL IMPACT

If knowledge is one of the fundamental pillars of an educational establishment, how much of the experiences, skills, upgrading, sharing, and innovations remain valuable, disseminated, retrievable, and accessible for external stakeholders? Are education establishments still perceived as delimitated spaces despite open digital networking opportunities?

There is a strong need for research that analyzes the effects of networking in public education, especially when public funds are involved. Patterns and relations mold the social capital of educators, which could identify hidden variables that may help understand networking patterns and their implications in the EU. The main collective entities are school establishments and other private or public organizations. To shift the examined investigation (involving Erasmus individual mobilities) to the new Erasmus Plus context, it would be reasonable to use these subjects as nodes and assign a weight to ties between organizations, program priorities, and locations. In addition, such a study may highlight the specific Erasmus Plus actions that have the most enduring lifelong learning networks, levels of geolocations, social and economic features, and types of outputs and innovations generated. Moreover, it would help establish whether there are further personal implications beyond the Erasmus Plus networks and how teachers can capitalize on these relations.

The complexity of such a research project could be extensively debated, but a few basic points can be indisputable; it must be international, cross-disciplinary, and involve EU central and national agencies to recover raw data. Reasonably, it would not be a short route, but most of all, it should be set, developed, and disseminated to foster teachers' awareness of their role in the emerging knowledge society.

REFERENCES

Avalos, B. (2011). Teacher professional development. *Teaching and Teacher Education over ten years. Teaching and Teacher Education*, *27*(1), 10–20. doi:10.1016/j.tate.2010.08.007

Barabási, A. L., Barzel, B., & Martino, M. (2012). *Introduction. In Network science*. Center for Complex Network Research - Northeastern University.

Boisot, M., & Child, J. (1999). Organizations as adaptive systems in complex environments: The case of China. *Organization Science*, *10*(3), 237–252. doi:10.1287/orsc.10.3.237

Bollinger, A. S., & Smith, R. D. (2001). Managing organizational knowledge as a strategic asset. *Journal of Knowledge Management*, *5*(1), 8–18. doi:10.1108/13673270110384365

Bucher, T., & Helmond, A. (2018). The affordance of social media platforms. In J. Burgess, A. Marwick, & T. Poell (Eds.), *The SAGE Handbook of Social Media* (pp. 233–253). Sage Publications. doi:10.4135/9781473984066.n14

Cabrera, A., & Cabrera, E. F. (2002). Knowledge-sharing dilemmas. *Organization Studies*, *23*(5), 687–710. doi:10.1177/0170840602235001

Cachia, R., Punie, Y., & Vuorikari, R. (2012). *Final report on the future of teacher networking. IPTS/JRC, European Schoolnet*. http://tellnet.eun.org/c/document_library/get_file?p_l_id=10704&folderId=18137&name=DLFE-817.pdf

Castells, M. (2013). *The impact of the internet on society: A global perspective. In 19 key essays on how Internet is changing our lives.* BBVA.

Cheng, E. C. K. (2012). Knowledge strategies for enhancing school learning capacity. *International Journal of Educational Management, 26*(6), 577–592. doi:10.1108/09513541211251406

Cheng, E. C. K. (2013). Applying knowledge management for school strategic planning. *KEDI Journal of Educational Policy, 10*(2), 339–356. http://repository.lib.eduhk.hk/jspui/handle/2260.2/14040

Cheng, E. C. K. (2017). Knowledge management strategies for capitalizing on school knowledge. *Journal of Information and Knowledge Management Systems, 47*(1), 94–109. doi:10.1108/VJIKMS-08-2016-0045

Cheng, E. C. K., & Chu, C. (2018). A normative knowledge management model for school development. *International Journal of Learning and Teaching, 4*(1), 76–82. Advance online publication. doi:10.18178/ijlt.4.1.76-82

Cheng, E. C. K., Wu, W. S., & Hu, J. (2017). Knowledge management implementation in the school context: Case studies on knowledge leadership, storytelling, and taxonomy. *Educational Research for Policy and Practice, 16*(2), 177–188. doi:10.100710671-016-9200-0

Cochran-Smith, M., & Lytle, S. (1999). Relationships of knowledge and practice: Teacher learning community. *Review of Research in Education, 24*, 249–305. https://www.jstor.org/stable/1167272

Collinson, V., & Cook, T. F. (2000). *I don't have enough time: Teachers' interpretations of time as a key to learning and school change.* Paper presented at the annual meeting of the American Educational Research Association, New Orleans, LA. https://files.eric.ed.gov/fulltext/ED446038.pdf

Commission of the European Communities. (2000). *A Memorandum on Lifelong Learning* (Commission staff working paper). https://arhiv.acs.si/dokumenti/Memorandum_on_Lifelong_Learning.pdf

Corredato Periotto, T. R., & Wessellenns, L. J. (2018). The school manager and the use of knowledge management practices for structuring organizational processes. *International Journal of Learning. Teaching and Educational Research, 17*(10), 43–54. doi:10.26803/ijlter.17.10.3

Dolton, P., Marcenaro, O., De Vries, R., & She, P. W. (2018). *The global teacher status index 2018.* London: The Varkey Foundation. https://www.varkeyfoundation.org/media/4867/gts-index-13-11-2018.pdf

European Commission. (2013). *Study on Policy Measures to Improve the Attractiveness of the Teaching Profession in Europe, Final Report, 1.* Publications Office of the European Union. Doi:10.2766/40827

European Commission/EACEA. (n.d.). *Erasmus Plus Programme Guide, Version 2 (26-02-2020).* https://ec.europa.eu/programmes/erasmus-plus/sites/erasmusplus2/files/erasmus_programme_guide_2020_v2_en.pdf

European Commission/EACEA/Eurydice. (2018). *Teaching careers in Europe: Access, progression and support.* Eurydice Report. Luxemburg: Publication Office of the European Union. https://op.europa.eu/en/publication-detail/-/publication/435e941e-1c3b-11e8-ac73-01aa75ed71a1/language-en European Commission/EACEA/

European Commission/EACEA/Eurydice. (2018). *The structure of the European education systems 2018/19: Schematic diagrams. Eurydice Facts and Figures*. Luxemburg. Publication Office of the European Union.

European Council. (2010). *Project Europe, 2030. Challenges and Opportunities*. Luxembourg: Publications Office of the European Union. https://www.consilium.europa.eu/media/30776/qc3210249enc.pdf

European Council. (2017). *The Rome Declaration. Declaration of the leaders of 27 member states and of the European Council, the European Parliament and the European Commission*. Brussels: Press office - General Secretariat of the Council. https://www.consilium.europa.eu/en/press/press-releases/2017/03/25/rome-declaration/

Eurydice. (2018). *Teachers' and school heads' salaries and allowances in Europe – 2016/17. Eurydice Facts and Figures*. Luxembourg: Publications Office of the European Union. https://eacea.ec.europa.eu/national-policies/eurydice/sites/eurydice/files/teacher_and_school_head_salaries_2016_17.pdf

Fox, A., & Wilson, E. (2015). Networking and the development of professionals: Beginning teachers building social capital. *Teaching and Teacher Education*, *47*, 93–107. Advance online publication. doi:10.1016/j.tate.2014.12.004

Gadár, L., Kosztyán, Z. T., Telcs, A., & Abonyi, J. (2020). A multilayer and spatial description of the Erasmus mobility network. *Scientific Data*, *7*(1), 1–11. doi:10.103841597-020-0382-1

Granovetter, M. S. (2001). The strength of weak ties. *American Journal of Sociology*, *78*(6), 1936–1380.

Klamma, R., Cao, Y., & Vuoriaky, R. (2009). Social network analysis of 45,000 schools: A case study of technology-enhanced learning in Europe. *Lecture Notes in Computer Science*. 10.1007/978-3-642-04636-0_18

Kools, M., & Stoll, L. (2016). What makes a school a learning organization? *OECD Education Working Papers*. doi:10.1787/5JLWM62B3BVH-EN

Lin, F., Lin, S., & Huang, T. (2008). Knowledge sharing and creation in a teachers' professional virtual community. *Computers & Education*, *50*(3), 742–756. doi:10.1016/j.compedu.2006.07.009

Linares Pons, N., Piñero Pérez, Y., Rodríguez Stiven, E., & Pérez Quintero, L. (2014). Diseño de un modelo de Gestión del Conocimiento para mejorar el desarrollo de equipos de proyectos informáticos. *Revista Espanola la de Documentacion Cientifica*, *37*(2), e044. Advance online publication. doi:10.3989/redc.2014.2.1036

Mansour, O., Askenas, L., & Ghazawneh, A. (2013). Social media and organizing – An empirical analysis of the role of Wiki affordances in organizing practices. *Thirty-Fourth International Conference on Information Systems*. https://portal.research.lu.se/portal/files/70684599/FULLTEXT01.pdf

Michos, K., & Hernández-Leoa, D. (2020). CIDA: A collective inquiry framework to study and support teachers as designers in technological environments. *Computers & Education*, *143*, 103679. Advance online publication. doi:10.1016/j.compedu.2019.103679

Moolenar, N. (2012). A social network perspective on teacher collaboration in schools: Theory, methodology, and applications. *American Journal of Education*, *119*(1), 7–39. doi:10.1086/667715

Nizzolino, S. (2020). *L'avvento della Open Education. L'Istruzione pubblica e l'educazione non formale nella Società della Conoscenza*. Edizioni Progetto Cultura.

Nonaka, I., & Konno, N. (1998). The Concept of "Ba": Building a Foundation for Knowledge Creation. *California Management Review*, *40*(3), 40–54. doi:10.2307/41165942

OECD Organisation for Economic Co-operation and Development. (2020). TALIS 2018 Results (Volume II): Teachers and School Leaders as Valued Professionals. TALIS, OECD Publishing. doi:10.1787/19cf08df-en

Parlar, H., Polatcan, M., & Cansoy, R. (2019). The relationship between social capital and innovativeness climate in schools. The intermediary role of professional learning communities. *International Journal of Educational Management*, *34*(2), 232–244. doi:10.1108/IJEM-10-2018-0322

Pateraki, I. (2018). Measuring the impact of eTwinning activities on teachers' practice and competence development - Monitoring eTwinning Practice Framework. Central Support Service of eTwinning - European Schoolnet.

Pil, F. K., & Leana, C. (2009). Applying organizational research to public school reform: The effects of teacher human and social capital on student performance. *Academy of Management Journal, 52*(6), 1101-1124. . doi:10.5465/amj.2009.47084647

Redecker, C., & Punie, Y. (2017). European framework for the digital competence of educators: DigCompEdu. *Publications Office of the European Union, Luxembourg., JRC107466*. Advance online publication. doi:10.2760/159770

Rismark, M., & Sølvberg, A. M. (2011). Knowledge sharing in schools: A key to developing professional learning communities. *World Journal of Education*, *1*(2), 150–160. doi:10.5430/wje.v1n2p150

Song, J. H., Kim, W., Chai, D. S., & Bae, S. H. (2014). The impact of an innovative school climate on teachers' knowledge creation activities in Korean schools: The mediating role of teachers' knowledge sharing and work engagement. *Journal of Education Policy*, *11*(2), 179–203.

Trust, T., Krutka, G. D., & Carpenter, P. J. (2016). "Together we are better": Professional learning networks for teachers. *Computers & Education*, *102*, 15–34. doi:10.1016/j.compedu.2016.06.007

Van Waes, S., De Mayers, S., Moonlenaar, N. M., Van Petegem, P., & Van de Bossche, P. (2018). Strengthening networks: A social network intervention among higher education teachers. *Learning and Instruction*, *53*, 34–49. doi:10.1016/j.learninstruc.2017.07.005

Volungevičienė, A., Teresevičienė, M., & Ehlers, U. (2020). When is open and online learning relevant for curriculum change in higher education? Digital and network society perspective. *The Electronic Journal of eLearning, 18*, 88–101. https://files.eric.ed.gov/fulltext/EJ1245114.pdf

Von Krogh, G. (2012). How does social software change knowledge management? Toward a strategic research agenda. *The Journal of Strategic Information Systems*, *21*(2), 154–164. doi:10.1016/j.jsis.2012.04.003

Vuorikari, R., Garoia, V., Punie, Y., Cachia, R., Redecker, C., Cao, Y., Klamma, R., Cuong, M., Pham, C. M., Rajagopal, K. P., Sibren, F., & Sloep, P. (2012). Teacher networks. Today's and tomorrow's challenges and opportunities for the teaching profession. *European Schoolnet (EUN Partnership AISBL).* https://www.academia.edu/13544915/Teacher_networks_Today_s_and_tomorrow_s_challenges_and_opportunities_for_the_teaching_profession

Vuorikari, R., Kampylis, P., Scimeca, S., & Punie, Y. (2015). Scaling up teacher networks across and within European schools: The case of eTwinning. In *Scaling Educational Innovations* (pp. 227–254). Springer Singapore. doi:10.1007/978-981-287-537-2_11

Vuorikari, R., Punie, Y., Carretero Gomez, S., & Van den Brande, G. (2016). *DigComp 2.0: The digital competence framework for citizens. Update phase 1: The conceptual reference model.* Luxembourg Publication Office of the European Union. doi:10.2791/11517

Wasserman, S., & Faust, K. (1994). *Social network analysis: methods and applications.* Cambridge University Press. doi:10.1017/CBO9780511815478

Wood, T. M. (2002). *Understanding and preventing teacher burnout.* ERIC Digest. https://www.ericdigests.org/2004-1/burnout.htm

Zhao, J. (2010). School knowledge management framework and strategies: The new perspective on teacher professional development. *Computers in Human Behavior, 26*(2), 168–175. doi:10.1016/j.chb.2009.10.009

KEY TERMS AND DEFINITIONS

E-Twinning: Refers to the major European educational network of teachers, schools, and students; all main users must be permanent or temporary staff employed in a public school (or recognized as such).

Edge: In a graphic representation of a social network, it is the visible link between two nodes.

Education Networking: Refers to when a teacher creates networks with other peers by professional social platforms or social networks, pursuing peer-to-peer exchange, and sharing experiences and materials.

Erasmus Plus: A flagship program of the EU for the education sector that funds partnerships, collaboration projects, exchange of staff and students across the EU, and other bordering countries.

EU Frameworks: A set of European schemes and guidelines oriented at harmonizing specific professional and social dimensions of the member states.

ISCED: International Standard Classification of Education; it is a framework for organizing information on education, and it helps to define education grades internationally to improve an immediate comparison among different national school systems.

Key Action 2: The specific approach of the European program, Erasmus Plus, that promotes cooperation for innovation and exchange of good practices among partner organizations, with a particular focus on schools in the EU.

Knowledge Management (KM): Refers to a set of good practices to deal with the process of selection, analysis, combination, storing, and retrieval of information and data that represent individual or collective knowledge. As a final step, the KM process generally aims at innovating the original knowledge encountered at the initial phase or during the process.

Knowledge Society: A term to describe societies that are economically and culturally dependent on their capacity to create, innovate, and share different forms of knowledge.

Mobility: Refers to the physical exchange of school staff and/or students between two or more educational institutions; it may last a week or several months, and offer opportunities for job shadowing, research, and/or training.

OER (Open Educational Resources): Any type of educational support or material publicly shared with an open license.

ENDNOTES

1 https://ec.europa.eu/education/policies/school/teaching-professions_en

2 Direct experience gained during 14 *job shadowing mobilities* in 14 foreign schools within the EU (from 2015 to 2019).

3 Public figures verified on eTwinning.net (05-08-2020)

4 Numbers officially reported in the platform at 05/08/2020.

5 https://eacea.ec.europa.eu/national-policies/eurydice/content/quality-assurance-42_en

6 The complete list of countries is available in the Erasmus+ official website: https://ec.europa.eu/programmes/erasmus-plus/about/who-can-take-part_en

7 "Commission adopts proposal for the next Erasmus programme 2021-2027". European Commission. 30 May 2018. Retrieved 8 December 2018. https://ec.europa.eu/programmes/erasmus-plus/news/commission-adopts-proposal-next-erasmus-programme-2021-2027_en

8 https://ec.europa.eu/programmes/erasmus-plus/about/who-can-take-part_en

9 Erasmus Plus programme guide 2020 version available at: https://ec.europa.eu/programmes/erasmus-plus/resources/documents/erasmus-programme-guide-2020_en

10 The author collaborates with the Italian National Agency *Erasmus+ INDIRE* as evaluator of Erasmus Plus proposals.

11 https://europa.eu/europass/en/national-europass-centres

12 Examples of Europass avaialbe at this link: https://europa.eu/europass/en/europass-mobility-examples-0

13 https://www.eter-project.com/#/home

14 https://www.grid.ac/

15 https://data.europa.eu/euodp/en/home

Chapter 11
Communication in the Age of a Global Pandemic:
Qualitative Remediation at the Community Level

Jean Constant
https://orcid.org/0000-0002-4941-3776
Hermay.org, USA

Sindy DeLaTorre Pacheco
Universidad Autónoma de Coahuila, Mexico

ABSTRACT

The COVID-19 pandemic is affecting communities worldwide today in many novel ways. The rapidity at which the disease is transmitted and the amount of information available in real-time creates a unique situation. This research, based on qualitative remediation at the community level, provides a fertile ground from which significant patterns are emerging. The authors reviewed the literature available as well as over 100 individual sites of local administrations, faith-based, NGOs, local charitable and community initiatives. It is premature to project an accurate picture of how to alleviate best the distress caused by a pandemic. However, some significant and credible patterns have emerged that lead to conclude that, next to transparency, initiatives based on proactive use of peer to peer e.communication, direct e.outreach, and e.collaboration between parties lead to constructive and successful initiatives.

INTRODUCTION

I recently was tasked by a Non-Profit organization to review effective remediation programs conducted at the community level. I am not a behavior analyst nor a trained scientist in Anthropology and Social Sciences. My field of expertise is Electronic Communication, and more specifically Visual Communication. It may seem odd to use my skills to find patterns and trends in a discipline I am not directly

DOI: 10.4018/978-1-7998-4891-2.ch011

Copyright © 2021, IGI Global. Copying or distributing in print or electronic forms without written permission of IGI Global is prohibited.

associated with. However, it is not uncommon to integrate communication and visual communication researchers in teams analyzing data in finance and economy, statistics, health, and even meteorology.

Dr. De La Torre Pacheco, who coordinated our effort, had the foresight to introduce her team to the Agile methodology. This multidisciplinary and collaborative approach is very similar to the Knowledge Visualization framework I currently use in my research projects. Agile is an umbrella term for several iterative, and incremental software development approaches, including Scrum, Crystal, Dynamic Systems Development Method, and Feature-Driven Development (Mendix, 2020). Its focus falls on empowering developers of all kinds to collaborate and make decisions together quickly and effectively. Knowledge visualization is information that has been made part of a specific context. In order for information to transform into knowledge, one must share some context, some meaning, in order to become encoded and connected to the pre-existing experience. In that sense, Knowledge Visualization can be considered as data visualization "in context" (Meyer, 2007)

BACKGROUND

The COVID 19 pandemic is unique in several ways. While pandemics have afflicted humanity since the beginning of time, this particular virus exploded in a manner never experienced before. The pandemic took less than two months to affect the whole planet. No place on earth has been immune to the virus's effect, from Iceland to the smallest atoll in the Pacific. Many reasons explain the speed and extent of the virus impact.

Transport

The 1918 Influenza (H1N1 virus) was a forewarner of things to come. It lasted for almost three years. The industrial age brought us trains and auto transportation. Today, all over the world, every day, millions travel every day across countries by air, ship, train, automobile, and other mechanical means of transportation. Over 500 million people, or one-third of the world's population, became infected with this virus. From Chicago to Mongolia's smallest community, all cities have in common an airport. According to ACI World's latest World Airport, Traffic Report passenger numbers are estimated to have reached 8.8 billion in 2018, growing by 6.4 percent compared to the previous year (ACI, 2019)

Economy

It is the first time in recorded history that the world economy is going through a global standstill for such an extended period. Except for food and utility services, all non-vital industries, such as manufacturing, services, and retail, had to close their doors. Workers were sent home to wait out the pandemic. This situation has created urgent financial, psychological needs. In many cases, it has affected household and individual properties as well. Millions of people have started to rely more and more on their network, family, friends, colleagues, support groups to find support and answers to their needs. This new situation affects everyone and, in particular, all the providers of services dedicated to helping and remediating individual needs. Staying relevant and continuing to grow in this unchartered new environment will require a thorough re-evaluation of the traditional methods and practices used to provide help and support, grow membership, and access funding.

Communication

1. Top Down Communication

SES's annual Satellite Monitor study, while limited to Europe and Africa shows that the number of global TV households it reaches directly or indirectly via satellite has increased by 12 million to 367 million in 2019. (FP, 2020). Traditionally, administrations are slow and prudent diffusing information of meaningful social significance. It has been experienced with China's slow response to the first warnings, US initial government release of real-time data, or Europe's almost non-existing information presence at the beginning of the pandemic. Most have corrected the course over time, and very proactive agencies participate in an extensive effort of transparency and accuracy, particularly at the local level (MSD, 2020). Non-governmental agencies and Community based support services have all faced a similar challenge. Very aware they were losing contact with their base, they responded with various degrees of effectiveness. While the situation is still very fluid, an outstanding effort is being made at replicating what large, better-funded agencies provide across the board to their constituents (Kilani, 2020). However, the short two-month time span in which individuals did not get information, got information of a debatable nature, and could not find appropriate answers to concrete questions created a novel and extraordinary landscape that will require urgent care and attention. Individuals that had lost hope or trust in their institutions found among each other help, peer support, and resources they did not know they had (NeoKosmos, 2020)

2. Peer to Peer Communication

Statista reveals that in 2015, there were approximately 1.5 billion PCs worldwide and 4.57 billion internet users. A number that reflects a trend as peer to peer communication moved from the office to the ubiquitous personnel cell phone. 4,68 billions of us have one (Statista, 2020). Consequently, it is not surprising to observe that the virus developed worldwide in less than two months. From China to North and South America, Europe, and Africa, we all got real-time information relating to the pandemic.

METHODOLOGY

Dr. Pacheco and I devised a simple research methodology to conduct our search. We focused on three main areas of remediation: heath, immediate needs, and long term support.

We also used a building-block approach to assess what makes a project work, why, and how. I visited over 100 websites based on three search criteria: official records, faith-based, charitable, community non-profit activities, and individual efforts. The information was compiled in a worksheet, where we both outlined, evaluated, and compared the most significant successes in each category. Indeed, more in-depth research will be needed to extract meaningful information. In the short time we were allowed to conduct this search, we already noticed a significant new pattern emerging from every data I collected.

QUALITATIVE REMEDIATION: COLLABORATION AND COMMUNICATION

The Administration

Administrations have a double handicap. Most of their workers were at home. By the nature of their work, they are wary of publishing information that has not been double fact-checked, discussed, and approved more broadly in committees. It takes time, and such framework is poorly adapted to an urgent response to a rapidly evolving landscape. However, and surprisingly, after a few months' delay, most are coming back with various degrees of success. They are now reporting facts, providing financial support, detailed public health advice, and meaningful positive information such as listing neighborhood by neighborhood services, non-profit and organized volunteer efforts participating in the remediation process at the local or individual level (MSD, 2020). Gathering real-time information necessitates a new, collaborative effort within each agency, agencies to agencies and an unusual proactive effort directed toward the community to collect and share information.

Often, this was made possible with a minimum of oversight from dedicated supervisors but by the sheer determination of personnel committed to their agency's relevance in this exceptional context. More significant, modern communication tools such as email, text messaging, group videocasts have allowed entire agencies to work on the same problem at the same time while respecting distancing and stay at home policies.

Faith Based Remediation in the Neighborhood

Most Faith-based and charitable organizations have had a long history of support within the community. They have stable structures in place, proper planning, logistics, and dedicated volunteers to reach out to those in need. The administrative policies in response to the pandemic, particularly concerning distancing and stay-at-home measures, created a direct problem and an unforeseen challenge. How to adjust to this new environment and continue providing needed services when most of their obligations rest on staff and volunteers direct participation? A renewed urgency in interfaith collaboration to share information, assess needs and help each other and their communities as best as they could. According to Dr. Brian J. Adams Director of the Centre for Interfaith & Cultural Dialogue at Griffith University, "This is a multi-faith, multi-cultural challenge in our society that is best combatted by a united community" (DKH, 2020).

Some have fared better than others. It is significant to notice that the most visible and successful intervention have all been based on excellent communication. Using their experience and expertise, identifying new urgent projects, and completing them successfully have been based on pro-active electronic communication. From email to website outreach and social platforms, projects were discussed, planning and logistics shared in real-time. Examples such as food collection, food distribution, home, and senior services have been aplenty here and abroad (NCC, 2020). For these organizations, the difference between failure and success seems to have been mostly based on communicating effectively or not, using all the wide variety of communication tools available on the internet to their advantage, or not. Indeed, more in-depth research on this newly available element to help conduct service efforts will provide additional consequential data. However, expert or ingenious use of electronic devices is the first clear, distinctive component that emerged from my short reviewing of numerous Faith based sites. It contributed meaningfully in the positive outcome of the organizations undertaking, kept their constituency involved, and possibly attracted new participants as well.

Faith-based organizations are often large groups, including a broad spectrum of the community—young, senior, and adults. Opinions may differ on this, but I did not notice any significant differences in age/gender disparities in adopting these tools and their enthusiastic response to it. In all successful projects, many over-50 staff and volunteers, well versed in technology or not, always found ways to be relevant, present, and active. The perception of the electronic media as means of communication and collaboration has changed in a very short time. It won't be possible to perpetuate older traditional approaches to build trust, support, and dedication from all involved. It will require that leaders demonstrate foresight, determination, and much listening to adjust to their base's newly acquired empowerment.

NGOs and NPOs Community Remediation

Significantly, because of communication or collaboration lack thereof, a very similar pattern emerged regarding NGOs' presence in community disaster remediation.

NGOs are trained and well equipped to respond to disasters worldwide. Their weakness is that it is mostly a top-down effort. What to do when staff and volunteers are sent home, when supplies and transport happen only at their bare minimum? Large multinational NGOs such as Red Cross or Red Crescent had no problem continuing their support, mainly because of governmental help and existing infrastructure (ReliefWeb, 2020). However, NGOs and NPOs at the regional and local level did not fare so well. Many have not updated their site since 2019 (Missing staff?). They provide next to no information relating to the pandemic or their involvement in remediation efforts in areas where they are supposed to be present and very involved. Among a few noticeable exceptions, the Getty Museum foundation directing financial support to the Los Angeles community. Direct knowledge of their community needs, granting expertise, and unique skills in the digital environment may have been among the decisive factors that led to the speed and success of their effort (CCF, 2020).The Nike Foundation, in addition to substantial financial support to regional and local community projects, used its brand name recognition and commercial strategy to provide support to grassroots organizations in the United States and Europe's neighborhood schools and community centers (Gilliland, 2020). The common thread that helped make these efforts successful has been an acute sense of effective communication, extensive use of electronic tools, on-location knowledge of the community needs and collaborative efforts between all involved.

Local Charitable Organizations

Like Faith-based organizations, NGOs, or NPOs, local organizations have fared with various degrees of success in their involvement with the community. Either because they are still following older, outdated models, or lack resources, most have had little to no impact in remediation drives. Sheltering and distancing may have been the main obstacle to their traditional modus-operandi. However, the ones that succeeded and flourished since the beginning of the pandemic have mostly based their efforts on networking, focusing on simple, identified objectives, and more significantly, used electronic communication tools in a very proactive manner (RI, 2020). The best equipped among them, Rotary International, Lions, Kiwanis, and others, all have continued to contribute to community remediation efforts [x] as best as they could. What they all have in common besides their name recognition is a dedicated membership. These active professionals look at the logistics of support projects as professionals would do. They practice networking every day in their professional and organizational life and have diverse expertise in communicating electronically. Within a few months of the stay at home restriction, more than 70% of New Mexico Rotary clubs were holding their weekly meetings online, planning, and completing new projects (Kays, 2020). In addition, their communication success rate has not so much been led by expertise, age, or gender, but the will to be of service. It certainly validates the old adage - when there is a will, there is a way!

Local Community Groups

Social and interest groups exist for various reasons. Special interest, fishing, bowling, etc. What they have in common is a network based membership of volunteers participating in a shared activity. The administrative lockdown policy eliminated their practice of meeting regularly in one dedicated place. One would think it would have eliminated or created extreme hardship to the very existence of these groups. Not always. Groups are built on friendship, quality time, and most important, communication. Abruptly sharing a concern much larger than their informal associative activity, some tapped their network to put their mind together and address immediate local issues relative to health, peer support, even community projects much beyond the scope of their association. In February of this year, the volunteer based Lake Huron Fishing Club received a $25,000 community sponsorship for a Stream Rehabilitation project. However, in light of the current situation, and in response to calls for community groups to redirect sponsorship funds, the LHFC board held a virtual meeting and approved the reallocation of their much-needed funds to Covid-19 Pandemic efforts in their community (LHFC, 2020).

Peer to Peer Collaboration and Communication

Workers of all walks of life share and network every day for multiple reasons. Information sharing, networking, peer support, among others. Sent home because of the pandemic did not stop their professional communication habits. Many have continued to interact with each other on their phone, FaceTime, or other video devices. That very informal setting motivated individuals to put their newly acquired free time and know-how to good use, participating in community-based relief efforts in a very informal but effective manner.

Individual professionals, especially in urban environments, could not provide much direct help because of the distancing restriction. However, they have quickly learned to bypass the existing limitations of their life and use electronic communication to build thriving networks and provide immediate, much-needed assistance. A librarian and cycling enthusiast started the CoronaCouriers in New York. A few days later, a software engineer stepped in to organize an online workplace. The group quickly gathered over 200 volunteers delivering to hospitals, nonprofits, food pantries, food banks, social workers, and individuals (Rivera, 2020). A father at home with his teenage kids steered their homeschooling activity into a more interactive and neighbor oriented type of study. They tapped the kids' network of friends to compose and write about their daily personal experience, put together the information, and publish a 29 pages online magazine (Colin, 2020). The response has been so enthusiastic that not only are they starting to receive responses from all over the world, parents ask for templates to replicate the process. Moreover, the on-going project is now about to join 826National, the largest youth writing network in the country.

COMMENTARY AND FINDINGS

What do all successful remediation efforts have in common?

1. Empathy

It is the first time in history that we all experience the same level of hardship, whether in Arizona, Korea, or South Africa. We have a common problem; we have a common issue to face. Empathy starts at home, and the planet has become our involuntary collective home.

2. Goodwill

Regardless of the situation, goodwill is the primary motivator that makes people dedicate time and effort to remediate difficult situations. While the assumption has been that most involuntary stay-at-home individuals and families would spend their time watching TV or baking, time and again, testimonies from around the world show that they chatted neighbors to neighbors, organized themselves, and moved quickly forward to address or solve community problems that

3. Communication

Distancing has been imposing unprecedented limitations on our traditional way of communication. The agencies, organizations, groups, and individuals who responded best to the challenge were the ones that used today's digital communication tools effectively, creatively, and with ingenuity, making them think innovatively to deliver much-needed services and support.

4. E. Collaboration

Aristotle claimed that "Man is by nature a social animal". When the philosopher suggested several thousand years ago that Man cannot live alone, his well-founded observation took an extraordinary turn in the environment we're living today. The uniqueness of the situation created by the stay at home, compounded by the electronic environment we are now surrounded by created a fertile ground for renewed direct communication and effective collaborative effort between participants.

In hindsight, one should not be surprised. For many years now, most of us carry a cell phone in our bag or our pocket. We all use the internet at work or at home, regardless of age, background, or geographical location. A little group in Fiji island (Vijay, 2020) was able to build a robust food relief effort in no time because from the most sophisticated banker in London or New York to a rural community on a small island, we all use electronic communication. Communication has become a vital component through which good intents failed, and projects have succeeded. Some may point out that not everyone is computer literate; not everyone owns a cell phone. I would argue that even the illiterate fisherman in Kenya knows how to use a cell phone to determine where to sell his catch. Even if you do not have a phone, someone in your family has one, a friend or a neighbor has one. When communicating becomes a vital priority, people find creative ways to meet the challenge.

NEW INDIVIDUAL DYNAMICS

When administrations, NGOs, and Charity fell short in providing the help we were accustomed to expect from them, individuals raised to the challenge. They addressed the issues at the building level, at the block level, at the neighborhood level, and all the while, respected the distancing regulations. Again, if motivation has been the critical engine of their determination, communication played a significant role in shaping and directing their effort.

Until recently, relief communications have been a top-down activity, an ideological message from the top conveyed by the elders, a newsletter vetted by the board. This structural model did not respond well to the unique new challenge created by the pandemic. Leaders and administrators will have to come to term with the fact that trust and individual engagement starts at home. It is probably the most meaningful new information emerging from the multitude of efforts being accomplished every day worldwide.

CONCLUSION

It is indeed a challenge to analyze an event developing in real-time and in which we are all involved. Regardless, the numerous reports I went through brushed again and again the same picture. Individual resilience, goodwill, and communication are among the key elements driving productive remediation efforts. Only yesterday, many among us were still debating how technology, the internet, cell phones were changing our social habits and were reluctant to commit to it. Today, individual resourcefulness has shown us that computer literacy is not just some credit needed to complete an education. Young and old, it is a skill everyone already possesses and knows how to put to good use.

As concluded Lisa Cornish, "Increased attention to more localized procurement processes and the procurement of local goods will support communities in being more efficient and proactive, along with facilitating access to real-time data to help with decision making. Everyone needs to take new risks and invest in emerging networks and relationships (Cornish, 2020). A recent report from the Aspen Institute recently highlighted that a successful nonprofit is digitally-savvy (Ottinger, 2018). It has the digital expertise at the senior management level and a willingness to embrace the digital in many, if not all, of its undertakings. Fostering a culture of feedback is crucial to the success of every organization. Creating an open, feedback-oriented company culture requires people to be able to give and receive feedback about any aspect of organizational life.

What was prescient two years ago has become today's reality and will shape our tomorrow. A new approach to communication well as more direct proactive collaboration between stakeholder is what is defining new pattern that can successful respond to a catastrophic event, and demonstrate the effectiveness of energetic, individual, social and community based networking.

ACKNOWLEDGMENT

The authors would like to acknowledge the Society of St. Vincent de Paul, Phoenix for its support and having made this research possible.

REFERENCES

Airports Council International. (2019). *Annual World Airport traffic. Forecast 2019-2040.* https://aci.aero/

California Community Foundation. (2020). *LA Arts Covid 19 Relief Fund Grantees.* Getty Foundation. https://www.getty.edu/foundation/initiatives/current/la_covid_fund.html

Colin, C. (2020). *Kid Reporters tackle the Coronavirus.* CondeNast publication. https://www.wired.com/story/kid-reporters-tackle-coronavirus-newspaper/

Cornish, L. (2020). *First came the coronavirus. And then the cyclone hit.* Devex. https://www.devex.com/news/first-came-the-coronavirus-and-then-the-cyclone-hit-97261

Financial Post. (2020). *SES Delivers over 8,300 TV channels to 367 Million homes.* Business Wire. Retrieved on 07/15/2020 at https://financialpost.com/pmn/press-releases-pmn/business-wire-news-releases-pmn/ses-delivers-over-8300-tv-channels-to-367-million-homes-worldwide

Gilliland, N. (2020*). How Nike is striking the right tone with its response to COVID 19.* Centaur Media plc. https://econsultancy.com/how-nike-is-striking-the-right-tone-with-its-response-to-covid-19/

KAICIID. (2020). *COVID 19 and Religion.* https://www.kaiciid.org/dialogue-knowledge-hub/webinars/covid-19-and-religion

Keys, A. (2020). *Rotary Club of Albuquerque offers support to food pantries, Navajo Nation.* KRQE. https://www.krqe.com/news/albuquerque-metro/rotary-club-of-albuquerque-offers-support-to-food-pantries-navajo-nation-during-covid-19-crisis/ Kinlani/Flagstaff

Lake Huron Fishing Club. (2020). *Message from the President.* LHSC. Retrieved on 07/15/2020 at https://www.lakehuronfishingclub.com/

Mendix.com. (2020). *A Brief introduction to Scrum.* https://www.mendix.com/agile-framework/#:~:text=Agile%20is%20an%20umbrella%20term,%2C%20and%20Feature%2DDriven%20Development

Meyer, R. (2007). *Knowledge Visualization.* LMU, Department of Informatics. https://www.medien.ifi.lmu.de/

Ministry of Social Development. (2020). *COVID-19 Community Wellbeing and Resilience Grant.* New Zealand Government. Retrieved on 07/15/2020 at https://www.msd.govt.nz/a

Mutual Aid. (2020). *Mutual aid needs list, summer 2020.* https://kinlanimutualaid.org/

NeoKosmos. (2020). *Xanthi teams makes 3D masks to help medical staff.* NeoKosmos publication. https://neoskosmos.com

North Coast Church. (2020). *Covid 19 resources.* https://www.northcoastchurch.com/covid-19-resources/

ReliefWeb. (2020). *COVID-19: The International Red Cross and Red Crescent Movement's Approach.* OCHA. https://reliefweb.int/report/world/covid-19-international-red-cross-and-red-crescent-movement-s-approach

Rivera, D. (2020). *A volunteer food courier talks about delivering food during the quarantine.* UPROXX. https://uproxx.com/culture/new-york-coronavirus-couriers/

Rotary International. (2020). *COVID 19 global grants listing.* https://www.rotary.org/en/top-global-grant-projects

Schuman Ottinger, C., & Bonilla, B. (2018). *Open Nonprofit Data Open Doors for Researchers.* The Aspen Institute. https://www.aspeninstitute.org/blog-posts/open-nonprofit-data-opens-doors-for-researchers/

Statista. (2020). *Electronic environment overview.* Retrieved on 07/15/2020 at https://www.statista.com/

Vijay. (2020). *Much needed assistance for Lautoka residents.* Fiji Village. https://www.fijivillage.com/news/Much-needed-assistance-for-Lautoka-residents-affected-by-lockdown--fx4r85/

ADDITIONAL READING

Covid19DVRN. (2020).COVID-19 DVRN Application https://airtable.com/shr7oLm0Ouxm5iNM8

DEVPB. (2020). Fiji civil society solidarity driving the COVID-19 humanitarian response https://devpolicy.org/fiji-civil-society-solidarity-driving-the-covid-19-humanitarian-response-20200604-2/

Exult. (2020) COVID-19 Response Funding Available for Non-Profits https://www.exult.co.nz/covid-19-response-funding/

Google. (2020) Our role in Asia's economic recovery. https://blog.google/around-the-globe/google-asia/our-role-in-asias-economic-recovery

IFRC. (2020). Community Feedback. https://media.ifrc.org/ifrc/cea_covid19_response/ Leyden Academy on Vitality and Aging, (2020). Verhalen in Coronatijd. https://wijencorona.nl/

Nature. (2020) Doing Science during the COVID-19 quarantine. https://www.nature.com/articles/d41586-020-01001-8

Orden Hospitalia de San Juan de Dios. (2020). Vencer el virus COVID-19. https://www.ohsjd.es/vencer-virus-covid-19-84-anos-experiencia-personal

Rotary International. (2020) Rotary response to the Corona pandemic. https://www.rotary.org/en/rotarys-response-coronavirus-pandemic

SIMAP. (2020). European public procurement. https://simap.ted.europa.eu/web/simap/covid-related-tenders

UNICEF. (2020). COVID-19) information centre https://www.unicef.org/coronavirus/covid-19#covid-19-stories-features

US-CCF. (2020) COVID-19 Business in Action. https://www.uschamberfoundation.org/aid-event/corporate-aid-tracker-covid-19-business-action

Chapter 12
Study of Increasing Adoption Trends of Digital Banking and FinTech Products in Indian Payment Systems and Improvement in Customer Services

Narinder Kumar Bhasin
https://orcid.org/0000-0001-7167-8730
Amity University, Noida, India

Anupama Rajesh
https://orcid.org/0000-0002-8421-473X
Amity University, Noida, India

ABSTRACT

The objective of massive adaptation of digital payments by the banks with the support of the central bank of any country along with their government agencies is to improve customer services and satisfaction in the online payment systems in place of cashless and paperless payment systems. There are very few researches that have focused to measure the higher customer satisfaction based on factors like trust, risk-free, secure, transparent, accountability of banks, fintech, regulator, and payment system operators. This chapter analyzes the impact of digital banking and fintech in the Indian banking system, initiatives taken by RBI, NPCI, and the government to build the strong trust of customers in online payment systems to ensure improvement in customer services with higher customer satisfaction.

DOI: 10.4018/978-1-7998-4891-2.ch012

Copyright © 2021, IGI Global. Copying or distributing in print or electronic forms without written permission of IGI Global is prohibited.

INTRODUCTION

Innovation is progressively turning into a piece of the banking system in India. Indeed, the speed with which various banks are moving toward this path may fluctuate, however the focus is to ensure to offer services to clients in an increasingly productive and innovative way. Fintech can possibly assume a major job in expanding access to finance, and in advancing the development of MSMEs in the nation. The development of Fintech, or the structuring and provisioning of financial services by utilizing new mechanical innovations, is one of the most critical advancements in the financial sector in the previous decade. The objective of financial services made accessible by means of digital stages is to add to neediness decrease and to add to the financial consideration targets of creating economies. There are three patterns that are molding the speed of the digital banking space in India:

- ***First***, and this maybe is the most significant, is the entire push government is providing for digital economy in the nation and which itself is actuating an adjustment in shopper conduct and causing clients to request more comfort from their banks.
- ***Second***, is the quick development of the more agile Fintech players that are attempting to convey services in a way never observed. Banks should work nearby such players to improve the client confronting side of their business just as their own inner procedures.
- ***Third***, the experience of clients in different ventures be it internet business, social insurance, instruction or transportation is improving at such a quick pace, that they are presently expecting comparative delivery and interface even in the banking business.

The Common people started to shift from traditional banking payment modes towards electronic funds transfer and digital payment solution based on the principle of safety, security, accountability, transparency, convenience, trust and final confirmation of successful funds transfer message on their Email id or mobile message. Easy internet connectivity, WIFI, smart phones has also played an important role in increasing usage and acceptance of digital and Fintech products in India. (Franciska A, Sahayaselvi S, 2017)

The objective of massive adaptation of digital payments by the banks with the support of the Central Bank of any country along with their Government agencies is to improve customer services and satisfaction in the online payment systems in place of cash less and paper less payment systems. There are very few researches which have focused to measure the higher customer satisfaction based on factors like trust, risk free, secure, transparent, accountability of banks, fintech, regulator and payment system operators. (Tiwari N, Singh N.K 2019)

Background of the Study

From Uber to Airbnb, disturbances have changed numerous sectors. As of not long ago, the financial sector remained generally immaculate. As of late, there has been a move in the focal point of digitalization from improving the delivery of traditional assignments to presenting on a very basic level new business openings and models for financial service organizations. Since decades, the financial business has encountered a persistent development in service delivery because of digitalization. This advancement is described by expanded network and improved speed of data preparing both at the client interface and in back-office forms. Digitalization offers new open doors for banks to put the client at the focal point of the improvement procedure. Indian Banking Payment System since last decade is undergoing through various phases of digitalization and digital disruptions coupled with banking reforms like push towards digital finance, financial inclusion. demonetization, GST Tax, Digital India connecting rural through micro ATMS and Payment Banks (Bhasin N.K., Rajesh A, 2018) New advances appear to be and remain in the market to upset the retail financial service value chain, just as bringing new players into the serious field. One of the fundamental changes in the business is turning out to be digitalization which is seeing a significant change to the banking framework. The ascent of Fintech new companies and the expanding aspirations of the world's digital titans are putting expanded weight on traditional banks, guarantors, and different players. The major issue the customers are facing in paper based payment systems are delays in collection of cheques, clearing settlement delays, loss in transit, frauds and lack of accountability of various parties involved in the process .Electronic payment systems were able to address many issues but the nature of customer`s complaint have changed like cybercrimes, lost cards, ATMs fraud, phishing attacks etc. .So all the good work done through digital payment by traditional banks and fintech goes in vain if the number of complaints and dissatisfaction increasing among the customers .This Chapter analyzes the Impact of Digital banking and Fintech in Indian Banking System, initiatives taken by RBI, NPCI and Government to build strong trust of customers in online payment systems to ensure improvement in customer services with higher customer satisfaction.

Objective of the Study

1. To understand the overview and increasing digital banking trends in Indian Banking Systems through comparative study between the period 2015-16 and 2018 -19
2. To study and review the initiatives taken by Reserve Bank of India through Payment System Vision 2019-2021.
3. To analyze the impact of digitalization on the Banks and Fintech in India
4. To measure the impact of digital banking and Fintech products adaptation on the improvement in customer services and satisfaction

Research Methodology

To understand the role of digital banking and Fintech in India and its impact on improving customer satisfaction, we used secondary online sources. The following sections were analysed on the basis to identify the Research Topic. They are as follows:

- Initiatives of Reserve Bank of India and Indian Government
- Digital Payments Actions for Enhancement through Payment System Vision Document
- Present scenario of increasing digital payments usage and acceptance by the customers.
- Improvement in customer services and customer satisfaction through online made of payments

The Secondary sources that we used were Online Article, Journals, and Issued Public Interest Booklets. Chapter has been divided into four sections focusing on overview of Indian banking and payment systems, increasing digital trends, initiatives by various stake holders to promote digital and fintech predicts and improvement in customer services on usage of digital payment systems.

Literature Review

Franciska A M, Sahayaselvi S. (2017) studied in their article on Overview of Digital Payments that the information technology has played an important role to revolutionize the traditional banking payment systems in India. The Study focus on the various electronic payment system methods used by the customers and various transaction routed by them through mobile and internet for day to day routine financial operations. Future of Indian banking payment system is focused on cashless financial transactions with the faster reach of mobile / internet connectivity and easily amiability of electricity in urban, semi urban and rural areas.

Bhasin N. K, Rajesh A (2018) in their research paper examine and analyze the major trends in digitalization and electronic payment system in India. The paper analyzes the Role of Fintech in the disruptive trends through next gen chatbots, machine learning, block chain, smart workflows, automated personalization, open banking, social media marketing, digital wallet, workable banking technology and contextual banking. The paper presents the four stages of evolution of digital banking in India and comparative study of various electronic payment system volumes and values between the two periods of 2013-14 and 2017-18.

Vasan M, Senthil B (2018) in their research paper on A study of payment and settlement system in the Indian Banking Sector explain the types and reasons for implementing electronic services in India. The paper traces the customer shift from cash or paper based payment systems from the year 2007 to 2017 and comparative study of volume of electronic funds like ATM, RTGS, NEFT, Cards, IMPS, Mobile banking were presented.

Mohan R, Ray P (2017) in their study on Indian Financial Sector: Structure, Trends and Turns traces the story of banking reforms in India since 1950 to 2015. Author classify the various innovative growth development into three phases of classification. First Phase 1950`s to 1970`s, Second Phase 1970`s to 1980`s and third phase from 1990`s to 2015.

Bhasin N. K (2019) in his research paper study define the function of digital banking and its evolution in Indian banking sector. The study further traces the story of Indian banking payment system reforms from the year 1980 to 2019. Paper also presents the review of success of RBI Payment System`s vision in India, increasing trends in adaptation, use of digital products by Indian bank` customers and new emerging Fintech products and advantages of E collaboration.

RBI Reports (2019) in their vision documents Payment and Settlement Systems in India Vision 2019-2021 explain the road map for substantial development to ensure "state of art", fast. efficient and affordable payment systems. Empowering exceptional E payment experience for the customer is main objective of this vision document and focus on growth of retail payments as well as systematically important financial market infrastructure. The paper focus on review of achievements of the vision 2018, payment system vision 2021, expected outcomes of vision 2021 and specific initiatives from customers, regulators like RBI and NPCI, payment system operators, card network operators and legal entity identifier.

KPMG Reports (2018) in their research reports on Bharat Bill Payment System (BBPS) explain the various bills payments in India as a game changer to increase adoption of online payment system and discuss various Global Case Studies. The paper focus on Integration of online utility bill payment system by RBI authorization to Banks and Non-Bank entities to connect their core banking system to offer a one common platform to the billers all over India to make the utility bills payment.

Manoj P.K, 2017 in his research study on Digital Transformation in Indian Banking focus on the implementation of Image Based Cheque Truncation System – A Clearance payment system which stop the physical movement of the paper based payment instruments. The paper explains the benefits of CTS System faster clearing cycle, efficient, effective, transparent and customer friendly system where customer can deposit the cheques at ATM, Kiosk and other digital cheque drop machines where the cheque is digitally scanned and settlement is based on the secured images.

Gupta, A and Xia, C (2018) in their chapter A Paradigm Shift in Banking: Unfold Asis`s Fintech adventures studies the new role of Fintech in traditional banking system and focus on evolution in Asia. The paper explains the process of technology revolution across various functions like deposit, lending, investment, capital raising, insurance and payments. The chapter focus on the important role that central banks of the country and government need to play to resolve various challenges faced due to disruptions in the economy.

Manser Payne, E., Peltier, J.W. and Barger, V.A. (2018) in their study investigate the various determining factors that influence the perception, attitudes and comfort of the people while using mobile banking and AI enabled mobile devices . The study was based on primary data with 218 digital natives and based on multivariate and multiple regression analysis. The findings of the research were the relative advantage construct has most impact on mobile banking usage and not on AI based mobile products.

Lavanya V, (2019) in his article on the Impact of Digital Banking in India explains the digital technology innovations and examine its impact in the Indian Economy. The paper explains the advantages and disadvantages of digital banking. The findings focus on various challenges in digitalization like the computer illiterate, poor and people living in rural areas who does not have access to electricity, server and computer virus problems.

PWC, Report, (2019) on Emerging Technogym disrupting the financial sector explains the key drivers of India`s Fintech revolution and segment overview of the Indian Fintech Market like digital payments, alternative lending, InsurTech and Wealth tech . The report focus on the emerging technologies reshaping the financial sector and recommendations for accelerating Fintech growth.

Tiwari N, Singh N.K (2019) in their research paper studies the various factors affecting the customer satisfaction in cash less payments systems in India with respect to digital payment platform like Paytm and Bhim. The study was conducted with close ended questionnaire with 200 respondents using sampling method, quantitative analysis and inferential analysis tools like correlation test, ANOVA and regression analysis. The findings of their research focus that there is a much impact on customer satisfaction subject to applicability, functionality and availability.

Sikdar P, Makkad M, (2015) in their paper Online bank adoption – A factor validation and satisfaction causation study in the context of Indian Bank Customers considers a five factor model tested for reliability and validity by factor analysis. The five factors which impact overall customer satisfaction on line banking system are trust, constraint, intention to use, ease of use and accessibility.

Monferer D, Moliner A.M, Estrada M (2019) in their research paper on increasing customer loyalty through customer engagement in the retail banking industry used structural equation modelling based on dyadic methodology of 225 dyads (bank branch manager – average of five branch customers). The findings of the research were the various factors which improves customer satisfaction in retail banking industry are customer engagement, customer loyalty, emotions, self-brand connection and branch market orientation.

SECTION 1: OVERVIEW AND INCREASING DIGITAL TRENDS IN INDIAN BANKING SECTOR

Indian payment System is the life line of the country and it connect the various banks, financial, institutions, customers, Fintech, IT vendors and various modes of funds transfer system like ATM, POS, Internet and Mobile Banking. Role of technology has enabled connecting the basic sectors of the economy and usher in another dawn of headway on the Indian horizon. The introduction of ICT – Information and Communication Technology has revolutionized the Indian banking sector with high level of acceptance of the electronic and digital banking products with new innovative technologies. (Vasan, M, Senthil B, 2018) Banking sector has deciphered the desires and wants of an enormous number of people into this present reality. Nevertheless, to do all things considered, it has expected to control miles and miles of irksome territory, persevere through the shock of foreign rule and the hurts of section. Today, Indian banks can positively match top banks of the world. In the Indian Banking System, Cooperative banks exist by one another with commercial banks and accept an advantageous activity in giving need-based service to local people, especially for horticultural and agribusiness based assignments including cultivation, dairy farming, milk products, hatchery in form of little businesses and independent work driven activities. Before the twentieth century, money lending by unorganized sectors at a high rate of interest, was commonly unavoidable in rural India.

With opening of rural branches by Public Sector Banks and Rural Banks like NABARD with focus on increased financial inclusion and financial literacy, customers have shifted their dependence on money loan masters / lenders to regulated financial institutes. Unorganized money lenders still exist in Indian Financial System but have lost their business as now common man is aware of their financial access. As the banking habits and number of bank`s branches started increasing and turn out to be logically preferred mode of customers for their financial needs, the impact of deregulation of interest rates, technology advancement and mechanical upgradation like ATMs has led to increase in number of bank`s account and deposit. Since Nationalization of Banks in India in 1969 and 1980, the economic development goals have impacted the financial markets in India with increase in the credit loans sanctioned to the priority sector of the country. Indian Banking industry underwent a change with new generation private sector banks with core banking system and advance technology opened from 1995 onwards. With the fifty years of bank`s nationalization and as a consequences of various banking reforms in the last 25 years with growth in interest rates, float management, and considerable competition still the extent of development is not uniform. (Mohan, Roy, 2017) The banks start shedding their traditional functions and focus on upgrading, improving and turning out with new innovative product and services to deliver customer satisfaction and delight by meeting expected needs of their customers. Speed, Accuracy, Safety and Security of advanced digital payments lead to reduction in costs and faster movement of funds transfer. The Banking Industry of India is unique and have huge network of branches connecting different states and remote areas considering the fascinating social, economic, legal, and geographic attributes. Banking Industry with collaboration with Fintech and IT vendors, expected to achieve all of the goals of the economic and highly digital payment systems and improving customer`s satisfaction.

Customer `s Increasing Adaptation and Usage of Digital Banking Products in Indian Banking System

Customer focus started to shift from paper-based clearing instruments like cheques, demand drafts and pay orders which have longer cycle of settlement of 3-4 days due to physical movement of the cheques from place of deposit to clearing centre and then to drawee bank for payment. In case cheques were not paid due to funds reason or technical reasons like incomplete date, signature differs, mutilation, then cheques are returned through return clearing house again. During this manual process or MICR, there were the chances of loss of cheques in transit, misplacement or cheques get torn, wrong capture of MICR data at time of encoding or at clearing centres. Since the Magnetic Ink Character Recognition Based Clearing System of processing cheques were discontinued by RBI in 2013 and As per RBI directives, periodicity for processing Non-CTS cheques in CTS clearing was reduced to 'once in a month' from 01.09.2018, i.e., second Wednesday of the month. (Bhasin N.K, 2019). No such cheques were accepted in CTS clearing after 31.12.2018., therefore at present:

Paper Based Clearing consists of two components:

1. **Non MICR Clearing:** is a process of manual clearing settlement adopted at the centres where the number of participating banks in clearing house are less as well as the low volumes of cheques. Cheques are physically delivered to drawee banks and in a time consuming process.
2. **Cheque Truncation System:** CTS was introduced in 2011 replacing MICR clearing with Image Based Processing of truncated cheques with essential data without physical movement of cheques are transferred electronically to clearing house and drawee banks for payments). CTS, though it's a paper based payment system has shown marginal increase because its more advance, faster, time and cost savings and more secure system. Figure 1 is reflecting 16% increase in volume and 17% increase during the period 2015- 16 and 2018-19 whereas Non MICR Clearing is reflecting 91% decrease in volume and 92% decrease in value reflecting the shift from the manual paper based payment instruments to CTS and other digital banking modes. (Manoj P.K, 2017)

Various Initiatives were taken by RBI, NPCI, Government of India and Banks in promoting the various types of electronics and digital banking products. Cash less and highly digital is the main objective of Payment System Vision 2021 and NPCI, an umbrella organization of retail payment system processes more than fifty person of digital payment transactions in India. Various new digital banking funds transfer systems were introduced and the following statistics shows that there has been continuous growth in individual segments of retail electronic payment systems such as:

- **Real Time Gross Settlement (RTGS):** is an electronic and continuous transfer of funds on real time gross basis without netting. This payment system is used for high value transactions above Rs. 2 lakh and beneficiary received funds instantly. Figure 2 reflects the 38% increase in volumes and 65% increase in values of RTGS transactions.

- **Electronic Clearing Service (ECS):** is a retail electronic payment funds transfer system for transactions of bulk collection and payments of repetitive in nature. An ECS Debit and Credit transaction facilitates fund transfer from one bank to many bank accounts and many banks to one bank

Figure 1. Comparative Study of Paper Based Payment Systems for the period 2015-16 and 2018-10
Source: RBI Bulletin Payment System Indicators

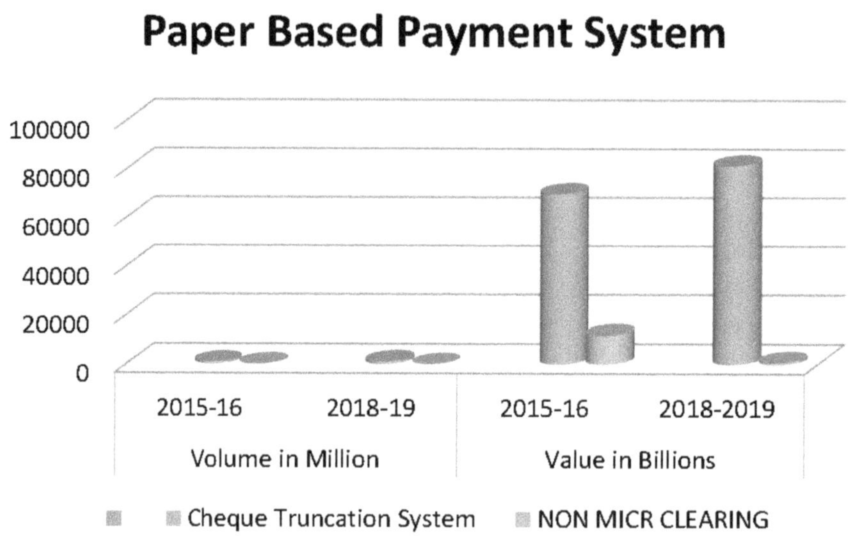

account. ECS volumes and values at RBI Platform are showing decreasing trends because w.e.f. 1st may, 2016 ECS was replaced by National Automated Clearing House (NACH) at NPCI Platform. NACH is more efficient and faster centralized electronic clearing system with various features of standardization and digitalization of mandates, minimum activation time and reduction of operational cost. A Figure 3 NACH transactions reflects the 105% increase in volumes and 260% increase in values from the period 2015-16 to 2018-19.

Figure 2. Comparative Study of RTGS for the period 2015-16 and 2018-10 Source RBI Bulletin Payment System Indicators

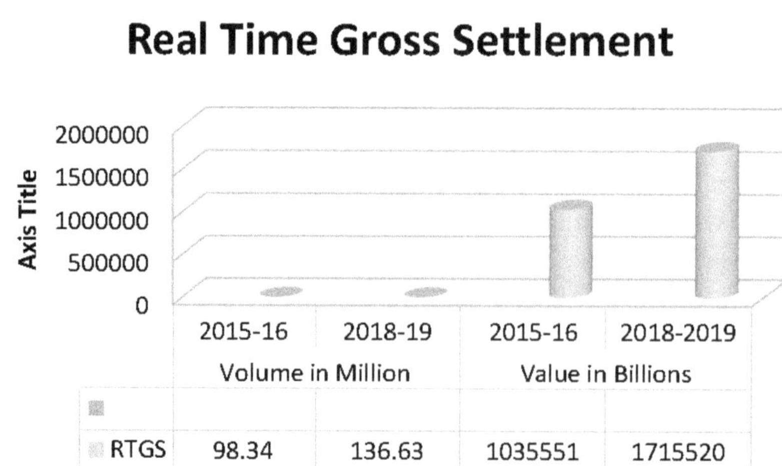

Figure 3. Comparative Study of ECS Debit, ECS Credit & NACH for the period 2015-16 and 2018-10 Source RBI Bulletin Payment System Indicators

- % increase in values from the period 2015-16 to 2018-19.

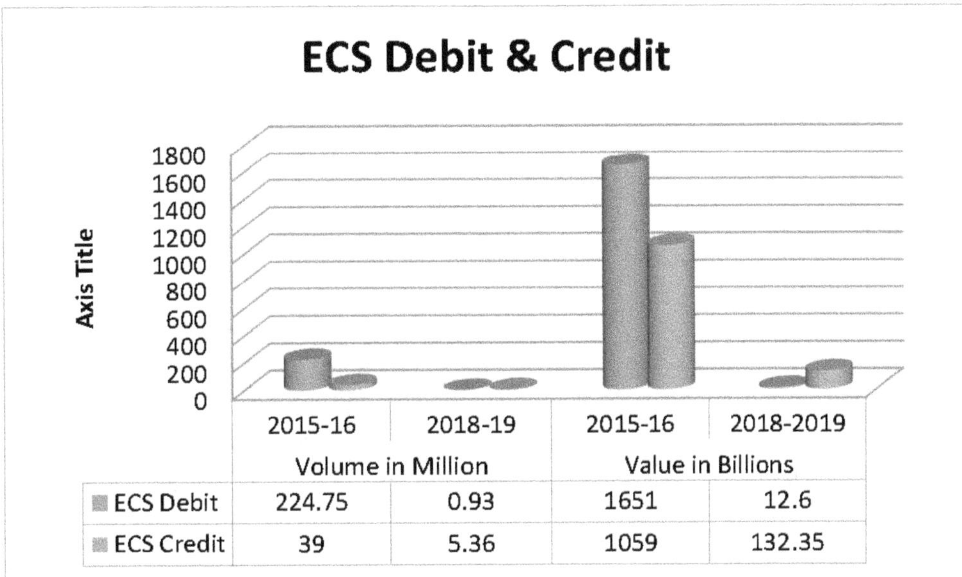

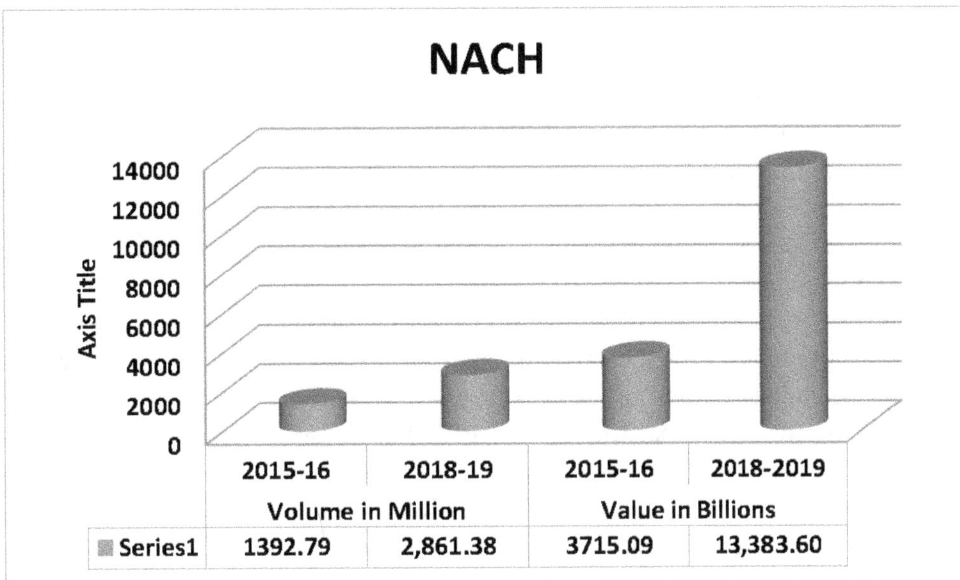

- **National Electronic Funds Transfer (NEFT)** is one to one nationwide electronic payment System where individuals, corporate, firms can transfer funds to others having a bank account throughout India. NEFT system is offered on RBI Platform in 23 batches from 8.00 AM TO 6.30 PM except 2nd and 4th Saturday. Figure 4 reflects the 85% increase in volumes and 173% increase in values

Figure 4. Comparative Study of EFT / NEFT for the period 2015-16 and 2018-10 Source RBI Bulletin Payment System Indicators

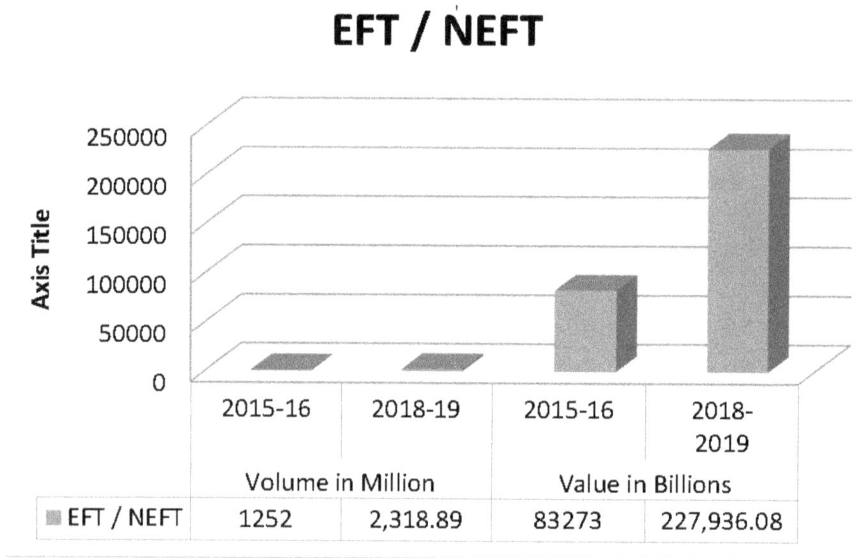

- **Immediate Payment Service (IMPS):** is 24 x7 instant electronic funds transfer systems between all the banks in India through ATM, Mobile and Internet. IMPS was launched by NPCI ON 22nd Nov, 2010 and the users can transfer the money through MMID and M Pin. Figure 5 reflects the tremendous 696% increase in volumes and 880% increase in values because of mobile and internet banking with benefits of safe, secure cost effective and 24 hours' availability and on holidays.

Mobile Banking Services are offered 24 by 7 by 365 by banks to their customers through Mobile Applications via internet banking or mobile data connection. Customers can download the mobile apps from play store and with internet banking password / customer id and can generate Mpin. Customers can do various transactions like view the account balances, credit card balance, transfer funds, create on line fixed deposits, change or block password, make investments etc. There has been increase in the registered customer base for mobile banking as well 1493% increase in volumes and 632% increase in value. The sharp increase in mobile banking was due to convenient, cost savings, reduced visits to branch, anywhere any time availability, P2P Payments, utility bill payments etc. Convenient fast banking was the relative advantage where people prefer as regards to complex layers in AI enabled mobile banking. (Manser Payne, E., Peltier, J.W. and Barger, V.A. (2018)

Card Payment System – Indian Customers are increasingly using the Cards more for shopping at point of sales, online shopping through internet and mobile banking as compared to cash with drawls at ATM. Figure 7 shows the Credit Card 124% increase in volume and 149% increase in value and Debit Card 54% increase in volume and 44% increase in value .RBI data shows that Point of Sales usage in Debit Card in 2018-19 was 4414.28 Million and Value 5934.75 Billion whereas Credit Card usage was 1773.26 Million and 6033.48 Billion.

Unified Payments Interface (UPI): is another important instant and real time initiative in retail electronic payment system introduced in 2016. This interface is regulated by RBI and facilitated by

Figure 5. Comparative Study of IMPS for the period 2015-16 and 2018-10 Source RBI Bulletin Payment System Indicators

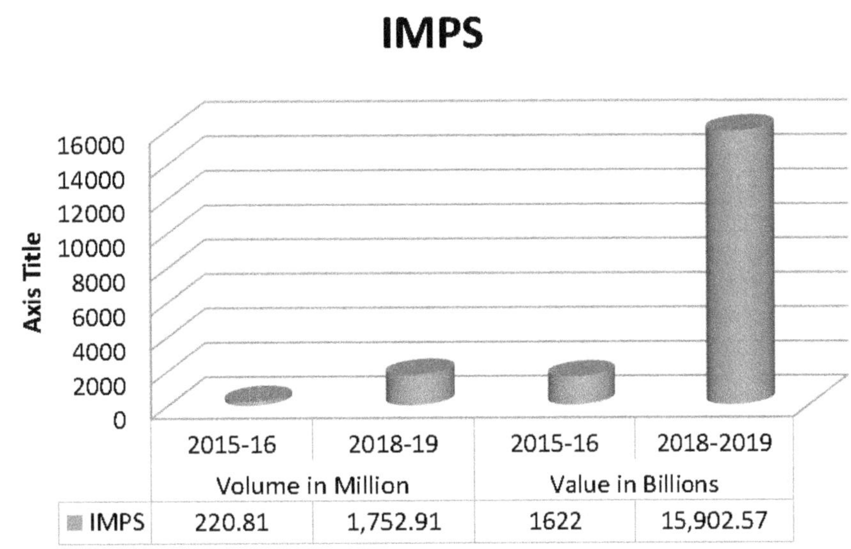

NPCI which connects multiple bank accounts than NEFT and customers can instantly transfer the funds through mobile device with virtual address of the customers. UPI has made processing simple to the extent of text message via mobile application without the requirement of bank account. Figure shows that UPI volume Rs. 5165.11 and Rs. 7970.69 Billion value during the financial year 2018-19 and increasing trends continues in FY 2019- 20 (April – June 2019) reflects volume 2223.16 Million and value 4215.83 billion. UPI transactions have exceeded all other modes of digital payment system and have become a

Figure 6. Comparative Study of Mobile Banking Volumes & Values for the period 2015-16 and 2018-10 Source RBI Bulletin Payment System Indicators

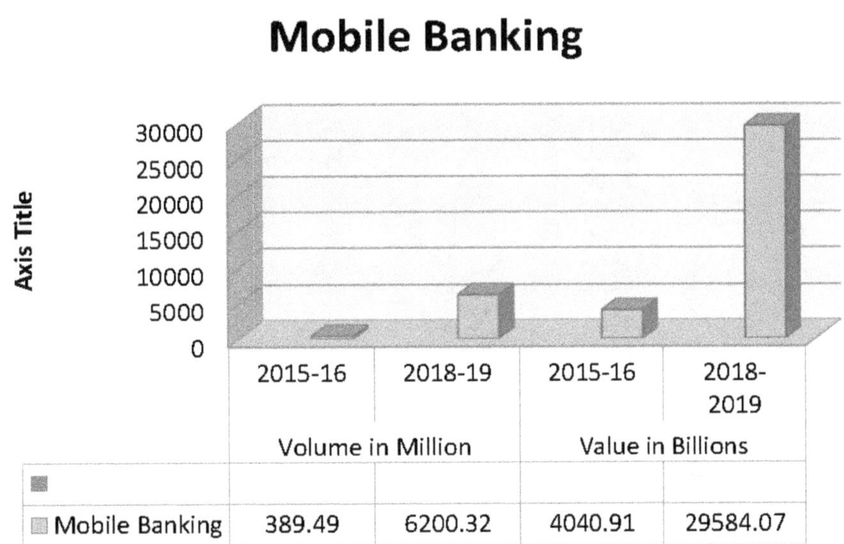

Figure 7. Comparative Study of Mobile Banking Volumes & Values for the period 2015-16 and 2018-10 Source RBI Bulletin Payment System Indicators.

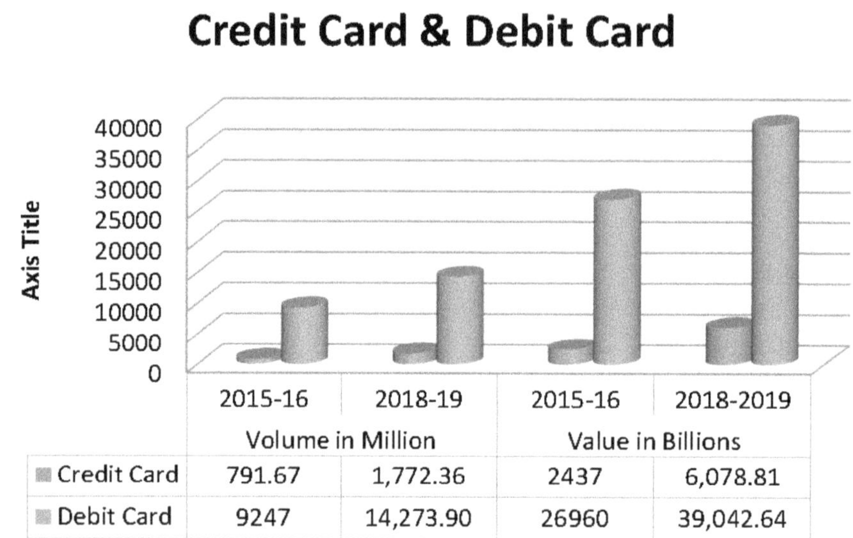

	2015-16	2018-19	2015-16	2018-2019
	Volume in Million		Value in Billions	
Credit Card	791.67	1,772.36	2437	6,078.81
Debit Card	9247	14,273.90	26960	39,042.64

role model of other countries. NPCI has provided UPI open architecture to more than 30 Non-Banking Players by closely working with Payments Council of India and Internet Mobile Association of India to provide solutions to Start Ups and Fintech Companies.

Bharat Interface for Money (BHIM) is funds transfer application on Unified Payment Interface (UPI) for quick transactions of payments in a simple and easy way. This application can be downloaded in play store in smart mobile devices with android version 5.0 and above. Customers can send and receive

Figure 8. Comparative Study of UPI, BHIM & USSD for the period 2015-16 and 2018-10 Source RBI Bulletin Payment System Indicators

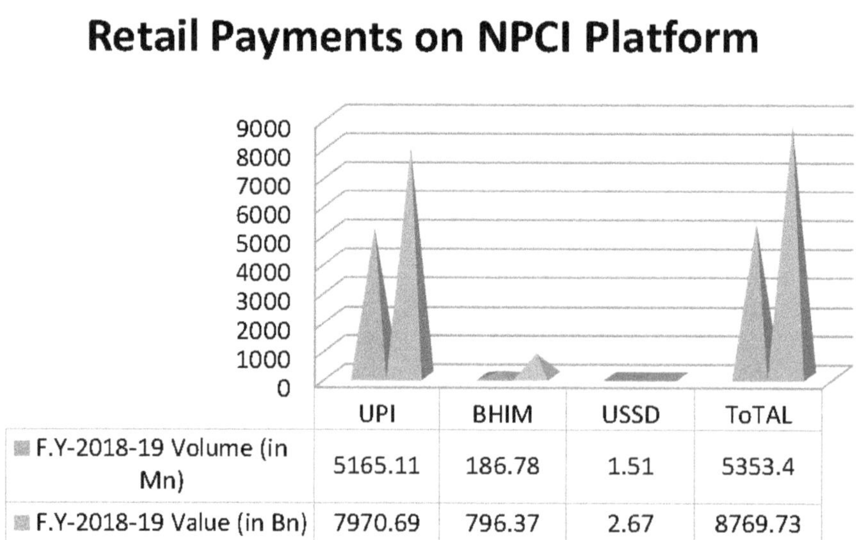

	UPI	BHIM	USSD	ToTAL
F.Y-2018-19 Volume (in Mn)	5165.11	186.78	1.51	5353.4
F.Y-2018-19 Value (in Bn)	7970.69	796.37	2.67	8769.73

money through BHIM Application by using Virtual Payment Address i.e. UPI ID and Mobile number. Figure shows that BHIM volume Rs. 186.78 Million and Rs. 796.37 Billion value during the financial year 2018-19 and increasing trends continues in FY 2019- 20 (April – June 2019) reflects volume 46.41 Million and value 194.13 Billion. **(KPMG, Reports 2018)**

USSD: *99# is Unstructured Supplementary Service Data launched by NPCI to offer common banking services through mobile devices initially by two telecom providers MTNL and BSNL. Banking Customers can dial *99# on their mobile devices and do various transactions like funds transfer, balance enquiry, changing UPI pin etc. All GSM service providers and 41 banks in India are offering USSD service. Figure8 reflects during the period 2018-19 USSD volumes have touched 1.51 Million and value of transactions 2.67 Billion.

ATMS and Point of Sales (POS) numbers are also increasing which another important factor is resulting in significant growth in acceptance infrastructure. Figure 9 shows 4.54% increase in ATM and 168% increase in point of sales during the four-year period from 2015-16 to 2018-19.

Figure 9.

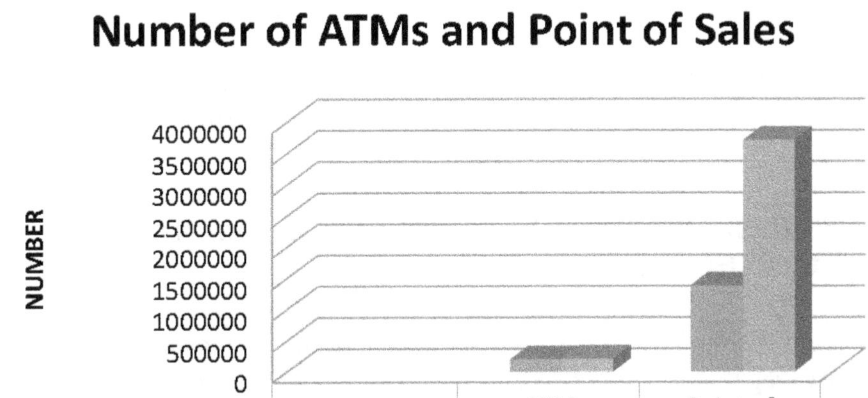

	ATM	Point of Sales
In Actuals 2015-16	212061	1385668
In Actuals 2018-19	221703	3722229

Aadhaar Based Retail Payment Systems consists of Aadhar Enabled Payment System (Inter Bank) Txn over Micro ATM (e.g. Cash withdrawal/ Cash Deposit) and APBS Credit (Disbursement based on UIDAI no.). These two initiatives were taken by NPCI to boost up Financial Inclusion. It's a very simple and easy to operate bank led model where the customers IIN (Bank identifier number), Finger print and Aadhar Number can do transactions at Micro ATM through the business correspondents. APBS enables to disburse Direct Benefit Transfers directly to customer's bank account after receiving the Aadhar numbers. Figure10 reflects increasing volumes and values both in AEPS and APBS credit.

An assessment of the achievements during the last four years covered by Vision 2018 reveals that the goals of (at market prices-current price) increased to 7.85 in 2017 from 7.14 in 2016, 7.85 in 2017

Figure 10.

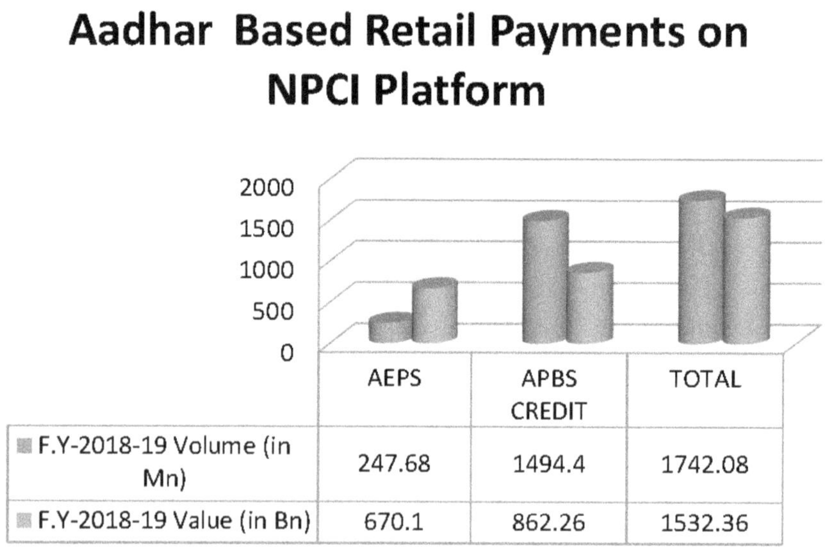

and further to 8.42 in 2018. RBI has an objective to increase digital payment transactions turnover as a percentage of GDP to 14.80 in 2021 from about 10.37 percent in 2019.

SECTION 2: REVIEW OF INITIATIVES AND ACHIEVEMENT OF PAYMENT SYSTEM VISION 2019 -21

RBI payment System Vision 2019- 21 was based on the four important strategic pillars of robust infrastructure, responsive regulation, customer centricity and effective supervision.

The Core theme of the Payment System Vision 2019-2021 is "Empowering Exceptional (E) payment Experience aims to empower every Indian Citizen with access to a bouquet of e-payment options that is safe, quick, secure, convenient and affordable. It recognizes the needs with continued focus on cyber security, innovation, financial inclusion, competition and customer protection. The vision statement has been formulated, based on the various suggestions and inputs from the various stakeholders of payment systems. RBI stated to continuously strive to achieve for a 'Cash Lite' and 'Highly Digital' society and intend to enhance the strong foundation of Indian Payment System built over the last two decades. Less Card India is another new ambition to ensured increased efficiency and uninterrupted payment systems to all the segments of Indian populations who are financially excluded and remain untouched by payment systems.

Two pronged approaches of Vision 2021 are:

(a) Exceptional Customer Experience;
(b) Enabling an Eco-system

With this in view, the Vision aims towards,

1. Enhancing the experience of Customers;
2. Empowering payment System Operators and Service Providers;
3. Enabling the Eco-system and Infrastructure;
4. Putting in place a Forward-looking Regulation;
5. Supported by a Risk-focussed Supervision.

Vision 2021 envisages the following 4 (four) Goal Posts (4C`s) Competition, Cost, Convenience and Confidence to achieve the above two approaches with 36 (Thirty-Six) action points as discussed below are:

1. **Competition:** On 29th March, 2019 RBI issued list of certificates of Authorisation issued to 80 entities under the payment system act, 2007 for setting up and operating payment systems in India. Financial market infrastructure by The Clearing Corporation of India, retail payment organisation by NPCI and various other entities for card payment networks, cross border money transfers, ATM network, prepaid instruments and instant money transfer.
   Summary of Action Points for Goals Post 1 - Competition
   1 Self-Regulatory Organisation for all PSOs
   2 Collaborative Competition - Encourage and facilitate innovation
   3 Feature phone- based payment services
   4 Off-line payment solutions
   5 USSD-based payment services
   6 Global Outreach of Payment Systems
   7 Fostering innovation through regulatory sandbox in a responsible environment
   8 Review of membership to centralised payment systems
   9 Inter-regulatory and intra-regulatory coordination
   10 Benchmarking India's Payment Systems
2. **Cost:** Migration of customers to digital mode from the cash mode of payment which carries cost in the whole economic system and with the presence of multiple players in the market is expected to achieve optimal Cost for the customers. With introduction of new digital financial products in the market will enable more options to the customers and give a delightful customer experience. Point of Sale Operators need to reduce the per transaction costs on the basis of marginal cost of pricing due to increase in number of transactions and value.
   Summary of Action Points for Goal Post 2 - Cost
   1 Accessible, Affordable and Inclusive Services
   2 Review of corridors and charges for inbound cross border remittances
   3 Capability Building and Inter-operability for transactions processing transactions of one system in another system
   4 Acceptance infrastructure to address supply side issues
   5 System Capacity and Scalability
   6 For High Value Cross Border Payments Increasing LEI usage
   7 Regulation of payment gateway service providers and aggregators

In order to ensure better risk management and to improve the accuracy and quality of financial data system, Legal Entity Identifier Code (LEI) is used as a key measure. Risk based Supervision post Global

Financial Crisis became important therefore 20-digit LEI unique code is used to identify parties in the global financial transactions.

3. **Convenience:** Freer access with availability of multiple payment system options anytime-anywhere should cater to the requirement of Convenience;
   Summary of Action Points for Goal Post 3 - Convenience
   1 Harmonizing TAT for resolution of customer complaints
   2 Setting up 24 x 7 helpline
   3 Enhancing awareness
   4 Conducting Customer awareness surveys
   5 Internal Ombudsman for digital payments
   6 National Settlement services for card schemes
   7 Enhanced Availability of retail payment systems and wide bouquets of offerings
   8 Widen scope / use of domestic cards
   9 New technology adoption like Distributed ledger Technology Platform for promotion of digital payment funds transfer services
   10 E-mandates / Standing Instructions for payment transactions
4. **Confidence:** The 'no-compromise' approach towards safety of payment systems should address security vulnerabilities to retain customer Confidence.
   Summary of Action Points for Goal Post 4 - Confidence
   1 Increased coverage of cheque truncations system
   2 Increased scope and coverage of Trade Receivables Discounting Systems (TreDS)
   3 Geo Tagging of payment systems touch point
   4 Contactless payments and tokenization
   5 Enhanced security of mobile based payments
   6 Oversight for maintaining integrity of payment systems
   7 Risk Management System wide security for Third party Transactions
   8 Framework for collection of data on frauds in payment systems
   9 Framework for testing resilience of payment systems
5. **Specific Outcomes:** The Following are the 12 (twelve) expected outcomes to achieve the four goals post with above 36 Specific Action Plan with the involvement and joint efforts of all stakeholders of payment system._

1. Decrease in Cheque / Paper based payments: As per the RBI, Bulletin May, 2019, the paper clearing volume stands at Rs.1123.76 Million consist of Cheque Truncation System and Non MICR Clearing in the financial year 2018-19. Numbers of paper instruments like cheque, demand draft, pay orders etc. processed in clearing centres are further decreasing as a total percentage of retail payments. It is expected that due to focus on shift from paper instruments to digital banking transactions volume of paper based instruments will further decrease to 2.0% of the total retail electronics volumes.

2. Accelerate Growth in Individual Retail Electronic Payments: Increased availability, number of transactions and volume of retail electronic payment systems are shown the growth trends. As per NPCI Statistics on Retail Payments April 2019, IMPS volumes have increased from 506.84 Million in 2016-17 to 1009.84 Million in 2017-18 and UPI volumes have increased from 17.86 Million to 915.23 Million in 2017-18. As per RBI Bulletin May 2019, a NEFT volume stands at 2318.89 Million in financial year

2018-19. It is expected that increase of 40% in NEFT Volumes and more than 100% growth expected in UPI / IMPS volumes. Total Digital transaction as on December 2018 stood at 2069 crore and likely to increase to 8707 crores in December 2019.

3. Increase in Digital Payment Turnover: Digital Payment Transaction is expected to increase vis-a-vis Gross Domestic Product in three important phases: 2019- 10.37, 2020 – 12.29 and in 2021 -14.80 times at market price - current price. Payment Transaction turnover in paper in CCIL Transactions likely to increase 22.30 times GDP by 2021.

4. Increase in Use of Digital Modes of Transactions: As per RBI Payment System Indicators, the total volume of Debit cards transactions at point of sales for purchases of goods and services in the financial year 2017-18 was 4414.28 Million and PPI Cards figures stood at 465 .00 Million. It is expected further increase of 35% at point of sales through debit cards transactions during the Vision period 2021.

5. Usage of Debit Cards at PoS Transactions in the Financial year 2018-19, total usage of debit cards volume of transactions inclusive of usage at ATMs and POS was 14273.90 Million out of which POS 4414.28 Million. Total value was 39042.54 Billion out of which POS was only 5934.75 Billion .it is expected to increase the usage of debit cards 44% of total debit cards transactions consisting of both ATM and Point of sales during the vision period. In value terms it is 15.2 per cent in 2018-19 (5.2 per cent in 2014-15) which is expected to be 22% by end 2021.

6. Increased Deployment of Card Acceptance Infrastructure: As on 31st March, 2019, Actual Point of Sales is 37.22,229 which are expected to increase up to active 5 million by end of 2021. To achieve the vision of cashlite economy and shift the focus of customers from cash on delivery transactions to digital payment card acceptance infrastructure, it is expected to increase substantially: "

b. Contactless processing of card payments
c. Up scaled the total card acceptance to 6 times of the present level

7. Enhanced Availability of POS Infrastructure: In order to achieve in reduction in demand for cash as well as cash in circulation the increase in number of POS Infrastructure is expected. Though no specific target is fixed during the Vision period but enhanced availability of POS is expected.

8. Facilitation of Mobile Based Payment Transactions: is expected to increase by 50% considering the base effect on the basis of registered customers.

9. Reduction in Pricing of Digital Banking Transactions is expected to show reduction of minimum 100 bps from current levels. Enhanced usage of electronic payment systems and shift from ad value rates to per transaction is expected to reduce the marginal cost given the additional volume. Since the usage of an electronic payment system is irrespective of the value of a transaction, it will ensure reduction in cost prices.

10. Security of Systems and Customer Centricity: (a) Decrease in Technical Declines reported across various payment systems by 10% year-on-year. (b) Reduction in Business Declines reported across various payment systems by 5% year-on-year. This will be achieved through Improvement in Turnaround Time (TAT) for resolution of customer complaints by PSOs.

11. Reduce Fraud to Sales Value: FTS [Fraud to Sales (Fraud value / Sales value) x 10000] count for payment systems is expected to be less than 10 bps for most of the payment systems.

12. Enhanced healthy competition: in the payments space and establishment of new PSOs during the Vision period is envisaged.

5. Specific Initiatives Reserve Bank of India, National Payment Corporation of India (NPCI) and Payment System Operators (PSO`s) together will take initiatives to increase the electronic payments transactions both in volume and value during the vision period 2021. These initiatives are broadly categorized under the following five heads:

5.1 Customers: plays an important role in the payment system and in order to increase the acceptance and usage of electronic payment systems the following action are specified in the visions statement 2019-21.

Simple Process
Wide Spread Access
Minimal Intervention of RBI in pricing
Transparency in Pricing
Harmonizing the TAT of customer Complaints
Optimal Timelines to resolve customer complaints
Technology Driven dispute redressal mechanisms
General Centralised 24 x 7 helpline
Customer Orientation Programmes
Conduct Customer Surveys on awareness and usage of payment systems
Formalize internal ombudsman scheme in the PSO`s
Source - RBI Payment & Settlement System Vision 2019- 2021

5.2 System Operators and Service Providers: On 29th March 2019, Reserve Bank of India has authorized and released the list of 82 payment System Operators and service providers for setting up and operating payments system in India. Self-Regulatory Organizations (SRO) is a non-government voluntary body generally appointed by the industry to conduct or monitor the functioning of the players in the financial market to bring degree of standardization in implementing the best practices in the industry. Vision 2021 states that such SRO`s can be appointed to monitor the complete process of digital PSO`s. SRO`s can create a both way communication between the payment systems players and supervisor / regulator. Other initiatives will be taken by RBI, NPCI, PSO`s and Card Network Associations during the vision period are listed as below:

Self Regulatory Governance Framework
Best Practices for security, customer protection and pricing
SRO to cover digital PSO`s
Encourage more players to participate
Promote Pan India payment platform
Facilitate Innovation through Collaborative Competition
To encourage competition in existing payment systems
Innovation in mobile payment services for feature phones
Resolve connectivity issues for mobile internet
Off line mobile payments through mobile devices
Scale up security of USSD Based payment services
Different settlement account for settlement of card transactions
Feasibility of having single national settlement account
Source - RBI Payment & Settlement System Vision 2019- 2021

5.3 Eco-system and Infrastructure: Ease of Use and Convenience are the two important reasons which impact customer`s choice to select one retail payment system platform for another. Various steps will be taken by RBI, NPCI and PSO`s to improve the acceptance infrastructure during the vision period are listed as below:

Need for extending availability of NEFT 24 X 7
Uninterrupted and round the clock availability of payment systems
Faster Settlements and Staggered Payments features in NEFT
To examine the extend timings of RTGS for customer transactions
Enhancing Global outreach of India`s Digital Payment
Expression of Interest received from many countries for partnering in implementation of CTS, NEFT, UPI and messaging solutions
RBI to engage in discussion in international standard setting bodies
Efforts to increase scope and coverage of RuPay Cards
need to increase penetration of card acceptance infrastructure like POS Terminal, mobile POS, and asset light terminals
Enhance security and efficiency of present CTS Scheme
To provide more traction to MSME financing through Trade Receivable Discounting systems
RBI to examine a framework to capture geographical location of touch points of payment system like Commercial Bank branches, ATM`S, POS Terminals and Business Correspondents pan India.
Source - RBI Payment & Settlement System Vision 2019- 2021

5.4 Regulation: To set up the regulatory frame work and to responds with increasing digital and Fintech scenario in Indian Banking Payment System, in June 2016 RBI set up an Working Group to study the regulatory implications. One of the important recommendations of the Group was to introduce regulatory sandbox frame work to manage risks, increasing efficiency and create new opportunities for customers. Regulatory Sandbox refers to testing of new fintech and digital products or services introduce in the financial markets. It permits all the stakeholders – The Innovators, Regulators, financial service providers and the final users – customers to measure and test the risks and benefits of new financial innovations. Vision 2021 focus on the regulatory sandbox frame work and various other steps to control regulations on electronic payment systems as mentioned below:

Regulatory Sand box approach to be designed for payment systems to avoid any Systemic Risk
Controlled Environment and certain regulatory exemptions
Allow experimentation of new payment products
Robust and Resilient Payment System
Criteria of payment systems – Explicit exit
To explore transparent point of arrivals metrics
RBI to explore broad based framework of other payment experiences
RBI authorized players to offer mobile payment solutions through secure tokenization standards
Explore the option of using LEI to identify the payment system providers in cross border transactions
Adaptation of Distributed ledger technology for financial services
To explore transparent point of arrivals metrics
To explore transparent point of arrivals metrics

RBI To consider implementation of e mandates and standing instructions for retail payment systems
RBI to issue specific security aspects on mobile technology and payment gateway
Source - RBI Payment & Settlement System Vision 2019- 2021

5.5 Risk-Focused Supervision: On 17th January, 2019 The Basel Committee on banking Supervision (BCBS) advises Supervisors, Regulators and banks across the Globe to establish robust liquidity risk management framework in their country. BCBS also reviewed the liquidity risk management developments in the financial markets since 2008. Vision 2021 statement also focused various initiatives to be taken during the vision period to further strengthen the regulatory framework as listed below:

Undertake oversight of payment systems through onsite supervision and off site surveillance
Self Assessment by the PSO`s
IS Audit through CERT in empanelled auditors
Need for disclosed supervisory framework for all stakeholders of payment systems
Need for publishing oversight reports in public domain by RBI
Need for separate regulatory framework for out surmising arrangements by non bank payment service providers
Adaptation of Payment Card Industry Standards
Need to share fraud related data on payment systems
Fraud data to be used to influence regulatory decisions
Reducing incidence and level of frauds in the payment landscape
Need for drafting guidelines for resilience of alternate mode of payment systems
RBI to conduct a study for benchmarking India`s payment system with payment systems of major countries
Efforts to Improve Indian Payment System performance with international / cross country best practices
Source - RBI Payment & Settlement System Vision 2019- 2021

SECTION 3: IMPACT OF DIGITALIZATION ON BANKING AND FINTECH

Digitalization is of critical significance to storage, data processing, and transmission, since it "permits data of different sorts in all organizations to be conveyed with a similar productivity and likewise blended". Digitalization is the way toward changing over data into a digital in which the data is sorted out into bits. The trendy expression in India today is making a cashless financial system. The traditional banking industry is in this way confronting the effect of digital innovation. Digital banking is the transition to web based banking where banking services are delivered over the web. The favourable circumstances for banks and clients are giving increasingly helpful and quicker banking services. A digital bank speaks to a virtual procedure that incorporates web based banking and past. As a start to finish stage, digital banking must incorporate the front end that shoppers see, the back end that bankers see through their servers and administrator control boards and the middleware that associates these hubs. The explanation digital banking is something other than a portable or online stage is that it incorporates middleware arrangements. Middleware is programming that extensions working systems or databases with different applications. Eventually, a digital bank ought to encourage every useful degree of banking on all service delivery stages. As such, it ought to have no different capacities as an administrative centre, branch office, online service, bank cards, and ATM and retail location machines. Customer services and satisfaction level with usage of digital banking products are increasing due to the following benefits:

Major benefits of digital benefits are:

- Cost savings
- Business efficiency
- Improved competitiveness
- Increased accuracy
- Enhanced security
- Greater agility

It includes elevated levels of procedure automation and online services and may incorporate APIs empowering cross institutional service arrangement to convey banking items and give exchanges. Instances of digital banking services and organizations are:

- ***Stripe*** - online installment condition for private people
- ***Adyen*** - internet business for digital organizations including Facebook
- ***TagPay*** - software organization that built up a Digital Banking System

The meaning of technology in banking initially meant that computerization or the utilization of web, which has now advanced to new universes of FinTech, Internet of Things and to even less wandered universes of Artificial Intelligence and Machine Learning. Throughout the years, Indian banks and financial service providers have warily embraced technology to enlarge reach to the clients, furnish services to and operational proficiency with developing market and technological advances. FinTech isn't tied in with unbundling of financial services, nor is it restricted to computerization of procedures. FinTech is about digital innovations and technology-empowered plans of action that make value and efficiencies in the financial sector. FinTech is the real sight in the use of technology to offer new financial items and services to new market fragments in an economically practical way. From a plan of action viewpoint, the FinTech sector is effort by technology organizations that either endeavor to disintermediate, or co-operate with occupant Banks and Financial Institutions trust in on vital record and market landscape. In obvious sense, the troublesome intensity of FinTech can be acknowledged just when there is infusion of economic value in the system, and it can bring social and conduct changes. In the course of the most recent five years, the Indian FinTech market has scaled new statures, both as far as financing got and the expanding buyer reception of FinTech arrangements. Demonetization and GST have both been drivers for digital appropriation. FinTech involves characteristic movement for India. Henceforth, FinTech is dynamically turning into a chief focal point of fascination for all the key partners in India's Financial Services industry – Regulators, Traditional Banks, NBFCs, Payment Banks, Investors, Payment Service Providers, Broking and Wealth Management Companies, Insurance providers and unadulterated play FinTech players. Government of India and Reserve Bank of India, being Central bank of the country needs to play an important role to support Fintech startups during this digital disruption period. (Gupta, A, Xia, C .2018). The telecom upheaval, web banking and infiltration of mobile services have been effective in onboarding a minimum amount of Indians to either banking or network. In 2018, India positioned second all around on FinTech reception, with its level of FinTech clients at 57.9%. Despite

Figure 11.

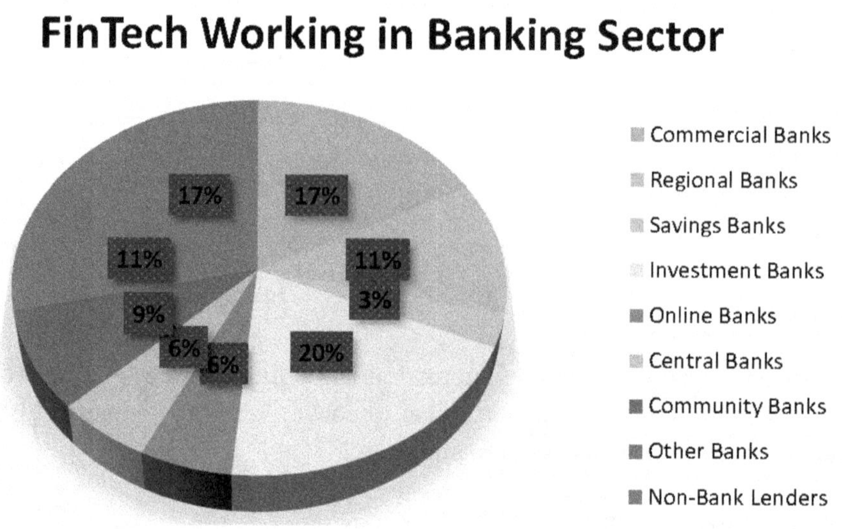

the fact that India's appropriation rate lingers behind China's 83.5%, it has outperformed that of created nations, which stands at 34.2%. (PwC Report, 2019)

FinTech or digital innovations have risen as a possibly transformative power in the financial markets. Fintech is yet young and India is advancing towards Tech-Finance coordinated effort. The unexpected upsurge of Fintech has changed the manner in which traditional banks used to work and thus banking sectors need progressively inventive answers for contend with the developing firms. This expects Banks to put resources into Fintech related services so as to profit themselves and give quality services to their clients when contrasted with traditional financial techniques. Starting at now just 64% of Fintech relationship in India is having a stable base. This will together assistance the Fintech new companies and the banking sector in improving the manner in which digital transaction based tasks are dealt with. As India is changing into a totally digital country throughout the years, even the banking business is attempting to redesign itself to the national just as worldwide standards to rival its adversary banks and additionally other nonbanking financial service providers. BFSI. Com, Economic Times dated 17th Feb, 2020 explains the eight factors that will drive Fintech in India in 2020 are:

1. Trust in Tech Firms
2. Demand for Banking
3. New Fintech Players
4. Blockchain increasing Security
5. NLP – Based Chatbots
6. Cloud Banking
7. Peer to Peer Lending
8. Insurance Technology

SECTION 4: IMPROVEMENT ON CUSTOMER SERVICES AND SATISFACTION

The digital upheaval is significantly changing the business environment and the financial services industry is no exemption. Albeit an essential presumption of technology improvement is the capacity to make things less difficult, from a key perspective, numerous financial establishments are confronting digitalization as a problem. Reserve Bank of India`s report that complaint to Banking Ombudsman have increased to 20% to over 1.96 Lakh in the financial year 2019 with debit cards complaints increased to 19%. (RBI Reports, 2019). The report further explains that the disposal rate of all such complaints were 94.03% in the financial year 2018-19. The major reason for concern is that the complaints on the ground of ATM and Debit card has increased to 18.65 per cent whereas credit card related issues, levy of charges without notice have declined in 2018-19. In order to resolve the digital banking complaints, RBI has introduced Ombudsman Scheme for Digital Transactions on 31st Jan, 2019. The Retail banks in India need to focus on customer digital literacy through customer engagements, market orientation, emotions, satisfaction, customer loyalty and self brand connection. (Monferer D, Moliner A.M, Estrada M, 2019). The findings of their study explains the customer satisfaction is the main antecedent of customer engagement and three important factors which have positive and significant influence of bank`s service for the customer satisfaction. We recommend that Indian retail banking industry which interact with the customer directly for digital payments must ensure the customer engagement as important parameter for improving customer satisfaction. Along with web based platform, there is a need of relationship managers to be in consistent touch with the customer to support off line also.

The main advancements that have improved customer services and enhanced customer satisfaction in Banking Services are due to Fintech and Digital Banking as well as various initiatives taken by RBI and Government of India are listed as below:

4.1 Customer Service Initiatives

- Services are progressively utilized independent of time and spot. The development of opening times of virtual services is affecting additionally increasingly traditional services, as consumers anticipate service nonstop, or even "24//365".
- The customer can accomplish the fund to someone else's Credit Card in a similar city.
- One of the associated patterns is that consumers are at the same time globally brought together and privately divided. Global brands imply that numerous items and services are today in reality accessible around the world, and likewise work on a global scale.
- The customer can report the loss in the neighborhood (across the country) when the customer's Credit Card or passbook is missing or taken.
- The customer can accomplish the fund transfer between his own bank investment accounts of his own Credit Card record and his own capital record in the protections organization. In addition, the customer can ask about the present parity at real time.
- In banking services, the development of elderly generations may make clashes with the present service advancement patterns, for example, the drive for web based self-services and chopping down the over-the-counter services.
- The customer can exchange the outside exchange, drop arranges and ask about the data of the transaction of remote exchange as indicated by the exchange rate given by our bank on net.

- Online peer-to-peer (P2P) loaning is empowered by the two consumers ready to attempt to utilize services outside the extent of old and set up banks and financial organizations, just as, the assistance of online networks with various kinds of services. Excluding the intercession of financial establishments is definitely not an original thought, however digital systems expand it to more extensive customer groups.
- The customer can do the real-time transfer and get the criticism data about installment from our bank when the customer does shopping in the named web-site.

4.2 Initiatives Taken by Indian Government for Promoting Digital Banking

- **Embracing neo technologies-** In the aftermath of the economic and pandemic uncertainties, emerging technologies will play a vital role in speeding up transactions and decreasing costs for banks. The Indian banking industry has already recognized the role of technology in obtaining the access as well as scale.
- We have foreseen above, increased rates of adoption of micro-service architecture by dropping vertically integrated stacks, cloud computing, containerization, APIs, AI and block chain. These technologies are going to play crucial roles in digital transformation of Financial Institutions and Banks and re imagine digital delivery of services.
- **Channels of digitization-** As per the 2017 worldwide findex report by the World Bank, India is actually house to the world's second largest unbanked population at 190 million adults with no access to a bank account. With improved penetration of mobile and Internet, the main target would accelerate know-how enabled digital monetary inclusion.
- The small business emphasis would likewise be creating a gradual change of customer preference out of visiting bank branches for using digital channels. Banks are going to enable the clients of its to work together over a number of automatic as well as digital channels to present the perfect channel blend. Banks are going to consider essential things like demographics, access to online, final mile connectivity, customer banking behavior patterns etc. to allow highly effective adoption by the Indian banking customers.
- **Protection, privacy as well as customer trust-** Based on RBI, because the fiscal season 2017-18, India's banking sector saw a spike in cyber frauds and pegged the losses during $13.7 million. With increased use of digital economy and cashless, it is going to be important for the banks to implement protected frameworks & solutions. Several of the apparent cyber consequences include privacy breaches, identity thefts, data loss, money laundering, and financial frauds.
- Banks have to draw stringent measures to determine both external and internal program vulnerabilities. They need to be commercially strengthened by arduous KYC, strong customer authentication (SCA), financial grade APIs, firewalls, sensible networks, etc., for seamless and secure transactions. Strong banking strategies as well as cyber security initiatives help safeguard against malicious attacks.
- **Compliance as well as policy-** The concentration must be on enhanced digital payment infrastructure, particularly in outlying India, with an objective to make a monetary ecosystem for the underbanked and unbanked population of the nation of ours.
- Originating from a security as well as privacy standpoint, India is currently on the road of its to expose the Personal Data Protection bill (PDP) on the lines of GDPR in the EU. This bill protects private info of customers including sensitive financial info. It will be in the very best interest to carry out strict penalties on erring entities seen in violation of the bill.

- India's banking revolution could be further catalyzed by the launch of the open banking directive on the lines of the EU and also the UK.
- The COVID 19 effect on the global as well as Indian monetary methods is going to be extraordinary and multi fold. It's crucial that you take the very long view and then prioritize accordingly. For Indian banks especially, resilience, driven by digital agility, is actually a means to attain good results as well as relevance on the additional side of COVID 19.

4. 3 Actions Taken by RBI and NPCI to Enhance Digital Payments

As stated by the Governor and also the RBI press release, the customer can use different digital payment channels for transacting in place of physical money. Digital payments channels including NEFT, UPI, IMPS, etc. with additional improvement in digital transactions to make it more safe as well as seamless in the past season.

Having NEFT Payments Free and Accessible 24/7

In 2019, RBI an RBI announced the removal of costs for payments by RTGS and NEFT and asked banks to pass on the advantages to customers. This attract the customers to use more payment transactions through RTGS as well as NEFT as fees have been considerably reduced or zero. This came in to effect from January 2020. Apart from this, the Reserve Bank likewise produced the accessibility of the NEFT process on a 24x7 schedule.

A Digital Payments Regulator

In February 2020, throughout the Monetary Policy committee meet, RBI has suggested to get a self-regulatory organization (SRO) by April 2020 to enhance security, customer shelter as well as pricing in India's digital payment feature. As per the RBI document, "With substantial development in digital payments as well as maturity acquired by entities of the payment ecosystem, it's appealing to possess a Self-Regulatory Organization (SRO) for orderly operations of the entities in the payment phone. The Reserve Bank is going to put in place a framework for setting up an SRO for the digital payment process by April 2020 with a view to fostering best practices on security, customer shelter & pricing, among others. The SRO is going to serve as a two-way communication channel between the regulator/supervisor." as well as the players

Bharat Bill Payment System to Cover Repeated Bill Payments

RBI expanded the scope of Bharat Bill Payment System (BBPS) to go over all repeated bill payments, which will include things like school costs, municipal taxes and insurance premiums. BBPS is actually an integrated bill payment process that provides interoperable bill payment service to clients online or even in by way of a network of agents on the ground. The device is going to provide several payment modes as well as immediate confirmation of payment.

All the above initiatives taken by the various stakeholders in Indian banking and payment system to improve customer services and satisfaction are focused to increase the trust, convenience, easy to use and accessibility of digital payment systems. (Sikdar P, Makkad M, 2015)

CONCLUSION

Indian digital banking payment system is a success story of transformation from paper based payment systems to electronic banking systems. The last decade has witnessed the revolutionary paradigm shift from cash and cheque system as a preferred mode of settling financial transactions to digital transactions. Various banking reforms like Demonetization, GST, Internet and Mobile banking and Fintech startups collaboration with traditional banks has resulted in the increasing adoption and usage. Above discussions in the four sections, presents the results of various initiatives taken by RBI, Government of India, NPCI and Banks to shift to new innovative products to meet customer`s requirements. To increase the customer satisfaction from the usage of digital banking products, the number of complaints need to be reduced for which RBI has recently taken few steps like Digital Banking Ombudsman. We recommend the two important factors need to be focused are, one customer`s digital financial literacy levels need to be increase through awareness and second the trust of customers need to be strengthened through reduction in cybercrimes and phishing attacks by ensuring safe and secure information technology structure. Many banks have adopted two factor authentication, OTP on mobile, secured passwords or Mpin when the customers access their digital accounts through various applications but still lot more to do to educate customers. The positive signs of higher acceptance of digital and Fintech products by Indian banking customers has paved the way for new digital banking innovative products and its likely to further grow in the future.

REFERENCES

Franciska A Martina, S. S. (2017, October). An *Overview of Digital Payments. International Journal of Research*, *4*(13), 2101–2111.

Kumar & Anupama. (2018). A Study of Digital Payments: Trends, Challenges and Implementation in Indian Banking System. *International Journal of Virtual Communities and Social Networking, 10*(1), 46 – 63.

Vasan, M., & Senthil, B. (2018). *A* Study of Payment and Settlement System in Indian Banking Sector. *Research magma Journal, 1*(11), 1-8.

Rakesh, M., & Partha, R. (2017). *Indian Financial Sector, Structure, Trends, and Turn.* IMF Working Papers No 17/7. Stock No WPIEA2017007

Bhasin, N. K. (2019). Study of increasing digital banking and financial technology – trends, challenges and opportunities in Indian Banking System. *Bank Quest, 90*(4), 33-44.

RBI Reports. (2019). *Vision documents. Payment and Settlement Systems in India Vision 2019 -2021.* www.rbi.org.in. https://www.rbi.org.in/Scripts/PublicationVisionDocuments.aspx?Id=921

Reports, K. P. M. G. (2018). *Bharat Bill Pay System – KPMG in India Perspective.* KPMG.com/in. https://www.npci.org.in/sites/default/files/Bharat%20Bill%20Payment%20System%20-%20KPMG.pdf

Manoj, P.K. (2017). Digital Transformation in Indian Banking: A Study of Cheque Truncation System and other Technolgical Advances. *International Journal of Emerging Trends & Technology in Computer Sciences, 6*(6), 172-179.

Gupta, A., & Xia, C. (2018). A Paradigm Shift in Banking: Unfolding Asia's FinTech Adventures. In Banking and Finance Issues in Emerging Markets. Emerald Publishing Limited.

Manser Payne, E., Peltier, J. W., & Barger, V. A. (2018). Mobile banking and AI-enabled mobile banking: The differential effects of technological and non-technological factors on digital natives' perceptions and behavior. *Journal of Research in Interactive Marketing, 12*(3), 328–346. doi:10.1108/JRIM-07-2018-0087

Lavanya, V. (2019). Impact of Digital Banking on Indian Economy. *Int J Recent Sci Res., 10*(09), 34633–34635. doi:10.24327/ijrsr.2019.1009.3937

BFSI.com. (2020). Eight factors that will drive fintech in India this year. *Economic Times*. https://bfsi.economictimes.indiatimes.com/news/fintech/eight-factors-that-will-drive-fintech-in-india-this-year/74167318

Neelu & Kumar. (2019). Factor affecting consumer satisfaction in cashless payment systems in India with respect to Paytm and BHIM. *International Journal of Recent Technology and Engineering, 8*(3S2), 10-15.

Monferrer, D., Moliner, M. A., & Estrada, M. (2019). Increasing customer loyalty through customer engagement in the retail banking industry. *Spanish Journal of Marketing – ESIC, 23*(3), 461–484.

Pallab, S., & Munish, M. (2015). Online banking adoption – A factor validation and satisfaction causation study in the context of Indian Banking Customers. *International Journal of Bank Marketing, 33*(6), 760–785.

Chapter 13
Vocational Education Paradigm Transformation Through Information Technology:
An Innovation Case Study of China

Jingyuan Zhao
Department of Political Science and Department of Geography, University of Toronto, Toronto, Canada

ABSTRACT

The advancement in information technology has transformed the world. There has been a tremendous impact of information technology on contemporary vocational education. This chapter highlights the impact of information technology on vocational education paradigm in China. In general, education paradigm has gone through three stages: empirical imitation education, computer-aided education, and data-driven education. China's vocational education is experiencing a transformation of paradigm from teaching support to learning support. This work is focused on how to construct a learning support paradigm in China's vocational education system through information technology. The Open University of China creating an innovative approach to learning support paradigm is discussed and three key elements of strategy for constructing a learning support paradigm of vocational education through information technology are presented in the chapter.

1. INTRODUCTION

EDUCAUSE (2019) provides a source how information technology in education has impacted education paradigm transformation. For over a decade these yearly reports detail those technologies' impact on colleges and universities (Gibson et al., 2018). This report describes the trends expected to have a significant impact on the ways in which colleges and universities approach their core mission of teaching, learning, and creative inquiry. Institutions of higher education are actively developing new strategies to rethink how they fulfill their mission. Not only are students more diverse, but a specific aspect of that

DOI: 10.4018/978-1-7998-4891-2.ch013

Copyright © 2021, IGI Global. Copying or distributing in print or electronic forms without written permission of IGI Global is prohibited.

diversity is the "new majority learner," who is older, is more likely to be balancing work and family with college, and has vastly different needs from those of a traditional-aged student navigating a residential college experience. Institutions of higher education are rethinking how to meet the academic and social needs of all students seeking credentials or degrees. This shift to student-centred learning requires faculty and academic advisors alike to act as guides and facilitators (The Horizon Reports of the New Media Consortium NMC, 2019).

China's vocational education industry has made great progress since China's opening-up and reform policies of mid-1980s. Currently China's education industry scale is the largest in the world. According to statistics from the Ministry of Education of China (MOE), there are 11,718 vocational colleges and universities in China in 2018. The annual enrollment of students is 9.3 million and the total number of students at school is 26.9 million. Of these, there are 10,300 secondary vocational schools, whose annual enrollment of students is 5.6 million and the total number of students at school is 5.5 million. There are 1,418 higher vocational schools, whose annual enrollment of students is 3.7 million and the total number of students at school is 11.3 million (MOE, 2019).

China's vocational education has a trend of online and lifelong education. The scale of vocational education is close to that of higher education. Since 2012, in order to cope with the requirement of human resources and provide talent support for national strategy, the State Council, the Ministry of Education, and the Ministry of Human Resources and Social Security of China, as well as related governments have been issued a series of policy measures, continuously promoting vocational education system by integrating multiple modes including university-enterprise cooperation, Internet Plus, life-long education, etc. At present, China's vocational education system is gradually complete.

Information technology applications in teaching and learning include enhancement of its presentation, design of different processes and phenomena, activation, individualization and differentiation of learning, formation of conditions for organizing independent educational activity, communication facilitation, and creative approach development. Informatization allows to modernize aims, contents, methods, means and organizational forms of teaching and learning; to facilitate the development of students' individual abilities and their personal qualities; to promote forming their cognitive abilities and aspiration for self-perfection; to provide the integrity of studying the phenomena of reality, indissoluble intercommunication between natural and technical sciences, the humanities and art; permanent dynamic upgrade of the content, forms and methods of education (Lytvyn et al., 2020).

Online vocational education has prominent advantages and the market scale is gradually expanding based on the development of information technology. The advantages of online vocational education are reflected in three aspects. First, it can make full use of the fragmented time, not limited by the scene and site. Second, the capital input for online vocational education is relatively low, and economic factors are no longer a burden. Thirdly, online vocational education can be targeted to meet diversified demands. From 2012 to 2019, China's online vocational education market grew rapidly, from 18.12 billion yuan to 80.64 billion yuan, with a compound annual growth rate of 23.77%.

Educational informatization 2.0 is committed to the deep integrative innovation of information technology and education paradigm. Hardware and software products, represented by IWB (Inside-the-Waistband Holsters), an interactive intelligent tablet, are in line with the trend of educational paradigm reform and development. In the context of Chinese government's continuous support for vocational education, the investment in education informatization is further increased, and these measures further promotes the in-depth application of information technology products in vocational education.

At present the mainstream of teaching design in developed countries is student-centered. The paradigm of vocational education in China is also changing from teaching support paradigm to learning support paradigm. Therefore, it is a task for the industry and the education, as well as the government to construct the learning support paradigm of vocational education by using educational information technology.

Representative sample of 16 vocational schools from Beijing regions of China, 57 instructors and school administrators, 14 specialists of related government departments, administrative centers and associations of vocational education allow to study and analyze the state of vocational education paradigm transformation, as well as to discuss the influence of information technology on the paradigm of vocational education. Our argument is organized as follows. In Section 2, a learner centred approach in vocational education is defined as theoretical background of this study. Section 3 discusses the development and change of education paradigm development. Section 4 presents empirical evidence regarding the role of information technology in vocational education paradigm, especially promoting learning support paradigm. Finally, section 5 concludes and presents policy implications and directions for future research.

2. LEARNER-CENTERED APPROACH IN EDUCATION

As early as the beginning of the 20th century, the educational concept and instructional design in developed countries in Europe and America began to change from the traditional style, teacher-centered to student-centered, a new mode. A revolution takes place in education, one that deals with the philosophy of how one teaches, of the relationship between teacher and student, of the way in which a classroom is structured, and the nature of curriculum (Norman & Spohrer, 1996). Learner-centered education (LCE) is a pedagogical framework that positions learners at the heart of the instructional process, not as passive recipients of information as in a traditional teacher- or content-centered approach. When instruction is learner-centered, the focus shifts from instructors only delivering content and controlling the learning environment to actively engaging students in creating their own learning (Mahendra et al., 2005).

Kember (1997) reviewed the teaching methods of 13 universities and divided teaching into two orientations: (1) the teacher-centered/contents-oriented approach and (2) the student-centered/learning-oriented approach. Teacher-centered orientation refers to the inculcation of information and transmission of structured knowledge; Student-centered orientation is to assist students in understanding, conceptual change and mental development. After that, Kember & Kwan (1999) interviewed professors from the universities in Hong Kong and found similar results. Research shows that teacher-centered pedagogical approach, despite the disadvantages of students becoming passive learners, is still widely adopted in universities due to the advantages of teachers' ability to systematically transfer knowledge (Hativa, 2000). According to the literature, more than 90% of college classrooms adopt this teaching method (Thielens, 1987), the researcher reported that rote teaching was in fact the main method of instruction (O'Sullivan, 1999), even in research universities of the Ivy League (Hativa, 1997).

In 1998, UNESCO (United Nations Educational, Scientific, and Cultural Organization) formally stated at the World Conference on Higher Education in Paris that, in today's rapidly changing world, higher education clearly needs a new perspective and model of student-centred. At present, developed countries attach great importance to the research and practice of student-centered teaching mode (Mcalpine,2004), and put the concept of student-centered into the training programs of teachers. Most representative training projects include ISW (Assignment Skills Workshop) and CDI (Curriculum Design Institute) (Ren et al., 2016). The training programs of teachers mainly help trainees to place student learning at the core of education from the learners' point of view. Student-centered/learning-oriented approach is achieved through rebuilding education, by the development of individual teachers and the transformation of the school (Nieto, 2005).

The focus of education is on learning itself, not on making machines for exams. In order to inspire students' inquiry learning, conduct teaching innovation towards literacy-oriented education, cultivate students' autonomous action, social participation as well as communication and interaction, the school is required to form a learning organization to mutually cooperate as network (Halinen & Holappa, 2013), which is a resource pool and circulation system to promote the curriculum reform of learner-centered.

Schools are aimed at assisting students to carry out meaningful and effective learning. A learning-centered school is characterized by spontaneous and interactive learning system and network. While students need access and support in order to learn with information technology, as important are the types of usage, for example to replace or extend traditional methods of teaching (Gibson et al., 2018). Hinostrosa & Labbe (2011) point out that the school and teacher's perspective contributed significantly to the variation in learning opportunities from simple operations to creative uses of information technology. While it is therefore important to continue tracking the progress of countries on infrastructure, access and teacher training, a shift toward learner-centred usage is of critical importance for evaluating and comparing how students are being prepared for participating in the digital age.

3. DEVELOPMENT OF EDUCATION PARADIGM

3.1 Three Stages of Education Paradigm

The world is moving from the era of information technology to the era of data technology. Big Data, as a new technological force is rapidly integrating into all industries. With the continuous advancement of China's education informationization strategy, the informationization environment of school at all levels has been rapidly improved, and accordingly a paradigm shift from empirical imitation teaching and computer-aided teaching to data-driven teaching takes place. Teaching paradigm is a general explanation of the complex activity of teaching and a manifestation of the comprehensive characteristics of teaching in a certain period or stage. It includes not only teaching theories and research methods, but also teaching modes, learning strategies and teaching evaluation methods. The human society has gone through the agricultural age, the industrial age and the information age since its birth. The educational system, as a subsystem of the society, has gone through many significant changes. In general, since the agricultural era, teaching paradigm has gone through three stages: empirical imitation teaching paradigm, computer-aided teaching paradigm and data-driven teaching paradigm (Yang & Tian, 2018). In the process of education paradigm transformation, the scientific nature of education and the intelligence of technology are gradually enhanced as shown as Figure 1.

3.1.1 Empirical Imitation Education

Empirical imitation teaching paradigm is the oldest paradigm in the history of teaching, prevailing in the agricultural and industrial era. Its core is to regard teaching as the transfer of knowledge and experience. The teaching in this stage emphasizes imitation of experience and giving and receiving of knowledge. Under the teaching paradigm of empirical imitation, the teacher occupies an absolute dominant position

Figure 1.

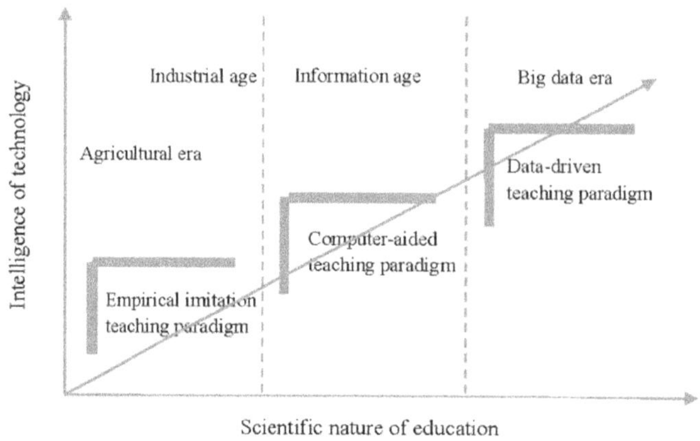

in the overall teaching structure, while the learner plays a role of passive receiver. The teaching content is mainly based on textbooks, existing experience and skills, while the teaching media is limited to traditional teaching tools such as paper and pen, books, blackboard and chalk. In the agricultural era, empirical imitation education was considered as an important way of knowledge transmission. With the advent of industrial society, in order to meet the practical needs of social production, empirical imitation teaching, which is good at the efficiency of knowledge transfer and acquisition, has been popularized rapidly in the school education. The talents trained by the school could be put into social production on a large scale, promoting the economic and social development and improving the social productivity in this period. But at the same time, empirical knowledge is overrated, and that has a profound impact on the view of knowledge and education. Under the influence of empirical imitation teaching, teaching often pays too much attention to learners' acquisition of explicit knowledge and neglects the practical activities and psychological activities necessary for learners to develop their perfect personality, resulting in trained talents' lack of basic ability of exploration and innovation.

Empirical imitation teaching paradigm is an important teaching paradigm in traditional teaching. It is also a necessary stage in the development of teaching paradigm. Although this paradigm has obvious drawbacks and has brought many problems to the innovative development of education, its contribution to human society is substantial. In the current information age, the empirical imitation teaching still exists, but its dominant position is gradually replaced by computer-aided teaching and data-driven teaching.

3.1.2 Computer-Aided Education

In the late 1940s and early 1950s, the third technological revolution led by information technology swept over the world. The emergence of multimedia, computer and network technology has changed human cognition and life style, and education has also begun to explore the way of reform under the support of technology. With the development of information technology and the change of educational concepts, the paradigm of computer-aided teaching is gradually formed. The original intention of this paradigm is to use the power of technology to solve the disadvantages of empirical imitation teaching, such as single content source, monotonous presentation mode and insufficient interest of learners, so as to improve the effectiveness of teaching and learning. The intervention of technology is the key characteristic of the computer-aided teaching paradigm. The application of various emerging technologies and media, such as the Internet, continually makes the generation and transmission of knowledge improved. The teaching content begins to surpass the traditional textbooks and teaching materials, extending to the broad Internet. The form of teaching content is gradually diversified. For example, audio and video, pictures, animation and other resources began to be widely used in teaching. The teaching media include computer, network, whiteboard, multimedia courseware more than blackboard, chalk, textbook.

Computer-aided teaching is an education paradigm transformation caused by technology. Under this paradigm, although the classroom teaching structure is still teacher-centered and knowledge-centered, learners begin to participate in the process of knowledge discovery and inquiry compared with the empirical imitation teaching paradigm. With the support of technology, the stage of the teaching mode is changed from lecture teaching to inquiry teaching and project teaching, during which the representative teaching models mainly include WebQuest teaching, just-in-time teaching (JiTT), inquiry learning and project learning, problem-based learning, resources-based learning, etc. Computer-aided teaching has played a positive role in cultivating learners' ability of knowledge inquiry and problem solving, and promoting the development of basic education innovation.

3.1.3Data-Driven Education

With the rapid development of data-intensive science, data has become an important indicator to drive the development of social innovation and comprehensive competition, as well as the main object of educational research and utilization. Meanwhile, new technologies represented by big data, cloud computing, ubiquitous network, virtual reality and artificial intelligence began to be applied in education. The learning space transcends the closed physical space and moves towards the borderless learning field based on the combination of virtual and actual reality. Learning is a continuous process through the home-school link, and online and offline integration, not only intermittent activities in classroom, home, library. In the meantime, more and more detailed behaviors of teaching and learning are truly recorded by online teaching platforms, mobile apps, wearable devices, etc. The continuous collection of teaching process and result data gradually forms teaching big data. Through deep mining and multiple analysis of teaching big data, the teaching meaning and value indicated in the data can be clearly presented, so as to assist teachers to teach more accurately and guide students more purposefully. With the generation and operation of data flow in all aspects of teaching, a teaching chain with a positive feedback mechanism begins to form, and the data-driven teaching paradigm has emerged.

Under the data driven teaching paradigm, as shown in Figure 2, through the learning analysis technology and education data mining, the teaching data generated in the environment of classroom and network can be interpreted into valuable information, such as identification of students with learning difficulties, discovery of knowledge defects, diagnosis of subject ability, achievement degree of teaching goal, etc., so as to provide a more accurate, more timely, more comprehensive support for teachers and learners to formulate strategies, promoting precision teaching and learning driven by data (Yang & Tian, 2018).

Data-driven teaching is expected to surpass computer-aided teaching and gradually become the mainstream teaching paradigm in the era of big data (Yang & Tian, 2018). In recent years, the application of big data technology in the field of education makes the data-driven teaching more scientific, precise, intelligent and personalized.

Figure 2.

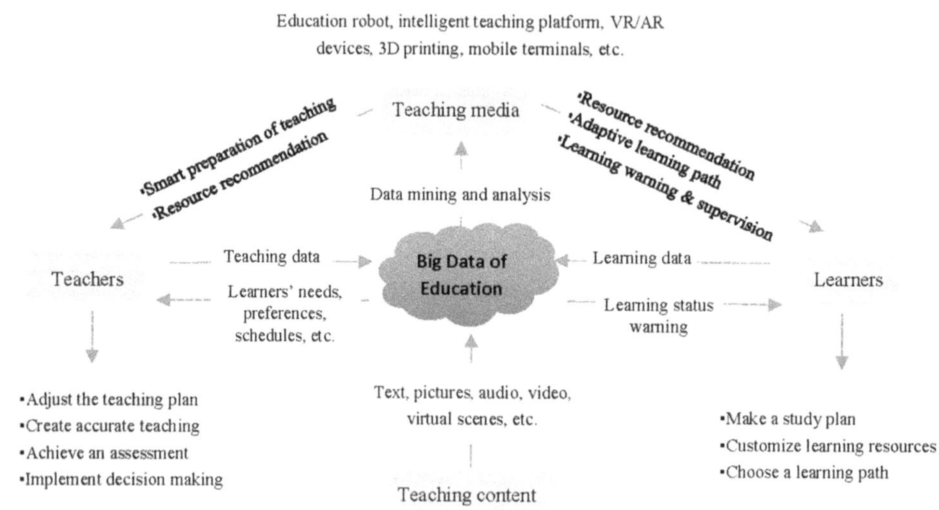

3.2 Education Paradigm Transformation: From Teaching Support to Learning Support

A paradigm is a generally accepted set of beliefs, theories, or world views. An established paradigm will directly provide practitioners with themes, tools, methods and premises. Paradigms are not static, but are constantly refined and expanded through application. A paradigm also needs further clarity and refinement in a new context. Through the choice of new practice, the new paradigm may replace the old paradigm and become the accepted paradigm of the discipline, which is called paradigm transformation (Yan & Zhang, 2008; Yang & Tian, 2018).

At the beginning of the 20th century, higher education was undergoing a paradigm transformation from teaching to learning. Whether it was the European Bologna Process or the American quality certification of higher education, student learning received unprecedented attention and the traditional view of teaching was challenged (Barr & Tagg, 1995). As was stated in Modernisation of Higher Education: "With this report, we put quality of teaching and learning centre stage" and "Our focus, therefore, is on the quality of teaching and learning for those who enter or who hope to enter higher education in the future" (Higher Level Group on the Modernization of Higher Education, 2013). Higher Level Group on the Modernization of Higher Education points out that the future higher education will be student-centered, and students' diverse needs must be taken into account. Clear goals and organizational structures should be established to drive and support the new paradigm, and the integration of information technology and teaching methods should be regarded as an important element in the transformation of learning paradigm (Higher Level Group on the Modernization of Higher Education, 2014). The development of information technology has made learning methods digital and learners self-directed and self-regulated so as to support learner-centered paradigm (Huh & Reigeluth, 2017). Nowadays, traditional lectures are considered insufficient to cover learners' needs (Higher Level Group on the Modernization of Higher Education, 2014) and the efficacy of more participatory and active methods has been pointed out (Ghislandi & Raffaghelli, 2014). The synergistic use of both traditional lectures and educational technologies supporting self-assessment, peer learning and peer evaluation alike, has been proved effective (Nulty, 2011; Bozzi et al., 2018).

With the aid of information technology, the education paradigm is shifting from teaching support paradigm to learning support paradigm. Information technology is not only an important driving force for the transformation of school to learning support paradigm, but also provides the support of method, means and culture for the transformation. Teaching support paradigm and learning support paradigm have completely different meanings in key elements, as shown in Table 1. Learning paradigm is an unprecedented paradigm revolution in the current world higher education field. It is not only the common result of the development of psychological science and educational science in the past hundred years, but also the urgent demand of higher education to cope with the rapid development of information technology and improve the quality of higher education.

Table 1. Key elements of teaching support paradigm and learning support paradigm

Key elements	Teaching support paradigm	Learning support paradigm
Application purpose	Helping the transmission of well-formed knowledge, improving teaching efficiency, and supporting individual learning (closed learning) and collective learning	Helping the construction of weakly structured knowledge, improving learning outcomes, promoting the cooperation and exchange of learning communities, providing channels for social participation, and supporting personalized learning (open learning) and cooperative learning
Application form	Lecture, tutoring, simulation, demonstration, practice	Tools related to research, communication, production, thinking, modeling
Student behavior	Passive practice, watch, and reflect	Hands-on operation, experience, application, cooperation, communication, participation
Teacher behavior	Focus of teaching content, design and development of courseware, correction and feedback	Focus of learning process, design and development of learning resources and learning environments, implementation of performance-based assessment
Technical evaluation	Verisimilitude, convenience and applicability	Intelligence, reusability, interoperability, standardization
Organizational architecture	Central processing architecture	Distributed architecture
Social influence	Aggravating the inequality between those who have devices and those who do not	Aggravating the inequality between those who have resources and those who do not

The transition to the paradigm of learning support is a new trend of vocational education reform in developed countries and an urgent demand for vocational education reform in China (Liu & Chang, 2018). Information technology provides support for the transformation of vocational education institutions to learning support paradigm from methods, technologies and cultures (Liu, 2012). With regard to methods, the integration of teaching methods and information technology to create interactive learning methods and learning environment (e.g., blended learning, online learning, flipped classroom, hybrid of online learning, real interaction and hands-on practice) is helpful to the interaction between teachers and students, making learning more active, interesting, enhancing the students' learning motivation, promoting deep learning. On the technological level, information technology breaks the boundary between traditional learning space and informal learning space, so that learners are not limited by time and space, and have convenient and fast access to all kinds of high-quality educational resources, so that learning has unprecedented flexibility. On the cultural level, the application of information technology can better meet students' personalized learning needs, endow learners with great learning freedom and choice, and enable learners to flexibly plan their learning process at anytime and anywhere, so as to achieve personalized growth and development to the maximum extent in a way suitable for themselves.

4. CONSTRUCTING LEARNING SUPPORT PARADIGM

4.1 Learning Support Paradigm Case: The Open University of China

The Open University of China is a representative of the learning support paradigm in China's vocational education field. The Open University of China provides students with a new learning system that is accessible to everyone, anytime and anywhere, and carries out lifelong education through Credit Bank System.

On July 31, 2012, the Open University of China was founded on the basis of China Central Radio and Television University. The Open University of China is committed to the realization of supported open learning, exploring a new learning paradigm that is learner-centered, based on the combination of online network of independent learning, distance learning support service and face-to-face tutoring. It aims to reform the teaching content and curriculum system, cooperate with industrial enterprises, and set up characteristic majors in the Open University of China in a scientific, flexible and targeted way. The university improves teaching methods, and provide learners with massive and high-quality online courses integrating multimedia resources, teaching interaction, learning evaluation and learning support services. Face-to-face tutoring is provided through learning centers all over the country, and real-time communication between teachers and students can also be promoted through high-definition and fast two-way video system, so as to provide distance learning support services for learners anytime and anywhere.

Online learning environment anytime, anywhere. The Open University of China's Learning Network provides learners with a one-stop learning service. Learning Network is an innovative talent training model of the Open University of China. It is a network learning platform featuring the six-network integration, including several subsystems such as network learning space, network teacher team, network core curriculum, network learning support, network teaching management and network learning evaluation. The interface design of the Learning Network reflects the concept of learners as the core, which is divided into three sections: student space, teacher space and curriculum recommendation. The Open University of China has established a one-stop and integrated Cloud Call remote reception center covering the whole country, which combines front-line seats, remote seats and expert seats, and can provide students with round-the-clock information inquiry, course selection guidance and other services.

Learning experience of walking in the clouds. As a new type of university, the Open University of China pays attention to providing educational services to disadvantaged areas and groups, and attaches importance to the needs of vocational education in ethnic minority areas. In order to solve these problems, the Open University of China has put forward the strategic planning of building cloud classrooms based on cloud computing technology, and put emphasis on the construction of cloud classrooms for China's central and western regions, giving priority to first-line learning centers in the central and western regions, so as to maximize the delivery of quality educational resources to students.

Massive digital learning resources. Five-minute course network has become a public platform for gathering and sharing high-quality micro and small course resources. In addition to micro courses such as the five-minute course, all kinds of resources including video open class, network core class, famous teacher classic class, domestic excellent class and foreign open class are available to meet different preferences of learners. Moreover, the Open University of China has set up 224 sub-centers of digital learning resources within its own educational system and in secondary and higher vocational colleges, realizing the sharing and co-construction of high-quality resources.

Lifelong learning files for learners. The Open University of China is committed to promoting lifelong learning for all people, building a Credit Bank System with the functions of credit certification, transfer and access, and setting up personal lifelong learning file for each learner. The so-called Credit Bank System is essentially a visual representation of the authentication, accumulation and conversion of different types of learning outcomes through referring to some functional characteristics of banks. Learners can apply for the corresponding certificates in accordance with the rule of credit accumulation. The university's Credit Bank System provides a basis for a mutual recognition and conversion of credits between all kinds of education training institutions, encourages social members to realize the communication between the academic education and non-academic education, and to accumulate credits through various forms of learning, promoting the formation of lifelong education system.

4.2 Information Technology Promotes Learning Support Paradigm

Information technology contributes to the transformation of vocational education paradigm towards learner-centred learning (Liu & Chang, 2018). In order to construct a learning support paradigm based on information technology in vocational education system, an empirical study was conducted. This study investigated 16 vocational education colleges in Beijing, and interviewed 25 experts from 57 instructors and administrators and 14 specialists of related government departments, administrative centers and associations of vocational education. Three strategies are summarized through empirical investigation. Three key elements of strategy of learning support paradigm are modularization, flexibility and globalization.

4.2.1 Modularization of The Curriculum Based on Learning Outcomes

With the development and popularization of the open education, vocational education more and more tends to personalized customization, that is, a flexible schooling system (Wang, 2017; Liu & Chang, 2018). In 2014, Task Force on the Future of MIT Education put forward 16 suggestions for schools, including suggestions to divide more courses into small module courses, explore modular teaching methods, and establish module course library and share module courses across departments to form more training schemes (Task Force on Future of MIT, 2014).

The foundation of modular courses is students' learning achievement. A course module is an independent learning unit based on certain learning achievement. Modular courses emphasize the construction of competency-based instruction, which can vary in size from a complete course, to a chapter of the course, a lecture, etc. Modules can be learned either sequentially or individually, and can be combined flexibly among modules. Modular courses can greatly promote the flexibility, mobility and malleability of learning. Because modules can be split and reorganized, students can freely choose what to study according to their interests, and future students can even customize degree courses through modules. Universities and colleges can also promote a portfolio of courses cross-curriculum, interdisciplinary, inter-college and even cross-university through modular courses to develop more minor degrees. The modular course can avoid the repetition and overlap of teaching content in the course mode through the effective reorganization of knowledge points of the course. Modularization also helps with the rapid development of online courses. It typically takes months to develop a complete online course, but it takes only a few weeks to develop a course module, greatly improving the timeliness of course development. In addition, the modularization of the curriculum is also conducive to the evaluation of learning outcomes to promote students' comprehensive mastery of learning content, to alleviate the shortage of existing teacher resources and realize the sharing of cross-school teacher resources, and to provide more learning practice opportunities for students with strong learning ability.

4.2.2 Flexibility of Learner-Centred Vocational Education

Barr & Tagg (1995) proposed that higher education paradigm is changing from teaching paradigm to learning paradigm, that is, from providing information to designing learning experience, from thinking input to focusing on output, and from decentralized activity design to integrated activity design. To redesign vocational education courses, the elements of high influence on learning are considered for designing curriculum and organizing class activities. For example, activities are designed to let students have more time and energy into the knowledge processing and application creation, so that more opportunities are available for teachers and classmates to communicate learned information. Also, the relevance between courses and other practical activities are provided, and assignments are designed to be more relevant, such as being related to life experiences, other courses or large practical communities, to create different experiences, and give students more frequent feedback to establish a community in which they have a sense of belonging helping each other. Obviously, in the process of constructing learning support paradigm in vocational education, technology plays an important role in the implementation of curriculum development.

The impact of MOOC (Massive Open Online Course) on vocational education is that new education institutions of network teaching supported by capital markets have emerged, such as Minerva Schools at KGI in USA. The infrastructure to support these new universities and colleges, which are democratizing and making affordable scarce education resources, is the Internet, digital resources and learning management systems.

In a word, the development of information technology has changed many aspects of vocational education, vocational education is towards to individualized adaptability, accordingly providing diversified choices, which not only increase the education opportunity, but also the way of education is varied, the education path is custom-made, and the time to obtain a degree is flexible.

4.2.3 Learning Ecosystem Through the Globalization of Vocational Education

As online education makes learning ubiquitous, traditional strict boundaries of campus and classroom timetable have been blurred. Universities and colleges have to shift their focus from the construction of a school to the construction of a global learning ecosystem, in which all resources, relationships and roles must be reshaped (Task Force on Future of MIT, 2014).

Information technology offers a huge opportunity of constructing a global learning ecosystem. First, educational functions can be broken up by using online technology. Second, satellite schools or flipped schools are founded around the world. Third, hybrid learning is promoted by collaboration. Deep interaction with the world enables students to have more international experiences, connect students with global research and innovation, and provide teachers with deeper insights into teaching and research, to better understand innovate teaching methods. Interaction with the global communities has various forms, such as global discussion. By setting up challenging courses and questions by schools, students are able to collaborate with global learners on projects that create global communities of thought and practice, and make problem solutions applicable to local realities (Liu & Chang, 2018).

5. CONCLUSIONS AND DISCUSSIONS

Vocational education in China is in a transitional period, and the traditional teaching support paradigm is being replaced by the learning support paradigm. In this process, how to build a learner-centred vocational education paradigm by using information technology is a key issue. Learning from the experience and theory of developed countries, investigating vocational education institutions as well as interviewing experts in Beijing, taking the Open University of China as a typical case to study its innovative initiatives, this study constructs an innovative paradigm of vocational education through information technology. The three key elements of strategy for constructing the learning support paradigm of vocational education are modularity, flexibility and globalization.

In a landscape of rapid technological advances and increasingly uncertain and complex work environments, lifelong learning will become part of vocational education if sustainable development is to be achieved. However, many systems and models of vocational education do not have clear mechanisms for lifelong learning, despite the fact that workers often undertake learning on their own, in non-formal and informal environments (Kanwar et al., 2019). UNESCO (2015) claims that for the transformation of vocational education, informal and non-formal learning must be encouraged, recognized and validated (Latchem, 2017, p. 8). At present, the development of vocational education is faced with rare opportunities and great challenges. Vocational schools should always take people's needs as the center, and run vocational education for everyone, anytime and anywhere, so that vocational education can truly become the backbone of the lifelong education system for all. Vocational education at anytime and anywhere means that vocational schools should break out of the shackle of full-time and fixed schooling, and focus on the needs of people for vocational knowledge and skills to provide vocational education that meets their timely needs. Moreover, in addition to academic education, vocational training for enterprises and society is also an important function of vocational education.

Under the background of lifelong learning, it is urgent to break through the limit of traditional vocational education mode, and gradually establish a management system of certification, evaluation, accumulation and mutual transformation for learning results obtained through various learning channels. Credit Bank System not only enables students to break through the limit of learning time, that is, the storage refers to cumulative credits of learning achievement, and also can break through traditional specialized limit, and combine learning results through different ways with related degree education, to implement mutual transformation of credits between the different types of education by means of expert assessment. It is an important strategic task of vocational education to establish a system of certification, evaluation and conversion, such as Credit Bank System, for different types of learning outcomes (Hao, 2012). Currently Credit Bank System is still lack of operational policies and measures for its implementation. Software and hardware platform of Credit Bank System should be actively constructed to solve the problem of mutual recognition of various learning credits, especially to explore the system in which non-academic continue education learning outcomes, relevant professional qualifications and skills are into course credits of vocational schools.

REFERENCES

Barr, R. B., & Tagg, J. (1995). From teaching to learning -A new paradigm for undergraduate education. *Change: The Magazine of Higher Learning*, *27*(6), 12–26. doi:10.1080/00091383.1995.10544672

Bozzi, M., Raffaghelli, J., & Zani, M. (2018). *Peer learning for large size Physics lectures in higher education: yes, we can. Proceedings of iCERi2018, 8739-8747*. IATED.

EDUCAUSE. (2019). *The Horizon Reports of the New Media Consortium NMC (2019)*. https://linhadeleitura.files.wordpress.com/2019/05/2019horizonreport.pdf

Ghislandi, P., & Raffaghelli, J. (2014). Quality teaching matters: Perspectives on quality teaching for the modernization of higher education. *Formazione & Insegnamento*, *12*(1), 57–86.

Gibson, D., Broadley, T., Downie, J., & Wallet, P. (2018). Evolving Learning Paradigms: Re-Setting Baselines and Collection Methods of Information and Communication Technology in Education Statistics. *Journal of Educational Technology & Society*, *21*(2), 62–73.

Halinen, I., & Holappa, A. (2013). Curricular balance based on dialogue, cooperation and trust-The case of Finland. In W. Kuiper & J. Berkvens (Eds.), *Balancing Curriculum Regulation and Freedom across Europe. CIDREE Yearbook 2013,39-62*. SLO.

Hao, K. (2012). Lifelong Learning and Management Models for the Credit Bank. *Open Education Research*, *18*(1), 12–15.

Hativa, N. (1997). *Teaching in a research university: Professors' conceptions, practices, and disciplinary differences* (An Unpublished report). Tel Aviv: Tel Aviv University.

Hativa, N. (2000). *Teaching for effective learning in higher education*. Kluwer Academic Publishers. doi:10.1007/978-94-010-0902-7

High Level Group on the Modernisation of Higher Education. (2014). *Report to the European Commission on New modes of learning and teaching in Higher Education*.

Higher Level Group on the Modernization of Higher Education. (2013). *Report to the European commission on improving the quality of teaching and learning in Europe's higher education institutions*. Publication Office of European Union.

Hinostrosa, J. H., & Labbe, C. (2011). *Policies and practices for the use of information and communications technologies (ICTs) in education in Latin America and the Caribbean*. https://unesdoc.unesco.org/images/0022/002232/223251e.pdf

Huh, Y., & Reigeluth, C. M. (2017). Self-Regulated Learning: The Continuous-Change Conceptual Framework and a Vision of New Paradigm, Technology System, and Pedagogical Support. *Journal of Educational Technology Systems*, *46*(2), 191–214. doi:10.1177/0047239517710769

Kanwar, A., Balasubramanian, K., & Carr, A. (2019). Changing the TVET paradigm: New models for lifelong learning. *International Journal of Training Research*, *17*(1), 54–68. doi:10.1080/14480220.2019.1629722

Kember, D. (1997). A reconceptualisation of the research into university academics' conception of teaching. *Learning and Instruction*, *7*(3), 255–275. doi:10.1016/S0959-4752(96)00028-X

Kember, D., & Kwan, K. P. (1999). Lectures' approaches to teaching and their relationship to conceptions of good teaching. In N. Hativa & P. Goodyear (Eds.), *Teacher thinking, beliefs and knowledge in higher education*. Kluwer Academic Publishers.

Kuhn, T. S. (1962). The Structure of Scientific Revolutions (2nd ed.). The University of Chicago Press.

Latchem, C. (2017). *Using ICTs and blended learning in transforming TVET*. UNESCO and Commonwealth of Learning.

Liu, H., & Chang, T. (2018). Modularity, Flexibility and Globalization: The Transformation of the University's learning paradigm based on information Technology - a case study based on MIT. *Open Education Research*, *24*(3), 19–26.

Liu, X. (2012). On student - centered. *Journal of Higher Education (Columbus, Ohio)*, *33*(8), 1–6.

Lytvyn, A., Lytvyn, V., Rudenko, L., Pelekh, Y., Didenko, O., Muszkieta, R., & Żukow, W. (2020). Informatization of technical vocational schools: Theoretical foundations and practical approaches. *Education and Information Technologies*, *25*(1), 583–609. doi:10.100710639-019-09966-4

Mahendra, N., Bayles, K. A., Tomoeda, C. K., & Kim, E. S. (2005). Diversity and Learner-Centered Education. *ASHA Leader*, *10*(16), 12–19. doi:10.1044/leader.FTR3.10162005.12

Mcalpine, L. (2004). Designing learning as well as teaching—A Research-based model for instruction that emphasizes learner practice. *Active Learning in Higher Education*, *5*(05), 119–134. doi:10.1177/1469787404043809

MOE. (2019). *Education Statistics 2019*. http://www.moe.gov.cn/s78/A03/moe_560/jytjsj_2019/qg/

Nieto, S. (2005). *Why we teach*. Teacher College Press.

Norman, D. A., & Spohrer, J. C. (1996). Learner-centered education. *Communications of the ACM*, *39*(4), 24–27. doi:10.1145/227210.227215

Nulty, D. (2011). Peer and self-assessment in the first year of university. *Assessment & Evaluation in Higher Education*, *36*(5), 493–507. doi:10.1080/02602930903540983

O'Sullivan, E. (1999). *Transformative learning: Educational vision for the 21st century*. Zed Books.

Ren, J., Zhao, W., Wang, Y., Xu, M., & Fu, S. (2016). Research and Practice of Student-centered Teaching Model - Introduction to Information Security teaching Reform of small Class. *Computer Education*, *09*, 106–110.

Task Force on Future of MIT. (2014). *Institute-wide Task Force on the Future of MIT Education Final Report*. http://web.mit.edu/future-report/TaskForceFinal_July28.pdf

Thielens, W., Jr. (1987). *The disciplines and undergraduate lecturing*. Paper presented at the annual meeting of the American Educational Research Association, Washington, DC.

UNESCO. (2015). *Revising the 2001 Revised Recommendation concerning Technical and Vocational Education* (Report of the UNESCO-UNEVOC special virtual conference 1–14 April 2014). https://unesdoc.unesco.org/images/0023/002341/234137e.pdf

Wang, Q. (2017, May). The development trend of global higher education from the perspective of informatization. *China Education Daily*. http://paper.jyb.cn/zgjyb

Yang, X., & Tian, X. (2018). *Big Data in China's Basic Education 2016-2017: Towards data-driven accurate teaching*. Science Press.

Compilation of References

Aalborg University. (2015). *Problem-based Learning. November 2015.* https://www.pbl.aau.dk/digitalAssets/269/269243_148025_pbl-aalborg-model_uk.pdf

Aalst, W. (2000). Loosely coupled interorganizational workflows: Modeling and analyzing workflows crossing organizational boundaries. *Journal of International Management*, *37*(2), 67–75.

Abdallah, S. (2020). Social Interactions in Electronic Networks of Practice: A Model for Effective Knowledge Construction, Problem Solving, and Learning. *International Journal of e-Collaboration (IJeC), 16*(2), 27-44. doi:10.4018/IJeC.2020040103

Academy, P. B. L. (2019). *The Problem-Based Learning Academy at Aalborg University*. http://www.pbl.aau.dk

Adkins, M., Younger, R., & Schwarz, R. (2003). Information technology augmentation of the skilled facilitator approach. In *Proceedings of the 36th Annual Hawaii International Conference on System Sciences*. Computer Society Press. 10.1109/HICSS.2003.1173776

Aeneis. (2014). *Aeneis Handbuch: intellior AG*. Retrieved from https://www.intellior.ag/wp-content/uploads/Handbuch_Aeneis_Anwender.pdf

Aiken, M., Wang, J., Gu, L., & Paolillo, J. (2011). An Exploratory Study of How Technology Supports Communication in Multilingual Groups. *International Journal of e-Collaboration*, *7*(1), 17–29. doi:10.4018/jec.2011010102

Airports Council International. (2019). *Annual World Airport traffic. Forecast 2019-2040*. https://aci.aero/

Ajzen, I. (1991). The theory of planned behavior. *Organizational Behavior and Human Decision Processes*, *50*(2), 179–211. doi:10.1016/0749-5978(91)90020-T

Ajzen, I., & Fishbein, M. (1980). *Understanding attitudes and predicting social behavior*. Prentice-Hall.

Albinsson, P. A., & Perera, B. Y. (2012). Alternative marketplaces in the 21st century: Building community through sharing events. *Journal of Consumer Behaviour*, *11*(4), 303–315. doi:10.1002/cb.1389

Albors, J., Ramos, J. C., & Hervas, J. L. (2008). New learning network paradigms: Communities of objectives, crowdsourcing, wikis and open source. *International Journal of Information Management*, *28*(3), 194–202. doi:10.1016/j.ijinfomgt.2007.09.006

Aleksander, I. (2017). Partners of humans: A realistic assessment of the role of robots in the foreseeable future. *Journal of Information Technology*, *32*(1), 1–9. doi:10.105741265-016-0032-4

Alshatnawi, E. A. R. (2014). Assessing communication skills among Jordanian tour guides: German tourists' perceptions. ***false***. *Journal of Management Research*, *6*(1), 1–11. doi:10.5296/jmr.v6i1.4361

Alter, C., & Hage, J. (1993). *Organizations working together*. Sage Publications, Inc.

American Distance Education Consortium (ADEC). (n.d.). *ADEC EdFuture 2014 Presentations*. Retrieved December 12, 2014 from http://www.adec.edu/conference/edfuture-2014/presentations

Anastasiadis, P. (2007). Advanced Learning Technologies of synchronous and asynchronous transmission serving ODL (in Greek). In A. Lionarakis, (Ed.), *Proceedings of 4th International Conference of Open and Distance Learning, Issue B*. Athens: Propompos.

Anderson, T. (2009). The dance of technology and pedagogy in self-paced distance education. *Proceedings of the 17th ICDE World Congress, Maastricht*. Retrieved November 8, 2013 from http://auspace.athabascau.ca:8080/dspace/bitstream/2149/2210/1/The%20Dance%20of%20technology%20and%20Pedagogy%20in%20Self%20Paced%20Instructions.docx

Anderson, T., & Dron, J. (2011). Three Generations of Distance Education Pedagogy. *International Review of Research in Open and Distance Learning*, *12*(3), 80-97.

Anderson, J., Rainie, L., & Luchsinger, A. (2018). *Artificial intelligence and the future of humans*. Pew Research Center.

Anderson, T., & Shattuck, J. (2012). Design-Based Research: A Decade of Progress in Education Research? *Educational Researcher*, *41*(1), 16–25. doi:10.3102/0013189X11428813

Anson, R., Bostrom, R., & Wynne, B. (1995). An experiment assessing group support system and facilitator effects on meeting outcomes. *Management Science*, *41*(2), 189–208. doi:10.1287/mnsc.41.2.189

Apker, J., Kathleen, M. P., Wendy, S. Z. F., & Hofmeister, N. (2006). Collaboration, credibility, compassion, and coordination: Professional nurse communication. *Journal of Professional Nursing*, *22*(3), 180–189. doi:10.1016/j.profnurs.2006.03.002

Armstrong, D., & Cole, P. (2002). Managing distances and differences in geographically distributed work groups. In P. Hinds & S. Kiesler (Ed.), Distributed Work (pp. 167-189). Cambridge, MA: MIT Press.

Armstrong, J. S., & Overton, T. S. (1977). Estimating nonresponse bias in mail surveys. *JMR, Journal of Marketing Research*, *14*(3), 396–402. doi:10.1177/002224377701400320

Arslanian-Engoren, C. M. (1995). Lived experiences of CNSs who collaborate with physicians: A phenomenological study. *Clinical Nurse Specialist CNS*, *9*(2), 68–74. doi:10.1097/00002800-199503000-00002

Athanasoula-Reppa, A. (2006). Tutor-counselor's role in Open and Distance Learning Lionarakis. In A. Lionarakis (Ed.), *Elements of theory and action*. Propompos. (in Greek)

Avalos, B. (2011). Teacher professional development. *Teaching and Teacher Education over ten years. Teaching and Teacher Education*, *27*(1), 10–20. doi:10.1016/j.tate.2010.08.007

Avouris, N., & Komis, B. (2003). Synchronous collaboration at a distance: community and interaction issues, (in Greek). In A. Lionarakis (Ed.), *2nd Hellenic Conference of Open and Distance Learning*. Patra: Hellenic Open University.

Axelsson, R., & Bihari-Axelsson, S. (2005). Intersectoral problems in the Russian organization of public health. *Health Policy (Amsterdam)*, *73*(3), 285–293. doi:10.1016/j.healthpol.2004.11.020

Babbie, E. (2015). *The practice of social research*. Nelson Education.

Baerg, K., Lake, D., & Paslawski, T. (2012). Learning needs and training interest in health professionals, teachers, and students: An exploratory study. *Journal of Research in Interprofessional Practice and Education*, *2*(2), 1–19. doi:10.22230/jripe.2012v2n2a47

Baggs, J. G., & Schmitt, M. H. (1997). Nurses' and resident physicians' perceptions of the process of collaboration in an MICU. *Research in Nursing & Health*, *20*(1), 71–80. doi:10.1002/(SICI)1098-240X(199702)20:1<71::AID-NUR8>3.0.CO;2-R

Baier, A. (1986). Trust and antitrust. *Ethics*, *96*(2), 231–260. doi:10.1086/292745

Bailey, K. (1983). Competitiveness and anxiety in adult second language learning: Looking at and through the diary studies. In H. Seliger & M. Long (Eds.), Classroom-oriented research in second language acquisition (pp. 67-102). Rowley: Mass Newbury House.

Bailey, P., Jones, L., & Way, D. (2006). Family physician/nurse practitioner: Stories of collaboration. *Journal of Advanced Nursing*, *53*(4), 381–391. doi:10.1111/j.1365-2648.2006.03734.x

Ball, M. J., & Lillis, J. (2006). E-health: Transforming the physician/patient relationship. *International Journal of Medical Informatics*, *61*(1), 1–10. doi:10.1016/S1386-5056(00)00130-1

Barabási, A. L., Barzel, B., & Martino, M. (2012). *Introduction. In Network science*. Center for Complex Network Research - Northeastern University.

Bardhi, F., & Eckhardt, G. M. (2012). Access-based consumption: The case of car sharing. *The Journal of Consumer Research*, *39*(4), 881–898. doi:10.1086/666376

Barimani, M., & Hylander, I. (2008). Linkage in the chain of care: A grounded theory of professional cooperation between antenatal care, postpartum care and child health care. *International Journal of Integrated Care*, *8*(4), 1–13. doi:10.5334/ijic.254

Barkley, E. F., Cross, K. P., & Major, C. H. (2014). *Collaborative Learning Techniques: A Handbook for College Faculty*. John Wiley & Sons.

Barnes, S. J., & Mattson, J. (2016). Understanding current and future issues in collaborative Consumption: A four-stage Delphi study. *Technological Forecasting and Social Change*, *104*, 200–211. doi:10.1016/j.techfore.2016.01.006

Barnes, S. J., & Mattson, J. (2017). Understanding collaborative consumption: Test of a theoretical model. *Technological Forecasting and Social Change*, *118*, 281–292. doi:10.1016/j.techfore.2017.02.029

Baron, N., Squires, L., Trench, S., & Thompson, M. (2005). Tethered or Mobile? Use of Away Messages in Instant Messaging by American College Students. In R. Ling & P. Pedersen (Eds.), *Mobile Communications: Renegotiation of the Social Sphere* (pp. 293–312). Springer. doi:10.1007/1-84628-248-9_20

Barrett, J., Curran, V., Glynn, L., & Godwin, M. (2007). *CHSRF synthesis: Interprofessional collaboration and quality primary healthcare*. Canadian Health Services Research Foundation.

Barr, R. B., & Tagg, J. (1995). From teaching to learning -A new paradigm for undergraduate education. *Change: The Magazine of Higher Learning*, *27*(6), 12–26. doi:10.1080/00091383.1995.10544672

Batt, P. J., & Purchase, S. (2004). Managing collaboration within networks and relationships. *Industrial Marketing Management*, *33*(3), 169–174. doi:10.1016/j.indmarman.2003.11.004

Baumgart, D. C. (2005). Personal digital assistants in health care: Experienced clinicians in the palm of your hand? *Journal of the American Medical Association*, *366*(9492), 1210–1222.

Bayne, S., & Ross, J. (2011). 'Digital Native' and 'Digital Immigrant' Discourses. In R. Land & S. Bayne (Eds.), *Digital Difference. Educational Futures Rethinking Theory and Practice* (Vol. 50). SensePublishers.

Belgavi, V., & Gandhi, M. (2020, April). *PWC India report - Impact of the Covid 19 outbreak on Digital Payments*. https://www.pwc.in/assets/pdfs/consulting/financial-services/fintech/point-of-view/pov-downloads/impact-of-the-covid-19-outbreak-on-digital-payments.pdf

Belk, R. (1988). Possessions and the extended self. *The Journal of Consumer Research*, *15*(2), 139–168. doi:10.1086/209154

Belk, R. (2010). Sharing. *The Journal of Consumer Research*, *36*(5), 715–734. doi:10.1086/612649

Belk, R. (2014). You are what you can access: Sharing and collaborative consumption online. *Journal of Business Research*, *67*(8), 1595–1600. doi:10.1016/j.jbusres.2013.10.001

Ben Said, I., Chaâbane, M. A., Andonoff, E., & Bouaziz, R. (2018). BPMN4VC-modeller: Easy-handling of versions of collaborative processes using adaptation patterns. *Journal of Information Systems and Change Management*, *10*(2), 140–189. doi:10.1504/IJISCM.2018.094604

Bernard, P. E., Chautemps, M. L., & Galaup, X. (2006). *Le rôle de réseaux sociaux dans la création et la structuration de l'information sur Internet, Initiation à la recherche*. École Nationale Supérieure des Sciences de l'Information et des bibliotheques. Working paper no DCB, 15, 6.

Berwick, D. M. (2003). Improvement, trust, and the healthcare workforce. *Quality & Safety in Health Care*, *12*(6), 448–452. doi:10.1136/qhc.12.6.448

BFSI.com. (2020). Eight factors that will drive fintech in India this year. *Economic Times*. https://bfsi.economictimes.indiatimes.com/news/fintech/eight-factors-that-will-drive-fintech-in-india-this-year/74167318

Bhasin, N. K. (2019). Study of increasing digital banking and financial technology – trends, challenges and opportunities in Indian Banking System. *Bank Quest, 90*(4), 33-44.

Bhasin, N. K. (2019). Study of Increasing Digital banking & Financial Technology Trends, Challenges and Opportunities in Indian Banking System. *Bank Quest*, *90*(4), 33–44.

Bhasin, N. K., & Rajesh, A. (2019). *Increasing Digital Banking Adoption and Usage Trends in India and its Impact on Financial Inclusion. International Journal of Recent Technology and Engineering.*

Biji Kurian John. (2020, June 10). *Bank and Fintech Collaboration –Lifeline for Economic Revival Post Covid 19.* Trade Finance Global Articles. https://www.tradefinanceglobal.com/posts/bank-and-fintech-collaboration-lifeline-for-economic-revival-post-covid19/

Birkhäuer, J., Gaab, J., Kossowsky, J., Hasler, S., Krummenacher, P., Werner, C., & Gerger, H. (2017). Trust in the health care professional and health outcome: A meta-analysis. *PLoS One*, *12*(2), e0170988. doi:10.1371/journal.pone.0170988

Blackboard, (2020). *Blackboard Collaborate*. Retrieved April 28, 2020 from https://www.blackboard.com/teaching-learning/collaboration-web-conferencing/blackboard-collaborate

Blanchard, A. L., & Markus, M. L. (2004). The experienced sense of a virtual community: Characteristics and processes. *ACM Sigmis Database*, *35*(1), 64–79. doi:10.1145/968464.968470

Blanchet, J. (2005). Innovative programs in telemedicine: The Arizona telemedicine program. *Telemedicine Journal and e-Health*, *11*(2), 116–123. doi:10.1089/tmj.2005.11.116

Boden, C., Sit, A., & Weinreb, R. N. (2006). Accuracy of an electronic monitoring and reminder device for use with travoprost eye drops. *Journal of Glaucoma*, *15*(1), 30–34. doi:10.1097/01.ijg.0000196654.77836.61

Bodenheime, T. (2007). Coordinating care: A perilous journey through the health care system. *The New England Journal of Medicine*, *358*(10), 1064–1071. doi:10.1056/NEJMhpr0706165

Boisot, M., & Child, J. (1999). Organizations as adaptive systems in complex environments: The case of China. *Organization Science*, *10*(3), 237–252. doi:10.1287/orsc.10.3.237

Bollinger, A. S., & Smith, R. D. (2001). Managing organizational knowledge as a strategic asset. *Journal of Knowledge Management*, *5*(1), 8–18. doi:10.1108/13673270110384365

Borghoff, U. M., & Schlichter, J. H. (2000). Computer-Supported Cooperative Work. In *Computer-Supported Cooperative Work* (pp. 87–141). Springer., doi:10.1007/978-3-662-04232-8_2

Botsman, R., & Rogers, R. (2011). *What's mine is yours: How collaborative consumption is changing the way we live.* HarperCollins.

Bouras, C., Giannaka. E., & Tsiatsos, T. (2008). *E-Collaboration Concepts, Systems, and Applications.* Retrieved April 28, 2020 from https://www.igi-global.com/chapter/collaboration-concepts-systems-applications/16849

Bozzi, M., Raffaghelli, J., & Zani, M. (2018). *Peer learning for large size Physics lectures in higher education: yes, we can. Proceedings of iCERi2018, 8739-8747.* IATED.

Brabham, D. C. (2008). Crowdsourcing as a model for problem solving: An introduction and cases. *Convergence (London)*, *14*(1), 75–90. doi:10.1177/1354856507084420

Bradley, F., Ashcroft, D.M., & Noyce, P.R. (2012). Integration and differentiation: a conceptual model of general practitioner and community pharmacist collaboration. *Res. Social Adm. Pharm, 8*(1), 36–46. . 005. doi:10.1016/j.sapharm.2010.12

Bradner, E., Mark, G., & Hertel, T. (2005). Team size and technology fit: Participation, awareness, and rapport in distributed teams. *IEEE Transactions on Professional Communication*, *48*(1), 68–77. doi:10.1109/TPC.2004.843299

Bray, J., Johns, N., & Kilburn, D. (2011). An exploratory study into the factors impeding ethical consumption. *Journal of Business Ethics*, *98*(4), 597–608. doi:10.100710551-010-0640-9

Brazil, K., Whelan, T., O'Brien, M. A., Sussman, J., Pyette, N., & Bainbridge, D. (2004). Towards improving the coordination of supportive cancer care services in the community. *Health Policy (Amsterdam)*, *70*(1), 125–131. doi:10.1016/j.healthpol.2004.02.007

Briggs, R. O., De Vreede, G. J., Nunamaker, J. F. Jr, & Tobey, D. (2001). ThinkLets: achieving predictable, repeatable patterns of group interaction with group support systems (GSS). In *Proceedings of the 34th Annual Hawaii International Conference on System Sciences*. Computer Society Press. 10.1109/HICSS.2001.926238

Briggs, R. O., de Vreede, G.-J., & Nunamaker, J. F. Jr. (2003). Collaboration engineering with ThinkLets to pursue sustained sucess with group support systems. *Journal of Management Information Systems*, *19*(4), 31–64. doi:10.1080/07421222.2003.11045743

Briggs, R. O., Reinig, B. A., & de Vreede, G.-J. (2006). Meeting satisfaction for technology-supported groups: An empirical validation of a goal-attainment model. *Small Group Research*, *37*(6), 585–611. doi:10.1177/1046496406294320

Brocke, J., Zelt, S., & Schmiedel, T. (2016). On the role of context in business process management. *Journal of International Management*, *36*(3), 486–495.

Brockner, J., & Siegel, P. (1996). Understanding the interaction between procedural and distributive justice: The role of trust. In R. M. Kramer & T. R. Tyler (Eds.), *Trust in organizations: Frontiers of theory and research.* Sage. doi:10.4135/9781452243610.n18

Broers, T., Poth, C., & Medeves, J. (2009). What's in a word? Understanding interprofessional collaboration from the students' perspective. *Journal of Research in Interprofessional Practice and Education, 1*(1), 3–9. doi:10.22230/jripe.2009v1n1a1

Bronstein, L. R. (2002). Index of interdisciplinary collaboration. *Social Work Research, 26*(2), 113–126. doi:10.1093wr/26.2.113

Bronstein, L. R. (2003). A model for interdisciplinary collaboration. *Social Work, 48*(3), 297–306. doi:10.1093w/48.3.297

Brown, M. (2013). Learning Spaces. In D. G. Oblinger & J. L. Oblinger (Eds.), *Educating the net generation.* Retrieved August 20, 2013 from https://net.educause.edu/ir/library/pdf/pub7101l.pdf

Brown, B., Crawford, P., & Darongkamas, J. (2000). Blurred roles and permeable boundaries: The experience of multidisciplinary working in community mental health. *Health & Social Care in the Community, 8*(6), 425–435. doi:10.1046/j.1365-2524.2000.00268.x

Brown, J. S., & Duguid, P. (2000). *The Social Life of Information.* Harvard University Press.

Bruckman, A., & Resnick, M. (1995). The MediaMOO Project: Constructionism and Professional Community. *Convergence, 1*(1), 94–109. doi:10.1177/135485659500100110

Bruner, J. (1966). *Toward a theory of instruction.* Belknap Press of Harvard University.

Bucher, T., & Helmond, A. (2018). The affordance of social media platforms. In J. Burgess, A. Marwick, & T. Poell (Eds.), *The SAGE Handbook of Social Media* (pp. 233–253). Sage Publications. doi:10.4135/9781473984066.n14

Burtscher, M. J., & Manser, T. (2012). Team mental models and their potential to improve teamwork and safety: A review and implications for future research in healthcare. *Safety Science, 50*(5), 1344–1354. doi:10.1016/j.ssci.2011.12.033

Butler, B. S., Bateman, P. J., Gray, P. H., & Diamant, E. I. (2014). An attraction-selection-attrition theory of online community size and resilience. *MIS Quarterly, 38*(3), 699-728. /2014/38.3.04 doi:10.25300/MISQ

Byrd, T. A. (1992). Implementation and use of expert systems in organizations: Perceptions of knowledge engineers. *Journal of Management Information Systems, 8*(4), 97–116. doi:10.1080/07421222.1992.11517941

Cabrera, A., & Cabrera, E. F. (2002). Knowledge-sharing dilemmas. *Organization Studies, 23*(5), 687–710. doi:10.1177/0170840602235001

Cachia, R., Punie, Y., & Vuorikari, R. (2012). *Final report on the future of teacher networking. IPTS/JRC, European Schoolnet.* http://tellnet.eun.org/c/document_library/get_file?p_l_id=10704&folderId=18137&name=DLFE-817.pdf

California Community Foundation. (2020). *LA Arts Covid 19 Relief Fund Grantees.* Getty Foundation. https://www.getty.edu/foundation/initiatives/current/la_covid_fund.html

Cameron, L. (2007). Scaffolding Effective Learning Design with Pre-Service Teachers. In C. Montgomerie, & J. Seale (Eds.), *Proceedings of World Conference on Educational Multimedia, Hypermedia and Telecommunications 2007* (pp. 195-202). Chesapeake, VA: AACE.

Canadian Health Services Research Foundation. (2006). *Teamwork in healthcare: Promoting effective teamwork in healthcare in Canada. Policy Synthesis and Recommendations.* Ottawa, ON: Canadian Health Services Research Foundation. URL: http://www.chsrf.ca/Migrated/PDF/ResearchReports/CommissionedResearch/teamwork-synthesis-report_e.pdf

Cao, Y. (2011). Comparison of Two Models of Foreign Language Classroom Anxiety Scale. *Philippine ESL Journal, 7*, 73–93.

Careau, E., Vincent, C., & Swaine, B. R. (2011). Consensus group session of experts to describe interprofessional collaboration processes in team meetings. *Journal of Interprofessional Care*, *25*(4), 299–301. Doi:10.3109/13561820.2011.566649

Carson, B. (2017, October 16). *Lime Bike Now Valued At $225 Million After Investors Go All In On Bike-Sharing Craze.* Retrieved from https://www.forbes.com/sites/bizcarson /2017/10/16/limebike-now-valued-at-225-illionafterinvestors-go-all-in-on-bike-sharing-craze /#4af3736d4a12

Cassel, C., Hackl, P., & Westlund, A. H. (1999). Robustness of Partial Least-Squares Method for Estimating Latent Variable Quality Structures. *Journal of Applied Statistics*, *26*(4), 435–446. doi:10.1080/02664769922322

Castells, M. (2013). *The impact of the internet on society: A global perspective. In 19 key essays on how Internet is changing our lives*. BBVA.

Chaâbane, M. A., Bouzguenda, L., & Bouaziz, R. (2011). Towards a Business Process Versions Querying and Manipulating Language. In *The International Conference on Information Technology and e-services* (pp. 12–19). Sousse, Tunisia: Academic Press.

Chandra, S., Mohammadnezhad, M., & Ward, P. (2018). Trust and communication in a doctor-patient relationship: A literature review. *Journal of Health Communication*, *3*(3), 31–36.

Chan, T.-W. (1995). Artificial agents in distance learning. *International Journal of Educational Telecommunications*, *1*(2), 263–282.

Cheney, G. (2011). *Organizational communication in an age of globalization: Issues, reflections, practices.* Waveland Press.

Cheng, E. C. K. (2012). Knowledge strategies for enhancing school learning capacity. *International Journal of Educational Management*, *26*(6), 577–592. doi:10.1108/09513541211251406

Cheng, E. C. K. (2013). Applying knowledge management for school strategic planning. *KEDI Journal of Educational Policy*, *10*(2), 339–356. http://repository.lib.eduhk.hk/jspui/handle/2260.2/14040

Cheng, E. C. K. (2017). Knowledge management strategies for capitalizing on school knowledge. *Journal of Information and Knowledge Management Systems*, *47*(1), 94–109. doi:10.1108/VJIKMS-08-2016-0045

Cheng, E. C. K., & Chu, C. (2018). A normative knowledge management model for school development. *International Journal of Learning and Teaching*, *4*(1), 76–82. Advance online publication. doi:10.18178/ijlt.4.1.76-82

Cheng, E. C. K., Wu, W. S., & Hu, J. (2017). Knowledge management implementation in the school context: Case studies on knowledge leadership, storytelling, and taxonomy. *Educational Research for Policy and Practice*, *16*(2), 177–188. doi:10.100710671-016-9200-0

Chen, H., Houston, A., Nunamaker, J. F. Jr, & Yen, J. (1996). Toward intelligent meeting agents. *Computer*, *29*(8), 62–70. doi:10.1109/2.532047

Chin, W. W. (1998). The Partial Least Squares Approach to Structural Equation Modeling. In G. A. Marcoulides (Ed.), *Modern Methods for Business Research* (pp. 1295–1336). Lawrence Erlbaum Associates.

Cho, E., Gupta, S., & Kim, Y. (2015). Style consumption: Its drivers and role in sustainable apparel consumption. *International Journal of Consumer Studies*, *39*(6), 661–669. doi:10.1111/ijcs.12185

Chotto & Dirckinck-Holmfeld. (2008). *Facilitating Communities of Practice in Teacher Professional Development* (Vol. 1). Lancaster University.

Clark, P. G. (2014). Narrative in interprofessional education and practice: Implications for professional identity, provider patient communication and teamwork. *Journal of Interprofessional Care*, *28*(1), 34–39. doi:10.3109/13561820.2013.853652

Clegg, S. (2003). Problematising ourselves: Continuing professional development in higher education. *The International Journal for Academic Development*, *8*(1-2), 37–50. doi:10.1080/1360144042000277928

Coats, M. (1992). *Open Teaching Toolkit – Effective Tutorials*. The Open University. Retrieved August 20, 2012 from http://labspace.open.ac.uk/file.php/5718/LDT_12_Intro.pdf

Cochran-Smith, M., & Lytle, S. (1999). Relationships of knowledge and practice: Teacher learning community. *Review of Research in Education*, *24*, 249–305. https://www.jstor.org/stable/1167272

Cognini, R., Corradini, F., Gnesi, S., Polini, A., & Re, B. (2018). Business process flexibility-a systematic literature review with a software systems perspective. *Journal of Information Systems Frontiers*, *20*(2), 343–371. doi:10.100710796-016-9678-2

Colin, C. (2020). *Kid Reporters tackle the Coronavirus*. CondeNast publication. https://www.wired.com/story/kid-reporters-tackle-coronavirus-newspaper/

Collinson, V., & Cook, T. F. (2000). *I don't have enough time: Teachers' interpretations of time as a key to learning and school change*. Paper presented at the annual meeting of the American Educational Research Association, New Orleans, LA. https://files.eric.ed.gov/fulltext/ED446038.pdf

Commission of the European Communities. (2000). *A Memorandum on Lifelong Learning* (Commission staff working paper). https://arhiv.acs.si/dokumenti/Memorandum_on_Lifelong_Learning.pdf

Contu, A. (2014). On boundaries and difference: Communities of practice and power relations in creative work. *Management Learning*, *45*(3), 289–316. doi:10.1177/1350507612471926

Contu, A., & Willmott, H. (2003). Re-embedding situatedness: The importance of power relations in learning theory. *Organization Science*, *14*(3), 283–296. doi:10.1287/orsc.14.3.283.15167

Cornelius, S., & Macdonald, J. (2008). Online informal professional development for distance tutors: Experiences from The Open University in Scotland. *Open Learning*, *23*(1), 43–55. doi:10.1080/02680510701815319

Cornish, L. (2020). *First came the coronavirus. And then the cyclone hit*. Devex. https://www.devex.com/news/first-came-the-coronavirus-and-then-the-cyclone-hit-97261

Coronado, M., Iglesias, C. A., Carrera, Á., & Mardomingo, A. (2018). A cognitive assistant for learning java featuring social dialogue. *International Journal of Human-Computer Studies*, *117*, 55–67. doi:10.1016/j.ijhcs.2018.02.004

Corredato Periotto, T. R., & Wessellenns, L. J. (2018). The school manager and the use of knowledge management practices for structuring organizational processes. *International Journal of Learning. Teaching and Educational Research*, *17*(10), 43–54. doi:10.26803/ijlter.17.10.3

Cox, W. (2009). Improving quality of life through telecommuting. *The Information Technology & Innovation Foundation*, *1*, 1–22.

Cramton, C. (2001). The mutual knowledge problem and its consequences for dispersed collaborations. *Organization Science*, *12*(3), 346–371. doi:10.1287/orsc.12.3.346.10098

Cramton, C. D., & Webber, S. S. (2005). Relationship among geographic dispersion, team process, and effectiveness in software development work teams. *Journal of Business Research*, *58*(6), 758–765. doi:10.1016/j.jbusres.2003.10.006

Crawford, K. (2008). Continuing professional development in higher education: The academic perspective. *The International Journal for Academic Development*, *13*(2), 141–146. doi:10.1080/13601440802076657

CTI. (n.d.). *CTI Diophantus*. Retrieved April 28, 2020 from www.cti.gr

Culnan, M. J., & Bies, J. R. (2003). Consumer privacy: Balancing economic and justice considerations. *The Journal of Social Issues*, *59*(2), 323–342. doi:10.1111/1540-4560.00067

Cummings, J., & Ghosh, T. (2005). *Teams as Networks in a Connected Organization: The Critical Role of Geographic Distance*. Academy of Management Conference, Honolulu, HI.

D'Amour, D. (1997). *Structuration de la collaboration interprofessionnelle dans les services de sante´de premie`re ligne au Que´bec*. The`se de doctorat. Montre´al: Universite´ de Montre´al.

D'Amour, D., Ferrada-Videla, M., Rodriguez, L. S. M., & Beaulieu, M. D. (2005). The conceptual basis for interprofessional collaboration: Core concepts and theoretical frameworks. *Journal of Interprofessional Care*, *19*(S1), 116 – 131. Doi:10.1080/13561820500082529

D'Amour, D., Sicotte, C., & Le'vy, R. (1999). L'action collective au sein d'e'quipes interprofessionnelles dans les services de sante´. *Sciences Sociales et Sante*, *17*(3), 68–94. doi:10.3406osan.1999.1468

Dadam, P., & Reichert, M. (2009). The ADEPT project: A decade of research and development for robust and flexible process support. *Journal of Computer Science-Research and Development*, *23*(2), 81–97. doi:10.100700450-009-0068-6

Dahl, B., & Kolmos, A. (2016). Students' attitudes towards group based project exams in two engineering programmes. *Journal of Problem Based Learning in Higher Education*, *3*(2).

Dalziel, J. (2010). *Practical e-Teaching Strategies for Predict – Observe – Explain, Problem-Based Learning and Role Plays*. Sydney: LAMS International. Retrieved October 13, 2014, from http://www.practicaleteachingstrategies.com/

Daneci-Patrau, D. (2011). Formal communication in organisationfalse. *Economics. Management and Financial Markets*, *6*(1), 487–497.

Danermark, B., & Kullberg, C. (1999). *Samverkan: välfärdsstatens nya arbetsform* [Collaboration: The new working methods of the welfare state]. Studentlitteratur.

Davies, C. (1996). The sociology of professions and the sociology of gender. *Sociology*, *30*(4), 661–678. doi:10.1177/0038038596030004003

Davies, H. (1994). Falling public trust in health services: Implications for accountability. *Journal of Health Services and Policy Research*, *4*(4), 193–194. doi:10.1177/135581969900400401

Davis, F. D. (1985). *A Technology Acceptance Model for Empirically Testing New End-user Information Systems: Theory and Results*. Massachusetts Institute of Technology.

de Vreede, G. J., & Briggs, R. (2018). *Collaboration Engineering: Reflections on 15 Years of Research & Practice*. Retrieved from https://aisel.aisnet.org/hicss-51/cl/processes_and_technologies_for_team/4/

de Vreede, G. J., Antunes, P., Vassileva, J., Gerosa, M. A., & Wu, K. (2016). Collaboration technology in teams and organizations: Introduction to the special issue. *Journal of Information Systems Frontiers*, *18*(1), 1–6. doi:10.100710796-016-9632-3

de Vreede, G.-J., & Briggs, R. O. (2019). A Program of Collaboration Engineering Research and Practice: Contributions, Insights, and Future Directions. *Journal of Management Information Systems*, *36*(1), 74–119. doi:10.1080/07421222.2018.1550552 de Vreede, G.-J., Briggs, R. O., van Duin, R., & Enserink, B. (2000). Athletics in electronic brainstorming: asynchronous electronic brainstorming in very large groups. In *Proceedings of the 33rd Annual Hawaii International Conference on System Sciences*. Computer Society Press. 10.1109/HICSS.2000.926627

Deci, E. L., & Ryan, R. M. (1985). *Intrinsic motivation and selfdetermination in human behaviour*. Plenum. doi:10.1007/978-1-4899-2271-7

Deng, H. (2008). A Case study on undergraduates' Informal learning supported by QQ. *2008 International Conference on Computer Science and Software Engineering*, 649-654. 10.1109/CSSE.2008.235

Denning, P. J., & Yaholkovsky, P. (2008). Getting to "we." *Communications of the ACM, 51*(4), 19–24. Retrieved from file:///Users/avd108/Documents/articles/Denning,Yaholkovsky-2008.pdf

Dennis, A. R., & Valacich, J. S. (1993). Computer brainstorms: More heads are better than one. *The Journal of Applied Psychology, 78*(4), 531–537. doi:10.1037/0021-9010.78.4.531

Dennis, A. R., Valacich, J. S., Connolly, T., & Wynne, B. E. (1996). Process Structuring in Electronic Brainstorming. *Information Systems Research, 7*(2), 268–277. doi:10.1287/isre.7.2.268

Dey, R. M., De Vries, M. J. W., & Bosnic-Anticevich, S. (2011). Collaboration in chronic care: Unpacking the relationship of pharmacists and general medical practitioners in primary care. *International Journal of Pharmacy Practice, 19*(1), 21–29. doi:10.1111/j.2042-7174.2010.00070.x

Diehl, M., & Stroebe, W. (1987). Productivity loss in brainstorming groups: Toward the solution of a riddle. *Journal of Personality and Social Psychology, 53*(3), 497–509. doi:10.1037/0022-3514.53.3.497

Dillenbourg, P. (1999). Collaborative learning: Cognitive and computational approaches. In *Advances in learning and Instruction Series*. Elsevier Science, Inc.

Django. (2019). https://www.djangoproject.com

Dobbs, R., Manyika, J., Woetzel, J., Remes, J., Perry, J., Kelly, G., & Sharma, H. (2016). *Urban world: The global consumers to watch*. Retrieved from https://www.mckinsey.com/global-themes/urbanization/urban-world-the-global-consumerstowatch

Doherty, W. J. (1995). The whys and the levels of collaboration. *Family Systems Medicine, 13*(3), 275–281. doi:10.1037/h0089174

Dolton, P., Marcenaro, O., De Vries, R., & She, P. W. (2018). *The global teacher status index 2018*. London: The Varkey Foundation. https://www.varkeyfoundation.org/media/4867/gts-index-13-11-2018.pdf

Downes, S. (2007). An introduction to connective knowledge. *The International Conference on Media, knowledge & education—exploring new spaces, relations and dynamics in digital media ecologies*. Retrieved May 10, 2013 from https://www.downes.ca/post/3303

Driskell, J. E., Radtke, P. H., & Salas, E. (2003). Virtual Teams: Effects of Technological Mediation on Team Performance. *Group Dynamics, 7*(4), 297–323. doi:10.1037/1089-2699.7.4.297

Dubey. (2019). FinTech Innovations in Digital Banking. *International Journal of Engineering and Research & Technology, 8*(10).

Dugan, D. (2012). Interdisciplinary hospice team processes and multidimensional pain: A qualitative study. *Journal of Social Work in End-of-Life & Palliative Care, 8*(1), 53–76. doi:10.1080/15524256.2011.650673

Dulebohn, J. H., & Hoch, J. E. (2017). Virtual teams in organizations. *Human Resource Management Review, 27*(4), 569–574. doi:10.1016/j.hrmr.2016.12.004

Dumas, M., La Rosa, M., Mendling, J., & Reijers, H. A. (2018). *Fundamentals of business process management* (2nd ed., Vol. 1). Springer. doi:10.1007/978-3-662-56509-4

Duranti, C. M., & de Almeida, F. C. (2012). Is More Technology Better for Communication in International Virtual Teams? *International Journal of e-Collaboration, 8*(1), 36–52. doi:10.4018/jec.2012010103

EDUCAUSE. (2019). *The Horizon Reports of the New Media Consortium NMC (2019).* https://linhadeleitura.files.wordpress.com/2019/05/2019horizonreport.pdf

Ekanayake, C. C., La Rosa, M., Ter Hofstede, A. H., & Fauvet, M. C. (2011). Fragment-based version management for repositories of business process models. In *Proceedings of the International Conferences OTM Confederated On the Move to Meaningful Internet Systems* (pp. 20-37). Hersonissos, Crete, Greece: Springer. 10.1007/978-3-642-25109-2_3

Ellouze, F., Chaabane, M. A., Bouaziz, R., & Andonoff, E. (2016). Addressing inter-organisational process flexibility using versions: The VP2M approach. In *Proceedings of the International Conference on Research Challenges in Information Science* (pp. 1-12). Grenoble, France: IEEE. 10.1109/RCIS.2016.7549280

Elson, J. S., Derrick, D., & Ligon, G. (2018). Examining Trust and Reliance in Collaborations between Humans and Automated Agents. *Hawaii International Conference on System Sciences 2018 (HICSS-51).* https://aisel.aisnet.org/hicss-51/cl/processes_and_technologies_for_team/6

Elson, J., Derrick, D., & Ligon, G. (2020, January 7). *Trusting a Humanoid Robot: Exploring Personality and Trusting Effects in a Human-Robot Partnership.* doi:10.24251/HICSS.2020.067

E-me. (2020). *E-me.* Retrieved April 28, 2020 from https://auth.e-me.edu.gr/?eme=https://e-me.edu.gr/&cause=no-token&eat=a6d5e70e1fad5db9975afe235d2c85fb&lang=en_US

Eraut, M. (2000). Non-formal learning and tacit knowledge in professional work. *British Journal of Educational Psychology, 70,* 113–136. doi:10.1348/000709900158001

Ertz, M., Durif, F., & Arcand, M. (2016). Collaborative Consumption: Conceptual Snapshot at a Buzzword. *Journal of Entrepreneurship Education, 19*(2), 1–23.

Estellés-Arolas, E., & González-Ladrón-De-Guevara, F. (2012). Towards an integrated crowdsourcing definition. *Journal of Information Science, 38*(2), 189–200. doi:10.1177/0165551512437638

etwinning program. (n.d.a). *The etwinning program.* Retrieved April 28, 2020 from https://www.etwinning.net/en/pub/index.htm

etwinning program. (n.d.b). *etwinning projects.* Retrieved April 28, 2020 from https://www.etwinning.net/en/pub/get-inspired/projects.cfm

etwinning program. (n.d.c). *Digital stories.* Retrieved April 28, 2020 from https://digitalstories2014.wordpress.com/making-of/

European Commission. (2013). *Study on Policy Measures to Improve the Attractiveness of the Teaching Profession in Europe, Final Report, 1.* Publications Office of the European Union. Doi:10.2766/40827

European Commission/EACEA. (n.d.). *Erasmus Plus Programme Guide, Version 2 (26-02-2020).* https://ec.europa.eu/programmes/erasmus-plus/sites/erasmusplus2/files/erasmus_programme_guide_2020_v2_en.pdf

European Commission/EACEA/Eurydice. (2018). *Teaching careers in Europe: Access, progression and support.* Eurydice Report. Luxemburg: Publication Office of the European Union. https://op.europa.eu/en/publication-detail/-/publication/435e941e-1c3b-11e8-ac73-01aa75ed71a1/language-en European Commission/EACEA/

European Commission/EACEA/Eurydice. (2018). *The structure of the European education systems 2018/19: Schematic diagrams. Eurydice Facts and Figures.* Luxemburg. Publication Office of the European Union.

European Council. (2010). *Project Europe, 2030. Challenges and Opportunities.* Luxembourg: Publications Office of the European Union. https://www.consilium.europa.eu/media/30776/qc3210249enc.pdf

European Council. (2017). *The Rome Declaration. Declaration of the leaders of 27 member states and of the European Council, the European Parliament and the European Commission.* Brussels: Press office - General Secretariat of the Council. https://www.consilium.europa.eu/en/press/press-releases/2017/03/25/rome-declaration/

European Union. (2010). *A Digital Agenda for Europe. Digital Agenda COM 245 final.* Retrieved April 29, 2015 from http://europa.eu/legislation_summaries/information_society/strategies/si0016_en.htm

Eurydice. (2018). *Teachers' and school heads' salaries and allowances in Europe – 2016/17. Eurydice Facts and Figures.* Luxembourg: Publications Office of the European Union. https://eacea.ec.europa.eu/national-policies/eurydice/sites/eurydice/files/teacher_and_school_head_salaries_2016_17.pdf

Fanariti, M., & Spanaka, Ad. (2010, November). Metacognition and learning autonomy during the implementation of essays (in Greek). In the *Open. Education Journal*, *6*(1), 138–151. Retrieved June 2, 2011, from http://journal.openet.gr/index.php/openjournal/article/view/105

Faraj, S., Jarvenpaa, S. L., & Majchrzak, A. (2011). Knowledge collaboration in online communities. *Organization Science*, *22*(5), 1224–1239. doi:10.1287/orsc.1100.0614

Farmer, R. (2006). Instant Messaging: Collaborative Tool or Educator's nightmare! *Proceedings of 2003 The Web Learning Conference.* https://www.unb.ca/naweb/proceedings/2003/PaperFarmer.html

Fehr, E., Fischbacher, U., & Gächter, S. (2002). Strong reciprocity, human cooperation, and the enforcement of social norms. *Human Nature (Hawthorne, N.Y.)*, *13*(1), 1–25. doi:10.100712110-002-1012-7

Felson, M., & Spaeth, J. L. (1978). Community structure and collaborative consumption: A routine activity approach. *The American Behavioral Scientist*, *21*(4), 614–624. doi:10.1177/000276427802100411

Feng, S., & Buxmann, P. (2020, January 7). *My Virtual Colleague: A State-of-the-Art Analysis of Conversational Agents for the Workplace.* doi:10.24251/HICSS.2020.020

Financial Post. (2020). *SES Delivers over 8,300 TV channels to 367 Million homes.* Business Wire. Retrieved on 07/15/2020 at https://financialpost.com/pmn/press-releases-pmn/business-wire-news-releases-pmn/ses-delivers-over-8300-tv-channels-to-367-million-homes-worldwide

Fincash. (2020, July 12*). Impact of Covid 19 on the Future of Fintech Industry.* Academic Press.

Finkbeiner, N., & Morner, M. (2015). The Role of Conditional Cooperation in Organizing Change. In *Management of Permanent Change* (pp. 49–64). Springer Gabler. doi:10.1007/978-3-658-05014-6_3

Fiol, C. M., & O'Connor, E. J. (2005). Identification in Face-to-Face, Hybrid, and Pure Virtual Teams: Untangling the Contradictions. *Organization Science*, *16*(1), 19–32. doi:10.1287/orsc.1040.0101

Fornell, C. (1987). A Second Generation of Multivariate Analysis: Classification of Methods and Implications for Marketing Research. In M. J. Houston (Ed.), *Review of Marketing* (pp. 1407–1450). American Marketing Association.

Fornell, C., & Larcker, D. F. (1981). Evaluating structural equation models with unobservable variables and measurement error. *JMR, Journal of Marketing Research, 18*(1), 39–50. doi:10.1177/002224378101800104

Foronda, C., MacWilliams, B., & McArthur, E. (2016). Interprofessional communication in healthcare: An integrative review. *Nurse Education in Practice, 19*(2), 36–40. doi:10.1016/j.nepr.2016.04.005

Foth, T., Block, K., & Stamers, M. (2015). The long way toward cooperation: nurses and family physicians in northern Germany. *Global Qualitative Nursing Research*, 1–14. Doi:10.1177/2333393614565185

Fox, S. (2011). The social life of health information, 2011. *Pew Internet & American Life Project*. Retrieved from http://pewinternet.org/Reports/2011/Social-Life-of-Health-Info.aspx

Fox, A., & Wilson, E. (2015). Networking and the development of professionals: Beginning teachers building social capital. *Teaching and Teacher Education, 47*, 93–107. Advance online publication. doi:10.1016/j.tate.2014.12.004

Fragaki, M., Reynolds, S., & Vanbuel, M. (2009). A pedagogical framework for the effective use of video in class & Exemplary video- based educational scenarios. In *D6.1- A pedagogical framework for the effective use of video in class / Exemplary video-based educational scenarios, EduTubePlus -A European Curriculum Related Video Library and Hybrid e- services for the Pedagogical Exploitation of Video in Class*. Research Academic Computer Technology Institute.

Francescato, D., Porcelli, R., Mebane, M., Cuddeta, M., Koblas, J., & Renzi, P. (2006). Evaluation of the efficacy of collaborative learning in face-to-face and computer-supported university contexts. *Computers in Human Behavior, 22*(2), 163–176. doi:10.1016/j.chb.2005.03.001

Franchi, E., Poggi, A., & Tomaiuolo, M. (2013). Open Social Networking for Online Collaboration. *International Journal of e-Collaboration, 9*(3), 50–68. doi:10.4018/jec.2013070104

Franciska A Martina, S. S. (2017, October). An *Overview of Digital Payments. International Journal of Research, 4*(13), 2101–2111.

Franklin, C. M., Bernhardt, J. M., Lopez, R. P., Long-Middleton, E. R., & Davis, S. (2015). *Interprofessional Teamwork and Collaboration between Community Health Workers and Healthcare Teams: An Integrative Review. In Health Services Research Management*. doi:10.1177/2333392815573312

Freake, St., & Papathanassiou, H. (2006). *Tutorial support for a Level 3 Electromagnetism course - using a blended approach*. Department of Physics and Astronomy, The Open University. Retrieved May 3, 2009 from http://www.open.ac.uk/picetl/activities/details/detail.php?itemId=4612257d02466&themeId=460d2aa4d3c48

Fung, Y., & Carr, R. (2000). Face-to-Face Tutorials in a Distance Learning System: Meeting student needs. *Open Learning, 15*(1), 35–46. doi:10.1080/026805100115452

Gaboury, I., Bujold, M., Boon, H., & Moher, D. (2009). Interprofessional collaboration within Canadian integrative healthcare clinics: Key components. *Social Science & Medicine, 69*(5), 707–715. doi:10.1016/j.socscimed.2009.05.048

Gadár, L., Kosztyán, Z. T., Telcs, A., & Abonyi, J. (2020). A multilayer and spatial description of the Erasmus mobility network. *Scientific Data, 7*(1), 1–11. doi:10.103841597-020-0382-1

Gagliardi, A.R., Dobrow, M.J., & Wright, F.C. (2011). How can we improve cancer care? A review of interprofessional collaboration models and their use in clinical management. *Surgical Oncology, 20*(3), 146–154. .004 doi:10.1016/j.suronc.2011.06

Gambetta, D. (2000). Can we trust trust? In D. Gambetta (Ed.), *Trust: Making and breaking cooperative relations* (pp. 213–237). Department of Sociology, University of Oxford, Retrieved from: http://www.sociology.ox.ac.uk/papers/gambetta213-237.pdf

Gatignon, H., & Jean-Marc, X. (1997). Strategic orientation of the firm and new product performance. *JMR, Journal of Marketing Research*, *34*(2), 77–90. doi:10.1177/002224379703400107

Ghislandi, P., & Raffaghelli, J. (2014). Quality teaching matters: Perspectives on quality teaching for the modernization of higher education. *Formazione & Insegnamento*, *12*(1), 57–86.

Gibson, D., Broadley, T., Downie, J., & Wallet, P. (2018). Evolving Learning Paradigms: Re-Setting Baselines and Collection Methods of Information and Communication Technology in Education Statistics. *Journal of Educational Technology & Society*, *21*(2), 62–73.

Gilliland, N. (2020). *How Nike is striking the right tone with its response to COVID 19.* Centaur Media plc. https://econsultancy.com/how-nike-is-striking-the-right-tone-with-its-response-to-covid-19/

Gilson, L. (2003). Trust and the development of health care as a social institution. *Social Science & Medicine*, *56*(7), 1453–1468. doi:10.1016/S0277-9536(02)00142-9

Gliner, J. A., & Morgan, G. A. (2000). *Research Methods in Applied Settings: An Integrated Approach to Design and Analysis.* Lawrence Erlbaum Associates Publishers. doi:10.4324/9781410605337

Global Alliance for ICT and Development (GAID). (2010). *Information and communication technologies for development: Health.* White Paper. http://www.scribd.com/doc/35120854/GAID-White-Paper-on-ICT4D-Health

Gnaur, D., & Hüttel, H. (2017). A Platform for Developing and Maintaining Competences in PBL Supervision. In *Emerging Technologies for Education - Second International Symposium, SETE 2017.* Springer. 10.1007/978-3-319-71084-6_33

Gnewuch, U., Morana, S., & Maedche, A. (2017). Towards Designing Cooperative and Social Conversational Agents for Customer Service. *ICIS 2017 Proceedings.* https://aisel.aisnet.org/icis2017/HCI/Presentations/1

Gocan, S., Laplante, M. A., & Woodend, A. K. (2014). Interprofessional collaboration in Ontario's family health teams: A review of the literature. *Journal of Research in Interprofessional Practice and Education*, *3*(3), 1–19. doi:10.22230/jripe.2014v3n3a131

Goldsberry, J. W. (2018). Advanced Practice Nurses Leading the Way: Interprofessional Collaboration. *Nurse Education Today*, *65*(1), 1–3. doi:10.1016/j.nedt.2018.02.024

Goleman, D. (2006). *Social Intelligence.* Ellinika Grammata. (in Greek)

González-Navarro, P., Orengo, V., Zornoza, A., Ripoll, P., & Peiró, J. M. (2010). Group interaction styles in a virtual context: The effects on group outcomes. *Computers in Human Behavior*, *26*(6), 1472–1480. doi:10.1016/j.chb.2010.04.026

Google. (2019). *Cloud Translate documentation.* https://cloud.google.com/translate/docs/

Goold, S. (1998). Money and trust: Relationships between patients, physicians, and health plans. *Journal of Health Politics, Policy and Law*, *23*(5), 688–695.

Granovetter, M. S. (2001). The strength of weak ties. *American Journal of Sociology*, *78*(6), 1936–1380.

Gravemeijer, K., & Cobb, P. (2006). Design research from a learning design perspective. In *Educational design research* (pp. 29–63). Routledge.

Green, B., & Johnson, C. (2015). Interprofessional collaboration in research, education, and clinical practice: Working together for a better future. *The Journal of Chiropractic Education*, *29*(1), 1–10. doi:10.7899/JCE-14-36

Griffith, T. L., Fuller, M. A., & Northcraft, G. B. (1998). Facilitator Influence in Group Support Systems: Intended and Unintended Effects. *Information Systems Research*, *9*(1), 20–36. doi:10.1287/isre.9.1.20

Grinter, R. E., & Palen, L. (2002). Instant Messaging in Teen Life. *Proceedings of the 2002 ACM conference on Computer supported cooperative work*, 21-30.

Grudin, J. (1994). Computer-supported cooperative work: History and focus. *Computer*, *27*(5), 19–26. doi:10.1109/2.291294

Gulzar, L., & Henry, B. (2005). Interorganizational collaboration for health care between nongovernmental organizations (NGOs) in Pakistan. *Social Science & Medicine*, *61*(9), 1930–1943. doi:10.1016/j.socscimed.2005.03.045

Gunet. (2020). *The Greek University Network (GUnet)*. Retrieved April 28, 2020 from https://www.gunet.gr/el/

Gupta, A., & Xia, C. (2018). A Paradigm Shift in Banking: Unfolding Asia's FinTech Adventures. In Banking and Finance Issues in Emerging Markets. Emerald Publishing Limited.

Guzman, A. (2017). *Making AI Safe for Humans: A Conversation With Siri*. Academic Press.

Hadzilakos, T., Papadakis, S., & Rossiou, E. (2007). Group Counseling Conferences (in Greek). *Open Education*. Athens: Propompos.

Haeuser, J. L., & Preston, P. (2005). Communication strategies for getting the results you want. *Healthcare Executive*, *20*(1), 16–22.

Hair, J. F., Black, W. C., Babin, B. J., Anderson, R. E., & Tatham, R. L. (2006). *Multivariate Data Analysis* (6th ed.). Prentice Hall.

Halinen, I., & Holappa, A. (2013). Curricular balance based on dialogue, cooperation and trust-The case of Finland. In W. Kuiper & J. Berkvens (Eds.), *Balancing Curriculum Regulation and Freedom across Europe. CIDREE Yearbook 2013,39-62*. SLO.

Hallerbach, A., Bauer, T., & Reichert, M. (2010). Capturing variability in business process models: The Provop approach. *Journal of Software: Evolution and Process*, *22*(67), 519–546.

Hall, M. A., Camacho, F., Dugan, E., & Balkrishnan, R. (2002). Trust in the medical profession: Conceptual and measurement issues. HSR. *Health Services Research*, *37*(5), 1419–1439. doi:10.1111/1475-6773.01070

Hall, P. (2005). Interprofessional teamwork: Professional cultures as barriers. *Journal of Interprofessional Care*, *19*(1), 188–196. doi:10.1080/13561820500081745

Hamari, J., Sjöklint, M., & Ukkonen, A. (2016). The sharing economy: Why people participate in collaborative consumption. *Journal of the Association for Information Science and Technology*, *67*(9), 2047–2059. doi:10.1002/asi.23552

Hansen, H. E., Biros, M. H., Delaney, N. M., & Schug, V. L. (1999). Research utilization and interdisciplinary collaboration in emergency care. *Academic Emergency Medicine*, *6*(4), 271–279. doi:10.1111/j.1553-2712.1999.tb00388.x

Hanson, C. M., Carr, D. B., & Spross, J. A. (2000). Collaboration. In A. B. Hamric, J. A. Spross, & C. M. Hanson (Eds.), *Advanced nursing practice. An integrative approach* (2nd ed., pp. 315–347). W. B. Saunders.

Hao, K. (2012). Lifelong Learning and Management Models for the Credit Bank. *Open Education Research*, *18*(1), 12–15.

Harris, J. (1999). First steps in telecollaboration. *Learning and Leading with Technology*, *27*(3), 54–57.

Hativa, N. (1997). *Teaching in a research university: Professors' conceptions, practices, and disciplinary differences* (An Unpublished report). Tel Aviv: Tel Aviv University.

Hativa, N. (2000). *Teaching for effective learning in higher education*. Kluwer Academic Publishers. doi:10.1007/978-94-010-0902-7

Haynes, S. N., Richard, D. C. S., & Kubany, E. S. (1995). Content validity in psychological assessment: A functional approach to concepts and methods. *Psychological Assessment*, *8*(3), 238–247. doi:10.1037/1040-3590.7.3.238

Health Care News. (2001). *The increasing impact of eHealth on physician behavior.* Available at: http://www.harrisinteractive.com/news/newsletters/healthnews/HI_HealthCareNews.2001vol1_Iss31.pdf

Heinemann, G. D., & Zeiss, A. M. (Eds.). (2002). *Team performance in health care*. Kluwer Academic Publishers.

Helquist, J. H., Kruse, J., & Nunamaker, F., Jr. J. (2010). Participant-driven approach to autonomously cluster brainstorming ideas. In E-Collaboration Technologies and Organizational Performance: Current and Future Trends. IGI Global.

Helquist, J. H., Kruse, J., Deokar, A., & Meservy, T. O. (2013). Enabling large group collaboration. In Collaboration Systems: Concept, Value, and Use (pp. 128–142). M.E. Sharpe, Inc.

Helquist, J. H., Kruse, J., Meservy, T. O., & Deokar, A. (2011). Facilitating large group collaboration. In Collaboration Science, Technologies, Processes and Applications: Vol. Advances i. Armonk, NY: M.E. Sharpe, Inc.

Helquist, J., Diller, C. B. R., & Kruse, J. (2019). Crowdsourcing Convergence: Aggregating Partial Clusters to Facilitate Collaborative Convergence. *Proceedings of the 52nd Hawaii International Conference on System Sciences. (HICSS 2019).* Retrieved from https://scholarspace.manoa.hawaii.edu/handle/10125/59492

Helquist, J. H., Deokar, A. V., Meservy, T. O., & Kruse, J. (2011). Dynamic collaboration: Participant-driven agile processes for complex tasks. *ACM SIGMIS Database*, *42*(2), 95–115. doi:10.1145/1989098.1989104

Helquist, J. H., Kruse, J., & Adkins, M. (2006a). Developing large scale participant-driven group support systems: An approach to facilitating large groups. In R. H. Sprague Jr, R. O. Briggs, & J. F. Nunamaker Jr. (Eds.), *First HICSS Symposium on Field and Case Studies of Collaboration*. Los Alamitos, CA: IEEE Computer Society Press.

Helquist, J. H., Kruse, J., & Adkins, M. (2006b). Group support systems for very large groups: A peer review process to filter brainstorming input. *Proceedings of the Americas Conference on Information Systems.*

Helquist, J. H., Kruse, J., & Adkins, M. (2008). Participant-driven collaborative convergence. In *Proceedings of the 41st Annual Hawaii International Conference on System Sciences*. Computer Society Press.

Helquist, J. H., Kruse, J., & Nunamaker, J. F. Jr. (2009). Synchronicity and group ability to autonomously cluster brainstorming ideas. *International Journal of e-Collaboration*, *5*(4), 67–81. doi:10.4018/jec.2009062605

Henault, R. G., Eugenio, K. R., Kelliher, A. F., Alexis, G., & Conlin, P. R. (2002). Transmitting clinical recommendations for diabetes care via e-mail. *American Journal of Health-System Pharmacy*, *59*(22), 2166–2169. doi:10.1093/ajhp/59.22.2166

Henneman, E. A. (1995). Nurse-physician collaboration: A poststructuralist view. *Journal of Advanced Nursing*, *22*(2), 359–363. doi:10.1046/j.1365-2648.1995.22020359.x

Henneman, E. A., Lee, J. L., & Cohen, J. I. (1995). Collaboration: A concept analysis. *Journal of Advanced Nursing*, *21*(1), 103–109. doi:10.1046/j.1365-2648.1995.21010103.x

Hennig-Thurau, T., Henning, V., & Sattler, H. (2007). Consumer file sharing of motion pictures. *Journal of Marketing*, *71*(4), 1–18. doi:10.1509/jmkg.71.4.001

High Level Group on the Modernisation of Higher Education. (2014). *Report to the European Commission on New modes of learning and teaching in Higher Education.*

Higher Level Group on the Modernization of Higher Education. (2013). *Report to the European commission on improving the quality of teaching and learning in Europe's higher education institutions*. Publication Office of European Union.

Hilliges, O., Terrenghi, L., Boring, S., Kim, D., Richter, H., & Butz, A. (2007). Designing for Collaborative Creative Problem Solving. *Proceedings of the 6th ACM SIGCHI Conference on Creativity & Cognition*, 137–146. 10.1145/1254960.1254980

Hinds, P., & Kiesler, S. (2002). *Distributed Work*. MIT Press. doi:10.7551/mitpress/2464.001.0001

Hinostrosa, J. H., & Labbe, C. (2011). *Policies and practices for the use of information and communications technologies (ICTs) in education in Latin America and the Caribbean*. https://unesdoc.unesco.org/images/0022/002232/223251e.pdf

Hojat, M., Nasca, T. J., Cohen, M., Fields, S. K., Rattner, S. L., Griffiths, M., Ibarra, D., de Gonzalez, A. A.-G., Torres-Ruiz, A., Ibarra, G., & Garcia, A. (2001). Attitudes toward physician-nurse collaboration: A cross-cultural study of male and female physicians and nurses in the United States and Mexico. *Nursing Research*, *50*(1), 123–128. doi:10.1097/00006199-200103000-00008

Ho, K., Jarvis-Selinger, S., Norman, C., Li, L., Olatunbosun, T., Cressman, C., & Nguyen, A. (2010). Electronic Communities of Practice: Guidelines from a Project. *The Journal of Continuing Education in the Health Professions*, *30*(2), 139–143. doi:10.1002/chp.20071

Homeyer, S., Hoffmann, W., Hingst, P., Oppermann, R., & Dreier-Wolfgramm, A. (2018). Effects of interprofessional education for medical and nursing students: Enablers, barriers andexpectations for optimizing future interprofessional collaboration – a qualitative study. *BMC Nursing*, *17*(1), 13. doi:10.118612912-018-0279-x

Horwitz, E., Horwitz, M., & Cope, J. (1986). Foreign language classroom anxiety. *Modern Language Journal*, *70*(2), 125–132. doi:10.1111/j.1540-4781.1986.tb05256.x

Hosmer, L. T. (1995). Trust: The connecting link between organizational theory and philosophical ethics. *Academy of Management Review*, *20*(2), 379–403. doi:10.5465/amr.1995.9507312923

Hossain, M. (2012). Users' motivation to participate in online crowdsourcing platforms. In *2012 International Conference on Innovation Management and Technology Research*, pp. 310-315. IEEE. 10.1109/ICIMTR.2012.6236409

Hosta, M., & Zabkar, V. (2020). Antecedents of Environmentally and Socially Responsible Sustainable Consumer Behavior. *Journal of Business Ethics*. Advance online publication. doi:10.100710551-019-04416-0

Howe, J. (2006) The rise of crowdsourcing. *Wired*, *14*(6). https://www.wired.com/wired/archive/14.06/crowds.html

Hudson, B. (2002). Interprofessionality in health and social care: The Achilles' heel of partnership? *Journal of Interprofessional Care*, *16*(1), 7–17. doi:10.1080/13561820220104122

Huh, Y., & Reigeluth, C. M. (2017). Self-Regulated Learning: The Continuous-Change Conceptual Framework and a Vision of New Paradigm, Technology System, and Pedagogical Support. *Journal of Educational Technology Systems*, *46*(2), 191–214. doi:10.1177/0047239517710769

Hur, J. W., & Hara, N. (2007). Factors Cultivating Sustainable Online Communities for K-12 Teacher Professional Development. *Journal of Educational Computing Research*, *36*(3), 245–268. doi:10.2190/37H8-7GU7-5704-K470

Igbaria, M., Guimaraes, T., & Davis, G. (1995). Testing the determinants of microcomputer usage via a structural equation model. *Journal of Management Information Systems*, *11*(4), 87–114. doi:10.1080/07421222.1995.11518061

Illeris, L. (2012). *International Perspectives on Competence Development: Developing Skills and Capabilities*. Routledge. doi:10.4324/9780203523032

infoDev. (2006). *ICT in Health: The Role of ICTs in the Health Sector in Developing Countries*. InfoDev Activity File #1254. Retrieved from: http://www.infodev.org/en/Project.38.html

Jackson, J., MacKean, G., Cooke, T., & Lahtinen, M. (2017). Patient and provider experiences with relationship, information, and management continuity. *Patient Experience Journal*, *4*(3), Article 8. Available at: http://pxjournal.org/journal/vol4/iss3/8

Jackson, N. (2012). *Exploring learning ecologies*. Lulu. Com.

Jacobsen, D. I. (1999). Trust in political administrative relations: The case of local authorities in Norway and Tanzania. *World Development*, *27*(5), 839–853. doi:10.1016/S0305-750X(99)00032-7

Jaime, A., Domínguez, C., Sánchez, A., & Blanco, J. M. (2013). Interuniversity telecollaboration to improve academic results and identify preferred communication tools. *Computers & Education*, *64*, 63–69. doi:10.1016/j.compedu.2013.01.008

Janiesch, C., & Kuhlenkamp, J. (2018). Enhancing business process execution with a context engine. *Journal of Business Process Management*.

Janz, B. D., Colquitt, J. A., & Noe, R. A. (2006). Knowledge Worker Team Effectiveness: The Role of Autonomy, Interdependence, Team Development, and Contextual Support Variables. *Personnel Psychology*, *50*(4), 877–904. doi:10.1111/j.1744-6570.1997.tb01486.x

Jekins, J., & Vissere, G. (2001). *E-learning-Everybody's Business*. Retrieved May 10, 2011 from www.imaginal.nl

Jessup, S., Gibson, A., Capiola, A., Alarcon, G., & Borders, M. (2020, January 7). *Investigating the Effect of Trust Manipulations on Affect over Time in Human-Human versus Human-Robot Interactions*. doi:10.24251/HICSS.2020.068

Jessup, L. M., Connolly, T., & Galegher, J. (1990). The Effects of Anonymity on GDSS Group Process with an Idea-Generating Task. *Management Information Systems Quarterly*, *14*(3), 313–321. doi:10.2307/248893

JISC. (2013*). Designing Spaces for Effective Learning - A guide to 21st century learning space design*. Retrieved July 20, 2013, from https://www.jisc.ac.uk/uploaded_documents/JISClearningspaces.pdf

Johnson, D. W., & Johnson, R. T. (1996). Cooperation and the use of technology. In D. H. Jonassen (Ed.), *Handbook of research for educational communications and technology* (pp. 170–198). Simon & Schuster Macmillan.

Johnson, K. K., Mun, J. M., & Chae, Y. (2016). Antecedents to internet use to collaboratively consume apparel. *Journal of Fashion Marketing and Management: An International Journal*, *20*(4), 370–382. doi:10.1108/JFMM-12-2015-0092

Joint Commission on Accreditation of Healthcare Organizations. (2006). *Critical Access Hospital and Hospital National Patient Safety Goals*. Retrieved from: http://www.jcaho.org/accredited+organizations/patient+safety/06_npsg/06_npsg_cah_hap.htm

Jonassen, D. (2000). Revisiting Activity Theory as a Framework for Designing Student- Centered Learning Environments. In D. Jonassen & S. Land (Eds.), *Theoretical foundations of Learning Environments*. LEA.

Jr, N. (1996). Lessons from a dozen years of group support systems research: A discussion of lab and field findings. *Journal of Management Information Systems*, *13*(3), 163–207. doi:10.1080/07421222.1996.11518138

Kadefors, A. (2004). Trust in project relationships—Inside the black box. *International Journal of Project Management*, *22*(3), 175–182. doi:10.1016/S0263-7863(03)00031-0

Kahn, W. A. (1990). Psychological conditions of personal engagement and disengagement at work. *Academy of Management Journal*, *33*(4), 692–724.

KAICIID. (2020). *COVID 19 and Religion*. https://www.kaiciid.org/dialogue-knowledge-hub/webinars/covid-19-and-religion

Kankanhalli, A., Tan, B. C. Y., & Wei, K.-K. (2005). Contributing Knowledge to Electronic Knowledge Repositories: An Empirical Investigation. *Management Information Systems Quarterly*, *29*(1), 113–143. doi:10.2307/25148670

Kanwar, A., Balasubramanian, K., & Carr, A. (2019). Changing the TVET paradigm: New models for lifelong learning. *International Journal of Training Research*, *17*(1), 54–68. doi:10.1080/14480220.2019.1629722

Kaplan, A., & Haenlein, M. (2010). Users of the world, unite! The challenges and opportunities of social media. *Business Horizons*, *53*(1), 59–68. doi:10.1016/j.bushor.2009.09.003

Karam, M., Brault, I., Van Durme, T., & Macq, J. (2018). Comparing Interprofessional and Interorganizational Collaboration in Healthcare: A Systematic Review of The Qualitative Research. *International Journal of Nursing Studies*, *79*(2), 70–83. doi:10.1016/j.ijnurstu.2017.11.002

Keegan, D. (1986). *The foundations of distance education* (2nd ed.). Routledge.

Keller, J. (2010, November). Stack Overflow's crowdsourcing model guarantees success. *Atlantic (Boston, Mass.)*, 18.

Kember, D. (1997). A reconceptualisation of the research into university academics' conception of teaching. *Learning and Instruction*, *7*(3), 255–275. doi:10.1016/S0959-4752(96)00028-X

Kember, D., & Kwan, K. P. (1999). Lectures' approaches to teaching and their relationship to conceptions of good teaching. In N. Hativa & P. Goodyear (Eds.), *Teacher thinking, beliefs and knowledge in higher education.* Kluwer Academic Publishers.

Këpuska, V., & Bohouta, G. (2018). Next-generation of virtual personal assistants (Microsoft Cortana, Apple Siri, Amazon Alexa and Google Home). *2018 IEEE 8th Annual Computing and Communication Workshop and Conference (CCWC)*, 99–103. 10.1109/CCWC.2018.8301638

Keys, A. (2020). *Rotary Club of Albuquerque offers support to food pantries, Navajo Nation.* KRQE. https://www.krqe.com/news/albuquerque-metro/rotary-club-of-albuquerque-offers-support-to-food-pantries-navajo-nation-during-covid-19-crisis/ Kinlani/Flagstaff

Keyton, J. (2011). *Communication and organizational culture: A key to understanding work experience*. Sage.

Khan, M. T. (2014). Relationship Marketing - Some Aspects (Review). *International Journal of Information. Business and Management*, *6*(2), 108–122.

Kietzmann, J. H., Hermkens, K., McCarthy, I. P., & Silvestre, B. S. (2011). Social media? Get serious! Understanding the functional building blocks of social media. *Business Horizons*, *54*(4), 241–251. doi:10.1016/j.bushor.2011.01.005

King, K. (2011). Professional learning in unlikely spaces: Social media and virtual com- munities as professional development. *Intenational Journal of Emerging Technologies in Learning*, *6*(4), 40–46. doi:10.3991/ijet.v6i4.1765

Kittler, A. F., Carlson, B. A., & Harris, C. (2004). Primary care physician attitudes towards using a secure web based portal designed to facilitate electronic communication with patients. *Informatics in Primary Care*, *12*(2), 129–138.

Klamma, R., Cao, Y., & Vuoriaky, R. (2009). Social network analysis of 45,000 schools: A case study of technology-enhanced learning in Europe. *Lecture Notes in Computer Science*. 10.1007/978-3-642-04636-0_18

Klavins, X. (2005). *Instant Messaging Tool for Collaboration in a Peer to-Peer Network: MyBook Instant Messenger.* Thesis Paper. https://www.ohiolink.edu/etd/sendpdf.cgi/KLAVINS%20AINARS.pdf?acc_num=ucin1109305316

Kleinmann, H. (1977). Avoidance behavior in adult second language acquisition. *Language Learning*, *27*(1), 93–107. doi:10.1111/j.1467-1770.1977.tb00294.x

Knight, P. T., & Trowler, P. R. (2001). *Departmental leadership in higher education.* Society for Research into Higher Education and Open University Press.

Kock, N. (2010). Using WarpPLS in e-collaboration studies: An overview of five main analysis steps. *International Journal of e-Collaboration, 6*(4), 1–11. doi:10.4018/jec.2010100101

Kock, N. (2011). Using WarpPLS in e-collaboration studies: Descriptive statistics, settings, and key analysis results. *International Journal of e-Collaboration, 7*(2), 1–18. doi:10.4018/jec.2011040101

Kock, N. (2013). Using WarpPLS in E-Collaboration Studies: What if I Have Only One Group and One Condition? *International Journal of e-Collaboration, 9*(3), 1–12. doi:10.4018/jec.2013070101

Kock, N. (2015a). Common method bias in PLS-SEM: A full collinearity assessment approach. *International Journal of e-Collaboration, 11*(4), 1–10. doi:10.4018/ijec.2015100101

Kock, N. (2015b). A note on how to conduct a factor-based PLS-SEM analysis. *International Journal of e-Collaboration, 11*(3), 1–9. doi:10.4018/ijec.2015070101

Kock, N., & Lynn, G. S. (2012). Lateral collinearity and misleading results in variance-based SEM: An illustration and recommendations. *Journal of the Association for Information Systems, 13*(7), 546–580. doi:10.17705/1jais.00302

Kokkos, A. (2001). Tutor-counselor's role in Open and Distance Learning: the case of Hellenic Open University (in Greek). In *Proceedings of 1st International Conference of Open and Distance Learning, issue A.* Patra: Hellenic Open University.

Kools, M., & Stoll, L. (2016). What makes a school a learning organization? *OECD Education Working Papers.* doi:10.1787/5JLWM62B3BVH-EN

Kordaki, M., & Siempos, H. (2010). The JiGSAW Collaborative Method within the online computer science classroom. In *The 2nd International Conference on Computer Supported Education,* (pp. 65-74). Academic Press.

Kradolfer, M., & Geppert, A. (1999). Dynamic workflow schema evolution based on workflow type versioning and workflow migration. In *Proceedings of the International Conference on Cooperative Information Systems,* (pp. 104-114). Edinburgh, UK: IEEE. 10.1109/COOPIS.1999.792162

Kraut, R. E., Fussell, S. R., Brennan, S. E., & Siegel, J. (2002). Understanding Effects of Proximity on Collaboration: Implications for Technologies to Support Remote Collaborative Work. In P. Hinds & S. Kiesler (Eds.), *Distributed Work* (pp. 139–162). MIT Press.

Kripalani, S., LeFevre, F., Phillips, C. O., Williams, M. V., Basaviah, P., & Baker, D. (2007). Deficits in Communication and Information Transfer between Hospital-Based and Primary Care Physicians Implications for Patient Safety and Continuity of Care Coordination. *Journal of the American Medical Association, 297*(8), 831–841. doi:10.1001/jama.297.8.831

Krogstad, U., Hofoss, D., & Hjortdahl, P. (2004). Doctor and nurse perception of inter-professional co-operation in hospitals. *International Journal for Quality in Health Care, 16*(6), 491–497. doi:10.1093/intqhc/mzh082

Kruse, J., Helquist, J. H., & Adkins, M. (2008). Large-scale collaboration for ill-structured problems. *Thirteenth International Command and Control Research Symposium.*

Kuhn, T. S. (1962). The Structure of Scientific Revolutions (2nd ed.). The University of Chicago Press.

Kumar & Anupama. (2018). A Study of Digital Payments: Trends, Challenges and Implementation in Indian Banking System. *International Journal of Virtual Communities and Social Networking, 10*(1), 46 – 63.

La Rosa, M., & Dumas, M. (2008). Configurable Process Models: How To Adopt Standard Practices In Your How Way? *BPTrends Newsletter.*

Lake Huron Fishing Club. (2020). *Message from the President*. LHSC. Retrieved on 07/15/2020 at https://www.lakehuronfishingclub.com/

Lambert, D. M., & Harrington, T. C. (1990). Measuring Nonresponse Bias in Mail Surveys. *Journal of Business Logistics*, *11*(1), 5–25.

Lamberton, C. P., & Rose, R. L. (2012). When is ours better than mine? A framework for understanding and altering participation in commercial sharing systems. *Journal of Marketing*, *76*(4), 109–125. doi:10.1509/jm.10.0368

LAMS Community. (n.d.). *LAMS community*. Retrieved from www.lamscommunity.org

LAMS. (n.d.). *What is LAMS?* Retrieved from http://www.lamsfoundation.org/

Landqvist, F., & Teigland, R. (2005). Collective Action in Electronic Networks of Practice: An Empirical Study of Three Online Social Structures. In P. Van Den Besselaar, G. De Michelis, J. Preece, & C. Simone (Eds.), *Communities and Technologies 2005*. Springer. doi:10.1007/1-4020-3591-8_19

Lassoued, Y., Bouzguenda, L., & Mahmoud, T. (2016). Context-aware business process versions management. *International Journal of e-Collaboration*, *12*(3), 7–33. doi:10.4018/IJeC.2016070102

Latchem, C. (2017). *Using ICTs and blended learning in transforming TVET*. UNESCO and Commonwealth of Learning.

Lauvås, P., Hofgaard Lycke, K., & Handa, G. (2004). *Kollegaveiledning i skolen (Professional guidance in schools)*. Cappelen Akademisk Forlag.

Lavanya, V. (2019). Impact of Digital Banking on Indian Economy. *Int J Recent Sci Res.*, *10*(09), 34633–34635. doi:10.24327/ijrsr.2019.1009.3937

Lave, J., & Wenger, E. (1991). *Situated Learning: Legitimate Peripheral Participation*. Cambridge University Press. doi:10.1017/CBO9780511815355

Lave, J., & Wenger, E. (1998). *Communities of Practice: Learning, Meaning, and Identity*. Cambridge University Press.

Lee, O. F., & Meuter, M. L. (2010). The adoption of technology orientation in healthcare delivery: Case study of a large-scale hospital and healthcare system's electronic health record. *International Journal of Pharmaceutical and Healthcare Marketing*, *4*(4), 355–374. doi:10.1108/17506121011095209

Lee, S., Lee, J., & Lee, K. (2017). Designing Intelligent Assistant Through User Participations. *Proceedings of the 2017 Conference on Designing Interactive Systems*, 173–177. 10.1145/3064663.3064733

Lemieux-Charles, L., & McGuire, W. (2006). What do we know about heath care team effectiveness? A review of the literature. *Medical Care Research and Review: MCRR*, *63*(3), 263–300. doi:10.1177/1077558706287003

Leonhardt, P. (2006, Apr. 19). Political clout in the age of out sourcing. *The New York Times*.

LessonLAMS. (n.d.). *LessonLAMS*. Retrieved from https://lessonlams.com/lams/

Liederman, E. M., Lee, J. C., Baquero, V. H., & Seites, P. G. (2005). Patient-physician web messaging: The impact on message volume and satisfaction. *Journal of General Internal Medicine*, *20*(1), 52–57. doi:10.1111/j.1525-1497.2005.40009.x

Liederman, E. M., & Morefield, C. S. (2003). Web messaging: A new tool for patient-physician communication. *Journal of the American Medical Informatics Association*, *10*(3), 263–274. doi:10.1197/jamia.M1259

Linares Pons, N., Piñero Pérez, Y., Rodríguez Stiven, E., & Pérez Quintero, L. (2014). Diseño de un modelo de Gestión del Conocimiento para mejorar el desarrollo de equipos de proyectos informáticos. *Revista Espanola la de Documentacion Cientifica*, *37*(2), e044. Advance online publication. doi:10.3989/redc.2014.2.1036

Lindeke, L. L., & Block, D. E. (1998). Maintaining professional integrity in the midst of interdisciplinary collaboration. *Nursing Outlook*, *46*(5), 213–218. doi:10.1016/S0029-6554(98)90052-5

Lindell, M. K., & Whitney, D. J. (2001). Accounting for Common Method Variance in Cross-Sectional Research Designs. *The Journal of Applied Psychology*, *86*(1), 114–121. doi:10.1037/0021-9010.86.1.114

Lindenberg, S. (2001). Intrinsic motivation in a new light. *Kyklos*, *54*(2–3), 317–342. doi:10.1111/1467-6435.00156

Lin, F., Lin, S., & Huang, T. (2008). Knowledge sharing and creation in a teachers' professional virtual community. *Computers & Education*, *50*(3), 742–756. doi:10.1016/j.compedu.2006.07.009

Lingard, L., Regehr, G., Orser, B., Reznick, R., Baker, G. R., Doran, D., Espin, S., Bohnen, J., & Whyte, S. (2008). Evaluation of a preoperative checklist and team briefing among surgeons, nurses, and anesthesiologists to reduce failures in communication. *Archives of Surgery (Chicago, Ill.)*, *143*(1), 12–17. doi:10.1001/archsurg.2007.21

Lingard, L., Reznick, R., Espin, S., Regehr, G., & DeVito, I. (2002). Team communications in the operating room: Talk patterns, sites of tension, and implications for novices. *Academic Medicine*, *77*(3), 232–237. doi:10.1097/00001888-200203000-00013

Lingard, L., Whyte, S., Espin, S., Baker, G. R., Orser, B., & Doran, D. (2006). Towards safer interprofessional communication: Constructing a model of "utility" from preoperative team briefings. *Journal of Interprofessional Care*, *20*(5), 471–483. doi:10.1080/13561820600921865

Lionarakis, A. (2001). Open and Distance polymorphic education: considerations on a qualitative approach of designing educational material (in Greek). In Views and considerations on ODL. Athens: Propompos.

Lionarakis, A. (1998). Polymorphic Education: A pedagogical framework for open and distance learning. In A. Szucs & A. Wagner (Eds.), *Transformation, Innovation and Tradition Roles and Perspectives of Open and Distance Learning* (pp. 499–504). University of Bologna, Universities in a Digital Era.

Liu, H., & Chang, T. (2018). Modularity, Flexibility and Globalization: The Transformation of the University's learning paradigm based on information Technology - a case study based on MIT. *Open Education Research*, *24*(3), 19–26.

Liu, X. (2012). On student - centered. *Journal of Higher Education (Columbus, Ohio)*, *33*(8), 1–6.

Luchs, M. G., Naylor, R. W., Rose, R. L., Catlin, J. R., Gau, R., & Kapitan, S. (2011). Toward a sustainable marketplace: Expanding options and benefits for consumers. *Journal of Research for Consumers*, *19*(1), 1–12.

Lu, H., Li, Y., Chen, M., Kim, H., & Serikawa, S. (2018). Brain Intelligence: Go beyond Artificial Intelligence. *Mobile Networks and Applications*, *23*(2), 368–375. doi:10.100711036-017-0932-8

Luhmann, N. (2000). Familiarity, confidence, trust: Problems and alternatives. In *Trust: making and breaking cooperative relations* (pp. 94–107). Department of Sociology, University of Oxford. Retrieved from: http://www.sociology.ox.ac.uk/papers/luhmann94-107.pdf

Lyngstad, M., Melby, L., Grimsmo, A., & Hellesø, R. (2013). Toward Increased Patient Safety? Electronic Communication of Medication Information Between Nurses in Home Health Care and General Practitioners. *Home Health Care Management & Practice*, *25*(5), 203–211. doi:10.1177/1084822313480365

Lynn, M. R. (1986). Determination and Quantification of Content Validity. *Nursing Research*, *35*(4), 382–385.

Lytvyn, A., Lytvyn, V., Rudenko, L., Pelekh, Y., Didenko, O., Muszkieta, R., & Żukow, W. (2020). Informatization of technical vocational schools: Theoretical foundations and practical approaches. *Education and Information Technologies*, *25*(1), 583–609. doi:10.100710639-019-09966-4

MacKenzie, S. B., & Podsakoff, P. M. (2012). Common method bias in marketing: Causes, mechanisms, and procedural remedies. *Journal of Retailing*, *88*(4), 542–555. doi:10.1016/j.jretai.2012.08.001

Maedche, A., Morana, S., Schacht, S., Werth, D., & Krumeich, J. (2016). Advanced User Assistance Systems. *Business & Information Systems Engineering*, *58*(5), 367–370. doi:10.100712599-016-0444-2

Mahendra, N., Bayles, K. A., Tomoeda, C. K., & Kim, E. S. (2005). Diversity and Learner-Centered Education. *ASHA Leader*, *10*(16), 12–19. doi:10.1044/leader.FTR3.10162005.12

Manaikkamakl, P. (2007). Personal technology orientation in R&D: A tool to intensify organizational learning. *Development and Learning in Organizations*, *21*(6), 18–20. doi:10.1108/14777280710828594

Mann, M. Y., Lloyd-Puryear, M. A., & Lizer, D. (2006). Enhancing communication in the 21st Century. *Pediatrics*, *117*(4, Supplement 3), 315–319. doi:10.1542/peds.2005-2633K

Manoj, P.K. (2017). Digital Transformation in Indian Banking: A Study of Cheque Truncation System and other Technolgical Advances. *International Journal of Emerging Trends & Technology in Computer Sciences, 6*(6), 172-179.

Manser Payne, E., Peltier, J. W., & Barger, V. A. (2018). Mobile banking and AI-enabled mobile banking: The differential effects of technological and non-technological factors on digital natives' perceptions and behavior. *Journal of Research in Interactive Marketing*, *12*(3), 328–346. doi:10.1108/JRIM-07-2018-0087

Mansour, O., Askenas, L., & Ghazawneh, A. (2013). Social media and organizing – An empirical analysis of the role of Wiki affordances in organizing practices. *Thirty-Fourth International Conference on Information Systems*. https://portal.research.lu.se/portal/files/70684599/FULLTEXT01.pdf

Markus, H., & Kitayama, S. (1991). Culture and the self: Implications for cognition, emotion, and motivation. *Psychological Review*, *98*(2), 224–253. doi:10.1037/0033-295X.98.2.224

Mathematics Educators. (2018). *Mathematics Educators. StackExchange Forum*. https://matheducators.stackexchange.com

Matralis, Ch. (1998). Goal and Objectives (in Greek). In The educational material and new technologies, Open and Distance Learning (vol. C). Patra: Hellenic Open University.

Matsagouras, E. (2002). *Critical thinking in teaching*. Gutenberg. (in Greek)

Mattson, T., & Davidson, E. (2018). Promoting Domain-specific Forum Participation via Off-topic ForumParticipation in Electronic Networks of Practice. *Communications of the Association for Information Systems*, *43*, 35. Advance online publication. doi:10.17705/1CAIS.04335

Matziou, V., Vlahioti, E., Perdikaris, P., Matziou, T., Megapanou, E., & Petsios, K. (2014). Physician and nursing perceptions concerning interprofessional communication and collaboration. *Journal of Interprofessional Care*, *28*(6), 526–533. doi:10.3109/13561820.2014.934338

Mayer, R. C., Davis, J. H., & Schoorman, F. D. (1995). An Integrative Model of Organization Trust.'. *Academy of Management Review*, *20*(3), 709–733. doi:10.5465/amr.1995.9508080335

Mcalpine, L. (2004). Designing learning as well as teaching—A Research-based model for instruction that emphasizes learner practice. *Active Learning in Higher Education*, *5*(05), 119–134. doi:10.1177/1469787404043809

McKenney, S., & Reeves, T. (2012). *Conducting educational design research*. Routledge.

McKenney, S., & Reeves, T. (2013). Systematic Review of Design-Based Research Progress: Is a Little Knowledge a Dangerous Thing? *Educational Researcher*, *42*(2), 97–100. doi:10.3102/0013189X12463781

McTear, M. F. (2017). The rise of the conversational interface: A new kid on the block? Lecture Notes in Computer Science (Including Subseries Lecture Notes in Artificial Intelligence and Lecture Notes in Bioinformatics), 10341, 38–49. Scopus. doi:10.1007/978-3-319-69365-1_3

McTear, M., Callejas, Z., & Griol, D. (2016). The conversational interface. Springer, 6(94), 102.

McTear, M. F. (2004). *Spoken dialogue technology: Toward the conversational user interface*. Springer Science & Business Media. doi:10.1007/978-0-85729-414-2

Mechanic, D. (1996). Changing medical organization and the erosion of trust. *The Milbank Quarterly*, *74*(2), 171–189. doi:10.2307/3350245

Mechanic, D. (1998). Trust in the provision of medical care. *Journal of Health Politics, Policy and Law*, *23*(411), 661–686. doi:10.1215/03616878-23-4-661

Mechanic, D., & Meyer, S. (2000). Concepts of trust among patients with serious illness. *Social Science & Medicine*, *51*(5), 657–668. doi:10.1016/S0277-9536(00)00014-9

Media, T. (2018). *Teaching Media*. http://www.teachingmedia.org

Mendix.com. (2020). *A Brief introduction to Scrum*. https://www.mendix.com/agile-framework/#:~:text=Agile%20is%20an%20umbrella%20term,%2C%20and%20Feature%2DDriven%20Development

Merriam-Webster OnLine Dictionary. (n.d.). http://www.merriamwebster.com/dictionary/communication

Meyer, R. (2007). *Knowledge Visualization*. LMU, Department of Informatics. https://www.medien.ifi.lmu.de/

Meyer, M. W. (1985). *Limits to bureaucratic growth*. De Gruyter. doi:10.1515/9783110865295

Michos, K., & Hernández-Leoa, D. (2020). CIDA: A collective inquiry framework to study and support teachers as designers in technological environments. *Computers & Education*, *143*, 103679. Advance online publication. doi:10.1016/j.compedu.2019.103679

Miller, K. (2005). *Communication theories: Perspectives, processes, and contexts* (2nd ed.). McGraw-Hill.

Ministry of Social Development. (2020). *COVID-19 Community Wellbeing and Resilience Grant*. New Zealand Government. Retrieved on 07/15/2020 at https://www.msd.govt.nz/a

Mior, S., Barnsley, J., Boon, H., Ashbury, F. D., & Haig, R. (2010). Designing a framework for the delivery of collaborative musculoskeletal care involving chiropractors and physicians in community-based primary care. *Journal of Interprofessional Care*, *24*(6), 678–689. doi:10.3109/13561821003608757

Misztal, B. A. (1996). *Trust in modern societies: The search for the bases of moral order*. Polity Press.

MOE. (2019). *Education Statistics 2019*. http://www.moe.gov.cn/s78/A03/moe_560/jytjsj_2019/qg/

Mohammed, S., Ferzandi, L., & Hamilton, K. (2010). Metaphor no more: A 15-year review of the team mental model construct. *Journal of Management*, *36*(4), 876–910. doi:10.1177/0149206309356804

Mohlmann, M. (2015). Collaborative consumption: Determinants of satisfaction and the likelihood of using a sharing economy option again. *Journal of Consumer Behaviour*, *14*(3), 193–207. doi:10.1002/cb.1512

Molleman, E., Broekhuis, M., Stoffels, R., & Jaspers, F. (2008). How health care complexity leads to cooperation and affects the autonomy of health care professionals. Health Care Analysis. An. *International Journal of Health Care Philosophy and Policy*, *16*(4), 329–341. doi:10.100710728-007-0080-6

Mondal, S., & Nandi, G. C. (2018). *Personal robot: Towards developing a complete humanoid robot assistant using the Internet of Things*. Scopus., doi:10.1109/UIC-ATC.2017.8397453

Money Control News. (2020, April 2). *Fintech: Banks play a vital role in engaging customers amidst the COVID 19 spread*. https://www.moneycontrol.com/news/technology/fintechs-banks-play-a-vital-role-in-engaging-customers-amidst-the-covid-19-spread-5101931.html

Monferrer, D., Moliner, M. A., & Estrada, M. (2019). Increasing customer loyalty through customer engagement in the retail banking industry. *Spanish Journal of Marketing – ESIC*, *23*(3), 461–484.

Moodle. (2020). *Moodle*. Retrieved April 28, 2020 from https://docs.moodle.org/38/en/About_Moodle

Moodle. https://moodle.org

Moolenar, N. (2012). A social network perspective on teacher collaboration in schools: Theory, methodology, and applications. *American Journal of Education*, *119*(1), 7–39. doi:10.1086/667715

Moore, M. G. (1973). Toward a theory of Independent Learning and Teaching. *The Journal of Higher Education*, *44*(9), 661–679. doi:10.2307/1980599

Moore, M. G. (1980). Independent study. In R. Boyd & J. Apps (Eds.), *Redefining the Discipline of Adult Education* (pp. 16–31). Jossey-Bass.

Moqbel, M., Nevo, S., & Kock, N. (2013). Organizational members' use of social networking sites and job performance. *Information Technology & People*, *26*(3), 240–264. doi:10.1108/ITP-10-2012-0110

Morgan, S., Pullon, S., & McKinlay, E. (2015). Observation of interprofessional collaborative practice in primary care teams: An integrative literature review. *International Journal of Nursing Studies*, *52*(7), 1217–1230. doi:10.1016/j.ijnurstu.2015.03.008

Murli Nagasundaram. (2008). E-Collaboration Through Blogging. Boise State University. Doi:10.4018/978-1-59904-000-4.ch031

Mutual Aid. (2020). *Mutual aid needs list, summer 2020*. https://kinlanimutualaid.org/

Nardi, B. A., & Whittaker, S. (2002). The Place of Face-to-Face Communication in Distributed Work. In P. Hinds & S. Kiesler (Eds.), *Distributed Work* (pp. 83–110). MIT Press.

Nass, C., & Moon, Y. (2000). Machines and Mindlessness: Social Responses to Computers. *The Journal of Social Issues*, *56*(1), 81–103. doi:10.1111/0022-4537.00153

Neelu & Kumar. (2019). Factor affecting consumer satisfaction in cashless payment systems in India with respect to Paytm and BHIM. *International Journal of Recent Technology and Engineering, 8*(3S2), 10-15.

NeoKosmos. (2020). *Xanthi teams makes 3D masks to help medical staff*. NeoKosmos publication. https://neoskosmos.com

Newman, J. (1998). The dynamics of trust. In A. Coulson (Ed.), *Trust and contracts: Relationships in local government, health and public services*. The Polity Press.

Nieto, S. (2005). *Why we teach*. Teacher College Press.

Nigam, A. (2020). *Future of Fintech in a Post Covid world*. https://timesofindia.indiatimes.com/blogs/voices/future-of-fintech-in-a-post-covid-world/

Nilsson, N. J. (2014). *Principles of Artificial Intelligence*. Morgan Kaufmann.

Nizzolino, S. (2020). *L'avvento della Open Education. L'Istruzione pubblica e l'educazione non formale nella Società della Conoscenza*. Edizioni Progetto Cultura.

Nonaka, I., & Konno, N. (1998). The Concept of "Ba": Building a Foundation for Knowledge Creation. *California Management Review*, *40*(3), 40–54. doi:10.2307/41165942

Norman, D. A., & Spohrer, J. C. (1996). Learner-centered education. *Communications of the ACM*, *39*(4), 24–27. doi:10.1145/227210.227215

North Coast Church. (2020). *Covid 19 resources*. https://www.northcoastchurch.com/covid-19-resources/

Nulty, D. (2011). Peer and self-assessment in the first year of university. *Assessment & Evaluation in Higher Education*, *36*(5), 493–507. doi:10.1080/02602930903540983

Nunnally, J. (1978). *Psychometric methods*. McGraw-Hill.

Nunnally, J. C., & Bernstein, I. H. (1994). *Psychometric Theory* (3rd ed.). McGraw-Hill.

O'Connor, M., & Das, A. (2009). SQWRL: a query language for OWL. In *Proceedings of the 6th International Conference on OWL: Experiences and Directions* (pp. 208-215). Chantilly, VA: Academic Press.

O'connor, P., O'dea, A., Lydon, S., Offiah, G., Scott, J., Flannery, A., Lang, B., Hoban, A., Armstrong, C., & Byrne, D. (2016). A mixed-methods study of the causes and impact of poor teamwork between junior doctors and nurses. *International Journal for Quality in Health Care*, *28*(3), 339–345. doi:10.1093/intqhc/mzw036

O'Sullivan, E. (1999). *Transformative learning: Educational vision for the 21st century*. Zed Books.

OECD Organisation for Economic Co-operation and Development. (2020). TALIS 2018 Results (Volume II): Teachers and School Leaders as Valued Professionals. TALIS, OECD Publishing. doi:10.1787/19cf08df-en

Online, E. T. (2020, June 17). *Coronavirus impact on motor insurance, health and life insurance*. PWC Report. https://economictimes.indiatimes.com/wealth/personal-finance-news/coronavirus-impact-on-motor-health-and-life-insurance-pwc-report/articleshow/76418575.cms?from=mdr

Open Clinical. (2011). eHealth. *Open Clinical: Knowledge Management for Medical Care*. Retrieved from: http://www.openclinical.org/e-Health.html#applications

Open eClass platform. (2020). *The Open eClass platform*. Retrieved April 28, 2020 from https://www.openeclass.org/en/about/

Oreg, S., & Nov, O. (2008). Exploring motivations for contributing to open source initiatives: The roles of contribution context and personal values. *Computers in Human Behavior*, *24*(5), 2055–2073. doi:10.1016/j.chb.2007.09.007

Ørngreen, R. (2015). *Reflections on Design-Based Research In Online Educational and Competence Development Projects*. Paper presented at Human Work Interaction Design (HWID), Denmark.

Pagaria, V. (2020, April 16). *The Fallout of Covid 19 on the BFSI Sector, ET BFSI.Com*. https://bfsi.economictimes.indiatimes.com/blog/the-fallout-of-covid-19-on-the-bfsi-sector/4170

Palanisamy, R., & Verville, J. (2015). Factors enabling communication based collaboration in interprofessional healthcare practice: A case study. *International Journal of e-Collaboration*, *11*(2), 8–27. doi:10.4018/ijec.2015040102

Palfrey, J., & Gasser, U. (2008). *Born digital: Understanding the first generation of Digital Natives*. Basic Books.

Pallab, S., & Munish, M. (2015). Online banking adoption – A factor validation and satisfaction causation study in the context of Indian Banking Customers. *International Journal of Bank Marketing*, *33*(6), 760–785.

Palloff, R., & Pratt, K. (1999). *Building Learning Communities in Cyberspace: effective strategies for the online classroom.* Jossey-Bass.

Papadakis, S., Kordaki, M., & Hadzilacos, T. (2007). Learning Design: the views of Prospective Computer Professionals. In *Proceedings of Informatics Education Europe II Conference*, (pp. 2-11). Academic Press.

Papadimitriou, S. (2013). Open Educational Resources and Practices Unfold a Brand New World Towards an Open Higher Education. In *Open Education 2030 Contribution to the JRC-IPTS Call for Vision Papers Part III: Higher Education.* Retrieved August 20, 2013 from http://is.jrc.ec.europa.eu/pages/EAP/documents/All_OE2030_HE_v%204_author%20 revised_OK.pdf

Papadimitriou, S., & Lionarakis, A. (2009). Tutor-counselor's role in Open and Distance Learning and the development of his support mechanism in ODL (in Greek). *The Open Education Journal*, *6*(1), 106-122. Retrieved on June 2, 2011 from: http://journal.openet.gr/index.php/openjournal/article/view/103

Papadimitriou, S., Papadakis, S., & Lionarakis, A. (2017). Supporting Electronic Collaborative Experiences at Universities based on Learning Spaces and LAMS in IGI Global. *Proceedings International Journal of e-Collaboration (IJeC).* Retrieved June 2, 2020 from https://www.igi-global.com/journal/international-journal-collaboration-ijec/1090

Papadimitriou, S., Papadakis, S., Lionarakis, A., & Kameas, A. (2011). A proposal of using Learning Activities Management System (LAMS) to support the work of Educators in HOU. In A. Lionarakis (Ed.), *Proceedings of the 6th International Conference in Open & Distance Learning - November 2011*. Retrieved March 21, 2012 from http://icodl.openet.gr/index.php/icodl/2011/paper/view/51

Papadimitriou, S., Lampropoulou, N., & Kampylis, P. (2007). The multiple use of videoconference in distance learning of Greek teachers via Greek School Network. (in Greek). In A. Lionarakis (Ed.), *Proceedings of the 4th International Conference Open and Distance Learning.* Athens: Propompos.

Papanikolaou, K. A., & Gouli, E. (2013). Investigating Influences among individuals and groups in a collaborative learning setting. *International Journal of e-Collaboration*, *9*(1), 9–25. doi:10.4018/jec.2013010102

Parlar, H., Polatcan, M., & Cansoy, R. (2019). The relationship between social capital and innovativeness climate in schools. The intermediary role of professional learning communities. *International Journal of Educational Management*, *34*(2), 232–244. doi:10.1108/IJEM-10-2018-0322

Pateraki, I. (2018). Measuring the impact of eTwinning activities on teachers' practice and competence development - Monitoring eTwinning Practice Framework. Central Support Service of eTwinning - European Schoolnet.

PBL Development Projects at Aalborg University. (2017). https://www.strategi.aau.dk/ AAU+strategy/Handleplaner+Viden+for+verden/Problem+based+learning/Problem+based+learning/

Pearce, W. B. (2003). *The coordinated management of meaning (CMM): Theorizing about communication and culture*. Sage.

Pearl, C. (2016). *Designing Voice User Interfaces: Principles of Conversational Experiences.* O'Reilly Media, Inc.

Pendry, L. F., & Salvatore, J. (2015, September). Individual and social benefits of online discussion forums. *Computers in Human Behavior*, *50*(C), 211–220. doi:10.1016/j.chb.2015.03.067

Perry, H., Robison, N., Chavez, D., Taja, O. O., Hilari, C., Shanklin, D., & Wyon, J. (1999). Attaining health for all through community partnership: Principles of the census based, impact-oriented (CBIO) approach to primary health care developed in Bolivia, South America. *Social Science & Medicine*, *48*(8), 1053–1068. doi:10.1016/S0277-9536(98)00406-7

Pfaff, K. A., Baxter, P. E., Jack, P. E., Jack, S. M., & Ploeg, J. (2014). Exploring new graduate nurse confidence in interprofessional collaboration: A mixed methods. *International Journal of Nursing Studies*, *51*(8), 1142–1152. doi:10.1016/j.ijnurstu.2014.01.001

Phipps, M., Ozanne, L., Luchs, M., Subrahmanyan, S., Kapitan, S., Catlin, J., Gau, R., Naylor, R. W., Rose, R. L., Simpson, B., & Weaver, T. (2013). Understanding the inherent complexity of sustainable consumption: A social cognitive framework. *Journal of Business Research*, *66*(8), 1227–1234. doi:10.1016/j.jbusres.2012.08.016

Pil, F. K., & Leana, C. (2009). Applying organizational research to public school reform: The effects of teacher human and social capital on student performance. *Academy of Management Journal, 52*(6), 1101-1124. . doi:10.5465/amj.2009.47084647

Piumsomboon, T., Lee, Y., Lee, G., & Billinghurst, M. (2017). CoVAR: A Collaborative Virtual and Augmented Reality System for Remote Collaboration. *SIGGRAPH Asia 2017 Emerging Technologies*, 3:1–3:2. doi:10.1145/3132818.3132822

Podsakoff, P. M., MacKenzie, S. B., Lee, J. Y., & Podsakoff, N. P. (2003). Common Method Biases in Behavioral Research: A Critical Review of the Literature and Recommended Remedies. *The Journal of Applied Psychology*, *88*(5), 879–903. doi:10.1037/0021-9010.88.5.879

Podsakoff, P. M., & Organ, D. W. (1986). Self-reports in Orgånizational Research: Problems and Prospects. *Journal of Management*, *12*(4), 531–544. doi:10.1177/014920638601200408

Polit, D. F., & Beck, C. T. (2004). *Nursing Research: Principles and Methods* (7th ed.). Lippincott, Williams, & Wilkins.

Polit, D. F., & Beck, C. T. (2006). The Content Validity Index: Are You Sure You Know What's Being Reported? Critique and Recommendations. *Research in Nursing & Health*, *29*(6), 489–497. doi:10.1002/nur.20147

Prensky, M. (2001). Digital natives, digital immigrants. The Horizon, 9(5), 1-6.

Prothero, A., Dobscha, S., Freund, J., Kilbourne, W. E., Luchs, M. G., Ozanne, L. K., & Thøgersen, J. (2011). Sustainable consumption: Opportunities for consumer research and public policy. *Journal of Public Policy & Marketing*, *30*(1), 31–38. doi:10.1509/jppm.30.1.31

PwC India Report. (2020, June). *Redefining the Fintech Experience: Impact of Covid 19*. https://www.pwc.in/assets/pdfs/services/crisis-management/covid-19/redefining-the-fintech-experience-impact-of-covid-19.pdf

Pyrko, I., Dörfler, V., & Eden, C. (2016). Thinking together: What makes Communities of Practice work? *Human Relations*, *70*(4), 389–409. doi:10.1177/0018726716661040 PMID:28232754

Question2answer. (2019). *Free Open Source Q&A Software for PHP.* https://www.question2answer.org/

Rakesh, M., & Partha, R. (2017). *Indian Financial Sector, Structure, Trends, and Turn.* IMF Working Papers No 17/7. Stock No WPIEA2017007

Ram, A., Prasad, R., Khatri, C., Venkatesh, A., Gabriel, R., Liu, Q., Nunn, J., Hedayatnia, B., Cheng, M., & Nagar, A. (2018). *Conversational ai: The science behind the alexa prize.* ArXiv Preprint ArXiv:1801.03604

Randrup, N., Druckenmiller, D., & Briggs, R. O. (2016). Philosophy of Collaboration. *2016 49th Hawaii International Conference on System Sciences (HICSS).*

RBI Reports. (2019). *Vision documents. Payment and Settlement Systems in India Vision 2019 -2021.* www.rbi.org.in. https://www.rbi.org.in/Scripts/PublicationVisionDocuments.aspx?Id=921

Redecker, C., & Punie, Y. (2017). European framework for the digital competence of educators: DigCompEdu. *Publications Office of the European Union, Luxembourg., JRC107466*. Advance online publication. doi:10.2760/159770

Reeves, S., McMillan, S. E., Kachan, N., Paradis, E., Leslie, M., & Kitto, S. (2014). Interprofessional collaboration and family member involvement in intensive careunits: Emerging themes from a multi-sited ethnography. *Journal of Interprofessional Care*, *29*(3), 230–237. doi:10.3109/13561820.2014.955914

Reeves, S., Pelone, F., Harrison, R., Goldman, J., & Zwarenstein, M. (2017). Interprofessional collaboration to improve professional practice and healthcare outcomes. *Cochrane Database of Systematic Reviews*, 6.

Reichert, M., & Weber, B. (2012). *Enabling flexibility in process-aware information systems: challenges, methods, technologies*. Springer Science & Business Media. doi:10.1007/978-3-642-30409-5

ReliefWeb. (2020). *COVID-19: The International Red Cross and Red Crescent Movement's Approach*. OCHA. https://reliefweb.int/report/world/covid-19-international-red-cross-and-red-crescent-movement-s-approach

Ren, J., Zhao, W., Wang, Y., Xu, M., & Fu, S. (2016). Research and Practice of Student-centered Teaching Model - Introduction to Information Security teaching Reform of small Class. *Computer Education*, *09*, 106–110.

Reports, K. P. M. G. (2018). *Bharat Bill Pay System – KPMG in India Perspective*. KPMG.com/in. https://www.npci.org.in/sites/default/files/Bharat%20Bill%20Payment%20System%20-%20KPMG.pdf

Resnick, M., Myers, B., Nakakoji, K., Shneiderman, B., Pausch, R., Selker, T., & Eisenberg, M. (2005). Design Principles for Tools to Support Creative Thinking. *Institute for Software Research*. http://repository.cmu.edu/isr/816

Ribak, A., & Jacovi, M. (2002). Ask Before You Search "Peer Support and Community Building with ReachOut. In *Proceedings of the 2002 ACM conference on Computer supported cooperative work*. ACM Press.

Rice, R. E., & Gattiker, U. E. (2001). New Media and Organizational Structuring. In F. M. Jablin & L. L. Putnam (Eds.), *The New Handbook of Organizational Communication* (pp. 544–584). Sage Publications. doi:10.4135/9781412986243.n14

Rice, S., & Gregor, M. N. (2016). *E-Learning and the Academic Library: Essays on Innovative Initiatives*. McFarland, Incorporated Publishers.

Riegelsberger, J., Sasse, M. A., & McCarthy, J. D. (2005). The mechanics of trust: A framework for research and design. *International Journal of Human-Computer Studies*, *62*(3), 381–422. doi:10.1016/j.ijhcs.2005.01.001

Rismark, M., & Sølvberg, A. M. (2011). Knowledge sharing in schools: A key to developing professional learning communities. *World Journal of Education*, *1*(2), 150–160. doi:10.5430/wje.v1n2p150

Rivera, D. (2020). *A volunteer food courier talks about delivering food during the quarantine*. UPROXX. https://uproxx.com/culture/new-york-coronavirus-couriers/

Rodriguez, L. S., Beaulieu, M., D'Amour, D., & Ferrada-Videla, M. (2005). The determinants of successful collaboration: A review of theoretical and empirical studies. *Journal of Interprofessional Care*, *19*(1), 132–147. doi:10.1080/13561820500082677

Rogelberg, S. G., & Stanton, J. M. (2007). Understanding and dealing with organizational survey nonresponse. *Organizational Research Methods*, *10*(2), 195–209. doi:10.1177/1094428106294693

Romano, N. C. Jr, Briggs, R. O., Nunamaker, J. F. Jr, & Mittleman, D. (1999). Distributed GSS facilitation and participation: Field action research. In *Proceedings of the Thirty-Second Annual Hawaii International Conference on System Sciences*. Computer Society Press. 10.1109/HICSS.1999.772737

Rönkkö, M., & Evermann, J. (2013). A critical examination of common beliefs about partial least squares path modeling. *Organizational Research Methods*.

Rosemann, M., Recker, J., & Flender, C. (2008). Contextualisation of business processes. *Journal of Business Process Integration and Management*, *3*(1), 47–60. doi:10.1504/IJBPIM.2008.019347

Rotary International. (2020). *COVID 19 global grants listing.* https://www.rotary.org/en/top-global-grant-projects

Roussinov, D. G., & Chen, H. (1999). Document clustering for electronic meetings: An experimental comparison of two techniques. *Decision Support Systems*, *27*(1–2), 67–79. doi:10.1016/S0167-9236(99)00037-8

Rowntree, D. (1998). Workshops role in Staff development. In C. Latsem & F. Lockwood (Eds.), *Staff development in open and flexible learning*. Routledge.

Rubio, D. M., Berg-Weger, M., Tebb, S. S., Lee, E. S., & Rauch, S. (2003). Objectifying Content Validity: Conducting a Content Validity Study in Social Work Research. *Social Work Research*, *27*(2), 94–104. doi:10.1093wr/27.2.94

Rusman, E., van Bruggen, J., Sloep, P., & Koper, R. (2010). Fostering trust in virtual project teams: Towards a design framework grounded in a TrustWorthiness ANtecedents (TWAN) schema. *International Journal of Human-Computer Studies*, *68*(11), 834–850. doi:10.1016/j.ijhcs.2010.07.003

Russell, S. J., & Norvig, P. (2016). *Artificial intelligence: A modern approach.* Pearson Education Limited.

Sacks, D. (2011). The sharing economy. *Fast Company*, *155*, 88-93.

Saffarizadeh, K., Boodraj, M., & Alashoor, T. (2017). Conversational Assistants: Investigating Privacy Concerns, Trust, and Self-Disclosure. *ICIS 2017 Proceedings.* https://aisel.aisnet.org/icis2017/Security/Presentations/19

Safran, C., Jones, P., Rind, D., Bush, B., Cytryn, K., & Patel, V. (1998). Electronic communication and collaboration in a health care practice. *Artificial Intelligence in Medicine*, *12*(2), 137–151. doi:10.1016/S0933-3657(97)00047-X

Safran, D. G. (2003). Defining the future of primary care: What can we learn from patients? *Annals of Internal Medicine*, *138*(3), 248–255. doi:10.7326/0003-4819-138-3-200302040-00033

Saidani, O., Rolland, C., & Nurcan, S. (2015). Towards a generic context model for BPM. In *Proceedings of the 48th Hawaii International Conference on System Sciences* (pp. 4120-4129). Kauai, HI: IEEE. 10.1109/HICSS.2015.494

Santra, D., & Choudhury, S. (2018). *C-BPMN: A Context Aware BPMN for Modeling Complex Business Process.* CoRR abs/1806.01333

Saunders, A. (2017, May 3). *Proud to Share! – The New Brand Claim Sums Up the car2Go.* Academic Press.

Scheer. (2015). *Scheer BPaaS. Scheer.* Retrieved from https://aws-institut.de/wp-content/uploads/2016/02/AWScheer_Whitepaper5_Industrie-4_0.pdf

Schofield, R. F., & Amodeo, M. (1999). Interdisciplinary teams in health care and human services settings: Are they effective? *Health & Social Work*, *24*(3), 210–219. doi:10.1093/hsw/24.3.210

Schroeder, J., & Schroeder, M. (2018, January 3). Trusting in Machines: How Mode of Interaction Affects Willingness to Share Personal Information with Machines. *Hawaii International Conference on System Sciences.* 10.24251/HICSS.2018.061

Schuman Ottinger, C., & Bonilla, B. (2018). *Open Nonprofit Data Open Doors for Researchers.* The Aspen Institute. https://www.aspeninstitute.org/blog-posts/open-nonprofit-data-opens-doors-for-researchers/

Schwartz, J., Hagel, J. III, Wooll, M., & Monahan, K. (2019). Reframing the Future of Work. *MIT Sloan Management Review*, *60*(3), 1–6.

Schwarz, R. (2002). *The skilled facilitator: A comprehensive resource for consultants, facilitators, managers, trainers, and coaches*. John Wiley & Sons.

Seeber, I., Merz, A., Maier, R., de Vreede, G.-J., & Weber, B. (2017). Convergence on self-generated vs. crowdsourced ideas in crisis response: comparing social exchange processes and satisfaction with process. *50th Hawaii International Conference on System Sciences (HICSS 2017)*. Retrieved from https://orbit.dtu.dk/en/publications/convergence-on-self--generated-vs-crowdsourced-ideas-in-crisis-response-comparing-social-exchange-processes-and-satisfaction-with-process(53fc726c-c3e5-4cd2-8810-1f860c9dbd92).html

Seeber, I. (2019). How do facilitation interventions foster learning? The role of evaluation and coordination as causal mediators in idea convergence. *Computers in Human Behavior*, *94*, 176–189. doi:10.1016/j.chb.2018.11.033

Seeber, I., Bittner, E., Briggs, R. O., de Vreede, T., de Vreede, G.-J., Elkins, A., Maier, R., Merz, A. B., Oeste-Reiß, S., Randrup, N., Schwabe, G., & Söllner, M. (2019). Machines as teammates: A research agenda on AI in team collaboration. *Information & Management*, *103174*. Advance online publication. doi:10.1016/j.im.2019.103174

Seeber, I., de Vreede, G.-J., Maier, R., & Weber, B. (2017). Beyond Brainstorming: Exploring Convergence in Teams. *Journal of Management Information Systems*, *34*(4), 939–969. doi:10.1080/07421222.2017.1393303 PMID:29399005

Senate Finance Committee. (2009). *Transforming the health care delivery system: proposals to improve patient care and reduce health care costs*. Retrieved August, 2, 2016, from: http://finance.senate.gov/sitepages/leg/LEG%202009/042809%20Health%20Care%20Description%20of%20Policy%20Option.pdf

Shaffer, K., & Speakman, E. (2014). Using Technology to Enhance Interprofessional Collaborative Practice: Creating Virtual Clinical Opportunities by Implementing Google Doc and Google Hangout in Clinical Rounding. *Collaborative Healthcare: Interprofessional Practice, Education and Evaluation*, *5*(1), Article 2. Available at: http://jdc.jefferson.edu/jcipe/vol5/iss1/2

Shah, I. (2020, March 8). *ET BFSI.Com. Covid 19 is a turning point for this Fintech*. https://bfsi.economictimes.indiatimes.com/news/fintech/covid-19-is-a-turning-point-for-this-fintech/74861775

Shahrawat, D., & Shah, V. (2020, March 3). *The Impact of COVID 19 on different Fintech Sectors*. Fintech.

Sharma, G., Qiang, Y., Wenjun,S., & Qi, L. (2013). Communication in virtual world: Second life and business opportunities. *Information Systems Frontiers*, *15*(7), 677–694. DOI doi:10.100710796-012-9347-z

Sharma, N. (2020, March 25). *Voices 3 emerging Robo trends amid Covid 19 market craziness*. Financial Planning.com. https://www.financial-planning.com/opinion/3-emerging-robo-trends-amid-coronavirus-stock-market-volatility

Shneiderman, B. (2007). Creativity Support Tools: Accelerating Discovery and Innovation. *Communications of the ACM*, *50*(12), 20–32. doi:10.1145/1323688.1323689

Shortell, S. M., Zimmerman, J. E., Rousseau, D. M., Gillies, R. R., Wagner, D. P., Draper, E. A., Knaus, W. A., & Duffy, J. (1994). The performance of intensive care units: Does good management make a difference? *Medical Care*, *32*(5), 508–525. doi:10.1097/00005650-199405000-00009

Sicotte, C., D'Amour, D., & Moreault, M. (2002). Interdisciplinary collaboration within Quebec community health care centers. *Social Science & Medicine*, *55*(6), 991–1003. doi:10.1016/S0277-9536(01)00232-5

Siegler, E. L., & Whitney, F. W. (1994). *Nurse-Physician collaboration. Care of adults and the elderly*. Stringer Publishing Company.

Siemens, G. (2005). A learning theory for the digital age. *Instructional Technology and Distance Education*, *2*(1), 3–10. Retrieved May 15, 2012 from http://www.elearnspace.org/Articles/connectivism.htm

Siemon, D., Eckardt, L., & Robra-Bissantz, S. (2015). Tracking Down the Negative Group Creativity Effects with the Help of an Artificial Intelligence-Like Support System. *2015 48th Hawaii International Conference on System Sciences (HICSS)*, 236–243. 10.1109/HICSS.2015.37

Siemon, D., Becker, F., Eckardt, L., & Robra-Bissantz, S. (2017). One for all and all for one—Towards a framework for collaboration support systems. *Education and Information Technologies*, 1–25. doi:10.100710639-017-9651-9

Siemon, D., Strohmann, T., & Robra-Bissantz, S. (2019). Towards the Conception of a Virtual Collaborator. *Proceedings of the Workshop on Designing User Assistance in Intelligent Systems,* 7–9.

Signavio. (2015). *Benutzerhandbuch. Signavio.* Retrieved from https://docs.signavio.com/userguide/editor/de/index.html

Singelis, T. M. (1994). The measurement of independent and interdependent self-construals. *Personality and Social Psychology Bulletin*, *20*(5), 580–591. doi:10.1177/0146167294205014

Singh, J., & Bodla, B. S. (2020). COVID-19 pandemic and lockdown impact on India's banking sector: A systemic literature review. In *COVID-19 Pandemic: A Global Challenge* (pp. 21–32). New Delhi: Aryan Publications.

Skalski, P., & Tamborini, R. (2007). The role of social presence in interactive agent-based persuasion. *Media Psychology*, *10*(3), 385–413. doi:10.1080/15213260701533102

Smith, M., Greene, B. R., & Meeker, W. (2002). The CAM movement and the integration of quality health care: The case of chiropractic. *The Journal of Ambulatory Care Management*, *25*(2), 1–16. doi:10.1097/00004479-200204000-00003

Snyder, J., & Field, M. (2006). We got the message: creating an instant messenger service point. *User Services Conference*. 10.1145/1181216.1181297

Solimeno, A., Mebane, M. E., Tomai, M., & Francescato, D. (2008). The influence of students and teachers characteristics on the efficacy of face-to-face and computer supported collaborative learning. *Computers & Education*, *51*(1), 109–128. doi:10.1016/j.compedu.2007.04.003

Song, J. H., Kim, W., Chai, D. S., & Bae, S. H. (2014). The impact of an innovative school climate on teachers' knowledge creation activities in Korean schools: The mediating role of teachers' knowledge sharing and work engagement. *Journal of Education Policy*, *11*(2), 179–203.

Spassova, G., & Lee, A. Y. (2013). Looking into the future: A match between self-view and temporal distance. *The Journal of Consumer Research*, *40*(1), 159–171. doi:10.1086/669145

Spinella, L. (2018). *Intelligent Virtual Assistants 101*. Interactions Resource Center. https://resources.interactions.com/library/intelligent-virtual-assistants-101/

Sproull, L., & Kiesler, S. (1986). Reducing social context cues: Electronic mail in organizational communication. *Management Science*, *32*(11), 1492–1512. doi:10.1287/mnsc.32.11.1492

Srinivasan, A. (1985). Alternative measures of system effectiveness: Associations and implications. *Management Information Systems Quarterly*, *9*(3), 243–253. doi:10.2307/248951

StackExchange. (2019). http://www.stackexchange.com

Starfield, B. (1998). *Primary care: Balancing Health Needs, Services, and Technology*. Oxford University Press.

Statista. (2020). *Electronic environment overview.* Retrieved on 07/15/2020 at https://www.statista.com/

Stein, L. I., Watts, D. T., & Howell, T. (1990). The doctor-nurse game revisited. *The New England Journal of Medicine*, *322*(6), 536–549.

Stichler, J. F. (1995). Professional interdependence: The art of collaboration. *Advanced Practice Nursing Quarterly*, *1*(1), 53–61.

Stille, C. J., Jerant, A., Bell, D., Meltzer, D., & Elmore, J. G. (2005). Coordinating Care across Diseases, Settings, and.: A Key Role for the Generalist in Practice. *Annals of Internal Medicine*, *142*(7), 700–708. doi:10.7326/0003-4819-142-8-200504190-00038

Stonebraker & Zhang. (2015). *Crowdsourcing reference help: using technology to help users help each other.* Libraries Faculty and Staff Scholarship and Research.

Stonebraker & Zhang. (2016). Participatory culture and e-learning. In E-Learning and the Academic Library: Essays on Innovative Initiatives, (pp. 201–213). McFarland.

Strang, T., & Linnhoff-Popien, C. (2004). A context modeling survey. *In Workshop Proceedings of the 1st International Workshop on Advanced Context Modeling, Reasoning And Management*, Nottingham, UK.

Strohmann, T., Fischer, S., Siemon, D., Brachten, F., Lattemann, C., Robra-Bissantz, S., & Stieglitz, S. (2018). Virtual Moderation Assistance: Creating Design Guidelines for Virtual Assistants Supporting Creative Workshops. *Proceedings of the 22nd Pacific Asia Conference on Information Systems.*

Supper, I., Catala, O., Lustman, M., Chemla, C., Bourgueil, Y., & Letrilliart, L. (2014). Interprofessional collaboration in primary health care: A Review of facilitators and barriers perceived by involved actors. *Journal of Public Health*, *37*(4), 716–727.

Suter, E., Arndt, J., Arthur, N., Parboosingh, J., Taylor, E., & Deutschlander, S. (2009). Role understanding and effective communication as core competencies for collaborative practice. *Journal of Interprofessional Care*, *23*(1), 41–51. doi:10.1080/13561820802338579

Szewkis, E., Nussbaum, M., Rosen, T., Abalos, J., Denardin, F., Caballero, D., Tagle, A., & Alcoholado, C. (2011). Collaboration within large groups in the classroom. *Computer-Supported Collaborative Learning*, *6*(4), 561–575. doi:10.100711412-011-9123-y

Tang, C. J., Zhou, W. T., & Liaw, S. Y. (2018). Interprofessional collaboration between juniordoctors and nurses in the general ward setting: A qualitative exploratory study. Journal of Nursing Management. *Journal of Nursing Management*, *26*(1), 11–18. doi:10.1111/jonm.12503

Tapscott, D. (1998). *Growing up digital: The rise of the Net Generation.* McGraw-Hill.

Tapscott, D. (2009). *Grown up digital: How the Net Generation is changing your world.* McGraw-Hill.

Task Force on Future of MIT. (2014). *Institute-wide Task Force on the Future of MIT Education Final Report.* http://web.mit.edu/future-report/TaskForceFinal_July28.pdf

Teigland, R., & Wasko, M. (2003). Integrating Knowledge through Information Trading: Examining the Relationship between Boundary Spanning Communication and Individual Performance. *Decision Sciences*, *34*(2), 261–286. doi:10.1111/1540-5915.02341

Terry, M. (2008). Text messaging in healthcare: The elephant knocking at the door. *Telemedicine Journal and e-Health*, *14*(5), 520–524. doi:10.1089/tmj.2008.8495

Thielens, W., Jr. (1987). *The disciplines and undergraduate lecturing.* Paper presented at the annual meeting of the American Educational Research Association, Washington, DC.

Thomas, E. J., Sherwood, G. D., Mulhollem, J. L., Sexton, J. B., & Helmreich, R. L. (2004). Working together in the neonatal intensive care unit: Provider perspective. *Journal of Perinatology*, *24*(9), 552–559. doi:10.1038j.jp.7211136

Thorpe, J., & Albrecht, C. C. (2004). Characteristics of large group support systems. In *Proceedings of the 37th Annual Hawaii International Conference on Systems Sciences*. Computer Society Press.

Thred, U. P. (2017). *ThredUP Annual Re-sale Report 2017*. Retrieved from https://www.thredup. com/re-sale/full

Tidwell, L. C., & Walther, J. B. (2002). Computer-Mediated Communication Effects on Disclosure, Impressions, and Interpersonal Evaluations. *Human Communication Research*, *28*(3), 317–348. doi:10.1111/j.1468-2958.2002.tb00811.x

Tourangeau, R., Rips, L. J., & Rasinski, K. (2000). *The Psychology of Survey Response*. Cambridge University Press. doi:10.1017/CBO9780511819322

Triandis, H. (1989). The self and social behavior in differing cultural contexts. *Psychological Review*, *96*(3), 506–520. doi:10.1037/0033-295X.96.3.506

Trust, T., Krutka, G. D., & Carpenter, P. J. (2016). "Together we are better": Professional learning networks for teachers. *Computers & Education*, *102*, 15–34. doi:10.1016/j.compedu.2016.06.007

Tussyadiah, I. P., & Pesonen, J. (2016). Impacts of peer-to-peer accommodation use on travel patterns. *Journal of Travel Research*, *55*(8), 1022–1040. doi:10.1177/0047287515608505

Tutty, J. I., & Klein, J. D. (2008). Computer-mediated instruction: A comparison of online and face-to-face collaboration. *Educational Technology Research and Development*, *56*(2), 101–124. doi:10.100711423-007-9050-9

Tyler, T. R., & Kramer, R. M. (1996). Whither trust? In R. M. Kramer & T. R. Tyler (Eds.), *Trust in organizations: Frontiers of theory and research*. Sage. doi:10.4135/9781452243610.n1

UNESCO. (2002). *How students learn* (in Greek). International Bureau of Education. Retrieved November 2, 2010 from http://www.ibe.unesco.org/fileadmin/user_upload/archive/publications/EducationalPracticesSeriesPdf/prac07gr.pdf

UNESCO. (2015). *Revising the 2001 Revised Recommendation concerning Technical and Vocational Education* (Report of the UNESCO-UNEVOC special virtual conference 1–14 April 2014). https://unesdoc.unesco.org/images/0023/002341/234137e.pdf

Urbach, N., & Ahlemann, F. (2010). Structural Equation Modeling in Information Systems Research Using Partial Least Squares. *Journal of Information Technology Theory and Application*, *11*(2), 5–40.

Valacich, J. S., Dennis, A. R., & Nunamaker, J. F. Jr. (1992). Group Size and Anonymity Effects on Computer-Mediated Idea Generation. *Small Group Research*, *23*(1), 49–73. doi:10.1177/1046496492231004

Van de Glind, P. B. (2013). *The consumer potential of Collaborative Consumption: Identifying the motives of Dutch Collaborative Consumers & Measuring the consumer potential of Collaborative Consumption within the municipality of Amsterdam* (Master's thesis). Retrieved from https://scholar.google.com/scholar?hl=en&as_sdt=0%2C34&q=Van+de+Glind++2013+collaborative+consumption&btnG

Van Waes, S., De Mayers, S., Moonlenaar, N. M., Van Petegem, P., & Van de Bossche, P. (2018). Strengthening networks: A social network intervention among higher education teachers. *Learning and Instruction*, *53*, 34–49. doi:10.1016/j.learninstruc.2017.07.005

Vance, A., Elie-Dit-Cosaque, C., & Straub, D. W. (2008). Examining Trust in Information Technology Artifacts: The Effects of System Quality and Culture. *Journal of Management Information Systems*, *24*(4), 73–100. doi:10.2753/MIS0742-1222240403

Vasala, P., Hatziplis, P., & Lionarakis, A. (2007). Views of undergraduate and postgraduate students at Hellenic Open University on essays: a comparative study of two courses, (in Greek). In A. Lionarakis (Ed), *Proceedings of 4th International Conference of Open and Distance Learning*, (pp. 296-308). Athens: Propompos.

Vasan, M., & Senthil, B. (2018). A Study of Payment and Settlement System in Indian Banking Sector. *Research magma Journal, 1*(11), 1-8.

Vasilescu, B., Capiluppi, A., & Serebrenik, A. (2012). Gender, Representation and Online Partici- pation: A Quantitative Study of StackOverflow. *2012 International Conference on Social Informatics*, 332–338. 10.1109/SocialInformatics.2012.81

Vazirani, S., Hays, R. D., Shapiro, M. F., & Cowan, M. (2005). Effect of a multidisciplinary intervention on communication and collaboration among physicians and nurses. *American Journal of Critical Care*, *14*(1), 71–77. doi:10.4037/ajcc2005.14.1.71

Veenstra, G., & Lomas, J. (1999). Home is where the governing is: Social capital and regional health governance. *Health & Place*, *5*(1), 1–2. doi:10.1016/S1353-8292(98)00037-9

Velasco, P. J., Learreta, B., Kober, C., & Tan, I. (2014). *Faculty Perspective on Competency Development in Higher Education: An International Study. Higher Learning Research Communications, December 2014.* Laureate Education, Inc. doi:10.18870/hlrc.v4i4.223

Venkatesh, V., Morris, M. G., Davis, G. B., & Davis, F. D. (2003). User Acceptance of Information Technology: Toward a Unified View. *Management Information Systems Quarterly*, *27*(3), 425–478. doi:10.2307/30036540

Verschuren, P. J., & Masselink, H. (1997). Role concepts and expectations of physicians and nurses in hospitals. *Social Science & Medicine*, *45*(6), 1135–1138. doi:10.1016/S0277-9536(97)00043-9

Vestergaard, E., & Nørgaard, B. (2018). Interprofessional collaboration: An exploration of possible prerequisites for successful implementation. *Journal of Interprofessional Care*, *32*(2), 185–195. doi:10.1080/13561820.2017.1363725

VIA University College. (2017). *VIA Connect.* https://challenges.dk/da/challenges

Vijay. (2020). *Much needed assistance for Lautoka residents.* Fiji Village. https://www.fijivillage.com/news/Much-needed-assistance-for-Lautoka-residents-affected-by-lockdown--fx4r85/

Voigt, M., & Bergener, K. (2013). Enhancing Creativity in Groups – Proposition of an Integrated Framework for Designing Group Creativity Support Systems. *2013 46th Hawaii International Conference on System Sciences (HICSS)*, 225–234. 10.1109/HICSS.2013.195

Volungevičienė, A., Teresevičienė, M., & Ehlers, U. (2020). When is open and online learning relevant for curriculum change in higher education? Digital and network society perspective. *The Electronic Journal of eLearning, 18*, 88–101. https://files.eric.ed.gov/fulltext/EJ1245114.pdf

Von Krogh, G. (2012). How does social software change knowledge management? Toward a strategic research agenda. *The Journal of Strategic Information Systems*, *21*(2), 154–164. doi:10.1016/j.jsis.2012.04.003

Vuorikari, R., Garoia, V., Punie, Y., Cachia, R., Redecker, C., Cao, Y., Klamma, R., Cuong, M., Pham, C. M., Rajagopal, K. P., Sibren, F., & Sloep, P. (2012). Teacher networks. Today's and tomorrow's challenges and opportunities for the teaching profession. *European Schoolnet (EUN Partnership AISBL).* https://www.academia.edu/13544915/Teacher_networks_Today_s_and_tomorrow_s_challenges_and_opportunities_for_the_teaching_profession

Vuorikari, R., Kampylis, P., Scimeca, S., & Punie, Y. (2015). Scaling up teacher networks across and within European schools: The case of eTwinning. In *Scaling Educational Innovations* (pp. 227–254). Springer Singapore. doi:10.1007/978-981-287-537-2_11

Vuorikari, R., Punie, Y., Carretero Gomez, S., & Van den Brande, G. (2016). *DigComp 2.0: The digital competence framework for citizens. Update phase 1: The conceptual reference model*. Luxembourg Publication Office of the European Union. doi:10.2791/11517

Wagner, E. H. (2004). Effective teamwork and quality of care. *Medical Care*, *42*(11), 1037–1039. doi:10.1097/01.mlr.0000145875.60036.ed

Walsh, C., Gordon, F., Marshall, M., & Hunt, T. (2005). Interprofessional capability: A developing framework for interprofessional education. *Nurse Education in Practice*, *5*(4), 230–237. doi:10.1016/j.nepr.2004.12.004

Wang, Q. (2017, May). The development trend of global higher education from the perspective of informatization. *China Education Daily*. http://paper.jyb.cn/zgjyb

Wang, C. Y., Yang, H. Y., & Sengcho, T. C. (2008). Using peer-to-peer technology for knowledge sharing in communities of practices. *Decision Support Systems*, *45*(3), 528–540. doi:10.1016/j.dss.2007.06.012

Wang, Y. Q., & Wan, Y. S. (2001). Anxiety in Foreign Language learning and its impact on foreign language learning. *Foreign Language Teaching and Research*, *33*(2), 122–126.

Waskett, C. (1996). Multidisciplinary teamwork in primary care: The role of the counsellor. *Counselling Psychology Quarterly*, *9*(4), 243–260. doi:10.1080/09515079608258706

Wasserman, S., & Faust, K. (1994). *Social network analysis: methods and applications*. Cambridge University Press. doi:10.1017/CBO9780511815478

Way, D., Jones, L., & Busing, N. (2000). *Implementation strategies: "Collaboration in primary care –Family doctors & nurse practitioners delivering shared care": Discussion paper written for the Ontario College of Family Physicians*. Ontario College of Family Physicians.

Weaver, B., Lindsay, B., & Gitelman, B. (2012). Communication technology and social media: opportunities and implications for healthcare systems. *OJIN: The Online Journal of Issues in Nursing, 17*(3), 17-24. Advance online publication. doi:10.3912/OJIN.Vol17No03Man03

Welton, W. E., Kantner, T. A., & Moriber, K. S. (1997). Developing tomorrow's Integrated Community Health Systems: A leadership challenge for public health and primary care. *The Milbank Quarterly*, *75*(2), 261–288. doi:10.1111/1468-0009.00054

Wenger, E. (2010). *Communities of practice and social learning systems 1: Communities of practice and social learning systems: the career of a concept*. Springer Publishing.

Wenger, E. (1998). *Communities of practice, Learning, meaning and identity*. Cambridge University Press. doi:10.1017/CBO9780511803932

Wikipedia. (2017). https://www.wikipedia.org/

Wilks, Y. (2006). *Artificial companions as a new kind of interface to the future internet*. Academic Press.

Williams, A. L., Lasky, R. E., Dannemiller, J. L., Andrei, A. M., & Thomas, E. J. (2010). Teamwork behaviours and errors during neonatal resuscitation. *Quality & Safety in Health Care*, *19*(1), 60–64. doi:10.1136/qshc.2007.025320

Wood, T. M. (2002). *Understanding and preventing teacher burnout*. ERIC Digest. https://www.ericdigests.org/2004-1/burnout.htm

Woods, J. A., Jackson, D. J., Ziglar, S., & Alston, G. L. (2011). Interprofessional communication. *Drug Topics*, *155*(8), 42–53.

Yang, H. Z. (2003). Fifteen years review on CET4 and CET6. *Waiguoyu, 145*(3), 21–29.

Yang, X., & Tian, X. (2018). *Big Data in China's Basic Education 2016-2017: Towards data-driven accurate teaching*. Science Press.

Ye, J. (2006). *Deliberate Learning in The Frontlines of Service Organizations* (Ph.D. Dissertation). Department of Marketing and Policy Studies, Case Western Reserve University.

Young, D. (1986). The relationship between anxiety and foreign language oral proficiency ratings. *Foreign Language Annals, 19*(5), 439–445. doi:10.1111/j.1944-9720.1986.tb01032.x

Young, D. J. (1991). Creating a low-anxiety classroom environment: What does language anxiety research suggest? *Modern Language Journal, 75*(4), 426–439. doi:10.1111/j.1540-4781.1991.tb05378.x

Yu, Z. (2018a). Differences in serious game-aided and traditional English vocabulary acquisition. *Computers & Education, 127*, 214–232. doi:10.1016/j.compedu.2018.07.014

Yu, Z. (2018b). Third-Level Digital Divide in English Teaching and Learning. *International Journal of Information and Communication Technology Education, 14*(3), 68–80. doi:10.4018/IJICTE.2018070106

Yu, Z. (2018c). Comparative effectiveness between game-enhanced and pencil-and-paper English vocabulary learning approaches. *International Journal of Gaming and Computer-Mediated Simulations, 10*(2), 1–20. doi:10.4018/IJGCMS.2018040101

Yu, Z. (2019a). A meta-analysis of use of serious games in education over a decade. *International Journal of Computer Games Technology, 1*, 1–8. doi:10.1155/2019/4797032

Yu, Z. (2019b). Mobile device- and video-aided flipped English classrooms. *International Journal of Mobile and Blended Learning, 11*(2), 19–32. doi:10.4018/IJMBL.2019040102

Yu, Z., & Zhu, Q. (2018d). Schema Theory-based Flipped Classroom Model Assisted with Technologies. *International Journal of Information and Communication Technology Education, 15*(2), 31–48. doi:10.4018/IJICTE.2019040103

Yu, Z., Zhu, Y., Yang, Z., & Chen, W. (2018). Student satisfaction, learning outcomes, and cognitive loads with a mobile learning platform. *Computer Assisted Language Learning*. Advance online publication. doi:10.1080/09588221.2018.1517093

Zhao, J. (2010). School knowledge management framework and strategies: The new perspective on teacher professional development. *Computers in Human Behavior, 26*(2), 168–175. doi:10.1016/j.chb.2009.10.009

Zhao, J. L., Nunamaker, J. F. Jr, & Briggs, R. O. (2002). Intelligent workflow techniques for distributed group facilitation. In *Proceedings of the 35th Annual Hawaii International Conference on Systems Sciences*. Computer Society Press. 10.1109/HICSS.2002.993940

Zhao, S. (2006). Humanoid social robots as a medium of communication. *New Media & Society, 8*(3), 401–419. doi:10.1177/1461444806061951

Zhao, X., & Liu, C. (2013). Version management for business process schema evolution. *Journal of Information Systems, 38*(8), 1046–1069.

Zwarenstein, M., Reeves, S., & Perrier, L. (2004). Effectiveness of pre-licensure interdisciplinary education and post-licensure interprofessional collaboration interventions. In I. Oandasan (Ed.), *Interdisciplinary education for collaborative patient-centred practice* (pp. 38–50). Health Canada.

About the Contributors

Jingyuan Zhao is a research fellow at University of Toronto, Canada. She is a also professor at Beijing Union University (China). She obtained her PhD in Management Science and Engineering from University of Science and Technology of China (China) and completed a postdoctoral program in Management of Technology from University of Quebec at Montreal (Canada). Dr. Zhao's expertise is on management of technological innovation, technological strategy, regional innovation systems and global innovation networks, knowledge management, management information systems, and science and technology policy.

* * *

Eric Andonoff is associate professor at UT-Capitole. His research work is in the field of business process management. It particularly addresses the issue of process adaptation. The field of crisis management is a privileged application framework for its research.

Narinder Bhasin is Professor, Amity University, Amity School of Insurance Banking and Actuarial Science.

Rafik Bouaziz is Professor Emeritus on computer science at the Faculty of Economic Sciences and Management of Sfax University, Tunisia. He was the president of this University during August 2014 – December 2017, and the director of its doctoral school of economy, management and computer science during December 2011 – July 2014. His PhD has dealt with temporal data management and historical record of data in Information Systems. The subject of his accreditation to supervise research was "A contribution for the control of versioning of data and schema in advanced information systems". Currently, his main research topics of interest are temporal databases, real-time databases, information systems engineering, ontologies, data warehousing and workflows. Between 1979 and 1986, he was a consulting Engineer in the organization and computer science and a head of the department of computer science at CEGOS-TUNISIA.

Mohamed Amine Chaâbane received a PhD degree from University of Toulouse, France in 2012. He is an associate professor at Higher Institute of Business Administration, University of Sfax – Tunisia and member of MIR@CL (Multimedia, InfoRmation systems and Advanced Computing Laboratory). His research interests focus on Business Process Management field. He is working on topics related to Business Process Modeling, Process Flexibility, Context of Process and Self-adaptation of process.

Jean Constant, past acting director of the Visual Communication program for the Northern New Mexico College, is presently researcher and lecturer in collaborative Math & Art projects. He publishes extensively on Mathematics and Art, Knowledge Visualization, and Visual Communication in various academic and professional publications. His most recent projects include "The Math-Art series", an ongoing series of mathematics and art visualizations; "Stochastic Processes and Art", an overview of stochastic processes visualizations in mathematics, applied sciences and visual communication; "Geometry of Nature", a visual exploration of 52 families of crystals with the support of UA GeoSciences department and Japan National Museum of Nature and Science in Ikabari.

Sindy De La Torre is a social scientist specializing in community institutions, food security, and education. During the last two years, Dr. De La Torre has worked on practical solutions to diminish poverty in the Phoenix metropolitan area. She utilizes qualitative and quantitative skills to improve non-profit programs based on the client's feedback. She is a full-time professor at the Universidad Autonoma de Coahuila and a level 1 member of Mexico's National Science and Technology Council.

Christopher Diller received a Ph.D. in Management Information Systems with a minor in Social Psychology from the University of Arizona. Dr. Diller has management- and executive-level experience in the telecommunications industry, where he directed advertising, marketing, public relations, and IT departments. For over 25 years, he has developed and led collaborative sessions (both in the lab and in the field), earning a reputation as an authority on effective facilitation techniques in challenging strategic environments. Currently, Dr. Diller serves as an instructor for the College of Business Administration at the University of Nebraska at Omaha. He is responsible for teaching courses in MIS, collaboration, and strategic management. His current research efforts support several federal agencies in the United States, including the Department of Homeland Security and the Department of Defense.

Fatma Ellouze is currently a contractual assistant at the Higher Institute of Business Administration, University of Sfax – Tunisia. She received her PhD in Computer Science from the Faculty of Economics and Management of the University of Sfax, Tunisia, in September 2018. She is a member of the Multimedia, Information systems and Advanced Computing Laboratory, since 2013. Her current research interests include Business process management, Business process modelling, Context Modelling and Information systems.

Dorina Gnaur is an associate professor in the Department of Culture and Learning at Aalborg University. Her research concerns learning in higher education and how technologies support learning.

Joel Helquist graduated with a Ph.D. in Business Management with an emphasis in Management Information Systems from the University of Arizona. Prior to completing his Ph.D., Dr. Helquist was a CPA and worked as a consultant for Arthur Andersen, LLP and KPMG, LLP in Seattle, Washington. As a consultant, he worked in the Technology Risk Consulting and Information Risk Management groups. The consulting work focused primarily on information and network security, IT audit, IT risks and controls, and privacy. Dr. Helquist is currently an Associate Professor at Utah Valley University in the Accounting Department. He is responsible for teaching the Accounting Information Systems, introduction to IT audit, and the MBA Information Systems and Project Management courses.

Hans Hüttel is an associate professor in the Department of Computer Science at Aalborg University. His research interests are programming language theory and technology in higher education.

John Kruse is a Lead Information Systems Engineer at the MITRE Corporation. Previously, he was the Director of Systems Development at the Center for the Management of Information at the University of Arizona. He received his Ph.D. in Management Information Systems with a minor in Management and Policy from the University of Arizona in 2001. He holds a B.S. in Management Information Systems and an M.B.A. from the University of Wyoming. He has worked extensively with a wide range of educational, governmental and military groups to help develop group processes and software that supports collaborative work. He is currently working to develop dynamic means for distributed groups to collaborate on complicated tasks and products.

Salvatore Nizzolino holds Diploma and Licence in Agrotechnology, a Degree in Language Teaching and two Masters in the field of Learning Design and Development of Teaching Programs. He serves as Contract Professor for Technical English at the Faculties of Information Engineering and Civil and Industrial Engineering, Sapienza University of Rome (Italy). He serves as a Lecturer and Tutor for the Advanced Course of European Project Management at the Facutly of Economics, Sapienza University of Rome. His research interests are Educational Networking, Lifelong Learning, Open Education, EU Projects and Knowledge Management. He is currently attenting the University Master's Degree in Strategic Management of Information and Knowledge in Organizations at Universitat Oberta de Catalunya (Spain).

Spyros Papadakis holds a PhD in Computer Science and Information Systems from the School of Science and Technology (HOU), a Master in Adult Education (HOU), a Postgraduate Certificate in Open and Distance Education (HOU) and a Bachelor in Mathematics from the University of Patras, Greece. His PHD dissertation titled "Online educational resource development: supporting the educator". He has extensive teaching experience as teacher and lecturer in the schools sector teaching Computer Science and Adult Education from secondary to professional development. He has participated in over 10 European and National research and development projects in the area of educational and Emerging Technologies for Learning.

Sofia Papadimitriou studied Mathematics and have a Master degree in Computer Science from the Athens National University. Her PhD regards the field of Open and Distance Learning in Higher Education and was developed at the Hellenic Open University. She is the Head of the Educational Radio-Television and she has been working as a tutor-counselor at the Hellenic Open University and the University of Piraeus in post graduate courses since 2017. She completed her postdoctoral reserach in 2020 at the Aegean University in the field of Digital Literacy in Audiovisual Media. She has also contributed in international conferences and scientific journals regarding Open and Distance Learning, Media and Information Literacy, and the use of Digital/Audiovisual Media in Learning. http://eap.academia.edu/SofiaPapadimitriou http://www.slideshare.net/sofipapadi

Dominik Siemon is a postdoctoral researcher of business information systems at Technische Universität Braunschweig. His work focuses specifically on how information technology can be designed to support collaboration and creativity. Furthermore, he researches collaboration with artificial intelligence, gamification, automated personality mining and Design Thinking, with an IT-based focus. His design-oriented research was published in various peer-reviewed journals and top ranked international conferences. He teaches E-Business, Information management and coaches Design Thinking workshops. He additionally acquired and works on third-party funded projects, such as Design Thinking for Industrial Services, where he supports companies in using Information Systems to apply digital Design Thinking.

Timo Strohmann is a doctoral researcher of Business Information Systems at Technische Universität Braunschweig. His design-oriented research is centered around the application of conversational agents in different contexts, like in-vehicle assistance, creativity support or virtual facilitation. His publications include studies of implemented conversational agents as well as prescriptive knowledge on how to design them. He especially focuses on designing the human-machine interaction in a forward-thinking manner by investigating the concept of virtual companionship.

Nazim Taskin is a Senior Lecturer at School of Management, Massey University, New Zealand. He holds a PhD in Interdisciplinary Studies from University of British Columbia, Okanagan, Canada. His research interests include Enterprise Systems, Strategic IS/IT Alignment, Knowledge Management, and Big Data. Nazim has published in various journals, conferences including Australasian Journal of Information Systems, Journal of Knowledge Management, Journal of Electronic Commerce, Journal of Enterprise Information Management, Business Strategy and the Environment, Hawaii International Conference on System Sciences (HICSS), Australasian Conference on Information Systems (ACIS), Americas Conference on Information Systems (AMCIS), and European Conference on Information Systems (ECIS). He has co-authored a book chapter as well.

Jacques Verville has a Doctor of Philosophy degree in Administrative Sciences with a concentration in Management of Information Systems from the Faculty of Administrative Sciences (AACSB accredited), University Laval; a Master of Science degree in Information Resource Management from Syracuse University; a Master of Arts in International Relations from Maxwell School, Syracuse University; and, a Bachelor of Arts degree from University of Alberta. Dr. Verville has published in peer review journals such as Decision Support Systems, Long Range Planning, Industrial Marketing, and International Business Review.

Zhonggen (中根) Yu (于), Professor in Beijing Language and Culture University, Ph.D. in English language, a dual Master-degree holder in applied linguistics and law, and a post-doctoral researcher in psycho-linguistics, has already published over 50 peer reviewed articles in distinguished journals based on rich teaching and research experiences. His research interest includes educational technologies, language attrition, and language acquisition.

Index

A

B

C

D

E

V

Purchase Print, E-Book, or Print + E-Book

IGI Global's reference books are available in three unique pricing formats:
Print Only, E-Book Only, or Print + E-Book.
Shipping fees may apply.

www.igi-global.com

Recommended Reference Books

ISBN: 978-1-5225-6201-6
© 2019; 341 pp.
List Price: $345

ISBN: 978-1-5225-7262-6
© 2019; 360 pp.
List Price: $215

ISBN: 978-1-5225-8003-4
© 2019; 216 pp.
List Price: $205

ISBN: 978-1-5225-5763-0
© 2019; 304 pp.
List Price: $205

ISBN: 978-1-5225-6980-0
© 2019; 325 pp.
List Price: $235

ISBN: 978-1-5225-7808-6
© 2019; 397 pp.
List Price: $215

Do you want to stay current on the latest research trends, product announcements, news and special offers?
Join IGI Global's mailing list today and start enjoying exclusive perks sent only to IGI Global members.
Add your name to the list at **www.igi-global.com/newsletters.**

Publisher of Peer-Reviewed, Timely, and Innovative Academic Research

IGI Global
DISSEMINATOR OF KNOWLEDGE

www.igi-global.com Sign up at www.igi-global.com/newsletters facebook.com/igiglobal twitter.com/igiglobal linkedin.com/igiglobal

Ensure Quality Research is Introduced to the Academic Community

Become an IGI Global Reviewer for Authored Book Projects

The overall success of an authored book project is dependent on quality and timely reviews.

In this competitive age of scholarly publishing, constructive and timely feedback significantly expedites the turnaround time of manuscripts from submission to acceptance, allowing the publication and discovery of forward-thinking research at a much more expeditious rate. Several IGI Global authored book projects are currently seeking highly-qualified experts in the field to fill vacancies on their respective editorial review boards:

Applications and Inquiries may be sent to:
development@igi-global.com

Applicants must have a doctorate (or an equivalent degree) as well as publishing and reviewing experience. Reviewers are asked to complete the open-ended evaluation questions with as much detail as possible in a timely, collegial, and constructive manner. All reviewers' tenures run for one-year terms on the editorial review boards and are expected to complete at least three reviews per term. Upon successful completion of this term, reviewers can be considered for an additional term.

If you have a colleague that may be interested in this opportunity, we encourage you to share this information with them.

IGI Global Proudly Partners With eContent Pro International

Receive a 25% Discount on all Editorial Services

Editorial Services

IGI Global expects all final manuscripts submitted for publication to be in their final form. This means they must be reviewed, revised, and professionally copy edited prior to their final submission. Not only does this support with accelerating the publication process, but it also ensures that the highest quality scholarly work can be disseminated.

English Language Copy Editing

Let eContent Pro International's expert copy editors perform edits on your manuscript to resolve spelling, punctuaion, grammar, syntax, flow, formatting issues and more.

Scientific and Scholarly Editing

Allow colleagues in your research area to examine the content of your manuscript and provide you with valuable feedback and suggestions before submission.

Figure, Table, Chart & Equation Conversions

Do you have poor quality figures? Do you need visual elements in your manuscript created or converted? A design expert can help!

Translation

Need your documjent translated into English? eContent Pro International's expert translators are fluent in English and more than 40 different languages.

Hear What Your Colleagues are Saying About Editorial Services Supported by IGI Global

"The service was very fast, very thorough, and very helpful in ensuring our chapter meets the criteria and requirements of the book's editors. I was quite impressed and happy with your service."

– Prof. Tom Brinthaupt,
Middle Tennessee State University, USA

"I found the work actually spectacular. The editing, formatting, and other checks were very thorough. The turnaround time was great as well. I will definitely use eContent Pro in the future."

– Nickanor Amwata, Lecturer,
University of Kurdistan Hawler, Iraq

"I was impressed that it was done timely, and wherever the content was not clear for the reader, the paper was improved with better readability for the audience."

– Prof. James Chilembwe,
Mzuzu University, Malawi

Email: customerservice@econtentpro.com **www.igi-global.com/editorial-service-partners**

IGI Global
DISSEMINATOR OF KNOWLEDGE
www.igi-global.com

Celebrating Over 30 Years of Scholarly Knowledge Creation & Dissemination

InfoSci®-Books

A Database of Over 5,300+ Reference Books Containing Over 100,000+ Chapters Focusing on Emerging Research

InfoSci®-Books Database

The **InfoSci®-Books** database is a collection of over 5,300+ IGI Global single and multi-volume reference books, handbooks of research, and encyclopedias, encompassing groundbreaking research from prominent experts worldwide that span over 350+ topics in 11 core subject areas including business, computer science, education, science and engineering, social sciences and more.

Open Access Fee Waiver (Offset Model) Initiative

For any library that invests in IGI Global's InfoSci-Journals and/or InfoSci-Books databases, IGI Global will match the library's investment with a fund of equal value to go toward **subsidizing the OA article processing charges (APCs) for their students, faculty, and staff** at that institution when their work is submitted and accepted under OA into an IGI Global journal.*

INFOSCI® PLATFORM FEATURES

- No DRM
- No Set-Up or Maintenance Fees
- A Guarantee of No More Than a 5% Annual Increase
- Full-Text HTML and PDF Viewing Options
- Downloadable MARC Records
- Unlimited Simultaneous Access
- COUNTER 5 Compliant Reports
- Formatted Citations With Ability to Export to RefWorks and EasyBib
- No Embargo of Content (Research is Available Months in Advance of the Print Release)

**The fund will be offered on an annual basis and expire at the end of the subscription period. The fund would renew as the subscription is renewed for each year thereafter. The open access fees will be waived after the student, faculty, or staff's paper has been vetted and accepted into an IGI Global journal and the fund can only be used toward publishing OA in an IGI Global journal. Libraries in developing countries will have the match on their investment doubled.*

To Learn More or To Purchase This Database:
www.igi-global.com/infosci-books

eresources@igi-global.com • Toll Free: 1-866-342-6657 ext. 100 • Phone: 717-533-8845 x100

IGI Global
DISSEMINATOR OF KNOWLEDGE
www.igi-global.com

IGI Global
DISSEMINATOR OF KNOWLEDGE
www.igi-global.com

Publisher of Peer-Reviewed, Timely, and Innovative Academic Research Since 1988

IGI Global's Transformative Open Access (OA) Model: How to Turn Your University Library's Database Acquisitions Into a Source of OA Funding

In response to the OA movement and well in advance of Plan S, IGI Global, early last year, unveiled their OA Fee Waiver (Read & Publish) Initiative.

Under this initiative, librarians who invest in IGI Global's InfoSci-Books (5,300+ reference books) and/or InfoSci-Journals (185+ scholarly journals) databases will be able to subsidize their patron's OA article processing charges (APC) when their work is submitted and accepted (after the peer review process) into an IGI Global journal. *See website for details.

How Does it Work?

1. When a library subscribes or perpetually purchases IGI Global's InfoSci-Databases and/or their discipline/subject-focused subsets, IGI Global will match the library's investment with a fund of equal value to go toward subsidizing the OA article processing charges (APCs) for their patrons.

   ***Researchers:* Be sure to recommend the InfoSci-Books and InfoSci-Journals to take advantage of this initiative.**

2. When a student, faculty, or staff member submits a paper and it is accepted (following the peer review) into one of IGI Global's 185+ scholarly journals, the author will have the option to have their paper published under a traditional publishing model or as OA.
3. When the author chooses to have their paper published under OA, IGI Global will notify them of the OA Fee Waiver (Read and Publish) Initiative. If the author decides they would like to take advantage of this initiative, IGI Global will deduct the US$ 2,000 APC from the created fund.
4. This fund will be offered on an annual basis and will renew as the subscription is renewed for each year thereafter. IGI Global will manage the fund and award the APC waivers unless the librarian has a preference as to how the funds should be managed.

Hear From the Experts on This Initiative:

"I'm very happy to have been able to make one of my recent research contributions, "Visualizing the Social Media Conversations of a National Information Technology Professional Association" featured in the *International Journal of Human Capital and Information Technology Professionals*, freely available along with having access to the valuable resources found within IGI Global's InfoSci-Journals database."

– **Prof. Stuart Palmer**,
Deakin University, Australia

For More Information, Visit: www.igi-global.com/publish/contributor-resources/open-access/read-publish-model or contact IGI Global's Database Team at eresources@igi-global.com.

Are You Ready to Publish Your Research?

IGI Global
DISSEMINATOR OF KNOWLEDGE

IGI Global offers book authorship and editorship opportunities across 11 subject areas, including business, computer science, education, science and engineering, social sciences, and more!

Benefits of Publishing with IGI Global:

- Free one-on-one editorial and promotional support.
- Expedited publishing timelines that can take your book from start to finish in less than one (1) year.
- Choose from a variety of formats including: Edited and Authored References, Handbooks of Research, Encyclopedias, and Research Insights.
- Utilize IGI Global's eEditorial Discovery® submission system in support of conducting the submission and blind review process.
- IGI Global maintains a strict adherence to ethical practices due in part to our full membership with the Committee on Publication Ethics (COPE).
- Indexing potential in prestigious indices such as Scopus®, Web of Science™, PsycINFO®, and ERIC – Education Resources Information Center.
- Ability to connect your ORCID iD to your IGI Global publications.
- Earn royalties on your publication as well as receive complimentary copies and exclusive discounts.

Get Started Today by Contacting the Acquisitions Department at:

acquisition@igi-global.com

www.igi-global.com/infosci-ondemand

InfoSci®-OnDemand

Continuously updated with new material on a weekly basis, InfoSci®-OnDemand offers the ability to search through thousands of quality full-text research papers. Users can narrow each search by identifying key topic areas of interest, then display a complete listing of relevant papers, and purchase materials specific to their research needs.

Comprehensive Service

- Over 125,000+ journal articles, book chapters, and case studies.
- All content is downloadable in PDF and HTML format and can be stored locally for future use.

No Subscription Fees

- One time fee of $37.50 per PDF download.

Instant Access

- Receive a download link immediately after order completion!

"It really provides an excellent entry into the research literature of the field. It presents a manageable number of highly relevant sources on topics of interest to a wide range of researchers. The sources are scholarly, but also accessible to 'practitioners'."

- Lisa Stimatz, MLS, University of North Carolina at Chapel Hill, USA

"It is an excellent and well designed database which will facilitate research, publication, and teaching. It is a very useful tool to have."

- George Ditsa, PhD, University of Wollongong, Australia

"I have accessed the database and find it to be a valuable tool to the IT/IS community. I found valuable articles meeting my search criteria 95% of the time."

- Prof. Lynda Louis, Xavier University of Louisiana, USA

Recommended for use by researchers who wish to immediately download PDFs of individual chapters or articles.

www.igi-global.com/e-resources/infosci-ondemand

IGI Global DISSEMINATOR OF KNOWLEDGE

www.igi-global.com

www.ingramcontent.com/pod-product-compliance
Lightning Source LLC
LaVergne TN
LVHW060422300926
849162LV00006B/1496

* 9 7 8 1 7 9 9 8 4 8 9 1 2 *